The Conquest of the Western Sudan

To my Wife

THE CONQUEST OF THE WESTERN SUDAN

A STUDY IN FRENCH MILITARY IMPERIALISM

by

A. S. KANYA-FORSTNER

Fellow of Gonville and Caius College
Cambridge

CAMBRIDGE

AT THE UNIVERSITY PRESS

1969

Published by the Syndics of the Cambridge University Press
Bentley House, 200 Euston Road, London N.W.1
American Branch: 32 East 57th Street, New York, N.Y.10022

© Cambridge University Press 1969

Library of Congress Catalogue Card Number: 69–11028
Standard Book Number: 521 07378 2

Printed in Great Britain
at the University Printing House, Cambridge
(Brooke Crutchley, University Printer)

Contents

MAPS

Preface

This book, as its sub-title suggests, is not primarily a military history of the Western Sudan. Its theme is the politics of military expansion. The problem is to explain why France found herself at the end of the nineteenth century in possession of a vast territorial empire in the West African interior. In attempting to explain it, I have concentrated upon the rôle of the French Military who undertook the conquest; their motives and their influence upon the formulation of policy are my principal concerns. But to study the Military in isolation would be both sterile and historically misleading; the significance of the military factor can only be assessed within a wider context. Accordingly, I have tried to present, if at times rather summarily, a more general picture of French African expansion, and to advance my views about its nature. More tentatively still, I have tried to arrive at some conclusions about the nature of Africans' responses to the forces which confronted and eventually overcame them during the era of the Partition. Historians in the past regarded the partition of Africa as no more than an aspect of European expansion. Those of the present have tended to see it merely as an episode in the much longer history of Africa. I believe it, as do many others, to be both. This book is therefore intended as a small and partial step towards a general interpretation of the Partition as a specific historical problem. For all its deficiencies, I hope it will be a useful or at least a provocative one.

The work in its present form is a revised and enlarged version of a doctoral dissertation submitted at Cambridge University in 1965. Its preparation has left me indebted to many people. I must first of all thank Madame Entremont–Archinard for permission to consult the papers of her great-uncle, General Louis Archinard; and Monsieur François Berge for permission to consult the papers of his grandfather, President Félix Faure. I must also express my gratitude to Monsieur C. Laroche, *Conservateur en Chef de la Section Outre-Mer des Archives Nationales*, and to Mademoiselle M-A. Ménier for their friendship and assistance while I was consulting the Colonial Ministry records at the Rue Oudinot; to Captain Désiré of the *Section Outre-Mer des Archives Historiques de l'Armée*, who helped my research at the Fort de Vincennes;

Preface

and to Professor Jean Ganiage, who acted as my supervisor during my year of research in Paris. Monsieur Yves Person, now Professor of History at the Université de Dakar, gave me much valuable information about Samori. Dr C. W. Newbury of the Institute of Commonwealth Studies, Oxford, gave me the benefit of his wide knowledge of West African trade and made many helpful criticisms. We also collaborated on a joint article about the origins of the scramble for West Africa. A fellow research-student, Dr J. M. A. Bakhiet, translated several Arabic documents for me. Professor J. D. Hargreaves of the University of Aberdeen, Dr E. T. Stokes of St Catharine's College, Cambridge, and Dr Anil Seal of Trinity College, Cambridge, all read the manuscript and made suggestions which greatly improved both its accuracy and its clarity. Failings on either count which remain are, of course, entirely my own.

Much greater still is my debt to my supervisors, Dr R. E. Robinson of St John's College, Cambridge, and Professor J. A. Gallagher of Balliol College, Oxford. They suggested the subject to me, guided my research, and gave me constant advice and encouragement. My conclusions may not have been those which they expected me to reach. Indeed this book is an attempt, at times implied, often explicit, to advance an alternative to their own interpretation of the Partition. But my concepts are theirs, and my frame of reference is one which they themselves established. There can be no better indication of their influence on me.

My greatest debt of all is to my wife.

A. S .K.-F.

Cambridge
February 1968

vii

Abbreviations used to refer to sources

AE	Archives du Ministère des Affaires Etrangères, Paris
AEMD	Archives du Ministère des Affaires Etrangères, Mémoires et Documents
AN	Archives Nationales, Paris
Arch. Guerre	Archives Historiques de l'Armée, Section Outre-Mer, Vincennes
B.C.A.F.	*Bulletin du Comité de l'Afrique française*
BN	Bibliothèque Nationale, Paris
D.D.F.	*Documents diplomatiques français*, $1^{\text{ère}}$ série
J.O.	*Journal Officiel de la République Française*
MFOM	Section Outre-Mer des Archives Nationales, formerly Archives du Ministère de la France d'Outre-Mer, Paris

I

Introduction: the Colonial Army and the Western Sudan

The conquest of the Western Sudan ranks as one of the most remarkable episodes in the history of European expansion in tropical Africa. During the second half of the nineteenth century the colonial troops of the French Navy penetrated deep into the savanna lands of the West African interior and carved out an empire larger than France itself. As a sustained and determined military endeavour this conquest had few parallels. Yet the reasons for it have still to be adequately explained.

By the standards of strategy and trade which governed the course of European expansion in the nineteenth century, empire-building on this scale should never have occurred in West Africa. Although France had a long and a glorious colonial tradition, her primacy in Europe had always been the measure of her greatness. It was on continental not colonial battlefields that her fortunes had always been decided; the *Ancien Régime* recovered from Quebec and Arcot, but the First Empire could not survive Moscow and Waterloo nor the Second, Sedan. In the years after 1871 the loss of Alsace-Lorraine and the growing power of Germany were the chief preoccupation of French statesmen. For the next fifty years the problem of the eastern frontier dominated their strategy, often to the detriment of French activity overseas.[1] Colonial rivalry with Great Britain did at times assume dangerous proportions; in 1898 it brought the two countries to the brink of war. But Anglo-French hostility, no matter how intense, did not alter the fundamental considerations of continental policy. Although a common distrust of

[1] The Radical Deputy Georges Périn, explaining his opposition to French participation in the Egyptian campaign of 1882, voiced sentiments which many shared: 'La France doit être économe du sang de ses soldats; ses malheurs passés, sa situation en Europe aujourd'hui, lui en font un devoir. Ce que les Anglais peuvent faire impunément nous n'aurions pu le faire sans péril. A ceux qui nous disent: "Vous êtes des timorés", je réponds: "Vous êtes des aveugles et des sourds. Aveugles qui ne voyez pas la frontière ouverte du côté des Vosges; sourds qui n'entendez pas ce grand bruit d'armes qui se fait en Allemagne..."' Georges Périn, speech at Limoges, 17 Sept. 1882, cited in: G. Clemenceau and H. Schirmer (eds.), *Georges Périn, 1838–1903: Discours politiques et notes de voyages* (Paris, 1905), p. xiv.

Introduction: the Colonial Army and the Western Sudan

British expansion occasionally drew France and Germany together, a genuine *rapprochement* was absolutely unthinkable until the Lost Provinces had been returned.[1] The colonial acquisitions of the Third Republic were certainly impressive, but they rarely if ever blinded her citizens to the overriding importance of continental strategy. In 1899 a future Minister of Colonies could still declare:

Happily, France is a great colonial power. But she is above all, and she must remain above all, a great European power. We have in Europe interests which outweigh all others, and to them our general policy must be subordinate.[2]

Commercially no less than strategically, French interests were focused in Europe. Until mid-century the French economy remained basically agricultural, and a nation of farmers could derive little concrete benefit from colonial possessions. By the 1850s the slow process of industrialisation had created some demand for tropical commodities, but the continued boom in public works, particularly in railway-building, kept economic energies concentrated on internal development. Even in the late nineteenth century French industry and capital sought continental rather than colonial outlets. Britain and Germany, the leaders of European industry, were France's main trading partners; Russian industrialisation provided the most attractive opportunities for investment. The colonies had nothing comparable to offer; before 1900 they accounted for less than 10 per cent of French foreign trade and investment.[3]

Not surprisingly, therefore, nineteenth-century French expansion was often a hesitant business, conducted in an atmosphere of public indifference or outright hostility. Although Algeria became the cornerstone of the French empire in Africa, the reasons for its original acquisition were those of internal political expediency. The expedition of 1830 was intended to bolster up the prestige of Charles X's faltering regime; but the manœuvre brought his Government no popularity, for

---

[1] E.g. Courcel [Ambassador, Berlin] to Ferry, 30 Aug. 1884; same to same, 29 Nov. 1884; same to same, 3 Dec. 1884; same to same, 27 Dec. 1884, *Documents diplomatiques français*, 1ère série [henceforth *D.D.F.*] v, nos. 385, 471, 475, 500; Courcel [now Ambassador, London] to Hanotaux, 31 July 1896, *ibid.* xii, no. 435; Hanotaux to Montebello [Ambassador, St Petersburg], 31 Jan. 1897, *ibid.* xiii, no. 87.

[2] Albert Decrais, speech on the Colonial Budget, cited in *La Dépêche Coloniale*, 30 June 1899.

[3] H. Brunschwig, *Mythes et réalités de l'impérialisme colonial français* (Paris, 1960), pp. 84–101; H. Feis, *Europe, the World's Banker, 1870–1914* (New Haven, 1930), pp. 49–57.

only the businessmen of Marseilles—who were bound to profit from the provisioning of the expeditionary force—welcomed the invasion. Three weeks after the capture of Algiers the Bourbons themselves were overthrown. The Orleanists came to power without an Algerian policy and vacillated for a decade before approving the 'total conquest' of the new colony.[1] During the Second Empire the pace of French expansion increased as Napoleon III sought to match the exploits of his more illustrious namesake. Yet the Emperor's attempts to enhance his prestige through overseas adventures never came to much. He sent an army to demonstrate French greatness in the Chinese campaigns of 1858–60, but his British allies secured the major political advantages from the Treaties of Tientsin and Conventions of Peking.[2] He had great plans for the creation of a satellite Arab empire in the Levant, but the first hint of British opposition was enough to dispel this particular dream.[3] He launched still more grandiose schemes for the creation of a powerful client state in Central America, but the Mexican expedition ended in total failure.[4] The men and money he so heedlessly squandered in America merely helped to weaken France in Europe, and in 1870 Napoleon paid the price.

Inevitably, the disasters of the Franco-Prussian war precluded any immediate possibility of further expansion overseas. Defeat cost France one hundred and fifty thousand men, an indemnity of 5,000,000,000 francs, the industries of Alsace and the iron deposits of Lorraine. It destroyed her ambitions for primacy in Europe and left her diplomatically isolated. It disrupted her political life and shattered her social stability. The continued survival of the new Republic remained in doubt for almost a decade; the self-inflicted wounds of the Commune took even longer to heal. In the aftermath of defeat, all the resources of the State had to be devoted to internal reconstruction. Colonial expenditure was cut to the bone, and the meagre credits available had to cover the mounting cost of the penal colonies as well. Not until the

[1] C-A. Julien, *Histoire de l'Algérie contemporaine* (Paris, 1964), caps. I–III; C. Schefer, 'La "Conquête Totale" de l'Algérie, 1839–1843', *Revue de l'histoire des colonies françaises*, IV (1916), 19–76. The views of the Marseilles merchants are discussed in P. Guiral, 'L'opinion marseillaise et les débuts de l'enterprise algérienne, 1830–1841', *Revue historique*, CCXI (1955), 9–34.

[2] J. F. Cady, *The Roots of French Imperialism in Eastern Asia* (Ithaca, 1954), pp. 181–206, 232–66.

[3] M. Emerit, 'La crise syrienne et l'expansion économique française en 1860', *Revue historique*, CCVII (1952), 232.

[4] C. Schefer, *La grande pensée de Napoléon III* (Paris, 1939), especially pp. 14–20, 243–66.

late 1870s did France feel herself able to afford the luxury of an active colonial policy.[1]

Worse still, the disastrous results of Napoleon's reckless ventures left Frenchmen profoundly suspicious of overseas commitments. *L'Empire a dégoûté notre pays d'aventures*, was Jules Ferry's famous complaint, and events seemed to prove him right.[2] The Tunisian expedition of 1881 provoked a political storm which threw the Chamber into utter chaos and brought down Ferry's Government. Anxious not to suffer the same fate, Freycinet handled the Egyptian crisis of 1882 with extreme circumspection, but when he finally requested approval even for limited participation in the Suez campaign, his fall from office was no less swift. When Ferry returned in 1883 and embarked upon a more serious policy of expansion in the Far East, the consequences were still more terrible. The retreat of the French expeditionary force from Lang-Son, of no great significance in military terms, destroyed the second Ferry Ministry and ruined its leader's political career. In the Chamber his opponents branded him a traitor and called for his impeachment; in the streets the mob branded him *Le Tonkinois* and called for his blood. The vote on the Tonkin credit in November 1885 confirmed Parliament's opposition to the enterprise and prompted the resignation of Ferry's successor, Brisson.[3]

Yet French policies in Tunisia, Egypt and Indochina, whatever their political repercussions, were all based on imposing economic or strategic considerations. The need to safeguard the security of Algeria, especially at a time of serious Muslim unrest, was a significant factor in the decision to occupy Tunisia. Major financial concerns had also invested heavily there, and the Tunisian bond-holders undoubtedly used their political connections to exert a very real pressure in favour of intervention. More important still, the Tunisian protectorate was intended to strengthen the preponderance of France in the western

[1]

COLONIAL BUDGETS: 1869–73			
Year	Credits Granted	Service Pénitentiaire	Net Credit
1869	27,207,217 fr.	5,129,580 fr.	22,077,637 fr.
1870	28,320,705 fr.	4,801,040 fr.	23,519,665 fr.
1871	24,737,595 fr.	5,034,011 fr.	19,703,584 fr.
1872	21,751,545 fr.	5,036,860 fr.	16,714,685 fr.
1873	24,889,484 fr.	8,678,866 fr.	16,210,618 fr.

Sources: Archives Nationales [henceforth AN] *Série* AD xviii^f (Budget Reports), 900, 913, 888, 892, 893.

[2] Preface to *Les affaires de Tunisie*, January 1882, cited in P. Robiquet (ed.), *Discours et opinions de Jules Ferry* (Paris, 1897), v, 522.

[3] See: F. Berge, *Le sous-secrétariat et les sous-secrétaires d'état aux colonies* (Paris, 1962), pp. 38–9.

4

Mediterranean and demonstrate her return to Great Power status.[1]
Egypt had been regarded as a special sphere of French cultural and
political influence ever since the Napoleonic invasion and the foundation of the *Institut d'Egypte*. French enterprise and technical expertise
had demonstrated its brilliance with the Suez Canal. French capital had
helped to finance the Khedive's extravagant programmes of moderni-
sation and to satisfy his increasingly desperate demands for loans.[2]
Although France herself was to blame for the eclipse of her position,
she still had good reason to make Britain's evacuation a prime objective
of her African policy in the two decades after 1882; for the British
occupation upset the balance of power in the eastern Mediterranean and
threatened the security of French routes to the East.[3] At the end of these
routes lay Indochina, the centre of French power in a region of growing
economic and strategic importance, and the base from which she hoped
to secure her share of the coveted Chinese market.[4] Developments in
North Africa and the Far East could affect the whole course of French
foreign policy and were therefore supervised by the major organs of
Government, by the Ministry of Foreign Affairs or by the Cabinet as a
whole.[5]

French expansion in the Western Sudan raised no issues of comparable importance. A Sudanese empire might contribute indirectly to the

[1] This was the reason why Gambetta made his vital decision to support the Tunisian expedition. See: Courcel's account of his conversation with Gambetta in March 1881, cited
in G. Hanotaux, *Histoire de la France contemporaine* (Paris, 1908), IV, 650–1, and Gambetta
to Ferry, 13 May 1881 [on the signature of the Treaty of Bardo], cited in D. Halévy and
E. Pillias (eds.), *Lettres de Gambetta, 1868–1882* (Paris, 1938), no. 474: '...je te félicite du
fond du cœur de ce prompt et excellent résultat. Il faudra bien que les esprits chagrins en
prennent leur parti un peu partout. La France reprend son rang de grande puissance.' For
financial pressures see: J. Ganiage, *Les origines du protectorat français en Tunisie, 1861–1881*
(Paris, 1959), esp. pp. 640–61.

[2] Feis, *op. cit.* pp. 383–4. See also: C. de Freycinet, *Souvenirs, 1878–1893*, 3rd ed. (Paris, 1913),
p. 216: 'Nous avons voulu sauvegarder les emprunts que nous avions consentis aux
gouvernants d'Egypte. L'année 1882 nous a trouvés dans la posture de créanciers inquiets
sur l'avenir de leurs titres. Cette question d'argent...a trop inspiré notre diplomatie. Le
souci...de protéger des intérêts particuliers a, par moments, empiété sur l'intérêt général
et permanent de la France.'

[3] E.g. Ribot [Minister of Foreign Affairs] to Paul Cambon [Ambassador, Constantinople],
30 Jan. 1892, *D.D.F.* IX, no. 180.

[4] See: M. Bruguière, 'Le Chemin de Fer du Yunnan: Paul Doumer et la politique d'intervention française en Chine, 1889–1902', part I, *Revue d'histoire diplomatique*, LXXVII (1963),
23–61.

[5] The Egyptian question was clearly one which belonged in the realm of foreign rather than
colonial policy. Tunisian affairs, because of the country's status as a Protectorate, were
also a matter for the Foreign Ministry. Even Tonkin and Annam were administered by
the Foreign Office from January 1886 to October 1887, although control was thereafter
shared with the Ministry of Marine and Colonies.

security of Algeria, but it had little bearing upon France's international position. High hopes were entertained about the commercial prospects of the interior, but existing trade in West Africa—gum and groundnuts in Senegal and palm oil on the Guinea coast—made only a small contribution to the development of French industry.[1] Capital investment was minimal; only local traders or small concerns based mainly in Bordeaux and Marseilles were interested in exploiting the available opportunities. Nor were the traders themselves wholeheartedly in favour of increased Government intervention, for they had to weigh the benefits of official protection against the disadvantages of tighter official control. Given the scale of the interests involved, West African policy could for the most part be safely relegated to the direction of the body responsible for the administration of colonial affairs, the Colonial Department of the Ministry of Marine.

Superficially, the place of the Colonial Department within the general framework of French policy-making reflected the low priority accorded to colonial questions in the nineteenth century. Until the 1880s it remained a minor adjunct of the Ministry of Marine, headed by a *directeur des colonies*, himself a civil servant.[2] Thereafter, its status was gradually raised to that of an Under-Secretaryship of State; but the Under-Secretary, now a politician and a junior member of the Government, remained directly responsible to his Minister, who decided the scope of his functions. Until 1889 his authority was delegated by ministerial *arrêté*. As the Department was shuttled between the Ministry of Marine and the Ministry of Commerce, so the confusion inherent in the system increased. Only in 1894 were the anomalies finally resolved by the creation of an independent Ministry of Colonies. Even then the Ministers were often minor figures in the Government.[3]

But, despite their modest position, the heads of the Colonial Department could exercise considerable influence upon the formulation of policy. The Ministers nominally responsible were generally too preoccupied with naval or commercial affairs to welcome the additional burden of supervising the colonies, and they were content to allow their

[1] In 1868 the total value of West African exports, mainly groundnuts, to France was estimated at 36,000,000 fr. See: C. W. Newbury, *The Western Slave Coast and its Rulers* (Oxford, 1961), pp. 99–100.

[2] For the history of the Colonial Department in the nineteenth century, see: Berge, *op. cit.* and A. Duchêne, *La politique coloniale de la France* (Paris, 1928).

[3] Of the seven holders of the office in the five years after its creation only one, Delcassé, was a major political figure. André Lebon achieved a measure of notoriety for the brutal treatment of Dreyfus on Devil's Island. The other five were political featherweights.

Directors or Under-Secretaries a wide measure of personal initiative. After 1889 the Under-Secretary's freedom of action amounted to virtual independence. Like his Minister, he was now appointed by Presidential Decree. He had powers of ministerial signature on all matters pertaining to the colonies. He had the right to attend Cabinet discussions on colonial affairs. He answered Parliamentary questions, and his replies were treated as ministerial statements. In effect the Under-Secretary, as his critics pointed out, enjoyed ministerial powers without ministerial responsibility.[1]

In the peculiarly confused state of French politics under the Third Republic the semi-bureaucratic status of the Under-Secretaryship could be highly advantageous to its occupant. The endless round of cabinet-making and cabinet-breaking which produced forty-two Governments in thirty years often left transient Ministers at the mercy of their permanent staffs. But the Under-Secretary, covered by his Minister's overall responsibility and free to concentrate exclusively upon the affairs of his own small department, was in a position to dominate his civil servants rather than be dominated by them. He was to some extent immune from the effects of ministerial reshuffling. He often had previous experience of colonial problems as *rapporteur* of the Colonial Budget or as the representative of one of the French ports. He could establish an intimate working relationship with his officials and had the right to appoint his own personal advisers. In practice, the powers which an Under-Secretary actually exercised depended upon his own capacity; but the post itself was by no means a political backwater. Its occupants were generally young men of high calibre and higher expectations. The three great Under-Secretaries, Félix Faure, Eugène Etienne and Théophile Delcassé, all became leading figures in the political life of the Third Republic. Even Amédée de La Porte and Emile Jamais, neither of them particularly successful in the office, were ranked among the most brilliant minds of their generation.[2]

Nowhere in Africa could the influence of the Under-Secretary be more widely exercised than in the Western Sudan. North Africa and Egypt lay outside his brief, and his views were rarely if ever solicited.

[1] *Journal Officiel de la République Française* [henceforth *J.O.*], *Débats Parlementaires, Sénat*, séance du 20 juin 1892, pp. 624 ff. The basis of the charge was that the Under-Secretary, while not directly responsible to Parliament, was no longer responsible to his Minister because he was now appointed by Presidential Decree.

[2] For their biographies, see: A. Robert, E. Bourloton, and G. Cougny (eds.), *Dictionnaire des parlementaires français* (Paris, 1891), iii, 396–7, 588–9.

Introduction: the Colonial Army and the Western Sudan

Only in the 1890s did the colonial administration become directly involved in the development of French policy on the Upper Nile. Even on the West African coast the presence of other European powers and the consequent threat of international complications often forced the Colonial Department to work in concert with the Ministry of Foreign Affairs and to subordinate local considerations to the more general objectives of foreign policy. On Sudanese affairs, however, the Under-Secretary could act more or less on his own. The Sudan's very isolation from the mainstream of *haute politique* reduced the need for continuous Cabinet supervision. Although senior Ministers did at times play a vital part in shaping the course of events, it was by no means impossible for the Under-Secretary and his staff to act without the approval or even the knowledge of their superiors. At the same time, this isolation freed Sudanese policy from the limitations of *haute politique*. The policy-makers had less need to worry about immediate consequences and more scope for long-term planning. Their decisions could thus mirror not only their views about the Sudan's actual economic or strategic significance but also their hopes about its future importance. And these hopes in turn could reflect their abstract assumptions about the benefits which Africa might one day yield to those who controlled her. Such aspirations and assumptions may well have been the crucial factors which determined the official motives for Sudanese expansion.

But the motives for Sudanese expansion cannot be explained simply in terms of the 'official mind'. The policy-makers in Paris could issue the directives governing the course of expansion, but the execution of their plans had to be entrusted to the agents of the Government on the spot. In the Sudan these were military men; through their efforts the territory was incorporated into the French empire not by the gradual diffusion of influence but by outright military conquest.

It was in Algeria that the process of nineteenth-century military expansion had its origins and reached its highest stage of development. Here the French Army first demonstrated its full potential as an independent force. From the start, the Algerian High Command set out to free itself from metropolitan control by systematically disregarding its instructions. During the Governorship of General Bugeaud (1840–7), military insubordination was raised to the level of an art.[1] Within the

---

[1] E.g. Bugeaud's reply to orders forbidding him to begin the conquest of Kabylia: 'Je reçois votre dépêche. Il est trop tard. Mes troupes...sont en marche...Si nous avons le succès, le Gouvernement et la France en auront l'honneur. Dans le cas contraire, la

colony itself, the Army laid the bases of administrative organisation and monopolised the sources of political power, deliberately excluding civilian colonists from any effective participation in political affairs. For forty years its mastery over Algeria was virtually absolute. Only in 1871, when its reputation had been destroyed on European battlefields, was its hold finally broken.[1]

Here in the harsh but exciting and none too dangerous circumstances of colonial war,[2] ambitious officers sought to make their careers. Algeria provided unique professional opportunities for those who served there. Officers received overseas supplements to their pay and could share in the spoils of war. Their periods of active service counted double for the purposes of seniority, and the order of seniority was the basic factor determining promotion. More important still, active service provided limitless prospects for the demonstration of military valour which might be rewarded with a decoration or a mention on the *ordre du jour de l'armée*, the only means of escape from the straitjacket of the seniority system. As a result, Algerian postings were the most coveted; the best graduates of the Infantry school at Saint-Cyr almost invariably chose to serve in the Algerian *zouaves*.

The Algerian experience shaped the outlook of two generations of the officer corps and influenced the development of French military theory for half a century. Here the Army learned the tactics of the rapid and daring advance; here it learned the organisation of the compact and mobile formations required to deal with an equally mobile and elusive enemy. Here too the officers of the *Armée d'Afrique* acquired the peculiar outlook of the colonial soldier. They were convinced that they alone had enough experience of local conditions to make decisions and resented any attempt to interfere with their freedom of action. They were supremely confident of their own military capacities and convinced that they alone knew how to wage war. They had a profound suspicion of anything that smacked of military science. For civilians they felt nothing but contempt. Through them this mystique came to pervade the whole Army, ultimately with terrible consequences; most of the

responsabilité toute entière retombera sur moi. Je la réclame.' Bugeaud to Minister of War, n.d., cited in H. d'Ideville, *Le Maréchal Bugeaud d'après sa correspondance intime* (Paris, 1882), III, 155–6.

[1] The best account of the Army's rôle in Algeria is Julien, *Histoire de l'Algérie contemporaine*, which also contains an exhaustive bibliography.

[2] Between 1830 and 1847 only 304 officers were actually killed in action. See: P. Chalmin, *L'officier français de 1815 à 1870* (Paris, 1957), p. 29. The rest of the paragraph is based on this work.

Generals who showed themselves so lamentably ignorant of modern warfare in 1870 were graduates of this Algerian school.[1]

Military expansion in the Western Sudan was of a quite different order. At the height of the Algerian conquest, 100,000 men, a third of the French Army, had been stationed there; the Sudanese garrisons never numbered more than 4,000. In Algeria, Field-Marshals and Generals had led the elite corps of the French Army; Sudanese troops were commanded by Majors and Colonels drawn not from the *armée de terre* but from the lowly *infanterie* and *artillerie de marine*.

During the mid-nineteenth century, service in the 'Marines' offered few of the advantages to be found in Algeria. Marine officers were despised by their naval superiors, deprived of top commands and discriminated against in the award of decorations. In common with the Army, the Marine corps drew their officers both from the ranks and from the *Grandes Ecoles*; but the intake from the latter was anything but distinguished. The level of instruction at Saint-Cyr was mediocre to begin with, and the cream of the graduating class was in any case drawn off by the *zouaves*, the *turcos* or the *chasseurs*. Only the dullest joined the *infanterie de marine*.[2] The Ecole Polytechnique provided a somewhat more respectable technical education, but its best graduates entered the civilian professions. Few actually chose a career in the *artillerie de terre*; virtually nobody joined the *artillerie de marine* of his own free will. The class of 1869 provides a striking example: of the fourteen postings available, thirteen were filled by the bottom of the class.[3]

If anything, the position of the colonial troops actually deteriorated in the years immediately after 1871. The nation's attention was now focused on the *armée de terre*. Defeat had left the Army in complete disarray, and military reorganisation was one of the Republic's most urgent tasks. The psychological need to restore faith in French military capacities was perhaps even greater. At all costs, the Army's reputation had to be saved. Defeat could only be blamed on individual failures or on deficiencies in organisation and training. The Army itself became a sacred institution, and for the next twenty years any criticism of it was regarded as tantamount to sacrilege.[4] But the emphasis was exclusively on its rôle in France and in Europe. It was supposed to remain the guardian of the social order as it had been during the Commune. Many

---

[1] For a discussion of military attitudes see: Julien, *op. cit.* pp. 297–330.
[2] Souvenirs inédits de Marie-Paul d'Ussel, cited in Chalmin, *op. cit.* p. 135.
[3] Class-list of Louis Archinard, Archinard Papers.
[4] See: R. Girardet, *La société militaire dans la France contemporaine* (Paris, 1953), pp. 161–247

wished to turn it into a vehicle for national regeneration, a school for the inculcation of patriotic virtues into all men of military age. Some wished to keep it a small, highly trained professional force; but all were agreed that its military function was to defend France against European aggression and to prepare for the day of retribution when the Lost Provinces would be retaken. There was little room in these schemes for colonial troops who could make only a marginal contribution to continental defence. Politicians were reluctant to vote the funds necessary for their maintenance. In 1876 Parliament refused to increase the permanent establishment of the *infanterie de marine* and regretted the impossibility of reducing its numbers still further. Gambetta himself, as staunch a defender of the Army as anyone, questioned the need to maintain the colonial infantry as a separate military formation in peacetime.[1]

Only after 1880 did the colonial troops begin to receive more attention. The *infanterie de marine*, with a strength of less than 19,000, was manifestly incapable of supplying the manpower for operations on the scale of the Tunisian or Indochinese expeditions. But the *Armée d'Afrique* was needed for Algerian security, and the use of metropolitan troops in colonial campaigns was both militarily questionable and politically most unwise. The only solution, as the Parliamentary Army Commission realised, was to create two separate military arms, 'one comprising all the forces of the nation gathered for the supreme effort of a continental war, the other consisting of mobile elements ready at all times for an expeditionary campaign'.[2] France, in short, needed a colonial army; yet it took her twenty years to acquire one.

Plans for the creation of a colonial army had first received the Army Commission's recommendation in 1881; but conflicts over its organisation and control, and the reversals of policy which followed ministerial changes, led only to four years of fruitless debate. In 1885 official proposals were withdrawn, and the matter was not raised again for six years.[3]

---

[1] Procès-Verbaux de la Commission du Budget, séance du 6 juillet 1876, AN C3150, pp. 809–10; *J.O. Déb. Parl. Chambre*, séance du 7 novembre 1876, p. 8036.

[2] Baron Reille, Rapport, 18 June 1883, *J.O. Documents Parlementaires, Chambre*, no. 2012, p. 1040.

[3] *Ibid.* Rapport, 5 July 1883, no. 2102, pp. 1087–90; Rapport, 28 Jan. 1884, no. 2583, pp. 20–3; Rapport, 29 Nov. 1884, no. 3267, pp. 2139–53; Rapport, 7 Mar. 1885, no. 3597, pp. 65 ff.; *J.O. Déb. Parl. Chambre*, séance du 18 mai 1885, pp. 846 ff.; *ibid.* séance du 3 août, 1885, pp. 1714 ff. The main point at issue was whether to attach the Colonial Army to the Ministry of Marine or to the Ministry of War.

Introduction: the Colonial Army and the Western Sudan

By 1891, however, the reorganisation of colonial administration had created an almost impossibly confused situation. Troops serving in the colonies were under the command of the colonial Governors who were responsible to the Colonial Department in Paris. As long as the Department remained attached to the Ministry of Marine the system retained some logic. But the Department's transfer to the Ministry of Commerce in 1889 deprived the Ministry of Marine of its executive powers over Marine contingents actually serving in the colonies, and in February 1890 the Ministry formally renounced its responsibility for colonial defence.[1] Unfortunately, these changes were technically illegal because the General Law on Recruitment of July 1889 had specifically placed the colonial troops under the control of a military Ministry. To resolve the difficulty, the Government now called for the creation of an autonomous Colonial Army attached to the Ministry of War, and it secured the approval of the Chamber for its plans. But the Senate rejected them, and by 1893 two years of debate had produced agreement merely on the method of recruitment for service in overseas campaigns.[2]

The formation of an independent Ministry of Colonies responsible for colonial defence in 1894 completed the confusion. Logically, this should have become the home of the Colonial Army; but all proposals to this effect ran into an insuperable barrier of prejudice against the creation of a third military Ministry.[3] All attempts to reach a more traditional solution—attaching the Army to the Ministry of War or to the Ministry of Marine—were blocked by the same bickering which had plagued the project from the start. Only in 1900, after almost two decades of interminable debate, was the *Armée Coloniale* as such brought into being.[4] In the meantime the colonial troops had completed the conquest of West Africa and had done so in conditions of almost total administrative anarchy.

In spite of their chaotic organisation, however, the colonial troops

---

[1] Presidential Decree, 14 Mar. 1889, *J.O.* 15 Mar. 1889, p. 1302; Presidential Decree, 3 Feb. 1890, *ibid.* 9 Feb. 1890, pp. 725–6. See also: Berge, *op. cit.* pp. 57–65.

[2] Projet de Loi, 16 Feb. 1891, *J.O. Doc. Parl. Chambre*, no. 1201, pp. 375–7; *J.O. Déb. Parl. Chambre*, séance du 12 juillet 1893, p. 2186. Politically, this was the key issue. The General Law on Recruitment of July 1889 had made provision for the despatch to the colonies of troops drawn by lot from the metropolitan forces. The new Law placed military service in the colonies on an entirely voluntary basis. If necessary, colonial contingents were to be supplemented by units of the Foreign Legion.

[3] Procès-Verbaux de la Commission de l'Armée, séance du 26 février 1896, AN C5541; *ibid.* séance du 28 février 1896.

[4] Law 7 July 1900, *J.O.* 8 July 1900, pp. 4373–5. The Colonial Army was constituted as an autonomous military formation under the supervision of the Ministry of War.

could still function as an effective political force. Indeed, their confused administration could actually work to their advantage. The colonial troops had two masters in Paris. The Colonial Department was responsible for their deployment in the colonies, and military commanders on active service took their orders from the Under-Secretary. But vital administrative matters such as pay, postings and promotion remained in the hands of the Ministry of Marine, and commanders retained the right to correspond directly with it on technical subjects. Moreover, Ministers of Marine, preoccupied with naval affairs, had little time for the direct supervision of their colonial charges.[1] By default, *de facto* control passed to the Inspectorates-General which handled the day-to-day affairs of the *infanterie* and *artillerie de marine* and were staffed by their senior officers. In effect, the colonial troops in the late nineteenth century ran themselves.

Despite their lowly status within the French military framework, the colonial troops could also offer attractions to those who wished to serve overseas. Colonial contingents had acquired a reputation for heroism during the Franco-Prussian war, and this in itself was enough to draw many to their colours. The *infanterie de marine* had been virtually annihilated at Sedan, but by the end of the war new volunteers had swelled its ranks to more than 13,000.[2] In years to come, politicians might question its usefulness, but they never forgot that 'it had been at Bazeilles'.[3] Once French expansion moved into its military phase after 1880, the professional advantages offered by Algeria earlier in the century were made available elsewhere. By 1885 the Army Commission was confident that the prospect of increased pay, limited periods of service, early retirement, and in particular the opportunities for rapid promotion, would persuade officers from the regular Army to volunteer for colonial expeditions. The colonial troops, incorporated into a Colonial Army, could thus be transformed from their present position as the *auxiliaire de la marine* into the *élite de l'armée de terre*.[4] And there were grounds for such optimism. Because of the seniority

---

[1] Throughout the late nineteenth century the Ministry of Marine was under constant fire in Parliament for its irregular financial practices and its inefficient administration of naval construction. See: Procès-Verbaux de la Commission du Budget, séance du 20 mai 1885, AN C3306, p. 143; séance du 28 mai 1890, AN C5541, pp. 386–7; *ibid.*, séance du 20 juin 1890, pp. 824–5; séance du 11 octobre 1895, AN C5548, p. 365.

[2] Ministère de la Marine, Notes sur les Troupes de la Marine, 7 Feb. 1871, AN C2874.

[3] *J.O. Déb. Parl. Chambre*, séance du 18 mai 1885, p. 850; séance du 17 décembre 1891, pp. 2721–4.

[4] Reille, Rapport, 29 Nov. 1884, *J.O. Doc. Parl. Chambre*, no. 3267, p. 2139; *J.O. Déb. Parl. Chambre*, séance du 18 mai 1885, pp. 853–4.

system, promotion in the metropolitan Army was dreadfully slow; it could take twenty-five years for an officer to reach the rank of Major.[1] But in the colonies, where disease and action took a heavier toll, vacancies occurred more frequently, and *actions d'éclat* could lead to still more rapid advancement. Not surprisingly, therefore, the *infanterie* and *artillerie de marine* drew into their ranks those who could not tolerate the monotony of garrison life and sought brilliant careers on colonial battlefields—'the most energetic adventurous elements of the Nation and of the Army'.[2]

Such men were particularly susceptible to the mystique of military expansion. They spent the major part of their careers overseas, often in positions of power and responsibility far greater than they could ever have exercised in France. Like their counterparts in Algeria they were confident of their own ability and experience, and they were contemptuous of the civilian politicians whom they considered unfit to give them orders.[3] Their prolonged absences from home and their close contacts with their fellow officers led them to develop an intense and exclusive *esprit de corps*. They despised the stultifying atmosphere of metropolitan life and all those, civilian or military, who breathed it.[4] For all its hardships, colonial service could at least provide excitement, satisfy their appetite for action, and provide a welcome release from the boredom which weighed so heavily on them in France.

The Western Sudan was to become their favourite place of refuge. This was not the only area where the colonial troops saw action in the nineteenth century, but it was the one theatre of operations where they were in sole command. In Tonkin, Dahomey and Madagascar, the Marines had to share control with the Army and the Navy; here they

---

[1] Girardet, *op. cit.* p. 268.

[2] Godefroy Cavaignac, Projet de Loi, 9 July 1895, *J.O. Doc. Parl. Chambre*, no. 1488, p. 1313.

[3] The views of the colonial troops on metropolitan control were well stated by Marshal Lyautey at a meeting of the *Société de l'histoire des colonies* held on the occasion of General Archinard's eightieth birthday: '*De propos délibéré*, mais voilà tout le secret de l'action coloniale efficace. Prendre l'initiative, concevoir et entreprendre sans attendre les ordres d'"En Haut" lesquels n'arrivent jamais ou n'arrivent que négatifs, cet "En Haut" que dans la construction de notre magnifique domaine colonial, il a toujours fallu mettre en présence du fait accompli.' *Revue de l'histoire des colonies françaises*, XVIII (1930), 132–3.

[4] E.g. General Borgnis-Desbordes to Félix Faure, May 1885, cited in M. Blanchard, 'Correspondance de Félix Faure touchant les affaires coloniales, 1882–1898', *Revue d'histoire des colonies*, XLII (1955), 159:'Quand le général Brière m'a annoncé le 28 au soir que la brigade rétrogradait sous les ordres du colonel Herbinger, je lui ai demandé quel était cet officier que je ne connaissais pas; et lorsque le général m'eut dit que c'était un ancien professeur à l'Ecole de Guerre, je lui répondis: "Alors nous sommes f..." et c'était vrai.'

did not. The conquest of the Western Sudan was carried out exclusively by the *infanterie* and *artillerie de marine* and by the African contingents which their officers led. Here at least the Marines were their own masters. What Algeria had once been for the Army the Sudan was to become for the *troupes coloniales*. The course of Sudanese expansion was to depend as much upon the attitudes and aspirations of the *officier soudanais* as it did upon those of the policy-makers. So the motives for the conquest must clearly be sought in the military as well as in the official mind of imperialism.

But European motives alone cannot explain the creation of the Sudanese Empire. Neither the policy-makers in Paris nor the Military on the spot could ignore the pressures of local circumstances. In the Western Sudan these pressures were very considerable; European expansion here had to contend with the forces of a militant Islamic revival which was sweeping over the whole of Muslim Africa.

When the European advance began, the history of Islam in the Western Sudan already stretched back over eight hundred years. Islam had been spreading south along the trans-Saharan trade routes ever since the Arab conquest of North Africa in the eighth century. By the beginning of the eleventh century the kingdom of Tekrur on the Lower Senegal had been converted. By its end the Almoravids, Sanhaja Berbers from Mauritania, had driven north to purify the Faith in the Maghrib and had overthrown the kingdom of Ghana. In ages to come the empires of Mali and Songhai, Muslim in name and partly in character, established their mastery over the Sudanese interior; the city of Jenné on the Upper Niger became an important centre of trade with North Africa; Timbuktu became a flourishing seat of Muslim learning. But Islam remained the religion of the towns—of rulers, administrators and traders—and even in royal courts animist practices continued to survive. Its impact upon the mass of the rural population was slight, and many regions, particularly the pagan kingdoms of the Niger Bend, escaped its influence altogether. By the sixteenth century, moreover, its expansive force was spent. The Moroccan invasion of 1591 and the fall of Songhai threw the Sudan into political confusion and allowed the forces of animism to reassert themselves. The Bambara kingdoms of Segu and Kaarta now rose to dominance. The remnants of the Moroccan garrisons, the *arma*, gradually lost contact with North Africa and became assimilated into the surrounding population. Although Muslim scholars continued to tend the embers of Islamic civilisation at Jenné, the leaders of the *arma*, the *Ardos*, acknowledged the suzerainty of Segu and paid tribute to their animist overlords.[1]

By the eighteenth century, however, Muslims everywhere were beginning to react against the religious decadence of the Islamic world and the appalling decline in its political and military power. Some tried to revitalise Islam by adapting its tenets to suit contemporary circumstances. Others altered circumstances to make them conform to the strict principles of orthodoxy originally proclaimed by the Prophet and his immediate successors. The Wahhabi movement in its attempt to re-create the conditions of primitive Islam in the Arabian desert was perhaps the purest example of this conservative revolution. In North Africa similar impulses tended to express themselves through sufism, a mystical strain of Islam which had developed in reaction to the excessive rationalism of the original creed.

In an attempt to make Islam more accessible to the uneducated, sufism preached the possibility of a mystical union with God through faith. Sufis approached this state through the practice of asceticism, the recitation of special prayers and the performance of religious exercises. Sufi beliefs had their institutional base in the religious brotherhoods, the *tariqas*, each with its own set of doctrines but all theoretically part of a single Sufi order. The heads of the brotherhoods, the *shaikhs*, all claimed their place in the mystical hierarchy of the Muslim sainthood and on a chain of apostolic succession stretching back to the spiritual founder of the order, al-Junaid (d. 916). They were said to possess supernatural powers and the ability to invoke the aid of the unseen forces which ruled the world. They acted as vessels through which the *baraka*, God's special grace, could be imparted to the faithful. After their death the continued outflow of their *baraka* turned their tombs into places of pilgrimage.[2]

By the eighteenth century the conditions of Ottoman rule in Algeria had enabled the brotherhoods to become an important social and political force among the rural tribes of the hinterland. The Government, concerned primarily with the maintenance of security and the

---

[1] For the early history of Islam in West Africa, J. S. Trimingham, *A History of Islam in West Africa* (London, 1962), pp. 16–103, remains a standard account although many of its conclusions are debatable. A brief but valuable discussion of the significance of Islam for Sudanese political development is presented in J. D. Fage, 'Some Thoughts on State-Formation in the Western Sudan before the Seventeenth Century', *Boston University Papers on African History*, 1 (Boston, 1964), 19–34.

[2] See: O. Depont and X. Coppolani, *Les confréries religieuses musulmanes* (Algiers, 1897), and J. M. Abun-Nasr, *The Tijaniyya, a Sufi Order in the Modern World* (London, 1965).

regular collection of revenue, interfered as little as possible with the daily lives of the indigenous Algerians, and the resulting administrative vacuum came to be filled by the *tariqas*. Their headquarters, the *zawiyya*, became hostels for travellers and traders, places of worship and centres of Koranic education. Representatives of the orders among the tribes acted as religious instructors and arbitrators of disputes. The *shaikhs*, exercising virtually total power over their adherents and commanding the veneration of all, possessed tremendous political influence, and by the end of the eighteenth century they had become the leaders of popular resistance against Ottoman rule.[1]

Sufi brotherhoods were to play a decisive rôle in the revolutionary movements which transformed Sudanese political life during the century or so after 1750. The Qadiriyya order, established in North Africa since the twelfth century, had long been active south of the Sahara, particularly among the Kunta Arabs of the Timbuktu region. The Tijaniyya, an Algerian order founded in the 1780s, also moved quickly into the missionary field, and by the end of the century its peculiarly exclusive doctrines were being preached along the Lower Senegal.[2] Generally speaking, their militant assertion of Islam made its greatest impact upon the Fulfulde-speaking peoples, Fulani and Tokolor, who ranged over the whole of the Sudan from their original homelands on the Senegal as far east as Lake Chad. As early as the 1720s Fulani immigrants from Macina had rebelled against the rulers of Futa Jallon in present-day Guinea, and after half a century of conflict they managed to establish a Muslim state there. The success of the revolution in Futa Jallon gave the signal for the *torodbe*, the Tokolor clerical aristocracy, to overthrow their political masters and create a loose confederation of theocracies in the Futa region of Senegal. Their success in turn inspired Uthman dan Fodio, a *torodo* preacher resident at the court of Gobir in Hausaland, to proclaim the *jihad* which would culminate in the creation of the Sokoto Empire. Following his example, an itinerant cleric, Ahmadu Hammadi Bari, led a successful rebellion against the *Ardos* and their Bambara masters and founded the Fulani Empire of Macina. Finally in the 1850s *al-hajj* Umar, himself a *torodo* and the chief representative of the Tijaniyya order in the Western Sudan, began the *jihad* which ultimately established his sway over all

---

[1] Julien, *Histoire de l'Algérie contemporaine*, pp. 15–17.
[2] The founder of the Tijaniyya, Ahmad al-Tijani, claimed for himself a unique place in the hierarchy of the Muslim sainthood and forbade members of his order to join other brotherhoods. For an account of his doctrines see: Abun-Nasr, *op cit.* pp. 27–57.

the territory from the outskirts of Timbuktu to the frontiers of French Senegal.[1]

The causes and nature of these revolutionary movements were matters of dispute in their own lifetime and have remained so ever since.[2] They have been described as a revolt against social oppression, and certainly elements of the Hausa peasantry joined the Fulani in their war against the Hausa ruling class. They have been seen as manifestations of Fulani nationalism, and they certainly resulted in the establishment of Fulani or Tokolor political hegemonies. But they were above all religious movements which by the tenets of Islam were bound to assume social and political forms. In theory there could be no distinction between the religious and the secular spheres of life. The true practice of Islam was possible only within the framework of an Islamic state, organised socially according to the principles of the Law, and governed politically by a righteous ruler pledged to the defence of the Faith. The creation of such a state by violent means was sanctioned by the rules of the *jihad*. Muslims had the duty to take up arms in the defence of their religion, to combat heresy, to punish apostasy, and in general to extend the political boundaries of the Islamic world.[3] Muslim clerics began the movements and in most cases retained control over their leadership. Their avowed objectives were to purify Islam by overthrowing those rulers who practised or sanctioned the practice of heresy, to spread the faith by converting the animists, and to create new societies based on the *Sharia*. With varying degrees of determination and success they all attempted to realise these ideals. They organised the financial and legal systems of their empires on religious principles;

---

[1] For the history of these revolutions, see, *inter alia*: H. A. S. Johnston, *The Fulani Empire of Sokoto* (London, 1967); A. H. Ba and J. Daget, *L'empire peul du Macina, 1818–1853* (Paris, 1962); Abun-Nasr, *The Tijaniyya*, pp. 106–41.

[2] Of the growing body of literature on this subject, M. R. Waldman, 'The Fulani *jihad*—a Reassessment', *Journal of African History*, VI (1965), 333–55, is particularly valuable. M. Hiskett, 'Material relating to the State of Learning among the Fulani before their Jihad', *Bulletin of the School of Oriental and African Studies*, XIX (1957), 550–78; and *idem*, 'An Islamic Tradition of Reform in the Western Sudan from the Sixteenth to the Eighteenth Century', *ibid.* XXV (1962), 577–96, deal with the intellectual foundations of the movement in Sokoto. J. R. Willis, '*Jihad fi sabil Allah*—its Doctrinal Basis in Islam and some Aspects of its Evolution in Nineteenth-Century West Africa', *Journal of African History*, VIII (1967), 395–415, discusses the doctrinal bases of the Fulani and Tokolor jihads. H. F. C. Smith, 'A Neglected Theme of West African History: The Islamic Revolutions of the Nineteenth Century', *Historians in Tropical Africa*, mimeographed (Salisbury, 1962), pp. 145–58, provides a brief but useful introduction to the revolutionary movement as a whole.

[3] Significantly, Muslims divided the world into the *Dar al-Islam* (Domain of Islam) and the *Dar al-Harb* (Domain of War).

as far as possible they levied only those taxes authorised by the Koran; they made provision for the spread of religious learning by building mosques and founding schools, and they enforced the strict observance of religious and social obligations.

Inevitably, the nature of these movements affected their response to the pressures of European expansion. The *jihadi* states were theocracies whose rulers' powers were sanctioned by divine laws. Peaceful acceptance of European political domination was out of the question; to acknowledge Christian suzerainty would destroy the religious foundation of the State and of its ruler's authority. The extension of European political control, as the French learned in Algeria, was likely to be violently resisted. Almost immediately after the invasion, the tribes of the interior declared war on the French, and in 1832 they proclaimed the *jihad*, appointing a member of the Qadiriyya order, Abd el-Kader, as their leader. It took fifteen years and ultimately a third of the French Army to break the back of their resistance. Even after Abd el-Kader's surrender in 1847, Muslim opposition remained a constant threat to French security.

Yet the confrontation between Europe and Islam was never quite as clear-cut as it appeared. Even in Algeria, the anti-European *jihad* was part of a tradition of resistance to alien domination. Abd el-Kader's principal objective was to weld the tribes into a unified Algerian nation, based on religious principles and strong enough to repel foreign aggression. What he demanded from the French was recognition of his sovereignty over the interior and non-interference in the affairs of his subjects. In return, he was prepared to accept a permanent French presence on the Algerian coast.[1] His militant nationalism was not an absolute bar to co-operation with the Europeans. On two occasions, in 1834 and in 1837, he signed treaties of peace and friendship with the French, and in neither case was there any reason to doubt his sincerity.[2] Nor was militant Islam in itself a bar to co-operation with the infidel. The Tijaniyya welcomed the French invasion as divine retribu-

---

[1] Abd el-Kader's declaration, cited in: M. Emerit, *L'Algérie à l'époque d'Abd-el-Kader* (Paris, 1951), p. 148: '...si vous borniez votre occupation à Alger, Bône, Oran, je pourrais vous souffrir près de moi, car la mer ne m'appartient pas, je n'ai pas de vaisseaux'. For the Emir's political objectives, see: R. Gallissot, 'Abd el-Kader et la nationalité algérienne', *Revue historique*, CCXXXIII (1965), 339–68.

[2] *Marabout* of Miliana to Desmichels, 21 July 1834 [quoting the orders of Abd el-Kader], cited in Emerit, *op. cit.* p. 42: 'J'ai fait la paix avec tous les Français qui sont en Afrique tout en me conformant aux lois de notre religion; ainsi faites attention de ne pas intercepter les communications...ne tuez aucun Français!'

tion for Turkish misrule. It steadfastly refused to participate in a *jihad* led by a member of the rival Qadiriyya order; instead it collaborated wholeheartedly with the Christian enemy.[1]

South of the Sahara the confrontation was still less sharply defined. Here the *jihads* had been proclaimed not against Christians but against animists or apostate Muslims. When the Islamic revival in the Western Sudan reached the peak of its intensity during the mid-nineteenth century, the era of European expansion was still in its infancy. By the time European expansion entered its most vigorous phase, the *jihadi* states were beginning to break up. For the *jihad* failed to provide a stable foundation for a lasting political structure. In practice, the true *Sharia* state could never be created; when organising their conquests the *jihadis* were forced to make compromises: to modify taxation in order to secure sufficient revenue, to make room in legislative systems for established local customs, or to make use of existing administrative forms.[2] The religious fervour which gave the revolutions so much of their dynamism proved difficult to sustain, and without it much of their strength and cohesion were lost. The death of the original leadership was often followed by succession disputes and factional rivalries which created deep divisions within the new ruling class. The territorial gains of the *jihad* were rarely consolidated effectively, and the animists were never completely subjugated. Theocracies were gradually transformed into secular despotisms maintaining an uneasy control over their largely hostile subjects. The secularisation and decay of the *jihadi* state could affect its response to European expansion as significantly as its original religious militancy.

But these are not the only factors which have to be considered. One cannot explain the conquest of the Western Sudan in exclusively African terms any more than one can in those exclusively European. The French had their own settled views about the nature of militant Islam and the dangers it posed for European security. In Algeria they had felt the full impact of an anti-European *jihad*, and this experience instilled in them both a pathological fear of Muslim resistance and a fanatical determination to eradicate all traces of independent Muslim power. 'The Arab nation must be overthrown and the power of Abd el-Kader destroyed', Bugeaud told the French Chamber in 1840,

---

[1] Abun-Nasr, *op. cit.* pp. 62–82.

[2] The Fulani administration of the Sokoto empire, for example, was to a remarkable extent based upon the previous Hausa system of government. See: M. G. Smith, *Government in Zazzau* (London, 1960).

Introduction: the Colonial Army and the Western Sudan

'otherwise France will never accomplish anything in Africa.'[1] Lasting accommodation with the Emir was never seriously considered; the French themselves provoked the final conflict after 1839 by violating the Treaty of Tafna. Once the 'total conquest' of Algeria had been authorised, the methods adopted were those of total war. Bugeaud's instructions were to destroy Abd el-Kader 'with all the means at your disposal',[2] and he acted accordingly. His assault on the Arab nation was merciless. Recalcitrant tribes were driven off their land; their crops were burnt, their livestock scattered, their possessions destroyed until they were forced to choose between unconditional surrender and annihilation. Atrocities were frequent, and they were committed with the Governor-General's full approval.[3] *Qui veut la fin veut les moyens*, was Bugeaud's maxim and that of his army as well.[4] In the Western Sudan the French were again confronted by Islamic polities, and the *officiers soudanais* who already had so much in common with their Algerian predecessors could easily have reacted in a similar fashion.

These then are the factors which this inquiry into the conquest of the Western Sudan will attempt to consider. As a study in military imperialism it will inevitably concentrate on the rôle of the Military in the process which led to the creation of a vast European empire in the African interior. To analyse the motives of military expansion will be its primary task. But this is not its only purpose. By seeking to determine the characteristics of official Sudanese policy as it evolved in Paris, it will attempt to throw new light upon the nature of French expansion in Africa during the era of its partition. Finally, by examining the African context within which the Military operated and by assessing the nature of the African response to European expansion, it hopes to make a small contribution to our understanding of African history during one of its crucial periods.

[1] Cited in d'Ideville, *op. cit.* II, 136.
[2] Minister of War to Bugeaud, 19 Jan. 1841, cited in Schefer, 'La "Conquête Totale" de l'Algérie, 1839–1843', *loc. cit.* p. 59.
[3] Bugeaud to Minister of War, 5 Jan. 1846, cited in Chalmin, *op. cit.* p. 56: 'L'affaire des grottes [les grottees of Dahra where 4,000 Arabs who had sought refuge were suffocated], tant reprochée à Pélissier...est à mes yeux un titre aux bontés du Gouvernement. Il n'est pas un homme dévoué...qui n'eût pas agi en pareille circonstance comme le colonel Pélissier.'
[4] E.g. le colonel de Montagnac, *Lettres d'un soldat*, cited in Chalmin, *op. cit.* pp. 53–4: 'Qui veut la fin veut les moyens...Voilà...comment il faut faire la guerre aux Arabes. Tuer tous les hommes jusqu'à l'âge de quinze ans, prendre toutes les femmes et les enfants, en charger les bâtiments, les envoyer aux Iles Marquises ou ailleurs; en un mot anéantir tout ce qui ne rampera pas à nos pieds comme des chiens.' For Bugeaud's personality, see: Julien, *op. cit.* pp. 164–78; G. Esquer and P. Boyer, 'Bugeaud en 1840', *Revue africaine*, CIV (1960), 57–98, 283–321.

2

The Background of Conquest

Timbuktu was the magnet which drew Europe into the heart of West Africa. The name of this mysterious city, symbol for the fabulous golden lands of the far interior, had excited European imaginations ever since the fourteenth century. Iberian courts and Italian bankers had heard of Mansa Musa, Emperor of Mali, whose display of wealth had so astounded the Cairenes when he made the pilgrimage to Mecca in 1324. They knew that gold from the Western Sudan swelled the coffers of the Muslim states in North Africa. Spurred on by the effects on the Mediterranean economy of a growing shortage of bullion, they too attempted to tap the riches of the interior. The Genoese merchant Antonio Malfante traded at the Tuat oasis in the 1440s. The Portuguese from their base at Arguin on the Saharan coast sought to establish commercial relations with Timbuktu during the 1480s. The Florentine Benedetto Dei actually reached the town in 1470. After the publication of Leo Africanus's *History and Description of Africa* in the sixteenth century, both the legends of Sudanese wealth and the marvels of Timbuktu became part and parcel of the European mythology about Africa.[1]

Thereafter, interest in the Western Sudan declined as the expansive energies of Europe became focused on the Indies and the Americas, and as the development of the slave trade concentrated its activities on the West African coast. But the attractions of the interior were never completely forgotten. European agents in Morocco were dazzled by the gold which the Sultan's conquering armies brought back from the Sudan in the 1590s, and for the next two centuries the Barbary consuls continued to transmit details of the trans-Saharan caravan trade.[2] By the

---

[1] See: C. de La Roncière, *La découverte de l'Afrique au moyen âge*, Mémoires de la Société Royale de Géographie d'Egypte (Cairo, 1924–7), I, 121–63; III, 27–31; E. W. Bovill (ed.), *Missions to the Niger* (Cambridge, 1964), I, 168–71; idem, *The Golden Trade of the Moors*, 2nd ed (London, 1963), pp. 91–2, 121–33; F. Braudel, *La Méditerranée et le monde méditerranéen à l'époque de Philippe II* (Paris, 1949), pp. 364–74.
Bovill, *The Golden Trade of the Moors*, pp. 179–90; P. Masson, *Histoire des établissements et du commerce français dans l'Afrique barbaresque, 1560–1793* (Paris, 1903), pp. 91–2, 177–8, 233, 605.

1790s the officials of the newly founded African Association were talking of 'countries new to the fabrics of England, and probably inhabited by more than a hundred millions of people...', of 'a lucrative Commerce...much underrated at a Million sterling per annum...'.[1] Timbuktu also retained the magic of its name. Trade with 'the luxurious city...whose opulence...attract[s] the merchants of the most distant states of Africa', the Association confidently predicted, 'may eventually prove of the greatest importance to the Commercial Interests of Britain'.[2]

Frenchmen had also been thinking in these terms. Geographically, they were well placed to penetrate into the interior. The Senegal River, despite the sandbanks at its mouth, was navigable to shallow-draft boats for six months of the year. By the end of the seventeenth century the French were trading in Galam, four hundred miles inland. During the administrations of André Brüe, the Senegal Company's energetic local director, forts were built on the Falémé river; agents were sent to explore the goldfields of Bambuk; attempts were made to encourage the gold trade, and plans were laid for sending a mission to explore the route to Timbuktu. For Brüe too was fascinated by the tales of its treasure.[3]

Nothing came of these early efforts. The gold of Bambuk failed to materialise, and the gum-trade remained the basis of the Senegalese economy. Brüe's successors failed to share his vision of a Sudanese Eldorado and did little to challenge the growing power of the Moorish tribes along the Senegal. After 1730 French influence in the interior was minimal. Senegal suffered heavily in the wars of the late eighteenth century. Saint-Louis was lost in 1758 during the Seven Year's War, recaptured in 1779 during the Revolutionary War and lost once more in 1809 during the War of the Third Coalition. As the great era of scientific exploration opened at the end of the eighteenth century, Britain took the lead in the penetration of Africa and retained it for fifty years. British explorers discovered the sources and mouth of the Niger; British missions crossed the Sahara and the Western Sudan, visited the courts of Bornu and Sokoto, and established consulates in the

---

[1] Resolution of the Committee of the African Association, 6 Aug. 1789; Paper submitted to...The Right Honourable Henry Dundas..., June 1793, cited in R. Hallett (ed.), *Records of the African Association, 1788–1831* (London, 1964), pp. 74, 144.

[2] Henry Beaufoy, Report, 1790, cited *ibid.* pp. 100–1.

[3] A. Delcourt, *La France et les établissements français au Sénégal entre 1713 et 1763*, Mémoires de l'Institut Français d'Afrique Noire, no. 17 (Dakar, 1952), pp. 169–75.

Saharan entrepôts of Murzuk and Ghadamès.[1] Fully committed in Europe and deprived of her base in West Africa, France could do little to dispute her rival's influence.

But she never abandoned her African ambitions. After the recapture of Saint-Louis, successive Governors were ordered to renew contacts with the Upper Senegal and encourage the supply of gum, slaves and gold.[2] In 1802 the Napoleonic regime ordered Governor Blanchot to infuse his colony with the same dynamic spirit which suffused the metropolis, to rebuild Fort Saint-Joseph on the Falémé, and by every means within his power 'to establish every possible sort of relationship between Senegal and the interior of Africa'. In 1808 similar instructions were given to his successor.[3] And, when Senegal was finally regained in 1817, the Government of the Restoration adopted the same policy.

FRENCH POLICIES TOWARDS THE WESTERN SUDAN, 1816–54

Optimism was the hallmark of the Restoration's initial approach to African questions. The Government in 1816 had no doubts about Senegal's brilliant future. It was confident that plantations of coffee, cotton, sugar cane and indigo would flourish, that African labour could be recruited on the spot, and that the colony could replace the West Indies as the principal supplier of tropical commodities to the French economy. It was equally hopeful that control over the Senegal would enable France to corner the European market for gum and to exploit the gold mines of Bambuk.[4]

Reports comparing the colony's fertility to that of the Nile Valley confirmed its brightest expectations, and in 1818 a detailed plan of action was drawn up. Over the next five years 11,000,000 fr. were to be made available for Senegalese development and a thousand colonists sent out from France. Three forts were to be built on the Senegal in order to secure communications with Galam; plantations were to be

---

[1] For British activities in the Western Sudan during the first half of the nineteenth century, see: A. A. Boahen, *Britain, the Sahara and the Western Sudan, 1788–1861* (Oxford, 1964).

[2] Mémoire du Roi, 1 Apr. 1782 [Instructions to Dumontet]; *idem*, 18 Nov. 1783 [Instructions to de Répentigny]; *idem*, 18 Nov. 1785 [Instructions to Boufflers], cited in C. Schefer, *Instructions générales données de 1763 à 1870 aux Gouverneurs et Ordonnateurs des établissements français en Afrique occidentale* (Paris, 1921), I, 87–96, 111–25, 136–42.

[3] Instructions to Blanchot, 29 Thermidor An X; Instructions to Pinoteau, 15 Sept. 1808, cited *ibid.* pp. 184, 197–8.

[4] Mémoire du Roi, 18 May 1816 [Instructions to Schmaltz], cited *ibid.* pp. 230–76. The best general work on this period is G. Hardy, *La mise en valeur du Sénégal de 1817 à 1854* (Paris, 1921).

set up, the gum trade encouraged and the gold mines explored. The Senegalese authorities were also to make contact with the populations of the interior, for Paris was convinced that millions of Africans were waiting there to be transformed into producers of tropical goods and consumers for French industry.[1]

But all these hopes were soon disappointed. The Senegal proved not to be a second Nile, and the plantations did not prosper. Africans failed to offer their services as cheap labour, and within a year Governor Schmaltz was embroiled in a major war with the Trarza Moors. By 1820 Paris had had enough; Schmaltz was recalled and the Senegalese estimates were drastically reduced. Despite Governor Roger's efficient administration of the plantations during the 1820s, the Ministry remained pessimistic about the future. At the end of 1830 the experiment was abandoned, and Senegal was reduced to its former status of 'a simple trading factory [comptoir]'.[2] Efforts to expand inland were no more successful. A fort was built at Bakel in 1818, and both Schmaltz and Roger sent missions into Bambuk; but practical results were negligible. Plans for expeditions to Timbuktu in 1824 and 1826 never got off the ground; proposals for installing a consul at Bamako on the Upper Niger were never followed up.[3] The *Compagnie du Galam*, granted a qualified monopoly over the Senegalese gum trade in 1824, was unable to break the control of the Moorish producers at the trading stations along the river. Prices remained high and profits too low to justify large-scale investment. The abolition of the Company's privileges in 1835 merely aggravated the situation by increasing competition, thus raising prices still higher.[4] Paris never lost sight of its long-term objectives; after the abandonment of the colonisation experiment it even ordered the Governor to focus all his attention 'on the commercial relations between Senegal and the African interior; [for] only a considerable extension of these relations can increase the colony's importance'.[5] But its grandiose declaration was not accompanied by any concrete measures.

[1] Schmaltz to Baron Portal, 8 July 1817; Fleuriau to Baron Portal, 28 Dec. 1817, cited in Hardy, *op. cit.* pp. 37, 45; Ministre de la Marine et des Colonies [henceforth M.M.C.] to Schmaltz, 31 Dec. 1818, cited in Schefer, *op cit.* I, pp. 280 ff.

[2] M.M.C. to Governor of Senegal, 28 Dec. 1830, cited in Hardy, *op. cit.* p. 246.

[3] P. Marty, *Etudes sénégalaises (1785–1826)* (Paris, n.d.), pp. 93–217; C. Faure, 'Le premier séjour de Duranton au Sénégal, 1819–26', *Revue de l'histoire des colonies françaises*, IX (1921), 189–263, 263–8; Schefer, *op. cit.* II, 639 [index: Caillié].

[4] For the activities of the *Compagnie du Galam* see: E. Saulnier, *La Compagnie du Galam au Sénégal* (Paris, 1921).

[5] M.M.C. to Gov. Sen., 15 Apr. 1831, cited in Schefer, *op. cit.* II, 24–5.

The Background of Conquest

It was the conquest of Algeria which revitalised the Government's expansionist plans. By the 1840s the military advance had extended French supremacy to the borders of the Sahara, so providing a northern base for penetration into the Sudan. René Caillié had already given the French first-hand information about the legendary Timbuktu, and although he found the city much less magnificent than its reputation, his report still described it as a major commercial entrepôt.[1] From hearsay, Algerian explorers sent to investigate the nature, value and itineraries of the trans-Saharan caravan trade confirmed the town's economic importance. They too urged its incorporation into the orbit of French trade.[2] During the Governorship of Marshal Randon (1851–8), the conquest of southern Algeria was completed and French influence extended into the Sahara itself. Relations were established with the Azjer Tuareg who controlled the northern half of the desert and supplied the escorts for the trans-Saharan caravans. An alliance was concluded with the Walad Sidi Shaikh confederation, and with their help the oasis of Wargla was occupied in 1853. French troops captured the oasis of Laghouat in 1852 and took Tuggurt in 1854.[3]

The implications of this activity for Senegalese expansion were not ignored. The authorities there were kept fully informed of the progress of Algerian exploration and urged to contribute what information they could about the Sudan.[4] Explorers were sent on extravagant missions to cross the length and breadth of Africa and investigate the routes between Algeria and Senegal.[5] In 1843 the staunchly expansionist Governor of Senegal, Bouët-Willaumez, sent new missions into Bambuk and signed a commercial agreement with the ruler of Bondu allowing the French to build a trading post in his territory. In 1844 the *Compagnie du Galam* established *comptoirs* at Sénoudébou and Sansanding.[6] By 1847 Paris was determined to establish an exclusive sphere

---

[1] R. Caillié, *Travels through Central Africa to Timbuctoo* (London, 1830), I, 285–6; II, 55.

[2] E.g. E. Carette and E. Renou, *Recherches sur la géographie et le commerce de l'Algérie méridionale*, Exploration scientifique de l'Algérie, no. 2 (Paris, 1844), pp. 116, 175–6.

[3] The standard work on French penetration into the Sahara is still A. Bernard and N. Lacroix, *La pénétration saharienne* (Algiers, 1906). See also: J-L. Miège, *Le Maroc et l'Europe (1830–1894)* (Paris, 1961–3), III, 74–95.

[4] M.M.C. to Gov. Sen., 9 Oct. 1847, cited in Schefer, *op. cit.* II, 184–6.

[5] A. Raffenel, *Nouveau voyage dans le pays des nègres*, 2 vols. (Paris, 1856); R. Mantran, 'Une relation inédite d'un voyage en Tunisie au milieu du 19ᵐᵉ siècle', *Cahiers de Tunisie*, no. 11 (1955), pp. 474–80.

[6] Hardy, *op. cit.* pp. 323–6; A. Raffenel, *Voyage dans l'Afrique occidentale* (Paris, 1846), pp. 337–42. See also: L. Capperon, 'Bouët-Willaumez en Afrique occidentale et au Gabon, 1836–1850', *Revue maritime*, n.s. LXXXIX (1953), 1085–1103.

of influence on the Upper Senegal. 'It is absolutely vital for us', declared the Minister of Marine, 'to prevent any European nation from challenging our pre-eminence...or from sharing in the commercial advantages we are seeking to develop there.'[1] In 1853 credits were allocated for the construction of a fortified post at Médine, the farthest point of navigability on the Senegal, and there was talk of building another post still further inland.[2] By now Senegal was being described as the colony with the brightest future in Africa, and the extension of trade to Timbuktu was soon established as a principal objective of Senegalese policy. By 1854 Timbuktu itself was seen as a sort of lynch-pin between French possessions in North and West Africa.[3]

The scope of these policies was certainly ambitious; but their nature was much more limited. The Government's aim was to increase French trade, to create new outlets for French manufactures, and so to further 'the cause of civilisation and humanity, for which so much remains to be done in Africa, and which cannot be better served than by the peaceful conquests of commerce and industry'.[4] Expansion was to be a peaceful process. From the first Paris had emphasised the need to avoid the use of force; Senegalese authorities were to give the populations of the interior 'a high opinion of the wealth, the power and above all the goodwill of the French'.[5] Like their contemporaries in London, the policy-makers were informal imperialists; they planned to create a trading empire held together by bonds of influence and commercial supremacy. They had no intention of bringing the Sudan under direct French rule by military conquest.[6]

At that, the Sudanese commercial empire was but a distant objective of policy; the Upper Senegal and Upper Niger were 'the fields on which the harvests of the future will one day be reaped'.[7] The French position on the Lower Senegal was a matter of more immediate concern. After the final revocation of the Galam Company's privileges in 1848, the volume of the gum trade had rapidly increased; but more

---

[1] M.M.C. to Gov. Sen., 16 Nov. 1847, cited in Schefer, *op. cit.* II, 188.
[2] M.M.C. to Protet, 4 Jan. 1853; same to same, 5 Jan. 1853, cited *ibid.* pp. 216–26, 226–9.
[3] M.M.C. to Ministre des Affaires Etrangères [henceforth M.A.E.], 18 Sept. 1852, Ministère des Affaires Etrangères, Mémoires et Documents [henceforth AEMD] Afrique 46; M.M.C. to Protet, 26 June 1854, Section Outre-Mer des Archives Nationales, formerly Archives du Ministère de la France d'Outre-Mer [henceforth MFOM] Afrique III 9.
[4] M.M.C. to Gov. Sen., 15 Apr. 1831, cited in Schefer, *op. cit.* II, 24–5.
[5] Mémoire du Roi, 18 May 1816 [Instructions to Schmaltz], cited *ibid.* I, 258.
[6] For the general theory of 'informal empire', see: R. E. Robinson and J. Gallagher, 'The Imperialism of Free Trade', *Economic History Review*, 2nd ser. VI (1953), 1–15.
[7] M.M.C. to Faidherbe, Instructions, 8 Dec. 1854, MFOM Sénégal I 41 (a).

vigorous commercial activity also underlined the precarious state of French political power on the river, where Moorish control over the trading stations remained as strong as ever. As a result, a Government Commission was set up in 1850 to investigate the economic position of the West African territories and to advise upon their future administration. Its conclusions on Senegal heralded the opening of a new era in West African expansion; for while it recognised the advantages of the free trade system and called for a relaxation of the regulations governing the gum trade, it also maintained that commercial prosperity was dependent on political security, and that security would require the establishment of French political supremacy over the whole course of the Lower Senegal. Accordingly, it recommended the retention of existing forts at Richard-Toll, Dagana and Bakel, the reinforcement of the post at Sénoudébou, and the reconstruction of the old fort at Podor.[1] The Minister of Marine and Colonies, Ducos, accepted the Commission's proposals. In December 1852 credits were made available for strengthening fortifications along the Senegal, and in January Governor Protet was ordered to break the hold of the Moors over the trading *escales*, if necessary by force. When the Governor put off the fortification of Podor he was sharply reminded of the urgency of his instructions; when he postponed action against the Moors he was reprimanded and recalled.[2] His replacement, Louis Faidherbe, was ordered to impose French dominance over the Senegal from Saint-Louis to the cataracts of Félu.[3] The new Governor turned out to be just the man for the job.

FAIDHERBE AND THE OCCUPATION OF THE SENEGAL

With the appointment of Faidherbe as Governor in November 1854 the new era in expansion formally began. Despite his youth—he was only thirty-six at the time—Faidherbe had already acquired considerable experience of conditions in the outposts of Empire and had demonstrated both a resolute character and a difficult temperament. Having gained a respectable entry into the Ecole Polytechnique in 1838, he frittered away his time and graduated with a reputation for idleness and

---

[1] For the composition, deliberations and recommendations of this Commission, see: Hardy, *op. cit.* pp. 331–42.

[2] M.M.C. to Protet, 4 Jan. 1853; same to same, 14 Dec. 1853; same to same, 19 July 1854 (Conf.), cited in Schefer, *op. cit.* II, 216–26, 239 ff., 248–9.

[3] M.M.C. to Faidherbe, 9 Nov. 1854, MFOM Sénégal I 41 (c).

dissipation, securing one of the last available vacancies in the corps of Military Engineers. Posted to Algeria in 1844, he served for three years in the campaigns against Abd el-Kader without distinguishing himself in any way. 'He seems capable and intelligent', ran his confidential report for 1845, 'but has so far shown a distaste for hard work.' In 1848 he was transferred to Guadeloupe, where his ardent Republican sympathies and his support for the Abolitionist Victor Schoelcher soon alienated both his fellow officers and the local settlers. Returning to Algeria in 1849, he took part in the conquest of Kabylia and was this time decorated for bravery. In 1852 he was posted to Senegal as *sous-directeur de génie* and Protet's expert on fortifications.[1] His relations with the Governor were anything but friendly; indeed his report on the mismanagement of a punitive expedition against the town of Dialmath contributed materially to Protet's dismissal.[2] Significantly, the reason for his animosity was the Governor's reluctance to oppose the exactions of upstart local rulers. Faidherbe despised such timidity and resented the military inactivity to which it condemned him.[3] He could be relied on to act much more energetically than his predecessor.

The new Governor's outlook was conditioned above all by his previous years of service in Algeria. His experience of military expansion in North Africa moulded his views about West Africa and served as the model for the policies he advocated. In the two colonies, he was later to declare, 'the objectives are the same...the difficulties to be overcome analogous, and the methods for overcoming them identical'. 'Having served in Algeria', he wrote in 1858, 'I had to be in favour of a more serious occupation of Senegal.'[4] For Faidherbe, military security was the overriding priority to which all other interests, including those of trade, had to be subordinated. It was useless to think in terms of economic development, he told the Minister in one of his first des-

---

[1] There is as yet no completely satisfactory biography of Faidherbe. The standard works are: G. Hardy, *Faidherbe* (Paris, 1947), and A. Demaison, *Faidherbe* (Paris, 1932). See also: R. Delavignette, 'Faidherbe', in C-A. Julien (ed.), *Les techniciens de la colonisation* (Paris, 1953).

[2] M.M.C. to Protet, 19 July 1854, cited in Schefer, *op. cit.* II, 248–9; M.M.C. to Faidherbe, 14 Nov. 1854, cited *ibid.* pp. 256–8.

[3] Faidherbe to Colonel Roux, 10 Sept. 1854, MFOM Dossier Administratif, Faidherbe: 'Le Gouverneur [Protet] regardait comme des cerveaux brûlés ceux qui demandent ici quelques réformes et qui disent qu'avec les forces dont on dispose la colonie ne doit pas céder partout et toujours à des petits états nègres qui n'ont jamais pu nous opposer 4000 hommes.'

[4] Faidherbe to Minister of Algeria and Colonies, 14 Oct. 1859, MFOM Sénégal I 46 (a); Faidherbe, Memorandum, 1 Oct. 1858, MFOM Sénégal I 45 (a).

patches, while French influence in the Futa region of Senegal remained negligible and Saldé province remained unpacified. Military domination was the sole guarantee for security and the essential precondition for any form of profitable commercial activity. Only those engaged in 'illicit operations', he wrote in one of his last reports, maintained that trade could flourish before the country had been effectively occupied.[1] Military domination meant more troops and more fortifications, and within weeks of his appointment Faidberbe was clamouring for reinforcements to be sent to Bakel; three months later he asked for permission to begin work on the new fort at Médine.[2]

The Governor's views on serious occupation were not fully shared by his superiors. Although Paris had agreed to the imposition of political control over the Senegal, its main pre-occupations were economic, and it rejected Faidherbe's North African analogy.[3] In 1854 the Ministry warned him not to regard his appointment as the start of 'a warlike era' and instructed him to concentrate on 'the peaceful development of commercial interests'. His first tasks were to ensure the freedom of the gum trade and to assist the local traders. At the same time, Paris was determined to prevent Senegal from becoming an excessive burden to the Treasury. The colony's total budget was less than 1,500,000 fr., and even this was described as 'a considerable... financial sacrifice'. The Governor was ordered on no account to exceed his estimates.[4] Not surprisingly therefore, Faidherbe's military demands were coolly received. Reinforcements were sent to Bakel in May 1855, but only after the garrison of Podor had been reduced. Faidherbe received permission to build Médine and was given an extra 30,000 fr. to cover the cost, but his request for a company of artillery to garrison the new fort was refused.[5]

Nevertheless, the two sides managed to work together in reasonable harmony. Paris had sanctioned the use of force against the Moors, and it cautiously approved a limited military campaign to suppress their influence over the trading stations. During the next three years Faidherbe was able to break their hold over the province of Walo on the

---

[1] Faidherbe to M.M.C., 19 Jan. 1855, MFOM Sénégal I 41 (b); Faidherbe to M.M.C., 27 Nov. 1864, MFOM Sénégal I 50 (b).

[2] Faidherbe to M.M.C., 22 Dec. 1854; same to same, 13 Mar. 1855, MFOM Sénégal I 41(b).

[3] Minister of Algeria and Colonies to Faidherbe, 21 Nov. 1859, MFOM Sénégal I 46(b).

[4] M.M.C. to Faidherbe, Instructions, 9 Nov. 1854, MFOM Sénégal I 41(c); same to same, Instructions, 8 Dec. 1854, MFOM Sénégal I 41(a).

[5] Note pour la direction des colonies, 7 June 1855, MFOM Sénégal I 41(c); M.M.C. to Faidherbe, 5 Apr. 1855; same to same, 17 Aug. 1855, *ibid.*

left bank of the Senegal and their control over the gum trade.[1] For his part, the Governor complied with his instructions to encourage peaceful economic activity. He was on friendly terms with the Saint-Louis merchants and gave them concessions around the forts. While ordering his commanders to be firm in their treatment of those who threatened security, he also reminded them that 'the aim of all our efforts is [the maintenance of] peace'.[2] 'I shall continue to carry out my orders...to the best of my ability', he assured the Minister in 1857, and the latter in turn complimented him on 'the vision, the...energy and the practical prudence which have governed all the acts of your administration'.[3]

But the subjugation of Moorish tribesmen and the protection of local traders could not keep the Governor contented for long. The colony, he thought, was destined for much greater things than the supply of acacia gum. He too had visions of a second India on the Senegal, and in September 1858 he returned to France in order to press his views on the Ministry.[4] The visit was well timed, for only three months before the Colonial Department had been transferred to the newly created Ministry of Algeria and Colonies headed by Prince Jerome Napoleon. The Emperor's cousin, a colonial enthusiast in his own right, responded to the Governor's call and approved his proposals for more vigorous action. In February 1859 new instructions were issued to consolidate the territories already occupied and to extend French power through the construction of new forts.[5]

Faidherbe was quick to seize the opportunity. Despite his protestations of loyalty and obedience, he was too much of an Algerian to resist such a tempting chance for asserting his independence. On his return to the colony, he immediately formed an expeditionary column and led it south on a punitive campaign into the province of Siné. Outrages committed against French nationals there, he later explained to the Ministry, had made it essential to restore French prestige by force, and

---

[1] M.M.C. to Faidherbe, 20 Feb. 1855, *ibid.* Faidherbe's campaigns against the Moors are described in L.L.C. Faidherbe, *Le Sénégal, la France dans l'Afrique occidentale* (Paris, 1889), pp. 121 ff.

[2] Faidherbe to M.M.C., 28 Dec. 1854, MFOM Sénégal I 41 (b); Faidherbe to *commandants de poste*, 3 Oct. 1855, MFOM Sénégal IV 44 (a); Faidherbe to Commandant of Bakel, n.d. [Copy], MFOM Sénégal I 41 (d). After the battle of Dialmath, the leading merchants of Saint-Louis had petitioned the Ministry to appoint Faidherbe as Governor. See: Faidherbe, *op. cit.* pp. 119–20.

[3] Faidherbe to M.M.C., 7 May 1857, MFOM Sénégal I 43 (a); M.M.C. to Faidherbe, 21 July 1857, MFOM Sénégal I 43 (b).

[4] Faidherbe, Memorandum, 1 Oct. 1858, MFOM Sénégal I 45 (a).

[5] Minister of Algeria and Colonies to Faidherbe, 22 Feb. 1859, MFOM Sénégal I 46 (b).

the need for prompt and decisive action had made it impossible for him to await instructions.[1] Unfortunately, Prince Napoleon was no longer in charge, and his replacement, the Marquis de Chasseloup-Laubat, took a much less tolerant view of the escapade than Faidherbe might have expected. A former Minister of Marine and a bureaucrat by profession and temperament, Chasseloup-Laubat was not prepared to see his authority flouted in such an off-hand fashion.[2] He rejected the Governor's excuses, reprimanded him for undertaking military operations without permission, and ordered him to halt his advance.[3]

Admittedly the tone of the reproof was severe, and for a moment Faidherbe thought of resigning.[4] But he retained enough composure to grasp its real significance. For all its bluster Paris had not ordered him to withdraw. His action had been condemned, but it had not been disavowed; tacitly, the *fait accompli* had been accepted. Faidherbe answered accordingly. The campaign, he told Chasseloup-Laubat, had not *compelled* the French to reoccupy their old positions at Rufisque, Portudal and Joal, as the latter seemed to think. On the contrary, the prestige gained by their victory now *enabled* them to hold these towns with only token garrisons, an opportunity which everyone in the colony agreed was too good to be missed. Nor was there any question of a deliberately planned *expédition de guerre*; the whole operation had been intended merely as 'a peaceful show of our force'.[5]

And these tactics succeeded. In effect, the Minister now apologised for suspecting his Governor of disobedience; he even accepted Faidherbe's laboured explanation about the supposedly peaceful nature of the expedition.[6] There was little else he could do. A second reprimand could only result in the Governor's recall, and Faidherbe had made himself too valuable to be lightly discarded.[7] Then too, the results of the expedition might further the interests of French trade in the area,

---

[1] Faidherbe to Minister of Algeria and Colonies, 14 June 1859, MFOM Sénégal I 46(a).
[2] For Chasseloup-Laubat's career see: A. Duchêne, *Un ministre trop oublié, Chasseloup-Laubat* (Paris, 1932).
[3] Chasseloup-Laubat to Faidherbe, 1 Sept. 1859, MFOM Sénégal I 46(b).
[4] See: Faidherbe to Marshal Randon [Minister of War], 14 Nov. 1859, cited in Demaison, *op cit.* pp. 129–30.
[5] Faidherbe to Chasseloup-Laubat, 16 Oct. 1859, MFOM Sénégal I 46(a).
[6] Chasseloup-Laubat to Faidherbe, 21 Nov. 1859, MFOM Sénégal I 46(b): 'J'admets aujourd'hui très volontiers les explications que vous présentez à ce sujet et d'après lesquelles vous avez été entraîné malgré vous, dans une expédition destinée à être tout à fait pacifique, à recourir à la force des armes pour faire respecter notre autorité et notre commerce dans ces contrées.'
[7] See: Prince Napoleon to Faidherbe, 22 Feb. 1859, MFOM Sénégal I 46(b); Faidherbe to Chasseloup-Laubat, 13 Oct. 1859, MFOM Sénégal I 46(a).

thus justifying its cost. And after all the deed was done. A withdrawal would certainly damage French prestige and so reduce the prospects for trade. By giving their enemies new heart it could also endanger the colony's security. Faidherbe's battle against ministerial control was as good as won, and he exploited his advantage to the full. Five months later he was outlining plans for a new campaign in the south. Nobody, he assured the Minister, was more opposed to a warlike policy than he; but the king of Cayor refused to sign a treaty and had to be taught a lesson.[1] This time there was no argument, and Faidherbe duly marched into Cayor, deposed the *damel* Macodou and installed the more amenable Madiodio in his place.

But his triumph was short-lived. In 1860 the Ministry of Algeria and Colonies was wound up, and the direction of colonial affairs reverted to the Ministry of Marine. The following year Faidherbe himself left Senegal for another tour of duty in Algeria, and Chasseloup-Laubat, more at ease in his old surroundings, took advantage of the Governor's absence to reimpose a semblance of metropolitan control. His instructions to Faidherbe's replacement, Jean Jauréguiberry, stressed the need for consolidation instead of expansion. The new Governor was ordered to encourage the peaceful extension of trade and to investigate the colony's potential as a producer of cotton now that regular supplies had been cut off by the American Civil War. Above all, he was to curb the steady rise in expenditure and ensure that the limits of the budget were not overstepped.[2] Chasseloup-Laubat could expect a greater degree of co-operation from his new subordinate; for as a naval Captain Jauréguiberry was dependent on the Ministry of Marine for his professional as well as administrative future.

In fact, Jauréguiberry was just as aggressive as his predecessor, but his attempts to maintain the impetus of military expansion met with no success. Committed now to a policy of peace, commercial development and economy, Paris generally ignored his proposals for new demonstrations of strength and rejected his demands for reinforcements.[3] Jauréguiberry himself did little to help his case. His unbounded talent for alienating his associates soon involved him in squabbles with the local merchants, the majority of his subordinates and in the end with

---

[1] Same to same, 13 Apr. 1860, *ibid.*
[2] M.M.C. to Jauréguiberry, Instructions, 17 Dec. 1861, MFOM Sénégal I 48 (a).
[3] Jauréguiberry to M.M.C., 17 Dec. 1861; same to same, 19 June 1862; same to same, 17 Oct. 1862 (with minute by Chasseloup-Laubat), MFOM Sénégal I 48 (b); Jauréguiberry to M.M.C., 16 Oct. 1862 [Copy], MFOM Sénégal I 48 (d).

the Colonial Department as well.[1] He failed to assist trade and could not prevent the political situation from deteriorating. The Trarza Moors grew restless; French influence in the riverine districts of Futa declined, and French supremacy in Cayor was again challenged by the rebellious Macodou and his kinsman Lat Dyor. In May 1863 Jauréguiberry was finally recalled, and Faidherbe, newly promoted to the rank of General, returned to repair the damage.

Predictably, his first concern was to restore security by another series of military campaigns. In August he told the Minister that a new expedition was required to crush resistance in Cayor and that an extra 100,000 fr. would be needed to cover the cost.[2] But the days of Siné were over. The Ministry's resources were now fully committed in the Far East and in Central America. The Mexican campaign alone was expected to cost 200,000,000 fr., to say nothing of Cochinchina, a subject of much greater interest to Chasseloup-Laubat than Senegal.[3] Although the Minister approved the Cayor campaign, he sharply rejected the request for additional funds. Instead, he ordered his Colonial Department to draft proposals for reducing Senegalese expenditure and warned Faidherbe to expect substantial cuts in his forces. Only when the expeditionary force sustained heavy casualties in a serious military reverse did he relent.[4] Faidherbe was warned that all projects involving costly military expeditions would in future be vetoed, and before he left the colony for good in 1865 he had been forced reluctantly to begin the evacuation of those forts no longer considered absolutely essential for the maintenance of security.[5]

It was a sad and an inappropriate end to Faidherbe's West African career. Through his energy and resolution, Senegal had in a decade been transformed from a collection of scattered and precarious trading

---

[1] The details of these disputes are to be found in MFOM Sénégal I 48(d).

[2] Faidherbe to M.M.C., 26 Aug. 1863, MFOM Sénégal I 50 (b).

[3] G. Gille, 'Les capitaux français et l'expédition du Mexique', *Revue d'histoire diplomatique* LXXIX (1965), 206. For Chasseloup-Laubat's interest in Indochina, see: Duchêne, *Un ministre trop oublié*, pp. 203 ff. The influence of the Mexican and Indochinese questions on West African policy is revealed in a postscript by Chasseloup-Laubat on M.M.C. to Faidherbe, 22 June 1864, MFOM Sénégal I 50(c).

[4] Minute by Chasseloup-Laubat on Faidherbe to M.M.C., 26 Aug. 1863, MFOM Sénégal I 50(b); M.M.C. to Faidherbe, 22 Oct. 1863, MFOM Sénégal I 50(c); Minute by Chasseloup-Laubat on Faidherbe to M.M.C., 18 Jan. 1864, MFOM Sénégal I 50(b). In December 1863 the expeditionary force lost over 100 men at the battle of Ngolgol. See: Faidherbe, *Le Sénégal*, pp. 271–2.

[5] M.M.C. to Faidherbe, 23 July 1864 [Copy], AEMD Afrique 47; Faidherbe to M.M.C., 28 Sept. 1864, MFOM Sénégal I 50(b).

posts into a powerful and vigorous colony dominating the lower reaches of the river. Much remained to be done; Cayor was still unpacified, and French mastery on the Senegal itself was still not absolute. But the Moors no longer threatened Saint-Louis; French military supremacy had been clearly established and her influence extended into the south. Trade was at last beginning to thrive, and the rapid increase in the production of groundnuts in particular seemed to provide a sound economic base for the colony's future development.

Yet the occupation of the Lower Senegal was not the Governor's chief preoccupation. As far as he was concerned his colony's future lay in the interior; Senegal itself was valuable mainly as the base from which to strike for the Niger. It was in the Western Sudan that the foundations of his new India were to be laid, and to lay them was his burning ambition. The pursuit of this ambition was to bring France up against the expanding empire of *al-hajj* Umar.

AL-HAJJ UMAR AND THE TOKOLOR JIHAD

Of the many outstanding leaders which the nineteenth century Islamic revolutions produced, few were more remarkable than Umar. He was born at the end of the eighteenth century in Futa Toro, where his father, Saïd Tall, belonged to the *torodbe* clerical caste which had come to power some twenty years before.[1] From his youth, Umar distinguished himself both by his intelligence and by his religious zeal. He studied under Abdul-Karim al-Naqil, a prominent Tijani scholar who initiated him into the order and persuaded him to undertake the pilgrimage in 1826, when he was about thirty-three years old. Umar reached Mecca in 1828 and there came under the protection of Muhammad al-Ghali, the *Khalifa* (chief representative) of the Tijaniyya in the Hijaz. After three years of instruction, Muhammad al-Ghali finally initiated him into the ultimate mysteries of the order and appointed

---

[1] There have been several accounts, both European and African, of Umar's career. The most recent work is Abun-Nasr, *The Tijaniyya*, pp. 106–28; See also: Ba and Daget, *L'empire peule du Macina*, pp. 233–880; E. Mage, *Voyage dans le Soudan occidental* (Paris, 1868), pp. 231–82; M. Delafosse, *Haut-Sénégal-Niger* (Paris, 1912), II, 305–38; M. A. Tyam (H. Gaden tr.), *La vie d'El Hadj Omar*, Mémoires de l'Institut d'Ethnologie, no. 21 (Paris, 1935); M. Delafosse, 'Traditions historiques et légendaires du Soudan occidental', *Afrique Française, Renseignements Coloniaux*, Oct. 1913, pp. 355–68; J. Salenc (tr.), 'La vie d'El Hadj Omar', *Bulletin du Comité des Etudes Historiques et Scientifiques de l'Afrique Occidentale Française*, I (1918), 405–13; J. Suret-Canale, 'El Hadj Omar', *Présence africaine* (1958), pp. 69–72.

him *Khalifa* to the Western Sudan.[1] On his return, he passed through the empires of Bornu and Sokoto and married into their ruling families. In Sokoto especially, he enjoyed a considerable reputation as a teacher and spiritual leader, and became an intimate friend of Sultan Muhammad Bello.[2] On the Sultan's death in 1837, Umar left the empire and resumed his journey home. After a less friendly reception by the Sultan of Macina and a short period of imprisonment at Segu, he finally settled in Futa Jallon and established a religious hostel at Diagouku.

Umar's prestige had already won him a numerous following and substantial wealth. Many disciples from Sokoto accompanied him to Futa Jallon, and many others made financial donations to further his religious work. Even the Bambara king of Segu was persuaded to give him gold on his release. At Diagouku he continued to proselytise and began to build up the bases of his economic and military strength. His followers worked the land, traded for gold dust in Buré and used the proceeds to purchase arms from Sierra Leone. A rapid tour through his native Futa in 1847 gained him many new adherents and further swelled his treasury. By now, however, his growing power had begun to alarm his hosts in Futa Jallon, and in 1849 he was forced to leave Diagouku for new headquarters in Dinguiray. From here he launched attacks on the small animist states of the region, and in September 1852 he declared the *jihad* against all those who refused to accept the rule of Islam. In a decade of religious war he established his supremacy over the whole of the Western Sudan, conquering Dinguiray and Buré, smashing the Bambara kingdoms of Segu and Kaarta, and overthrowing the Muslim empire of Macina. By 1863 his envoys were demanding tribute from Timbuktu.

Religion was undoubtedly the most important factor which inspired Umar's career of conquest and brought him his phenomenal success. The *Khalifa* did not consider himself a secular leader but a religious reformer with a divinely inspired mission to sweep the Sudan free of animism and establish the rule of the *Sharia*.[3] His travels and studies had made him intimately aware of the revivalist tradition, and his experience of similar movements elsewhere on the continent, particularly

[1] According to Abun-Nasr, Muhammad al-Ghali appointed Umar as *muqaddam* to the Western Sudan; but Tyam's praise poem states that the appointment was as *khalifa*, and this is confirmed by the traditions collected by Ba and Daget. Abun-Nasr, *op. cit.* pp. 108, 110–11; Tyam, *op. cit.* p. 12; Ba and Daget, *op. cit.* p. 239.

[2] *al-hajj* Saïd, *Tarikh Sokoto*, (O. Houdas tr.), Publications de l'Ecole des Langues Orientales Vivantes, IVe série, xx (Paris, 1901), 308–10, 314; Ba and Daget, *op. cit.* p. 135.

[3] Tyam, *op. cit.* p. 135.

in Sokoto, affected the course of his own. In common with other *jihadis* he modelled his actions as closely as possible on those of the Prophet, describing his flight from Diagouku as his *hijra*, those who accompanied him as the *muhajirin*, and those who later joined him in Dinguiray as the *ansar*. From Sultan Bello he probably learned the theoretical subtleties of the *jihad*; certainly he justified the legitimacy of his campaign against Muslim Macina on the same theologically suspect principles which Bello had advanced in support of his war against the Muslim empire of Bornu.[1] Umar's avowed intention was to extirpate animism, and he pursued his goal relentlessly. Defeated pagans were obliged to accept the new faith and its obligations, and death was often the penalty for their refusal.[2] The judicial and fiscal systems of his empire were ordered according to the precepts of the *Sharia*. The *talibés* (students of religion), for the most part Tokolor emigrants from Futa, filled most of the key posts in the administration. Mosques were built, and provision was made for the instruction of the people in the doctrines of Islam and of the Tijaniyya.

Religion was also the source of the *Khalifa*'s temporal power. His disciples were drawn to his banner by his prestige as a latter-day evangelist, and he commanded their loyalty primarily through his position as a religious leader. Religious enthusiasm inspired his troops and sustained their morale. Infused with the spirit of the *jihad* and led by the *talibés* who also formed its élite corps, Umar's army became a courageous and formidable fighting force. 'They march against our fire as if to martyrdom', wrote Faidherbe of the warriors who attacked Médine in 1857, 'it is clear that they wish to die.'[3]

But religion was not the sole foundation of the state nor the only element in its strength. Although the *talibés* constituted the administrative and military elite, maintained by special grants of land and exempt from taxation, the positions of greatest responsibility were entrusted to those most loyal to the *Khalifa* personally. The province of Kaarta, for example, was governed by his faithful slave Mustafa. Converted animists also remained in positions of power; organised into

---

[1] Abun-Nasr, *op. cit.* pp. 122–4. The argument was that Muslims who supported infidels against another Muslim power were themselves to be considered as infidels against whom the *jihad* could legitimately be waged.

[2] For Umar's policies of forceful conversion in Kaarta, see: G. Boyer, *Un peuple de l'ouest soudanais, les Diawara*, Mémoires de l'Institut Français d'Afrique Noire no. 29 (Dakar, 1953), pp. 43–7.

[3] Faidherbe to M.M.C., 19 July 1857, MFOM Sénégal I 43 (a); also cited in Abun-Nasr, *op. cit.* p. 130.

regiments of *sofas*, they even formed the basis of the army's fighting strength. Umar's followers included many simple adventurers attracted by the prospect of participating in his successful and profitable military campaigns. Recruits from the European colonies made a particularly significant contribution to the movement's military success, for they brought with them the skills which they had acquired from their former masters. Samba N'Diaye, a house servant from Saint-Louis, became Umar's chief engineer and supervised the construction of his fortifications. Trained gunsmiths capable of manufacturing gunpowder accompanied his armies on their campaigns. By the late 1850s the Tokolors also possessed four small cannons which had been captured in early skirmishes with the French. These were kept in good repair by Samba N'Diaye and were used to good effect, not least for their psychological value, at the capture of Segu.[1]

Material considerations determined Umar's relations with the French. The progressive extension of European control over the Tokolor homelands could not have pleased the *Khalifa*, but he also realised that the French could become valuable suppliers of arms, and he was anxious to stay on good terms with them. During his visit to Futa Toro in 1847, he assured the French authorities that his forthcoming campaigns would be directed only against animists. He promised protection for French trade if they agreed to sell him arms and allowed him to levy customs duties. Even when the French began to fortify Podor, a stone's-throw from the village where he was born, he made no attempt to interfere with their activities and again asked them to sell him arms.[2]

But the French would have none of it. They dreaded the effects of Umar's preaching on the Muslims of Saint-Louis, and they had no intention of contributing to the rise of a strong Muslim power on the Lower Senegal. Accordingly, they refused to supply the *Khalifa* with weapons and began to arm his enemies instead. As their intentions became clear, Umar's attitude also changed. Early in 1855 his supporters raided the French trading posts, seizing stocks of merchandise at Bakel and kidnapping the Commandant of Sénoudébou. More menacingly, Umar himself issued an open declaration of war, promising to

---

[1] For the importance of artillery in Tokolor campaigns, see: Y. Saint-Martin, 'L'artillerie d'El Hadj Omar et d'Ahmadou', *Bulletin de l'I.F.A.N.*, série B, xxvii (1965), 560–72.
[2] F. Carrère and P. Holle, *De la Sénégambie française* (Paris, 1855), p. 195; Mage, *op. cit.* p. 236.

continue the struggle until the Christians submitted and paid him tribute, and calling on his correligionists in Saint-Louis to have no dealings with the infidel.[1] Whether his manifesto was seriously meant as a proclamation of the *jihad*, however, is uncertain. By now Umar was fully committed to the conquest of Kaarta, and he had little to gain from attacking the much more formidable Europeans. His provocative letter was not the signal for an immediate outbreak of hostilities; indeed he soon renewed his offer to live in peace with the French and protect their trade, provided it were carried out under his control.[2] But certainly the Senegalese authorities had good reason to fear for the security of their colony, and nobody was more worried about the situation than Governor Faidherbe.

FAIDHERBE, ISLAM AND THE NIGER

Faidherbe's experience of Muslim resistance in Algeria was bound to affect his response to Umar's challenge. Admittedly, the Governor was much less influenced by crude anti-Muslim prejudices than many of his contemporaries. He had a passionate interest in Africa, a genuine sympathy for its peoples, and a deep concern for the interests of all those who accepted French authority. But there was a world of difference between Muslims living peacefully in Saint-Louis and the crusading warriors of a religious fanatic who seemed bent on disputing French supremacy along the Senegal. Faidherbe was too keenly aware of the power of militant Islam to relish the prospect of another anti-European *jihad*. From the first, therefore, he was profoundly suspicious of the *Khalifa*'s designs. The attacks on French traders and Umar's manifesto confirmed his worst fears that the *Khalifa* was becoming a second Abd el-Kader. 'God help us', he warned the Governor of the

[1] Umar to the Muslims of Saint-Louis, January 1855, cited in Faidherbe, *Le Sénégal*, pp. 163–4; 'Maintenant je me sers de la force et je ne cesserai que lorsque la paix me sera demandée par votre tyran, qui devra se soumettre à moi suivant les paroles de notre maître: Fais la guerre aux gens qui...ayant reçu une révélation ne suivent pas la vraie religion jusqu'à ce qu'ils paient le djezia par la force et qu'ils soient humiliés. Quant à vous, enfants de N'Dar [Saint-Louis], Dieu vous défend de vous réunir à eux; il vous a déclaré que celui qui se réunira à eux est un infidèle comme eux.' The significance of this letter is discussed in: J. D. Hargreaves, 'The Tokolor Empire of Ségou and its Relations with the French', *Boston University Papers on African History*, II (1966), 130.
[2] Umar's declaration, cited in Faidherbe, *Le Sénégal*, p. 170: 'Les blancs ne sont que des marchands; qu'ils m'apportent des marchandises dans leurs bateaux, qu'ils me payent un fort tribut lorsque je serai maître des noirs, et je vivrai en paix avec eux. Mais je ne veux pas qu'ils forment des établissements à terre ni qu'ils envoient des bâtiments de guerre dans le fleuve.'

Gambia in May 1855, 'if a holy war against the Christians is declared here as it was in Algeria...'[1]

To meet the danger Faidherbe sought to extend French military power into the disputed areas and to build up a network of alliances among the chiefs of the Upper Senegal whose own authority was being undermined by the *Khalifa*'s agitation. Bubakar Saada, ruler of Bondu, was actively supported against his rival Eli, a partisan of the Tokolors. Sambala, ruler of Khasso, received similar assistance against his brother, and in return he signed a treaty authorising the construction of a fort at Médine on his territory. Médine itself was intended to serve as a rallying point for the *Khalifa*'s opponents and a refuge for all those who looked to France for protection against the *talibés*.[2]

But the advance up the Senegal was not purely defensive in its purpose, and Médine was not merely a barrier to Tokolor expansion. Its construction was also the first move in Faidherbe's grand strategy for extending French power to the Niger and beyond. Ever since he took office, the Governor had been emphasizing the unlimited prospects for French trade in the interior. He too was dazzled by the legendary wealth of the Sudan, and he too sought to tap its hidden reserves of gold.[3] By 1858 he was ready to submit the broad lines of his imperial programme to Prince Napoleon. From their base at Médine the French were to penetrate deeper still into the Western Sudan, build a second fort at the confluence of the Senegal and the Bafing rivers, and ultimately occupy some point on the Upper Niger. Having asserted their political control over the Senegal–Niger valley, they could establish relations with the heavily populated regions of the far interior, capture their trade, and so create a West African empire worthy of comparison with Canada or India.[4]

These ambitions made accommodation with the Tokolors doubly impossible. As Faidherbe realised, the build-up of Tokolor strength on the Upper Senegal not only threatened the security of existing French possessions on the river; it also barred their gateway to the Niger. 'The pursuit and destruction of *al-hajj* Umar', was thus an integral part of the new policy; for both Faidherbe and the Minister were convinced

---

1 Faidherbe to M.M.C., 26 Dec. 1854, MFOM Sénégal I 41(b); Faidherbe to the Governor of the Gambia, 31 May 1855 [Copy], AEMD Afrique 47.
2 Faidherbe to M.M.C., 13 May 1855, MFOM Sénégal I 41(b). See also: Faidherbe, *Le Sénégal*, pp. 180–1; Abun-Nasr, *op. cit.* pp. 115–16.
3 Faidherbe to M.M.C., 22 Dec. 1854, MFOM Sénégal I 41(b); M.M.C. to Faidherbe, 20 Jan. 1857, cited in Schefer, *op. cit.* II, 297–9.
4 Faidherbe, Memorandum, 1 Oct. 1858, MFOM Sénégal I 45(a).

that 'the extension, [or] even the maintenance of our power makes [his] annihilation imperative'.[1] On the other hand, the French advance presented a challenge to Tokolor ambitions which Umar could not ignore. Until Faidherbe had intervened, the *Khalifa* and his supporters had been winning the struggle for power in Khasso and the neighbouring states of the Upper Senegal; now the French at Médine threatened to rob them of their gains. Accordingly, as soon as his military position in Kaarta improved, Umar launched a determined attack on the fort. Throughout the spring of 1857 its tiny garrison withstood the assaults of 20,000 warriors; only the last-minute arrival of reinforcements averted its surrender. Over the next two years, many smaller battles were fought along the Senegal as far west as Matam, and from their fort at Guémou the Tokolors constantly harassed the trade of Bakel.[2]

But the conflict was not as clear-cut as it seemed. Umar himself had never been anxious to test his strength against the Europeans; much of his apparent aggressiveness stemmed from his inability to control the more hot-headed among his *talibés* who urged him to free their homelands from European domination. The *Khalifa* had been strongly opposed to the attack on Médine and gave in to the *talibés* only when his enemy Sambala took refuge in the fort. His heavy losses and his failure to capture the town dealt his prestige a severe blow and persuaded him not to dispute French claims on the Lower Senegal any further. His subsequent skirmishes did not constitute a campaign of conquest but arose from his attempts to secure reinforcements for Nioro, his capital in Kaarta, or for Koundian, his fortress in Bambuk. After the French captured his stronghold at Guémou in October 1859, he abandoned the struggle and turned his energies against the animist Bambaras on the Upper Niger. Once embarked upon the conquest of Segu, he found it expedient to settle his differences with the French, and in 1860 he sent an envoy to propose the negotiation of a truce.[3]

Faidherbe also had good reason to welcome an end to the hostilities. Although Prince Napoleon had approved his plans for expansion to the Niger in principle, he had refused to authorise the construction of a new fort until further studies had been completed. Nor did the Minister

---

[1] *Ibid.*; Minister of Algeria and Colonies to Faidherbe, 22 Feb. 1859, MFOM Sénégal I 46(b).
[2] Faidherbe, *Le Sénégal*, pp. 182–215.
[3] *Ibid.* pp. 233–7; For Umar's views on the expedition against Médine, see: Tyam, *op. cit.* p. 101; Delafosse, 'Traditions historiques et légendaires...', *loc. cit.* p. 362.

consider the concentration of Tokolor power in Kaarta an immediate threat to French security, and he advised the Governor to postpone 'the decisive conflict which will enable us to finish with [Umar] once and for all'.[1] Faidherbe was inclined to agree. He had always been ready to temporise with the *Khalifa* until he had made his Senegalese base absolutely secure and had sufficient troops to ensure certain victory.[2] The growth of new difficulties in Cayor made it advisable to put off the final day of reckoning; so he accepted the overture and concluded a cease-fire. The Senegal from Médine to Bafoulabé and the Bafing to its source was defined as the boundary between the two states. The two sides promised protection and support for each other's trade. and each undertook not to force subjects of the other to emigrate. Provisions were also made for the appointment of a French ambassador to Umar.[3] The treaty of 1860 did not solve all the colony's problems; Umar's supporters continued to make trouble on the Senegal, and by 1862 the situation in Futa was again becoming critical.[4] But its commercial clauses did at least offer some prospect of Franco-Tokolor co-operation in the Western Sudan.

This was certainly a possibility which Faidherbe considered during his second Governorship. He had not forgotten about his Niger plan during his absence, and shortly before his return to the colony he published a fuller statement of his views in the *Revue maritime et coloniale*, the Ministry's official periodical. In addition to the chain of fortified posts beyond Médine, he now proposed to build a base at Bamako from which gunboats could control the Niger as far as Bussa, and to complete the establishment of French influence over the river by moving upstream from the Delta in concert with the English.[5] As soon as he arrived back at Saint-Louis, Faidherbe sent Lieutenant Mage to prepare the way for the eventual construction of the fortified posts by exploring the route from Médine to Bamako. Mage was also accredited as ambassador to the Tokolor empire and instructed to secure Umar's

[1] Minister of Algeria and Colonies to Faidherbe, 22 Feb. 1859, MFOM Sénégal I 46(b).

[2] Before the attack on Médine, Faidherbe had even considered offering the *Khalifa* recognition of his authority over Kaarta if he agreed not to oppose the French in Senegal. See: Abun-Nasr, *op. cit.* p. 116.

[3] An account of the negotiations and the text of the treaty is given in: Y. Saint-Martin, 'Les relations diplomatiques entre la France et l'empire toucouleur de 1860 à 1887', *Bulletin de l'I.F.A.N.*, série B, xxvii (1965), 184–8.

[4] Jauréguiberry to M.M.C., 26 Oct. 1862, MFOM Sénégal I 48(b); M.M.C. to Jauréguiberry, 20 Nov. 1862, MFOM Sénégal I 48(c). See also: Faidherbe, *Le Senegal*, pp. 240–8.

[5] L.L.C. Faidherbe, *L'avenir du Sahara et du Soudan* (extract from the *Revue maritime et coloniale*, June 1863) (Paris, 1863), pp. 22–7.

approval for the project, for the latter's support was considered essential for its success.[1]

Short-term co-operation with the Tokolors was thus both desirable and essential. The French could not reach the Niger overnight; they would have to proceed slowly and cautiously, gradually extending their influence by building a fort at Bafoulabé and then a line of trading posts to the Niger. In these preliminary stages Tokolor acquiescence was vital; until the French were firmly established they could not risk a full-scale war. The political situation in Senegal made it all the more important to avoid war. Jauréguiberry's disastrous administration had sapped the colony's military strength and seriously undermined its security. On his return, Faidherbe found the provinces in varying stages of anarchy and the *tirailleurs sénégalais*, the African contingents which formed the backbone of his fighting force, in a deplorable state of disorganisation.[2] Accordingly, the Governor was ready to pay a high price for the *Khalifa*'s good-will. He was prepared to lease the land required for the trading posts and to pay duty on French trade. Mage was authorised to promise recognition for Umar's future conquests along the Upper Niger; if necessary he could offer to supply the *Khalifa* with cannon as well.[3]

But Faidherbe could have envisaged a permanent alliance with Umar only if his objectives were limited to the peaceful extension of trade, and his 'noble enterprise' clearly involved much more than mere commercial gain. His goal, as in 1858, was the creation of an empire. His plans for commercial expansion were but the prelude to the imposition of French political hegemony. His 'simple *comptoirs*', he told the *Conseil d'Administration* in May 1864, were bound to be transformed 'by local rivalries, by political disruption and by civil wars in which our allies would always be the strongest', into fortified strongholds dominating the route to the Niger.[4] A line of forts from Saint-Louis to Bamako and possession of the coastline from Saint-Louis to the northern frontier of Sierra Leone—to be secured by exchanging French possessions further down the coast for the Gambia—would give France undisputed claim to the vast territories in between. With this Senegambian

[1] Faidherbe to Mage, 7 Aug. 1863 [extract from the *Délibérations du Conseil d'Administration*, 10 Aug. 1863], MFOM Sénégal III 9(c); Faidherbe to Mage, 7 Oct. 1863, cited in Mage, *op. cit.* pp. 17–18.
[2] Faidherbe to M.M.C., 17 Sept. 1863; same to same, 28 Mar. 1864, MFOM Sénégal I 50(b).
[3] Faidherbe to Mage, 7 Nov. 1864, cited in Mage, *op. cit.* p. 559.
[4] Délibérations du Conseil d'Administration, 21 May 1864 [Copy], AEMD Afrique 47.

Triangle as the power base and Bamako as the river port for the gun-boats, France could overthrow the Tokolors, control the whole course of the Niger to the limits of its navigation and occupy Timbuktu. This was imperialism on a grand scale, and Faidherbe's language reflected his sentiments. The feat of raising the *tricolore* over the fabled city, he declared when asking for his plans to be submitted to the Emperor, might itself merit the attention of 'the Sovereign who was taken Peking and Mexico City, who will have conquered Cochinchina and Mexico and opened the isthmus of Suez...'[1]

Unfortunately, the very features which made the plan so attractive to Faidherbe ensured its rejection by the Ministry. Chasseloup-Laubat was prepared to sanction measures for the encouragement of trade, and he had gladly approved the Mage mission.[2] But he was absolutely opposed to the more costly and more difficult business of political expansion, and when the Governor's flights of fancy assumed more concrete shape he unceremoniously shot them down. Faidherbe's request for permission to build a fort at Bafoulabé was rejected because he had neglected to mention how he intended to pay for it. His views on trading posts were scouted because the transformation of *comptoirs* into forts would create a permanently precarious situation and involve France in arduous and expensive military campaigns. Nor was it certain that the commercial prospects of the interior would justify the cost of the programme. Problems of transport and communications between Saint-Louis and Médine were already formidable; between Médine and the Niger they might well be impossible. Faidherbe's concept of a Senegambian Triangle was admittedly more seductive; but Chasseloup-Laubat doubted whether the Gambia would be worth the cession of Gabon, and he failed to see how the Portuguese were to be compensated for the loss of their enclave. The Minister sugared the pill with renewed expressions of confidence and assurances of support for missions to study commercial possibilities and extend French influence. But Faidherbe was left in no doubt that, in the Western Sudan no less than on the Senegal, actual expansion was not to be contemplated.[3]

[1] Faidherbe to M.M.C., 18 Jan. 1864; same to same, 23 Apr. 1864, MFOM Sénégal I 50(b).
[2] M.M.C. to Faidherbe, 24 Dec. 1863, MFOM Sénégal I 50(c).
[3] Same to same, 23 June 1864, *ibid.*; same to same, 23 July 1864 [Copy], AEMD Afrique 47.

The Background of Conquest

When Faidherbe left Senegal in 1865, the plans he had so vigorously advocated went with him. After his departure, the trends in official policy towards the peaceful development of commercial interests and the reduction of expenditure were accentuated. In 1867 Faidherbe's successor, Pinet-Laprade, ordered his *commandants de poste* to avoid military action except in cases of absolute necessity.[1] In 1869 Laprade's successor, Colonel Valière, was forbidden to annex new territory. 'What we must seek to extend', he was told, 'is our influence and trade.' By the following year the Ministry was actually contemplating a withdrawal from occupied positions. Territorial expansion, wrote the Minister of Marine in a report to the Emperor, had transformed Senegal from a collection of trading posts into a fully fledged colony much too large to be effectively administered. The construction of new forts dispersed their forces and often led to military operations which were both costly and injurious to trade. In order to reduce their commitments to more manageable proportions, he suggested a renunciation of French authority—more nominal than effective anyway—over the provinces of Dimar, Futa Toro, Cayor, and Saniokhor.[2]

The disasters of the Franco-Prussian War dealt Senegal a still more painful blow. The needs of internal reconstruction now monopolised the financial resources of the State. The metropolitan subvention to the colony's local budget, progressively reduced from 500,000 fr. in 1866 to 350,000 fr. in 1869, was slashed to 153,650 fr. in 1871 and abolished completely in 1873.[3] Senegal's status as *un grand comptoir colonial* rather than *une colonie proprement dite* was confirmed,[4] and even as such its position was precarious. A fall in European prices for groundnuts and gum cut the total value of Senegalese trade from 38·3 million francs in 1868 to 28·8 million in 1874.[5] In Cayor the French were forced to co-operate with their former enemy Lat Dyor, while in the Futa provinces another Tokolor leader, Ahmadu Cheikou, was exploiting the loss

[1] Pinet-Laprade to *commandants de poste*, 1 Nov. 1867, MFOM Sénégal IV 44(a).
[2] M.M.C. to Valière, Instructions, 25 Sept. 1869, MFOM Sénégal I 56 (a); M.M.C., Rapport à l'Empéreur, June 1870, *ibid*.
[3] B. Schnapper, *La politique et le commerce français dans le Golfe de Guinée de 1838 à 1871* (Paris, 1961), p. 250; C. W. Newbury, 'The Protectionist Revival in French Colonial Trade: The Case of Senegal', *Economic History Review*, 2nd ser. xxi (1968), 340.
[4] Note sur...[les] colonies françaises, Rapport de la 3e souscommission, 7 Mar. 1871, AN C2874.
[5] Newbury, 'Chambers of Commerce and the Protectionist Revival in French African Trade' (unpublished draft).

of French prestige to rally support for a new holy war against the Europeans. His preaching kept the area in turmoil until his defeat and death in 1875.[1]

The outlook on the Upper Senegal was just as gloomy. The Mage mission was less successful than its sponsors had hoped. The outbreak of an anti-Tokolor rebellion in Macina prevented it from exploring the Niger beyond Segu, where Mage and his companions were kept virtually prisoner for two years. Although the Ambassador was finally able to sign a treaty of friendship and commerce with Umar's son Ahmadu, its terms were more favourable to the Tokolors than to the French. In return for the right to trade, the French had to pay an import duty of 10 per cent, recognise Ahmadu's authority over his future conquests, allow his agents to buy what they wished in Saint-Louis and guarantee the freedom of his communications with Futa. Despite Mage's entreaties and his promises of cannon, Ahmadu categorically refused to permit the construction of trading posts on his territory. When the disillusioned Ambassador returned to Senegal in 1866, he warned that the route from Bafoulabé to Bamako was difficult and that Tokolor opposition would make the construction of forts expensive and their provisioning impossible if war broke out. He therefore thought it wiser to abandon the plan and persuade the Tokolors to trade at existing French *comptoirs* instead.[2]

By now Paris had lost almost all interest in the interior. There had been attempts throughout the 1850s to extend commercial influence southward from Algeria; in an effort to revive Algeria's participation in the trans-Saharan caravan trade, the customs regulations along its southern frontier had been eased in 1860, and in 1862 a commercial agreement was signed with the Azjer Tuareg at Ghadamès. But any hope that a commercial current might develop was killed in 1864 by the outbreak of a serious rebellion among the Walad Sidi Shaikh which blocked the northern avenues into the Sudan.[3] Mage's pessimistic conclusions strengthened the Ministry's determination to proceed no further from the west. Thereafter, the focus of French activity shifted

[1] Valière to M.M.C., 25 Dec. 1870, MFOM Sénégal I 56(b); Faidherbe, *Le Sénégal*, pp. 292–5.

[2] Mage, analyse succincte, 21 July 1866; *idem*, Rapport, n.d., MFOM Sénégal III 9(c). The negotiations are described and a copy of the treaty printed in Mage, *op. cit.* pp. 587 ff.

[3] C. Trumelet, *Histoire de l'insurrection dans le sud de la province d'Alger en 1864* (Algiers, 1879). For the Ghadamès mission see: [le cdt. Mircher], *Mission de Ghadamès: Rapports officiels et documents à l'appui* (Algiers, 1863).

from the Upper Senegal to the Southern Rivers, the groundnut-producing regions north of Sierra Leone. During the administration of Pinet-Laprade, several treaties of protectorate were signed with local chiefs; in 1866 a small fort was built at Boké on the Rio Nunez, and the following year another post was established at Benty on the Mellacourie.[1] Governor Valière's instructions in 1869 no longer mentioned the Upper Senegal, and by 1870 the Ministry, as part of its economy drive, was considering the evacuation of Médine. Only Valière's dire predictions about the disastrous consequences for French prestige and hence for trade managed to save the fort.[2]

Meanwhile, the Tokolor empire was also experiencing a period of severe dislocation. By 1862 Umar had completed his conquest of the Fulani empire of Macina; but in the spring of 1863 his attempt to appoint his son Ahmadu as Sultan sparked off a rebellion which soon united the whole country against him. Led by Ahmad al-Bakkay, Umar's long-standing religious adversary,[3] the inhabitants of Timbuktu and their Tuareg allies drove the Tokolors from the town, killing Umar's military commander, and besieged the *Khalifa* himself at Hamdallahi. These reverses encouraged the Bambaras in Segu to throw off their Tokolor yoke, and by the summer the whole of the province was in revolt. All communications between the two territories were cut, and no supplies reached the embattled garrison at Hamdallahi. Early in 1864 Umar himself was killed in a desperate attempt to break out.[4]

The Macinan disaster and the death of the *Khalifa* confronted his son with tremendous problems. Hitherto, the unity and the strength of the empire had rested upon Umar's undisputed religious and political leadership, and on the military success of his armies. Both these foundations now began to crumble. Ahmadu spent the first two years of his reign attempting, not always successfully, to crush the Bambara rebellion. The Tokolor army of 30,000 which had originally invaded Macina had been decimated during the rebellion and had lost two of its cannons at Timbuktu. By 1866 Ahmadu's troops, according to Mage,

---

[1] J. D. Hargreaves, *Prelude to the Partition of West Africa* (London, 1963), pp. 129–36; Schnapper, *op. cit.* pp. 227–39.

[2] M.M.C. to Valière, 26 May 1870, MFOM Sénégal I 56(c); Valiere to M.M.C., 14 Aug. 1870, MFOM Sénégal I 56(b).

[3] al-Bakkay was the head of the Bakkaiyya branch of the rival Qadiriyya order. The two men had been at odds ever since they had first met at Sokoto in the 1830s. See Abun-Nasr, *op. cit.* pp. 108–9, 124–5.

[4] *Ibid.* pp. 125–8.

47

numbered no more than 4,000 *talibés* and 11,000 *sofas*.[1] The new Sultan lacked his father's religious standing and was unable to maintain either the cohesion of the state or the crusading spirit of the army. His assumption of the title *amir al-muminin* (Commander of the Faithful) in 1868 failed to augment his authority; by 1871 small groups of *talibés* were deserting his ranks and returning to their homes in Futa.[2] Two years later he was faced with another rebellion, led this time by his own brothers. Although Ahmadu was Umar's eldest son and designated successor, he was born of a commoner, and the *Khalifa*'s children of nobler stock resented their subordination to a half-brother whom they considered socially inferior. In 1873 Abibou and Mukhtar, sons of a princess of Sokoto, joined forces in an attempt to overthrow him but were defeated and imprisoned. Having dealt with his recalcitrant brothers, the Sultan then had to suppress yet another Bambara rebellion which had been raging since 1870 and had severed communications between Segu and Kaarta.[3]

That the empire was able to survive these shocks was a tribute to the considerable political skill of its new ruler. Anxious to prevent fresh challenges to his authority, Ahmadu placed the administration of his more important territories in the hands of those brothers who had remained loyal to him in 1873. But he forced them to share their power with councillors whom he appointed and who were directly responsible to him. He was also careful to maintain his personal control over the provincial garrisons by making them dependent as far as possible on supplies drawn from the central treasury. All provincial governors were obliged to visit him once a year at Segu.[4] Under this system, which seemed to work remarkably well, Ahmadu was gradually able to restore order and consolidate his power.

But the empire never again approached the heights which it had reached in the early 1860s. Unable to base his authority on religious charisma, Ahmadu was forced to place a special premium on the personal loyalty which he could command through his powers of patronage. The consequent growth of an entourage of favourites, very

[1] Mage, Rapport, n.d., MFOM Sénégal III 9(c).
[2] Valière to M.M.C., 15 May 1871, MFOM Sénégal I 56(b). Abun-Nasr's research has shown that Ahmadu adopted the title *amir al-muminin* in 1868, not 1873 as hitherto supposed. See: Abun-Nasr, *op. cit.* pp. 129–30.
[3] A. de Loppinot, 'Souvenirs d'Aguibou', *Bulletin du Comité des Etudes Historiques et Scientifiques de l'A.O.F.*, II (1919), 24–61; Abun-Nasr, *op. cit.* p. 132.
[4] Valière to M.M.C., 20 July 1874 (based on information supplied by Ahmadu's ambassador), cited in Saint-Martin, 'Les relations diplomatiques...', *loc. cit.* p. 193.

often slaves or recent converts, alienated the original *talibés*. However, the *talibés* continued to provide much of the personnel of government, and they were allowed to retain their privileges because Ahmadu had to attract new recruits from Futa in order to keep his administration at full strength. Overshadowing these internecine conflicts was the constant threat of rebellion by subject peoples whom the exactions of their rulers often goaded into violent resistance.[1]

The territorial extent of the empire was also much reduced and its physical unity weakened. Although the rebellion in Macina was eventually crushed, Ahmadu was unable to reassert his authority. Instead, Macina became an independent and rather unfriendly state ruled by Tijani, one of Umar's nephews who had managed to escape from Hamdallahi before the *Khalifa*'s death. In the far south the province of Dinguiray, governed by Ahmadu's brother Aguibou, became virtually independent as well. On the left bank of the Upper Senegal effective Tokolor control was limited to the two fortresses at Koundian and Murgula, whose spheres of influence were never very extensive. On the right bank, immediately above Médine, the provinces of Diambouku and Diafunu, ruled by Ahmadu's brothers Bassiru and Nouru, were the scene of a major rebellion which was finally crushed in 1877. The position of his brother Muntaga in Kaarta was relatively strong, as was the Sultan's own position in Segu. But between the two central provinces of the empire the turbulent region of Beledugu, never completely subjugated, was in a quasi-permanent state of rebellion which often interrupted communications between Segu and Nioro.

The internal problems of the empire forced the Sultan to be extremely cautious in his dealings with the French. As his refusal to allow the construction of trading posts revealed, Ahmadu appreciated the dangers of a permanent European presence in regions of his empire where his authority was already weak. But like his father he could also see the positive advantages to be gained from limited co-operation. Duties on French trade could provide valuable revenue. French acquiescence was essential for the maintenance of free communications between the empire and Futa, the source of its reinforcements. Above all, French logistic support could tilt the military balance in his favour and enable him to keep the rebellious Bambaras in check. This was probably the decisive factor in his negotiations with Mage. His reluctance to con-

---

[1] Mage, *op. cit.* pp. 305, 422, 662–3; P. Soleillet, *Voyage à Ségou, 1878–1879* (G. Gravier ed.) (Paris, 1887), pp. 355–88.

clude the talks seemed to stem less from his suspicion of the French than from his desire to use them as allies in his campaigns against the rebels.[1] It was Mage's promise of cannon, too, which finally persuaded him to sign the agreement and allow the embassy to return. Although the Senegalese authorities refused to ratify the treaty, he remained on friendly terms with the French and encouraged trade between Kaarta and Médine.[2] Once he had dealt with his brothers, moreover, he sent an envoy to the fort with a proposal to revive the Mage agreement and a request for the sale of a dozen cannons.[3]

Valière was willing to respond. The Governor had remained apprehensive about the danger of Tokolor expansion to French security, and some months before he had expressed great satisfaction over rumours that Ahmadu had been killed. But he had also admitted that the Tokolor empire's inevitable disintegration was bound to hurt French trade in the Upper Senegal,[4] and when the rumours proved unfounded he decided to work for trade rather than for political expansion. Although he refused the request for cannons, he confirmed the guarantee of free communication between the two states, accepted a new boundary running some twenty kilometres east of Médine and undertook not to construct any permanent trading establishment in Tokolor territory without the Sultan's permission. In return, the 10 per cent duty of the Mage treaty was to be replaced by an export tax of one piece of *guinée* on every 1,000 kg of top-quality gum, and Ahmadu was to direct his trade towards the French posts in Senegal.[5] This agreement also remained unratified, but the atmosphere of cordiality was not disturbed. When Valière left the colony in 1876 he could report that the situation was absolutely calm and likely to remain so.[6]

THE SIGNIFICANCE OF THE EARLY YEARS

In practical terms, the results of half a century of French activity in West Africa were disappointingly few. The establishment of undisputed political supremacy over the Lower Senegal was still a long way short of complete realisation. The extension of French influence to the Niger

[1] Mage and his party accompanied the Tokolors on three expeditions against the Bambaras. Mage, *op. cit.* pp. 425–30, 464–74, 501–41.
[2] Valière to M.M.C., 15 Mar. 1871; same to same, 15 June 1872, MFOM Sénégal I 56(b).
[3] Valière to M.M.C., 24 Sept. 1874, MFOM Sénégal I 58(a).
[4] Same to same, 12 Jan. 1874, cited in Saint-Martin, 'Les relations diplomatiques...', *loc. cit.* pp. 192–3.   [5] A copy of this treaty can be found in MFOM Sénégal III 10(*bis*)(b).
[6] Valière, Notes pour mon successeur, 26 May 1876, MFOM Sénégal I 61(b).

and the creation of a commercial empire in the Western Sudan were still a dream. The prospects of vast profits which had shaped French policies both on the Senegal and in the Western Sudan had proved illusory. The chronic failure of the colony to measure up to expectations had gradually sapped the Government's enthusiasm and had driven it along the road of retrenchment. By 1876 the vision of an African empire had apparently faded, and Senegal itself had again become no more than a commercial emporium.

Yet by then most of the principles which were to govern French policy for the rest of the century had been firmly established. First of all, Senegal and the Western Sudan had clearly become the centres of French activity in Western Africa as a whole. French possessions on the Guinea Coast were never of more than marginal interest to the policy-makers. The *comptoirs* at Assinie, Grand Bassam and Gabon, built in 1843 as a riposte to the reassumption of British sovereignty over the Gold Coast, had failed to develop a thriving trade or, with the exception of Gabon, to provide useful *points d'appui* for the French Navy. The commanders of the West African naval squadrons charged with the supervision of French interests on the coast were reluctant to commit themselves politically or militarily in support of traders whom they generally despised. The Ministry of Marine was itself mainly concerned by the threat of British expansion, and this the Select Committee Report of 1865 seemed to remove. Thereafter, expenditure on the Guinea Coast fell rapidly. In 1868 Admiral Rigault de Genouilly, Chasseloup-Laubat's successor, vetoed proposals for the occupation of Porto Novo; in 1870 he was already considering the evacuation of existing posts in the interests of economy. In 1871 French garrisons were withdrawn completely from the Ivory Coast. Only Gabon was retained on a shoestring budget.[1]

Indeed, from the late 1860s onward, the policy-makers were ready to abandon the Guinea Coast entirely in favour of a more solid position on the Senegal. Faidherbe's proposals for a territorial exchange, rejected in 1864, were revived by the Government itself in 1866. Britain was now offered the Ivory Coast settlements and if necessary the Mellacourie and Rio Nunez in return for the Gambia. By 1867 the Ministry of Marine was prepared to add Gabon to the list. Nothing came of the proposal, but the French raised the matter once more in 1874 and

[1] For the development of French policy along the Guinea Coast before 1871, see: Schnapper, *op. cit.*; Hargreaves, *Prelude to the Partition of West Africa*, pp. 110–20; P. Atger, *La France en Côte d'Ivoire de 1843 à 1893* (Dakar, 1962), pp. 21–63.

4-2

agreed to British demands for the surrender of all claims between the Pongos River and the northern frontier of Gabon. They would have thrown in Gabon as well if the British had asked for it. Whitehall's capitulation to domestic pressure against the exchange, not any reluctance in Paris, finally killed the negotiations in 1876.[1] There could have been no clearer indication of French priorities in West Africa. The French Government wanted the Gambia primarily in order to 'give our possessions in Senegambia the unity they lack, [to] secure our influence and military domination over the native population, and [to] enable us to suppress all the uprisings which too often disturb our trade'. They were also aware that the Gambia River could serve as an alternative access route into the Upper Niger valley. If France could secure it, Governor Valière had told the Ministry in 1873, then the repercussions would be felt as far afield as Nioro, Segu and Timbuktu.[2]

And the far interior was to provide the greatest scope for future expansion; for by the 1860s Britain had withdrawn from the race for the Sahara and the Western Sudan. The British Government had been disillusioned by its failure to expunge the trans-Saharan slave trade and by the reluctance of traders to exploit the commercial opportunities which its efforts created for them. Once the possibilities of the Niger as a safer and more practicable outlet for Sudanese trade were appreciated, its interest in the Sahara rapidly declined. In 1857 al-Bakkay's appeals for protection against the threat of French expansion were firmly rejected. In 1860–1 the vice-consulates at Ghadamès and Murzuk, the last centres of British influence in the Sahara, were closed down. Britain at least now recognised that the future here belonged to France. In Algeria she had the most solid base and the most pressing reasons for expansion. The security of Algeria, declared the British Consul-General in Tripoli, made the extension of French military control over the northern reaches of the Sahara inevitable. From there it was only logical for her to advance into Tuat and transform the oasis into 'a vast commercial entrepôt through which will flow into Algeria all the trade of the Sahara and the basins of the Upper Niger and the Lake Tshad'.[3]

Consul Herman was not entirely mistaken. Although Algeria failed to

---

[1] Hargreaves, *Prelude to the Partition of West Africa*, pp. 125–8, 136–95; R. Catala, 'La question de l'échange de la Gambie britannique contre les comptoirs français du Golfe de Guinée', *Revue d'histoire des colonies*, XXV (1948), 114–37.

[2] M.M.C. to M.A.E., 16 Apr. 1874, AEMD Afrique 48; Valière to M.M.C., 23 Feb. 1873 [Copy], *ibid.*

[3] Herman to Hammond [Under-Secretary of State, Foreign Office], 26 July 1857, cited in Boahen, *op. cit.* p. 226; and see: *ibid.* pp. 213–34.

capture the trade of the interior and Tuat itself was not occupied until the early twentieth century, the seeds of French African imperialism had been sown. In Algeria France had created an empire based firmly on political supremacy and military domination. During the 1850s and the early 1860s she had tried to do the same on the Lower Senegal. From both bases she had sought to extend her influence into the Western Sudan. For over half a century the establishment in the African interior of commercial empire, however loosely constituted, for the nation's exclusive benefit had been a recognised if distant objective of French African policy.

It was Faidherbe, however, who envisaged the future African empire most clearly. Spurred on by his experience of military conquest in Algeria, he moved beyond the informal imperialism of his superiors and advocated the extension not of indirect commercial influence but of direct military occupation. Nothing came of his schemes because he failed to persuade the Ministry to authorise the necessary increases in expenditure and military effort. Miscalculating the Government's intentions, he pictured his plans as a brilliant new chapter in the history of the Second Empire, only to find that his visions had little appeal for policy-makers busy fashioning new empires enough in Mexico and Indochina. But his proposals did at least provide a detailed blueprint for African expansion, whose value later generations could more fully appreciate. When the policy-makers in the late nineteenth century finally set out to claim the Niger and construct the Sudanese empire, Faidherbe's was the master-plan which they adopted.

On the Lower Senegal, the Governor had a better understanding of the principles which determined official policy. Here at least Paris seemed to accept the axiom that trade could only flourish in conditions of political and military security. No matter how frequently it repeated its desire for peaceful commercial development, it never forgot the overriding importance of maintaining security. No matter how strongly it opposed the extension of military control, it could not risk the consequences of retreat; for in territories where security rested upon the demonstrated superiority of French arms, the least sign of weakness might lead to disaster. Only once, briefly, were these principles questioned.[1] Faidherbe grasped their significance for his own dealings

---

[1] As late as 1869 the Ministry of Marine had told Valière: '...il serait impolitique d'abandonner les territoires que nous possédons'. M.M.C. to Valière, Instructions, 25 Sept. 1869, MFOM Sénégal I 56(a).

with the Ministry. He realised that official policy had to be formulated on the basis of information which he himself supplied. He saw that if he argued for his proposals emphatically enough on the grounds of security they would generally be approved, that if he defended his independent initiatives forcefully enough in the same language they would probably be accepted. He achieved neither a complete nor a lasting independence from Paris, but he did demonstrate the essential weakness in the Government's position and the way for an energetic governor to exploit it. What he could do, those of his successors astute enough to appreciate the reasons for his success could emulate, and in 1876 just such a man, Colonel Brière de l'Isle, moved into the Governor's Mansion at Saint-Louis.

3

The Revival of the Niger Plan, 1876-80

The state of affairs in Senegal when Governor Brière de l'Isle took office in June 1876 left much to be desired. The colony's economic position had improved a little since 1874; but European prices for West African commodities remained low, and Senegal's total trade still ran almost 20 per cent below the 1868 level. The abolition of the metropolitan subsidy, now compounded by the adoption of an ambitious public works programme for Saint-Louis, continued to place a heavy strain upon the local revenue.[1] Politically, the outlook was not much brighter. French control over the Southern Rivers, never very secure to begin with, was being rendered still more precarious by Sierra Leone's efforts to extend British influence and customs regulations into the Mellacourie. Without adequate naval support Governor Valière could do little, and by 1876 he was having to advocate withdrawal from the area since he lacked the resources either to administer or to defend it effectively.[2] The situation on the Senegal was just as grave. Valière's defeat of Ahmadu Cheikou and his deposition of chief Sidia of Walo had at least strengthened the security of Saint-Louis and its immediate environs. But in order to gain support against Ahmadu Cheikou, the Governor was forced to come to terms with Lat Dyor and recognise him as *damel* of Cayor.[3] More seriously, Valière was unable to check the rising power of yet another Tokolor leader, Abdul-Bubakar, in the Futa region of Senegal. By 1876 French influence was limited to the provinces of Dimar and Futa-Toro. In the territories beyond, from Saldé to the outskirts of Bakel, Abdul-Bubakar was effectively in command and thus in a position to threaten French communications

[1] I am grateful for this information about the Senegalese economy to Dr C. W. Newbury.
[2] Valière to M.M.C., 22 Jan. 1876, cited in Y. Saint-Martin, 'Une source de l'histoire coloniale du Sénégal: Les rapports de situation politique (1874–1891)', *Revue française d'histoire d'outre-mer*, LII (1965), 171. For British activities in the Mellacourie, see: Hargreaves, *Prelude to the Partition of West Africa*, pp. 214–20.
[3] Saint-Martin, 'Une source de l'histoire coloniale du Sénégal', *loc. cit.* pp. 192–202. For subsequent difficulties with Lat Dyor, see: G. Ganier, 'Lat Dyor et le chemin de fer de l'arachide, 1876–1886', *Bulletin de l'I.F.A.N.*, série B, XXVII (1965), 223–81.

with Médine.[1] And on the Upper Senegal there were alarming signs that the Kaarta Tokolors were beginning to expand into Logo and Bambuk on the French side of the river.[2]

The uncertain prospects of Senegal offered the Government no incentive to change its policies. In 1876 internal reconstruction was still regarded as the first duty of the State. The effects of a disastrous war, Brière was warned, made it impossible for France to accept colonial commitments which might weaken her means of European defence. Peace and retrenchment were to remain the watchwords of Senegalese policy, the encouragement of trade and the limitation of political activity its basic objectives. The Governor was expressly forbidden to annex new territory; he was authorised to take military action only when absolutely necessary to protect existing commercial interests, and he was ordered on no account to exceed the limits of his budget.[3] Yet within five years all these sacrosanct principles had been swept aside. Political expansion had replaced commercial development as the keystone of French policy; new tracts of the Western Sudan had been brought under military control, and in the process budgetary provisions had gone completely by the board. The Governorship of Brière was destined to become as momentous for the history of Sudanese expansion as that of Faidherbe.

IN THE FOOTSTEPS OF FAIDHERBE

Colonel Louis-Alexandre Brière de l'Isle came to Senegal at the age of forty-nine with a long and distinguished career in the *infanterie de marine* behind him. A graduate of Saint-Cyr, he had gained military experience in the Chinese campaign of 1860 and the occupation of Cochinchina in 1866. After 1871 he had learned the techniques of administration as the *chef du bureau des troupes coloniales* in the Ministry of Marine. But his most brilliant achievement was to have led the *infanterie de marine* in its heroic if futile resistance at Bazeilles, a feat which had won for him the rank of *Commandeur* in the Legion of Honour, and most probably the Governorship of Senegal as well.[4]

---

[1] Saint-Martin, 'Une source de l'histoire coloniale du Sénégal', *loc. cit.* pp. 203–9.
[2] Brière de l'Isle to M.M.C., 23 Oct. 1876, same to same, 20 Dec. 1876, MFOM Sénégal I 61 (c).
[3] M.M.C. to Brière de l'Isle, Instructions, 19 July 1876, MFOM Sénégal I 61 (a).
[4] Fourichon [M.M.C.], Rapport au Président de la République, 20 Apr. 1876, MFOM Dossier Administratif, Brière de l'Isle.

In the Footsteps of Faidherbe

Brière was above all a soldier, and he brought with him to Senegal all the traditions of his profession. Authoritarian by temperament, accustomed to command the unquestioning obedience of his subordinates, intolerant of opposition, particularly from civilians, he quickly transformed the colony into a quasi-military dictatorship. Civilian adminitrators were systematically replaced by military men whose loyalty and support were further guaranteed by the Governor's frequent tours of inspection. The wishes of the civilian population and the local traders were just as systematically ignored. By 1881 the Deputy from Senegal, A-S. Gasconi, could justly complain: 'the colony is not being *administered* but *commanded*'.[1]

But this prickly Governor did at least inject a new energy into the conduct of the colony's affairs. To place the shaky finances of Senegal on a sounder footing was an obvious and urgent need. Forbidden to raise direct taxes, Brière campaigned vigorously for higher customs duties and differential tariffs on foreign goods. The decision to levy a duty of 10 per cent on imports of foreign cloth in 1877—at a time when France still paid lip-service to the principles of free trade—was in no small measure due to the Governor's agitation.[2] The erosion of French political influence in the Southern Rivers called for equally drastic remedies; so in 1877 Brière sent his *directeur politique* to reaffirm French sovereignty between the Pongos and the Mellacourie. On his own initiative he also ordered the occupation of Kakoutlaye, a small island near Benty to which the British had laid claim; when these measures failed to halt the extension of British fiscal control he again reacted sharply, ordering the occupation of Matacong in 1879.[3]

It was on the Senegal, however, that decisive action was most urgently needed, and it was here that Brière revealed himself most clearly as a true disciple of Faidherbe. Military security was also Brière's burning obsession, and he too saw the force of militant Islam as the greatest threat to it.[4] Abdul-Bubakar's attempt to revive the old Futa confederation presented the most immediate danger, and to meet it the Governor advocated direct military intervention. Non-inter-

[1] See: Saint-Martin, 'Une source de l'histoire coloniale du Sénégal', *loc. cit.* pp. 185–8.
[2] Newbury, The Protectionist Revival in French Colonial Trade', *loc. cit.* pp. 340–4.
[3] See: Hargreaves, *Prelude to the Partition of Wes Africa*, pp. 219–23.
[4] E.g. Brière to M.M.C., 7 Apr. 1877, MFOM Sénégal I 61(b): 'L'importance de cette question du Baol n'échappera pas à Votre Excellence...Laisser le Damel [Lat Dyor] prendre le Baol, ce serait lui donner les moyens de tendre la main à bref délai aux marabouts du Rip, qui de leur côté étendent leurs relations religieuses et entretiennent le fanatisme jusque dans le Fouta et à Bakel.'

ference in the affairs of Futa, he warned the Minister, would permit the growth of a strong anti-Christian power on the very doorstep of the colony and would thus lead to war just as surely as direct provocation.[1]

At first the Ministry refused to change its policies and vetoed Brière's plans for a preventive campaign.[2] Encouraged by the success of his policies in the south, however, the Governor drafted new proposals for an expedition in October 1877, and this time he was determined not to be overruled. Abdul-Bubakar's activities, he now maintained, threatened French influence in Futa-Toro and so endangered the security of Senegal. At the same time he announced his intention to send a strong force to the Toro frontier unless he received orders to the contrary. Less than a week later his column set out and soon bullied Abdul-Bubakar into recognising French protectorates over Toro and the disputed provinces of Lao and Irlabé.[3] Brière's unauthorised action left the Ministry just as powerless to control events as Faidherbe's expedition into Siné had done twenty years before. For all its abhorrence of military complications, Paris had to accept the importance of maintaining security. It could do no more than order the Governor to settle matters peacefully if at all possible and to hold back his column until all opportunities for conciliation had been exhausted. When the Minister learned that the expedition had already taken place, he merely congratulated Brière on its successful outcome.[4]

Having restored French predominance over the Lower Senegal, the Governor next turned his attention to the Upper River. Although Tokolor influence on the left bank had long been a source of concern, his general policy had hitherto been one of cautious observation.[5] But in 1878 his attitude suddenly changed. The Tokolors, he reported in January, had consolidated their position in Kaarta and were again beginning to advance towards Futa. Firm measures were needed to prevent them from joining their correligionists there and so threatening the very foundations of French rule in Senegal. To make matters worse,

---

[1] Brière to M.M.C., 9 Dec. 1876, MFOM Sénégal I 61(c). See also: Saint-Martin, 'Une source de l'histoire coloniale du Sénégal', *loc. cit.* pp. 209–10.
[2] M.M.C. to Brière, 16 Nov. 1876, MFOM Sénégal I 61 (d).
[3] Brière to M.M.C., 7 Oct. 1877, MFOM Sénégal I 61(c); Saint-Martin, 'Une source de l'histoire coloniale du Sénégal', *loc. cit.* p. 216.
[4] M.M.C. to Brière, 7 Nov. 1877, same to same, 16 Nov. 1877, MFOM Sénégal I 61(d).
[5] Brière to M.M.C., 22 Aug. 1877, MFOM Sénégal I 61(c). The French, however, did support Moriba, the Bambara chief of Diafunu, in his rebellion against his Tokolor overlords. Procès-Verbal...[negotiations at Nango], 1ère séance, 31 Oct. 1880, MFOM Sénégal III 10(bis).

the British were now making determined efforts to establish relations with Ahmadu and the states of the Upper Senegal in order to divert the trade of the Western Sudan towards the Gambia. There was evidence that even Bubakar Saada of Bondu was now in their pay. Only by reaffirming her intention to dominate the Upper Senegal could France meet this danger. To parry the English thrust, Sénoudébou would have to be reoccupied and another fort built on the Falémé. To counter Tokolor expansion, Khasso would have to be made into a strong buffer-state and the aged Sambala supported in his war against Tokolor-dominated Logo.[1] Before Brière went home on leave in June 1878, he gave orders for the reoccupation of Sénoudébou and the organisation of a column to be sent, if necessary, against Logo.[2]

The same preoccupation with security which had led Paris to sanction the Futa campaign now forced it to approve the Governor's new initiative. No Minister could ignore the risk of renewed Tokolor expansion into the Lower Senegal; still less could he allow the Senegal–Niger valley to pass into the hands of the English. On 3 July, therefore, instructions were sent for the despatch of an expedition to help Sambala. Its objective was to capture and destroy the Tokolor stronghold of Sabouciré. Brière may have reached Paris in time to press his case on the Ministry in person.[3]

The attack on the fortress was a complete success. Niamody, the chief of Logo and a vassal of the Tokolors, was killed; his followers were dispersed, and the province was incorporated into the Khasso federation. The power of French arms, Brière reported on his return, had impressed friend and foe alike. The authority of their allies had been confirmed and their confidence fully restored. Tokolor prestige had been severely shaken, and Ahmadu had been shown that the French were ready to protect their rights by force if necessary.[4]

The improvement of French security on the Upper Senegal was not the expedition's sole purpose. Despite his emphasis on its strictly defensive nature, Brière had more ambitious objectives in mind; for by now he had decided to revive Faidherbe's old plan for a Sudanese empire. In October 1877 he had already described his Futa campaign as

[1] Brière to M.M.C., 23 Jan. 1878; same to same, 5 June 1878, MFOM Sénégal I 61 (c). The charges against the British were first made in Brière to M.M.C., 22 Dec. 1877 [Copy], AEMD Afrique 49.
[2] Brière to *Ordonnateur* Leguay, 10 June 1878, MFOM Sénégal I 62 (a).
[3] M.M.C. to Leguay, 3 July 1878, MFOM Sénégal I 62 (e). Brière had left the colony on 11 June.
[4] Brière to M.M.C., 22 Nov. 1878, MFOM Sénégal I 63 (a).

a definite extension of French political influence. By January 1878 he was hinting that British rivalry made it essential for France to enter and win the race for the interior.[1] Five months later he was writing as if his proposals had already been accepted. 'Their instinct tells them', he declared in a report on Tokolor hostility, 'that France...must advance inland, and they can sense that our interests are driving us on towards the Niger.'[2] More significantly, by basing his proposals on solid arguments of security instead of insubstantial calls to empire, Brière succeeded in forcing the Ministry to approve a limited advance. But local initiative alone could not completely reverse the direction of French West African policy. Before the vision of a Niger empire could be resurrected as a serious political objective, the Government itself would have to revise its attitude to African questions and abandon its long-standing commitment to retrenchment. In 1879 this is precisely what happened.

THE ORIGINS OF THE SENEGAL–NIGER RAILWAY

In the decade after the Franco-Prussian War there seemed little reason to expect such a radical change in French African policy. The political climate for it was less than favourable. Domestic politics and internal reconstruction were the dominant concerns of the day; *recueillement* was the motto in foreign affairs, and colonial entanglements were generally regarded with profound suspicion. But the prospects were not quite as unpromising as they appeared. The prevailing disenchantment with overseas adventures was not universally shared. To some the imperialist cause was as worthy an outlet for nationalist sentiment as the cult of *La Revanche*. Expansion for them was not the cause of France's downfall but the source of her regeneration. Only the creation of a new empire overseas, they believed, would enable France to regain her rightful place among the great nations of the world. The most active exponents of this doctrine were the Geographical Societies. In the aftermath of the Prussian disasters they added political overtones to their traditional scientific objectives and adopted colonial expansion as an integral part of their programme.[3]

---

[1] Brière to M.M.C., 7 Oct. 1877, MFOM Sénégal I 61(c); same to same, 23 Jan. 1878 *ibid*.: 'La question du haut-fleuve doit fixer l'attention du département; elle devient de plus en plus importante à mesure que les Anglais de Sierra Leone et de la Gambie font des efforts pour nouer par le Fouta Djalon des relations avec Ségou et le haut Niger.'

[2] Same to same, 5 June 1878, *ibid*.

[3] The standard works on the rôle of the Geographical Societies are: D. V. McKay, 'Colonialism in the French Geographical Movement', *The Geographical Review*, XXXIII (1943),

The Origins of the Senegal–Niger Railway

The old dream of a North-West African empire was bound to excite their interest. Here French explorers could still make a useful contribution; after all, no Frenchman had visited Timbuktu since Caillié. Here too there was ample scope for the more technically minded to plan the railway systems which would open up Africa just as the transcontinental railways had opened up North America. And the reward for all these efforts would be the supposedly limitless wealth of the Western Sudan. To bring these vast regions under French political, commercial and cultural influence, and to unite Algeria with Senegal, was a fitting goal for the aspirations of the new imperialists. In 1873 the Paris Geographical Society subsidised the ill-fated Saharan expedition of Dournaux-Dupéré, and the Algiers Chamber of Commerce financed Paul Soleillet's mission to the Tuat oasis.[1] Two years later both Soleillet and his compatriot Adolphe Duponchel were outlining proposals for the construction of a trans-Saharan railway to link Algeria with the Niger.[2] For them at least the myth of the Sudanese Eldorado had lost none of its fascination. According to Eugène Warnier, the Deputy from Algiers and a patron of Soleillet, trade between Algeria and Tuat could easily total a hundred million francs a year. By 1880 the Deputy from Senegal, Gasconi, was predicting a Sudanese trade of three hundred million annually.[3] Their policies were equally optimistic. Soleillet dreamt of a French commercial empire stretching from the Mediterranean to the Gulf of Guinea and from the Atlantic to Lake Chad. Duponchel was even more explicit. The purpose of his railway, he proclaimed, was to create

a vast colonial empire...a French India rivalling its British counterpart in wealth and prosperity; to open up unlimited markets for trade and industry, [and] to give free rein to our civilising impulses.[4]

By the late 1870s, such views were making some impact upon French public opinion. The Geographical Societies—through the pages of

---

214–32; A. Murphy, *The Ideology of French Imperialism* (Washington, 1948). H. Brunschwig, *Mythes et réalités de l'impérialisme colonial français*, pp. 23–8, stresses the connection between colonialism and nationalism.

[1] Murphy, *op. cit.* p. 77; P. Soleillet, *L'Afrique occidentale, Algérie, Mzab, Tildikelt* (Avignon, 1877), p. 90.

[2] P. Soleillet, *Avenir de la France en Afrique* (Paris, 1876); A. Duponchel, *Le Chemin de Fer Trans-Saharien, jonction coloniale entre l'Algérie et le Soudan* (Montpellier, 1878). Duponchel had lectured on his project to the International Congress of Geography which met in Paris in 1875.

[3] Warnier to the Algiers Chamber of Commerce, 25 Apr. 1873, cited in Soleillet, *Avenir de la France en Afrique*, pp. 71–4; Gasconi in evidence to the Budget Commission, séance du 25 juin 1880, AN C3176, pp. 740–1.

[4] Soleillet, *Avenir de la France en Afrique*, p. 1; Duponchel, *op. cit.* p. 218.

their *Bulletins* and their allies in the Press, through their conferences, their exhibitions and their lecture tours—had long sought to win popular support for expansion. As the rapid increase in the membership of the Geographical Movement showed, their efforts did not go entirely unrewarded.[1] African expansion had its advocates in Parliament as well; even in times of financial stringency modest funds had been approved for projects no less fantastic than the Trans-Sahara Railway.[2] By the end of the decade Parliament could afford to be more generous. The era of *recueillement* was now drawing to a close. On the domestic front, Republican successes in the elections of 1877 and the Senatorial election of 1879 dispelled what doubts there remained about the Third Republic's continued survival. At the same time, the Congress of Berlin and the easing of Franco-German tensions improved the Republic's diplomatic position and permitted it greater freedom of manœuvre in foreign affairs. In Egypt, Tunisia and Morocco France could again begin to act more assertively, and public opinion approached the question of the Trans-Sahara Railway in the same confident spirit. Here was the opportunity to increase the nation's political and economic strength, to demonstrate her scientific genius, and to show the world that she was again a Power to be reckoned with. The current of interest generated by the publication of Duponchel's *Chemin de Fer Trans-Saharien* quickly swelled into a tidal wave of enthusiasm which swept aside all mundane questions of cost and technical feasibility.[3] In May 1879 Paul Bert, the young disciple of Gambetta, proposed the grant of 200,000 fr. to cover the costs of preliminary surveys. Maurice Rouvier, another member of Gambetta's entourage, expressed the Budget Commission's approval in terms which would have done Soleillet or Duponchel proud. 'France', he exclaimed,

closer to [Africa] than most other nations, more interested than they in the future of this continent because of her possessions in Algeria, Senegal [and] Gabon..., must participate in the movement which is drawing the nations of Europe into the [African interior]. Concern for the greatness and for the

[1] Between 1871 and 1881 twelve new Geographical Societies were founded. In the same period the membership of the Paris Geographical Society rose from 600 to 2,000. Murphy, *op. cit.* pp. 5–8.

[2] The most striking example was the vote of credits for Captain Roudaire's scheme for the creation of an interior sea in the Southern Tunisian depression. See: *ibid.* pp. 70–5.

[3] P-L. Monteil, 'Contribution d'un vétéran à l'histoire coloniale', *Revue de Paris*, xxx (1 Sept. 1923), 110: 'En 1879 l'opinion publique fut brusquement orientée vers une idée assez utopique en elle-même, imprécise dans sa réalisation, vague dans les conséquences qui pourraient en surgir, mais qui, en raison même de toutes ses données assez chaotiques, passionna les masses...'

interests of our country commands us to place ourselves at the head of this movement. A few days sail from our shores there lie vast regions watered by great rivers and great lakes, regions of unbelievable fertility inhabited by 200,000,000 people. Shall not these regions provide unlimited opportunities for our trade, inexhaustible supplies and unhoped for markets for our industries?

The response in the Senate was equally enthusiastic; and in November a further credit of 600,000 fr. was voted almost unanimously.[1]

This evidence of popular support for African expansion undoubtedly influenced the formulation of official policy. Before its appearance the Government had shown little interest in plans for a trans-Saharan union. When Soleillet urged the Ministry of Public Works to encourage the development of trade between Algeria and Senegal in 1871, his letter was not even acknowledged. His railway proposals were given the same treatment by the Ministry of Commerce in 1875.[2] In 1872 the Ministry of Education granted Dournaux-Dupéré no more than a pittance of 2,000 fr.; the Ministry of Foreign Affairs refused to make any contribution at all.[3] Only in 1877 did the Ministry of Public Works give Duponchel 4,000 fr. as a token of its interest in his work.[4] But once the publication of Duponchel's report had revealed the extent of the Railway's popular appeal, the Ministry was quick to respond. In May 1879 the Minister, Charles de Freycinet, set up a Preliminary Commission to investigate the technical aspects of the project, and on the basis of its favourable report he convened a full *Commission Supérieure du Trans-Saharien*. Recent expressions of support in both Houses of Parliament, he told the President of the Republic, also affected his decision to give the project his official sanction.[5]

There were, however, more fundamental reasons for the Govern-

[1] Rouvier, Rapport, 10 June 1879, *J.O. Doc. Parl. Chambre*, no. 1497, p. 6328; *J.O. Déb. Parl. Chambre*, séance du 13 décembre 1879, p. 11052; *ibid. Déb. Parl. Sénat*, séance du 16 décembre 1879, pp. 11199–200. The vote in the Chamber was 364 to 14, in the Senate 227 to 3.

[2] Soleillet to Minister of Public Works, October 1871, cited in J. Gros (ed.), *Les voyages de Paul Soleillet dans le Sahara et dans le Soudan en vue d'un projet de chemin de fer transsaharien racontés par lui-même* (Paris, 1881), p. xv; Soleillet to Minister of Commerce, 13 Jan. 1875, cited in Soleillet, *Avenir de la France en Afrique*, pp. 48–9.

[3] Murphy, *op. cit.* p. 77.

[4] Jacqmin, Rapport au Ministre des Travaux Publics [henceforth M.T.P.], 7 May 1879, AN F14 12438. Duponchel had first written to the Ministry about his project in 1875. Duponchel to M.T.P., 18 Aug. 1875, *ibid.*

[5] Freycinet to Pérouse, 10 May 1879, AN F14 12437; Freycinet, Rapport au Président de la République, 12 July 1879, *J.O.* 14 July 1879, pp. 6633–5. In May Freycinet had given the publicity created by the publication of Duponchel's report as one of the reasons for setting up the Preliminary Commission. Duponchel's report, later published as *Le Chemin de Fer Trans-Saharien*, had been presented to the Ministry on 22 February 1878, AN F14 12436.

ment's new attitude. An engineer and a *Polytechnicien*, Freycinet himself had long been passionately interested in railways. Since 1877 he had been hard at work on the *Programme des Travaux Publiques*, his grandiose project for reorganising the whole French railway system. At the instigation of President MacMahon he had extended his plans to cover the Algerian railway system and had completed his studies by the end of 1878.[1] For the Minister and his advisers, the Trans-Sahara was merely a further extension of a much wider programme of railway-building; significantly, his clearest statement on the rôle of railways in opening up the African interior was made at the end of his general report on the *Programme des Travaux Publiques*.[2] As a politician, moreover, Freycinet was a convinced partisan of overseas expansion. His later vacillation over the Suez campaign has all too often obscured his importance as a founding father of the Third French Empire. At a time when the most famous of the colonialists, Jules Ferry, was still exclusively preoccupied with his educational reforms, Freycinet had already begun to pave the way for the eventual occupation of Tunisia and Morocco.[3]

The appointment of Admiral Jean Jauréguiberry as Minister of Marine in February 1879 was even more significant. As Governor of Senegal Jauréguiberry had been an ardent if unsuccessful expansionist, and he had lost none of his enthusiasm during the intervening years. Within three months of his arrival at the Rue Royale he had committed his Department to a more vigorous Sudanese policy.[4] Here too the Railway was to be the vehicle for expansion. Soleillet had proposed the construction of a railway link between Saint-Louis and the Niger as part of his Trans-Sahara scheme in 1875. In order to explore the route, he even went on a private mission to Segu in 1878.[5] Soleillet's plans neatly complemented Brière's new initiatives on the Upper Senegal; so the Governor paid for his journey out of the colony's Exchequer and

[1] Freycinet, *Souvenirs*, I, 78–9; II, 7–12, 78–81.
[2] See: Jacqmin, Rapport au Ministre des Travaux Public, 7 May 1879, AN F¹⁴ 12438; Freycinet, Rapport au Président de la République, 31 Dec. 1879, *J.O.* pp. 11698–700.
[3] The definitive study of Freycinet's expansionist policy remains to be written, but W. B. Thorson, 'Charles de Freycinet, French Empire-Builder', *Research Studies of the State College of Washington*, XII (1944), 257–82, and idem, 'Reappraisal of a Diplomatist', *Historian* (1945), pp. 91–112, provide full accounts based on published documentary material.
[4] Procès-Verbaux de la Commission préliminaire..., séance du 30 mai 1879, AN F¹⁴ 12437, statement by N. C. Legros, *Inspecteur-Général des travaux maritimes*.
[5] Soleillet, *Avenir de la France en Afrique*, pp. 48–50. For Soleillet's mission to Segu, see: idem, *Voyage à Ségou, 1878–1879*.

urged the Ministry to give his railway project its serious consideration.[1] Freycinet and Jauréguiberry did the rest. The two men were intimate friends and close political allies, and their two Departments worked hand in hand on the preparation of the railway programme. N. C. Legros, the Ministry of Marine's chief technical adviser, sat on Freycinet's Preliminary Commission and secured its approval for the Senegal–Niger Railway as well. Freycinet offered his colleague similar facilities on the full Commission whose official title was to be: *Commission supérieure pour l'étude des questions relatives à la mise en communication, par voie ferrée, de l'Algérie et du Sénégal avec l'intérieur du Soudan.*[2] The union of Algeria and Senegal now became an officially sanctioned objective of African expansion once more.

This change in the Government's attitude rather than the growth of an expansionist spirit in public opinion marked the crucial turning point in French African policy. The Geographical Societies and the explorers had played their part in persuading the Ministries to act; but thereafter unofficial pressures ceased to have any significant influence upon the official mind. Freycinet and Jauréguiberry, not Soleillet or Duponchel, were the real architects of the new African empire. Their plans were not drafted in response to appeals from private economic circles; industrialists and financiers did not press for the opening up of the Western Sudan as they would for the occupation of Tunisia.[3] Those commercial interests in Saint-Louis who saw the Railway as a threat to their monopoly over the trade of the Upper Senegal were positively inimical to the Government's projects and actively conspired against them.[4] The Ministers acted according to their own firmly held views about the rôle of the State in African expansion. They considered it their function as statesmen to further the long-term national interest by extending French influence over the African interior. 'It is the duty of the Government', Freycinet declared on becoming Prime Minister in December 1879, 'to look beyond the frontiers and investigate what peaceful conquests it can undertake... Africa, on our doorstep, has a special claim

---

[1] Brière to M.M.C., 21 Apr. 1878, Sénégal I 61(c).

[2] Rapport de la Commission..., 12 June 1879, AN F14 12437; Freycinet to Jauréguiberry, 11 June 1879, AN F14 12438; Freycinet, Rapport au Président de la République, 12 July 1879, *J.O.* 14 July 1879, pp. 6633–5.

[3] The Paris Society of Commercial Geography did set up its own Commission, but, contrary to the claims of its President, there is no evidence that it had any influence upon the Government. See: Gazeau de Vautibault, *Le Trans saharien* (Paris, [1879]).

[4] Brière to Jauréguiberry, 7 Feb. 1880 (Conf.), MFOM Sénégal I 63(a); Jauréguiberry to Brière, 4 Feb. 1880, MFOM Sénégal I 63(b).

to our attention.'[1] Both he and Jauréguiberry believed the Sudan to be well worth the costs of its acquisition; their descriptions of its wealth were no less extravagant than those of Duponchel or Rouvier.[2] Their main concern was to secure for France the greatest possible benefit from the future exploitation of its economic potential. They were convinced that the race for Africa was about to begin; they were determined to win it, and the prize they aimed for was nothing less than the major portion of the West African interior. By the end of 1879 the Ministry of Public Works was planning to send a mission to Agadès and thence to Sokoto in the hope that the Fulani Empire might thus be opened to French trade and influence from Algeria.[3]

But if Freycinet and Jauréguiberry shared a common belief in African empire, each had his own distinctive view about its nature and about the way it was to be acquired. Freycinet's objective was a traditional one: the creation of a loosely held commercial empire based on trade and influence. Except for the Railway, his policies were basically the same as those of his predecessors half a century before. The methods he adopted were also broadly similar. French influence was to be extended by peaceful means, not by military conquests. The maintenance of peace, he warned Colonel Flatters before sending him out to survey the route for the Trans-Sahara Railway, 'is the essential condition for your mission'.[4] Unfortunately, such a policy was no more realistic than the exaggerated estimate of Sudanese wealth which formed its major premise. Blinded by its enthusiasm, Freycinet's *Commission Supérieure* took no account of the immense technical difficulties which railway-building in the Sahara involved. Almost wilfully, it ignored the existing state of North African politics which made peaceful penetration manifestly impossible. Both in Tunisia and in Egypt events were rapidly moving towards a crisis. In southern Algeria the Walad Sidi Shaikh, quiescent since 1873, were again in revolt. In the Sahara itself the friendly Azjer Tuareg had been heavily defeated by the rival Hoggar confederation which was much more hostile to European expansion. And from Tripoli came alarming reports about a determined Ottoman effort to drive France out of North Africa by unleashing the forces of Muslim

[1] Freycinet, Rapport au Président de la République, 31 Dec. 1879, *J.O.* p. 11700.
[2] Freycinet spoke of a Sudanese population of 100,000,000, Jauréguiberry of 80,000,000. Rapport au Président de la République, 12 July 1879, *J.O.* 14 July 1879, p. 6633; *ibid. Déb. Parl. Chambre*, séance du 13 juillet 1880, p. 8143.
[3] Projet d'instructions complémentaires, encl. in M.T.P. to M.A.E., 16 Jan. 1880, AEMD Afrique 75.
[4] Freycinet to Flatters, Instructions, 7 Nov. 1879, AN F14 12436.

fanaticism against her.[1] The massacre of the second Flatters expedition, almost certainly at the instigation of Turkish officials in Ghadamès and Ghat, finally shattered the illusory hopes which had surrounded the project from its inception. The policy-makers were now forced to realise that the security essential for railway-building would have to be imposed by military means. As the Governor-General of Algeria warned, any attempt to proceed with the Railway before French political and military domination had been effectively established over the Algerian Sahara was completely unthinkable. But with the French Army already engaged against the tribesmen of southern Tunisia and the rebels of southern Oran, a policy of military expansion in the Sahara was quite out of the question; so in June 1881 the whole Trans-Sahara Railway project was postponed indefinitely.[2] Once more the political realities of Africa had dispelled the extravagant aspirations of Paris.

The fate of the Railway, however, did not surprise the Ministry of Marine. The officials at the Rue Royale had never had much faith in its feasibility and had always tried to have the Senegal–Niger Railway considered (from a technical point of view) as an entirely separate project. Once Legros had obtained a declaration of approval for the latter scheme, he took no further part in the *Commission Supérieure*'s deliberations.[3] Henceforth, the direction of Sudanese policy was kept exclusively in the hands of the Ministry of Marine. When drafting its plans, it did not seek the technical advice of the Ministry of Public Works; it did not consult the Ministry of Finance on the question of costs; it did not even bother to keep Freycinet fully informed.[4] And it had good reason for this secretiveness, for its policies bore little resemblance to the vague commercial aspirations of the Prime Minister.

Ostensibly, the objectives of the Rue Royale were the same as those of Freycinet. 'Nothing is further from our minds than military ex-

---

[1] Referred to in M.A.E. to Tissot [Ambassador, Constantinople], 13 June 1881, *D.D.F.* IV, no. 33. See also M.A.E., Circular to London, Vienna, Berlin, Saint Petersburg, Rome, 31 July 1881, *ibid.* no. 88. For developments in the Sahara, see: C. Trumelet, *Histoire de l'insurrection dans le sud de la province d'Alger, 1864–1880* (Algiers, 1884).

[2] Grévy to M.A.E., 18 May 1881, cited in H.M.P. de la Martinière and N. Lacroix (eds.), *Documents pour servir à l'étude du nord-ouest africain* (Lille, 1894–7), III, 21–8; Rapport de la Commission Supérieure..., 18 June 1881, AN F14 12437. Grévy's letter was crucial to its decision.

[3] See: Legros, Note pour le cabinet du Ministre, 11 June 1879, MFOM Afrique XII 2 (a); Rapport de la 2e souscommission, 27 Oct. 1879, AN F14 12437. The minutes of the Trans-Sahara Commission are to be found *ibid.* and in MFOM Afrique XII 2.

[4] These facts emerged during the discussions of the Budget Commission. See: Procès-Verbaux de la Commission du Budget, séances du 17 mars, 4 juin 1880, AN C 3176.

pansion', Jauréguiberry assured him in November 1879, 'the aim of [my] Department is simply to participate in the general movement which is drawing the nations of Europe, in search of new outlets for their trade, into the heart of Africa'.[1] But the Ministry's real motives were political, not economic. No matter how profitable the Senegal Railway might become, wrote the Director of Colonies in 1880, the extension of French political influence would in itself justify the cost of its construction.[2] As far as Jauréguiberry and his advisers were concerned, the purpose of the Railway was to establish French control over the Niger, and to achieve this goal they were prepared to authorise the military occupation of the Western Sudan. In order to protect the Railway, Legros warned the Trans-Sahara Commission in 1879, it would be necessary to build a line of forts between Médine and the Niger and place gunboats on the river.[3] Faidherbe's blueprint for the Sudanese Empire had at last received the stamp of official approval.

Jauréguiberry now threw the whole weight of his authority behind the advance to the Niger. In July he ordered Brière to submit detailed plans for occupying Bafoulabé and linking it to Médine by a road.[4] When the Trans-Sahara Commission refused to sanction any expenditure without the prior consent of Parliament, he took advantage of the summer recess to have the estimated cost of 500,000 fr. approved by Presidential Decree.[5] In October Senegal's young *directeur politique*, Joseph Simon Gallieni, was sent to carry out the necessary surveys, establish relations with the Malinké tribes in the area and win their support for French expansion. His mission was successful, and in November both he and Brière reported that the road to the Niger was wide open. Tokolor influence in the area, they claimed, was negligible, and the local populations could be counted on to co-operate wholeheartedly. The British threat, of course, made it essential for them to exploit their advantage while they still retained it.[6] Jauréguiberry

---

[1] Jauréguiberry to Freycinet, 8 Nov. 1879, MFOM Sénégal XII 76(a).
[2] Michaux, Note pour le Ministre, 6 Jan. 1880, MFOM Missions 15, Carrey 1880.
[3] Procès-Verbaux...2ᵉ souscommission, séance du 21 juillet 1879, AN F¹⁴ 12437.
[4] M.M.C. to Brière, 19 July 1879, referred to in Brière to M.M.C., 9 Aug. 1879, MFOM Missions 15, Mousnier 1879.
[5] Procès-Verbaux...Commission Supérieure, séance du Iᵉʳ août 1879, MFOM Afrique XII 2(b); Decree, 25 Sept. 1879, *J.O.* 28 Sept. 1879, p. 9361. The credit was later approved by the Law of 24 Dec. 1879.
[6] Gallieni to Brière, 30 Oct. 1879; same to same, Rapport, 17 Nov. 1879; MFOM Sénégal III 10(*bis*); Gallieni, Note sur Ségou, 18 Nov. 1879, MFOM Missions 15, Gallieni 1879; Brière to M.M.C., 30 Oct. 1879; same to same, 9 Nov. 1879, no. 820, *ibid.*; same to same, 9 Nov. 1879, no. 821, MFOM Missions 16 Gallieni 1880; same to same, 9 Dec. 1879, MFOM Sénégal I 63(a).

needed little urging, and when funds ran out he immediately authorised an additional expenditure of 500,000 fr., again without Parliamentary approval.[1] Meanwhile, the Ministry itself had been hard at work on the details of the railway programme, and by November Legros was able to produce a general estimate of the cost. The Railway was to consist of three sections. Two of them, a line from Dakar to Saint-Louis and a branch line to Médine, were to be built by private enterprise, the third from Médine to the Niger at state expense. The total cost to the State, including the construction of six forts beyond Médine, was to be slightly more than 49,000,000 fr.[2] In February 1880 Jauréguiberry submitted the whole project to Parliament, assuring it that the promising results of work already in progress gave every reason to hope that the Niger could be reached in six years. In order to get the necessary material to Médine before the dry season made navigation on the Senegal impossible, he requested the immediate vote of 9,000,000 fr. to cover the costs of the first campaign.[3] And then the Minister's troubles began.

To begin with, Jauréguiberry soon learned that the situation in Senegal was much less rosy than Brière and Gallieni had pictured it. Construction of the road to Bafoulabé was severely hampered by an outbreak of yellow fever. The Commandants of Bakel and Médine were slapdash and inefficient; the chief engineer seemed interested only in prospecting for gold. The site chosen by Gallieni for the fort proved to be unhealthy and dangerously exposed to attack. Moreover, it displeased the local chiefs, who now refused to provide labour. Worst of all, the costs of the operation threatened to exceed even the revised estimate of 1,000,000 fr. By May Brière was forced to admit that the whole wretched business was seriously undermining French prestige.[4]

---

[1] Michaux, Note pour le Ministre, 6 Jan. 1880, MFOM Missions 15, Carrey 1880. A formal demand was later submitted and approved by the Law of 24 June 1880.

[2] Legros, Note sommaire, 9 Nov. 1879, MFOM Missions 109, Derrien 1880–1; Michaux, Note pour le Ministre, 6 Jan. 1880, MFOM Missions 15, Carrey 1880. The total cost of the project would be 107,148,400 fr., of which 49,270,000 fr. would be borne by the State.

[3] Jauréguiberry, Projet de Loi, 5 Feb. 1880, *J.O. Doc. Parl. Chambre*, no. 2266, pp. 2028–9. The Minister's estimate of the total cost was 120,000,000 fr., and of public expenditure 54,183,800 fr. The increase over the estimates of Legros is accounted for by the inclusion of provisions for unforeseen expenses.

[4] Brière to M.M.C., 9 Jan. 1880; same to same, 7 Feb. 1880 (Conf.), MFOM Sénégal I 63(a); Brière to M.M.C., 8 Mar. 1880, MFOM Sénégal I 99(a), Correspondance du Gouverneur; Legros, Note pour la direction des colonies, 10 Jan. 1880, MFOM Sénégal IV 73(a); Brière to M.M.C., 8 May 1880, MFOM Sénégal I 99 (a), Correspondance du Gouverneur.

The Revival of the Niger Plan, 1876–80

This news could hardly have reached Paris at a more embarrassing moment, for Parliamentary approval of the railway credit was turning out to be anything but the formality which the Ministry had expected. Jauréguiberry had counted on an easy passage through the Parliamentary Budget Commission which had already demonstrated its support for the Trans-Sahara Railway; but he soon discovered that its sanction was not to be taken for granted. Although the Commission had readily voted funds for preliminary surveys, it was not prepared to accept a hasty and ill-prepared scheme which could very well commit the State to a possible expenditure of 120,000,000 fr.[1] Its President, Brisson, and the *rapporteur* for the Colonial Budget, Blandin, were both highly sceptical. Blandin criticised the Ministry's failure to provide sufficient evidence in support of the project and refused to make any recommendation until he had received all the necessary details. More seriously, Jauréguiberry's determination to begin work immediately had led him to present his proposal as a supplementary credit on the Extraordinary Budget. For the self-styled guardians of the French economy such a procedure was financial heresy, and Brisson, as a matter of principle, absolutely refused to approve it.[2]

The Minister's customary tactlessness complicated matters still further. He made no attempt to satisfy the Commission's demand for more information, and, although he knew by the middle of April that his credit would be rejected,[3] he waited for two months before submitting an alternative plan. The programme which he finally presented in June limited the first stage of construction to the section of the line between Médine and Bafoulabé and reduced the initial grant to 4,000,000 fr. But the proposal came much too late to have any chance of acceptance. The Commission, determined not to commit itself, rejected it out of hand and agreed to recommend no more than 833,000 fr. for further surveys. On 12 July Jauréguiberry persuaded it to raise the

[1] The Budget Commission rejected the Minister's division between public and private expenditure, and it feared that the Treasury might have to meet the total cost of the enterprise. Procès-Verbaux de la Commission du Budget, séance du 17 mars 1880, AN C3176.

[2] Ibid.; see also: J.O. Déb. Parl. Chambre, séance du 13 juillet 1880, p. 8143 [Blandin]: 'Vous savez quelle est la règle, et cette règle...est qu'on n'accorde et qu'on ne vote jamais de crédits supplémentaires ou de crédits extraordinaires au budget extraordinaire.' On the composition and functions of the Budget Commission, see: L. Rogers, 'Parliamentary Commissions in France', *Political Science Quarterly*, xxxviii (1923), 413–42, 602–35; R. K. Gooch, *The French Parliamentary Committee System* (New York, 1935).

[3] Jauréguiberry to Brière, 5 Apr. 1880; same to same, 16 Apr. 1880, MFOM Sénégal I 63(b).

figure to 1,300,000 fr., thus managing to save something from the debacle.[1]

The Budget Commission's unexpected assault shook the Minister's confidence. He had already begun to have second thoughts about the project and had warned Brière against any illusions about the difficulties involved. Once the Budget Commission's attitude became clear, he absolutely forbade any expenditure over the authorised million.[2] But Jauréguiberry did not reckon with the stubbornness of his subordinate. Brière was determined to maintain the impetus of the French advance, and he had not forgotten how to overcome ministerial hesitations. He assured Paris that he was doing everything humanly possible to minimise costs, and he reaffirmed his conviction that the Railway was still a practical proposition if only the Government would provide the necessary funds. But any failure to do so, he was careful to add, could only have the most disastrous consequences for French security. To leave Bafoulabé unfinished would endanger its garrison. To abandon the telegraph would be a sign of French weakness and lack of resolution. If work already under way were halted, it would be extremely difficult to restart; all the materials collected on the Upper Senegal would thus be lost and the money already spent completely wasted. If petty financial considerations were allowed to stand in the way, then the field would be left clear for their British rivals.[3] These arguments were as effective as ever. Confronted by the problem of security, the harassed Jauréguiberry could only order the Governor to maintain the strictest financial control and to draft a detailed estimate of the losses which a suspension of the work would incur.[4]

The Minister's performance in the House completed his discomfiture. He defended his Bill with all the limited powers of rhetoric at his command, but his strident appeals to the Chamber's spirit of patriotism made no impression upon it. When he tried to argue that approval for surveys implied approval, in principle at least, for railway-construction, he was immediately challenged by Blandin and forced to withdraw his

---

[1] Procès-Verbaux de la Commission du Budget, séances du 4 juin, 19 juin, 25 juin 1880, AN C3176; Blandin, Rapport, 29 June 1880, *J.O. Doc. Parl. Chambre*, no. 2813, pp. 8541–2; Blandin, Rapport supplémentaire, 13 July 1880, *ibid.* no. 2948, p. 9204.
[2] Jauréguiberry to Brière, 4 Feb. 1880; same to same, 5 Apr. 1880; same to same, 16 Apr. 1880; same to same, 21 Apr. 1880, MFOM Sénégal I 63 (b).
[3] Brière to M.M.C., 7 Feb. 1880 (Conf.); same to same, 8 Feb. 1880; same to same, 8 Mar. 1880, MFOM Sénégal I 63 (a); same to same, 29 Apr. 1880; same to same, 8 May 1880, MFOM Sénégal I 99 (a), Correspondance du Gouverneur.
[4] Jauréguiberry to Brière, 20 May 1880, MFOM Sénégal I 63 (b).

remark. After this there was little left to oppose, and the credit was voted by a comfortable majority. Mercifully, the Senate followed suit without causing him any further embarrassment.[1]

Certainly, Jauréguiberry's handling of the railway Bill was hardly a model of Parliamentary expertise, and the pittance he finally received was a mere shadow of his original demand. But what the Minister lacked in finesse he made up for in energy and persistence. As soon as Parliament had relieved some of the financial burden, he authorised the construction of a second fort at Kita, a hundred miles beyond Bafoulabé. The extra 467,000 fr. which he had wheedled out of the Budget Commission were used to form a new battalion of *tirailleurs sénégalais*.[2] In June he had already transferred control over colonial construction to the *artillerie de marine*, and on 6 September he appointed a *Commandant-Supérieur du Haut-Fleuve* with full powers over all operations in the Upper Senegal.[3] Within the Ministry itself, a special department, the *Bureau du Haut-Fleuve*, was created to deal with Sudanese affairs. Jauréguiberry might have botched the railway credit, but he did demonstrate his readiness to bear the financial cost of Sudanese expansion, and he placed the Sudan under military command. In so doing he set French policy firmly on an imperialist course.

FRANCO-TOKOLOR RELATIONS: GALLIENI'S MISSION TO SEGU

The revival of the Niger plan was bound to affect French policies towards Ahmadu and his Tokolors. The alternatives were still the same as they had been since the 1850s. If the French wished merely to create a loose sphere of trade and influence, then it was both possible and desirable to co-operate with the Tokolor empire. But if their objective was to establish themselves as a political power on the Niger, then a military confrontation was sooner or later inevitable. Brière appreciated this fundamental reality as much as Faidherbe had done; from 1878 on-

[1] *J.O. Déb. Parl. Chambre*, séance du 13 juillet 1880, pp. 8142–4; *ibid. Sénat*, séance du 15 juillet 1880, p. 8193. The vote in the Chamber was 405 to 7 (72 abstentions), in the Senate 229 to 0 (63 abstentions).

[2] Jauréguiberry to Brière, 31 July 1880, MFOM Sénégal I 63(b); same to same, 4 Aug. 1880, MFOM Sénégal I 99(a), Correspondance Générale. See also: Blandin, Rapport supplémentaire, 13 July 1880, *J.O. Doc. Parl. Chambre*, no. 2948, p. 9204. 350,000 fr. were to be spent on the *tirailleurs*.

[3] Decree, 26 June 1880, *J.O.* 29 June 1880, pp. 7185–6; Decree, 6 Sept. 1880, *ibid.* 9 Sept. 1880, p. 9876.

ward he made no secret of his conviction that war with Ahmadu would have to come in the end. But like Faidherbe he also realised that premature hostilities might well have fatal consequences for the security of Senegal. Ahmadu was no Abdul-Bubakar to be cowed into submission by a judicious demonstration of French military might. Conflict had to be postponed until the French were firmly established on the Niger and controlled the river with their gunboats. Somehow or other, the Sultan had to be prevented from attacking the French while they were still weak; and this could only be done by negotiating a new treaty with him.

Brière had long recognised the need to re-establish diplomatic relations with the Tokolors. In 1878, even as he warned of the growing menace of Tokolor expansion and called for military action to combat it, he suggested the despatch of a mission to renegotiate the Mage treaty.[1] The adoption of the Senegal–Niger Railway project and the continuing danger of British expansion from the Gambia made it all the more essential to reach a settlement which would keep the British off the Niger and allow work on the Railway to proceed in an atmosphere of relative security. In July 1879 the Ministry authorised a mission to deal with any possible difficulties which might arise over the occupation of Bafoulabé; so, when Gallieni completed his surveys in the Bafing area, Brière sent him off again to Segu.[2]

The Governor's priorities were clear. His main objective was to extend French political control over the Niger. 'I consider Bamako to be an even more important goal than [Segu]', he had told Jauréguiberry in November.

All our efforts must be directed...at reaching the Niger as quickly as possible, not just to show our flag there but to plant it at some important spot which would then become the capital of a French protected state...

This, he claimed, was the only way to block the ambitions of their British rivals. Accordingly, Gallieni's first tasks were to secure local support for the construction of two forts at Fangala and Kita, to survey the route to the Niger, and to sign a treaty of protectorate with Bamako. Only when this had been accomplished was he to continue

[1] Brière to M.M.C., 5 June 1878, MFOM Sénégal I 61(c); same to same, 22 Nov. 1878, MFOM Sénégal I 63 (a). Ahmadu's repudiation of the Senegal–Bafing boundary which his father had accepted in 1860 provided an additional reason for reopening talks.
[2] M.M.C. to Brière, 19 July 1879 (Conf.); Brière to M.M.C., 9 Aug. 1879 (Conf.), MFOM Missions 15, Mousnier 1879.

on to Segu and sign a treaty of peace, friendship and trade with Ahmadu. Gallieni was to secure the Sultan's permission for the French to build and maintain roads in his empire and to introduce a steamboat service on the Niger. He was to obtain the grant of exclusive navigation rights on the river, the right to keep a French Resident in Segu and a promise not to sign any treaties with other European powers. In return, the French would recognise Ahmadu's authority over all territories 'effectively occupied by him and living in peace under his rule', as well as over future extensions of his empire in any direction other than towards the French. If necessary, Gallieni could also offer him cannon. To dispel the Sultan's suspicions, Brière also sent him a letter proclaiming his desire to maintain peace and his exclusive interest in the extension of French trade.[1]

The Governor's protestations of friendship were, of course, pure sham. In November he had ordered the Commandant of Bafoulabé to maintain an outward show of cordiality towards the Tokolors while secretly offering their rebellious Bambara subjects French protection and support.[2] The establishment of a French protectorate over Bamako clearly involved an assault upon the territorial integrity of the Tokolor Empire. The proposed treaty was conceived in the same spirit. In secret notes, Gallieni was ordered to leave the recognition clause as vague as possible and to insist on the wording: *vivant en paix sous sa domination*. This was designed to exclude all the Sultan's rebellious provinces. The envoy was instructed to press hard for permission to build and maintain roads, as this would enable the French to build the Railway, and forts to protect it, wherever they wished. The Niger steamboats were merely the cover for gunboats.[3] Brière was prepared to negotiate with the Tokolors only in order to deceive them, and in Gallieni he found a willing partner to the deception. Despite his later reputation as a subtle theorist of colonial administration, this future

---

[1] Brière to M.M.C., 9 Nov. 1879, no. 821 (Conf.), MFOM Missions 16, Gallieni 1880; Brière to Gallieni, Instructions, 1 Feb. 1880, with enclosures: Draft treaty of protectorate over Bamako, draft treaty with Ahmadu; Brière to Ahmadu, n.d., *ibid.*

[2] Brière to Marchi [Commandant, Bafoulabé], 8 Nov. 1879, MFOM Sénégal IV 73(a): 'Si l'on vous parle de nos relations avec le sultan de Ségou vous direz aux Toucouleurs qu'elles sont excellentes...aux Malinkés et Bambaras, c'est à dire aux indigènes du sol... vous direz que partout où nous sommes nous protégeons la race à qui appartient le sol... [mais] qu'il faut pour avoir cette protection venir en aide dans notre établissement ...que sans doute les Toucouleurs ne doivent pas nous voir d'un bon œil nous établir chez des peuples qu'ils avaient l'intention de soumettre tôt ou tard...'

[3] Confidential notes on draft treaty with Ahmadu, encl. in Brière to Gallieni, Instructions, 1 Feb. 1880, MFOM Missions 16, Gallieni 1880.

Franco-Tokolor Relations: Gallieni's Mission to Segu

Maréchal de France was in 1880 a young, impulsive, and bellicose Captain in the *infanterie de marine*, and certainly no friend of Islam. After his survey of Bafoulabé in November 1879, he had called for active if secret support for the rebellious Bambaras against their Tokolor oppressors. 'It has always been in the name of [the Prophet]', he added, 'that our worst enemies have marched against us.'[1]

Gallieni's first reports were uniformly promising. On 3 April he signed treaties of protectorate with the chiefs of the Bakhoy region and on the 16th with those of Fuladugu. On the 25th he established a protectorate over Kita and obtained permission to build a fort there during the next dry season.[2] But thereafter the mission began to encounter difficulties. At Kita Gallieni learned that the Beledugu region was in turmoil and dangerous for travellers, but he felt obliged to risk the journey lest he alienate his potential allies at Bamako by travelling along the safer route via the Tokolor stronghold of Murgula. He would have done better to choose the latter route, for on 11 May the Bambaras ambushed his mission at Dio, killing fourteen men and capturing most of the baggage, including Ahmadu's presents. Gallieni hurried on to Bamako, only to discover that it was merely a large village, not the important political centre he had been led to believe. Although he did establish relations with its chiefs, he made no attempt to install a French Resident; instead he quickly crossed the Niger and commended himself to the goodwill of Ahmadu.[3]

Despite his efforts to make light of the disaster at Dio, Gallieni was forced to admit that French plans would have to be seriously modified. Bamako was clearly unsuitable for their purposes; other means would have to be found to establish French power on the Niger. As far as Gallieni could see, only two options were open to the French. One was to negotiate with Ahmadu and obtain trading and navigation rights in his empire. Because the Sultan was the only strong ruler in the area and his capital the only fit place to receive a French Resident, it was essential to reach a settlement with him before the British did. The other (and in Gallieni's opinion preferable) course of action was to advance in force and take the Niger by military means. A well-organised column

[1] Gallieni to Brière, Report, 17 Nov. 1879, MFOM Sénégal III 10(*bis*).
[2] Gallieni to Brière, 10 Apr. 1880, no. 7; same to same, 25 Apr. 1880, no. 12, MFOM Missions 16, Gallieni 1880. Copies of these treaties can be found in MFOM *Recueil des Traités, Afrique: Soudan.*
[3] Same to same, 26 Apr. 1880, no. 16, *ibid.*; same to same, Nango, 7 July 1880, no. 5, MFOM Sénégal III 10(*bis*).

of five or six hundred men, he confidently declared, could reach the Niger in ten days, build a fort, and place gunboats on the river. Once French gunboats controlled the Niger as far as Timbuktu, the question of Tokolor opposition would become a strictly academic one.[1] It took more than an ambush to curb the Captain's spirit or alter his views.

Under the circumstances, Gallieni got a better reception than he deserved. Although Ahmadu was well aware of the mission's activities in Beledugu, he recognised its diplomatic status, provided it with food and shelter, and made arrangements for the care of the wounded.[2] But the Sultan's conciliatory attitude did not surprise the French; over the past months they had received ample proof of his desire to avoid a fight. Despite the capture of Sabouciré, Brière reported in November 1879, Ahmadu had made no move against the French and would probably remain quiet unless directly attacked. Three months later the Governor could add that Ahmadu had given orders not to interfere with the construction of Bafoulabé.[3]

According to Brière, the reason for the Sultan's inactivity was his political and military weakness. The capture of Sabouciré had been a severe blow to his prestige and had destroyed his influence in Bambuk. From Bafoulabé to Bamako, the fortresses of Koundian and Murgula were the only centres of Tokolor power. Beledugu was completely independent; indeed its inhabitants had only recently routed the Tokolor army and burned down the market town of Guigné. Gallieni's reports were still more emphatic. 'The Tokolor Empire', he wrote in October 1880, 'is nothing more than the debris of [Umar's] vast conquests with none of the political and territorial unity which that brilliant Negro was able to achieve...Today, the army of el Hadj [Umar] no longer exists...'[4]

These assessments were not far short of the truth. Although the Tokolor position in Kaarta was relatively secure after 1877, the Sabouciré

---

[1] Gallieni to Brière, 15 May 1880; same to same, 12 June 1880, Nango, no. 1, MFOM Missions 16, Gallieni 1880; same to same, 7 July 1880, Nango, no. 5, MFOM Sénégal III 10 (*bis*).

[2] Same to same, 2 Sept. 1880, Nango, no. 8, MFOM Missions 16, Gallieni 1880.

[3] Brière to M.M.C., 9 Nov. 1879, no. 821 (Conf.), MFOM Missions 16, Gallieni 1880; same to same, 7 Feb. 1880 (Conf.), MFOM Sénégal I 63 (a). See also: same to same, 8 May 1880, no. 281, *ibid*.

[4] Brière to M.M.C., 30 Oct. 1879, MFOM Missions 15, Gallieni 1879; same to same, 9 Nov. 1879, no. 820, *ibid*.; same to same, 9 Dec. 1879, MFOM Sénégal I 63 (a); same to same, 7 Feb. 1880 (Conf.), *ibid*.; Gallieni to Brière, 14 Oct. 1880, Nango, no. 14, MFOM Missions 16, Gallieni 1880.

campaign undoubtedly caused many former allies to desert to the French.[1] Gallieni's successful treaty-making and his passage through Beledugu confirmed the waning of Tokolor influence between Bafoulabé and the Niger. Although descriptions of Ahmadu's military weakness may have been exaggerated,[2] the Sultan was certainly finding it increasingly difficult to suppress the rebellions which now posed a constant threat to his empire's existence. In his dealings with the French, Ahmadu was thus faced once more with two alternatives: he could either seek to reunify his empire and recapture its old enthusiasm by proclaiming a new *jihad* against the European invader, or he could co-operate in the hope of securing European support. Once more he chose to co-operate.

But the Sultan was determined to exact a heavy price for his friendship. As in the past, his objectives were to obtain a generous supply of European weapons and at the same time prevent an undue extension of French influence into his empire. And he approached his task with considerable diplomatic skill. Despite his relatively friendly reception of the embassy, Ahmadu refused to meet any of its members or to allow them into Segu. Much more seriously, he ignored Gallieni's extravagant promises of military assistance and refused to open negotiations.[3] Throughout the summer the French envoys vegetated in the unhealthy surroundings of Nango, the village where they were confined. As the weeks went by, Gallieni became increasingly alarmed by the apparent extent of British influence in the Tokolor empire. Both the Gambia and Sierra Leone, he claimed, had tried to establish commercial relations with Ahmadu. Governor Rowe of Sierra Leone had even sent a treaty-making mission, and one of its members, the Native Agent Makka, had so far managed to persuade the Sultan to delay the start of

[1] E.g. Badou [chief of Logo] to Brière, n.d. [rec'd 23 June 1879], MFOM Sénégal III 10(*bis*)(b): 'Nous tous, les gens du Logo, nous avons pris la détermination de nous placer sous votre gouvernement et de devenir vos fidèles sujets. Nous venons aussi vous prier de nous rendre notre pays en le laissant sous votre protection. Nous désirons qu'il échappe à la domination d'Ahmadou Sheickou et qu'il soit placé sous la vôtre.'

[2] In the published account of his mission Gallieni again stressed Ahmadu's weakness but gave the strength of the Tokolor army as 12,000. J. S. Gallieni, *Voyage au Soudan français (Haut-Niger et pays de Ségou), 1879–81* (Paris, 1885), pp. 609–10. This estimate coincided fairly closely with that of Mage in 1866. See above: p. 48.

[3] Gallieni to Ahmadu, n.d. [but probably 13 June 1880], BN n.a.fr. 25070, Documents relatifs au Sultanat de Ségou: 'La France désire autant que toi-même ta puissance...Nous te donnerons des canons, des canoniers, des boulets pour détruire des tatas; nous te rendrons le maître absolu du Niger jusqu' à Tombouctou qui sous ta domination deviendra la Mecque de l'Afrique.' A revised version of this letter is printed in Gallieni, *op. cit.* p. 368.

negotiations.[1] But the Sultan himself supplied much of the information on which these panicky reports were based, and he certainly exaggerated the British threat in order to improve his bargaining position.[2] Although Gallieni dismissed this possibility as much too subtle a manœuvre for 'such ignorant people as we are dealing with here'; he eventually had to admit that '[Ahmadu], who does not lack a certain shrewdness, fully understood the importance we attached to our rapid installation on the banks of the Niger, and he did not hide the fact that the English were also intending to establish close relations with him.'[3] When negotiations were finally opened at the end of October, the Tokolors continued to make good use of the *bâton anglais*. 'We do not know the English', Ahmadu's councillor Seydou Djeylia told Gallieni at their first meeting, 'and for sentimental reasons we would always favour the French. But a man who cannot suck from his mother will suck from his grandmother. We shall go to the English if we cannot reach agreement with the French ...A girl', he added, changing the metaphor, 'will always choose the man who gives her the most and best assures her peace and tranquillity.'[4]

What Seydou demanded first of all was a general assurance that the French would pay a fair price for Tokolor concessions and honour any agreement which they concluded. Promises of cannon were not much good if, as in the case of Mage, the cannon failed to arrive.[5] He then insisted on the recognition of Ahmadu's authority over all lands conquered by his father except those actually paying taxes to the French, free communications between Segu and Futa, and the destruction of Bafoulabé. In return, the Tokolors would allow the French to build

---

1 Gallieni to Brière, 20 Aug. 1880, Nango, no. 6; same to same, 10 Sept. 1880, Nango, no. 9, MFOM Missions 16, Gallieni 1880; same to same, 25 Oct. 1880, MFOM Sénégal III 10(*bis*). See also: Same to same, 14 Nov. 1880, Nango no. 17, *ibid*. Rowe's mission was led by a Sierra Leone Government messenger, Sanoko Madi. The Makka whom Gallieni referred to was almost certainly a member of this party, Momodu Wakka, who had remained in Dinguiray after the main party had returned to Freetown. See: Hargreaves, *Prelude to the Partition of West Africa*, p. 259, n.2.

2 Lieutenant Vallière, who had been sent to allay the suspicions of Murgula while the mission proceeded through Beledugu, reported that he had found no evidence of any direct contact between Sierra Leone and the territories through which he had passed. The last Englishman to have visited the sources of the Niger, he claimed, had died in Buré forty years before. Vallière, Rapport, 15 June 1880, MFOM Missions 16, Gallieni 1880.

3 Gallieni to Brière, 10 Sept. 1880, Nango, no. 9, MFOM Missions 16, Gallieni 1880; same to same, 18 Nov. 1880, Nango, no. 19, MFOM Sénégal III 10(*bis*).

4 Procès-Verbal..., 1ère séance, 31 Oct. 1880, *ibia*.

5 The Government of Senegal did send Ahmadu a cannon in 1869, but the Sultan refused to accept it because it was too heavy to be transported easily along the empire's primitive roads. What Ahmadu wanted were smaller mountain guns. See: Saint-Martin, 'Les relations diplomatiques...', *loc. cit.* p. 192.

trading posts but not out of brick or stone, to permit free movement but not the construction of new roads, to give navigation rights on the Niger but not for steamboats, and to accept a French Resident at Segu but only if he were a Negro and a Muslim. Their asking price was an annual payment of 50,000 fr., 4,000 rifles, 4,000 barrels of powder, 4,000 sabre blades and 5,000 *guinées*.[1]

Gallieni could see that these cleverly phrased conditions neutralised every major element in the French programme, and he therefore rejected them. Instead, he demanded the acceptance of a French protectorate over the Niger.[2] But he was prepared to pay for it. The final agreement provided for a single payment of 4 mountain guns with full accessories and 20 cases of ammunition, 1,000 rifles and 4,000 cartridges, plus an annual rent of 10,000 fr., 200 flintlocks, 200 cannon balls, 200 barrels of gunpowder and sundry other articles. In addition, Gallieni solemnly pledged that France would never invade the Tokolor Empire nor construct fortified posts on the Sultan's territory.

Having gained satisfaction on their two essential conditions, the Tokolors gave way on the rest. Seydou retracted his refusal to allow steamboats on the Niger and did not insist on the destruction of Bafoulabé. The French were granted freedom of commercial movement and exclusive navigation rights. A French protectorate over the Niger and the establishment of a European Resident at Segu were accepted without demur.[3] After some hesitation, Ahmadu affixed his seal to the agreement and sent the mission back to Senegal with gifts for the Governor.

Gallieni himself was quite pleased with the outcome. He had managed to avoid making any definite commitment on Bafoulabé or setting any definite limits to the Tokolor Empire. The French, he claimed, could thus advance as far as the Niger without actually violating the treaty. Exclusive navigation rights, the protectorate clause, and the Resident, neutralised the danger of a British take-over. Although the payment of cannons was regrettable, he was sure that the Tokolors would not know how to use or maintain them. But Gallieni never considered the treaty

[1] *Ibid.* 1ère séance, 31 Oct., 2e séance, 1 Nov., 3e séance, 2 Nov. 1880.

[2] Gallieni to Brière, 2 Sept. 1880, MFOM Missions 16, Gallieni 1880. In a note attached to the draft treaty, however, Brière had instructed Gallieni: 'On devra éviter de parler de protectorat pour ne pas froisser l'orgueil du grand prophète; si cependant les Toucouleurs étaient tout à fait compromis par le mouvement bambara et qu'on jugeât qu'ils pourraient rattraper à cette branche, on pourrait tâter le terrain et ne s'y engager qu'à bon escient.' Encl. in Brière to Gallieni, 1 Feb. 1880, *ibid.*

[3] Procès-Verbal..., 3e séance, 2 Nov. 1880, MFOM Sénégal III 10(*bis*). An original copy of the treaty can be found in: BN n.a.fr. 25070, Documents relatifs au Sultanat de Ségou.

by itself as sufficient guarantee of French interests. He remained convinced that only the military occupation of the Niger could effectively secure French preponderance over the Western Sudan.[1] Nor did the negotiations alter his basic attitude towards the Tokolors. For a moment he had recognised Ahmadu's sagacity and his empire's relative strength; but he quickly reverted to his old opinions. Even before he left Nango he was again describing the Tokolors as 'our natural enemies... completely opposed to any idea of progress or civilisation', and their empire as a predatory tyranny rent by dissension and doomed to crumble under the assaults of its rebellious subjects. In his opinion, the industrious Bambaras were powers of the future and the ones most worthy of French support.[2]

By the time he returned from his mission, Gallieni was advocating nothing less than the empire's complete destruction. The animist rebels were to be given material support and incited to attack the fortress of Koundian, while the Sultan's brothers in Kaarta were to be encouraged to defy his authority. The French themselves should dismember Futa, occupy Beledugu, build forts at Niagassola and Bamako, place a gunboat on the Niger and send it to Segu with a Resident. In the meantime, the Sultan was to be lulled into a false sense of security and kept out of the arms of the English by the ratification of the treaty and the payment of the stipulated rent. This would in no way hamper the progress of French plans. The pledge not to build forts was made meaningless by the right to build trading posts which could easily be turned into forts. Permission to open and maintain new commercial routes allowed for the construction of the Railway; navigation rights without specification of vessels cleared the way for the gunboats. Above all, the protectorate gave France a solid diplomatic title to the Niger and opened the route to Timbuktu. The only risk lay in the payment of cannons, and these could be rendered non-serviceable before delivery. For Gallieni the treaty of Nango was nothing but a temporary expedient to be denounced as soon as Ahmadu had been reduced to impotence. If there were ever any doubts about his views on the possibility of Franco-Tokolor co-operation, this report dispelled them.[3]

---

[1] Gallieni to Brière, 14 Nov. 1880, Nango, no. 17; same to same, 16 Nov. 1880, Nango, no. 18; same to same, 18 Nov. 1880, Nango, no. 19, MFOM Sénégal III 10(*bis*).

[2] Same to same, 24 Dec. 1880, Nango, no. 22; same to same, 28 Feb. 1881, MFOM Missions 16, Gallieni 1880.

[3] Gallieni, Rapport au Ministre, 12 Oct. 1881, *ibid*. Cf. Hargreaves, *Prelude to the Partition of West Africa*, pp. 261–3; and *idem*, 'The Tokolor Empire of Ségou and its Relations with

The Government's reactions to the treaty were equally instructive. Gallieni's first report incorrectly describing the financial terms as a present of four mountain guns and a yearly rent of 25,000 fr. was welcomed in Paris. The Director of Colonies optimistically declared that railway-construction could now proceed in complete safety and urged an immediate payment to make the agreement binding.[1] But when the actual terms became known, Director Michaux changed his mind. In a letter accompanying the treaty, Ahmadu claimed sovereignty over Beledugu and demanded an immediate end to French operations there. He also emphasised the French pledge never to construct fortifications in his territory and therefore demanded the destruction of Bafoulabé and Kita as a sign of good faith. Michaux had to admit the technical validity of the Sultan's argument. He also considered an annual as opposed to a single payment of arms dangerous and unacceptable. The treaty, he concluded, would have to be modified.[2] Accordingly, the Governor of Senegal was ordered to negotiate new terms recognising French rights 'to establish our communications system wherever we wish and to protect it with whatever buildings we consider necessary'. In return, the Sultan could be sent only one consignment of arms and allowed an increase in his annual grant of not more than 5,000 fr.[3] In fact, the Tokolor ambassador who accompanied Gallieni back to Saint-Louis was persuaded to accept terms even more favourable to the French. The payment of arms was now replaced by a single grant of 30,000 fr. and a yearly rent of 20,000 fr. In addition, the promise never to construct forts on Tokolor territory was removed from the pledge never to invade the empire.[4] Not surprisingly, however, Ahmadu refused to ratify the new agreement.

the French', *loc. cit.* pp. 140–2. Professor Hargreaves attributes Gallieni's hostility to the influence of the *Commandant-Supérieur*, Lieutenant-Colonel Borgnis-Desbordes. But Gallieni had already demonstrated his feelings before he left Nango.

[1] Michaux, Note pour le Ministre, 19 May 1881, MFOM Sénégal III 10(*bis*)(b). The report was based on a despatch from the new Governor of Senegal, Delanneau, 23 Apr. 1881 (Conf.), MFOM Sénégal I 64(b), itself based on an inaccurate summary of the terms of the treaty contained in Gallieni to Brière, 9 Mar. 1881, MFOM Missions 16, Gallieni 1880.

[2] Ahmadu to Brière, n.d. [rec'd 12 May 1881], MFOM Sénégal IV 73 (c), transmitted along with the full terms of the treaty in Delanneau to M.M.C., 23 May 1881; same to same, 24 May 1881, MFOM Sénégal I 64(b). Michaux, Note pour le Ministre, 15 June 1881, MFOM Sénégal III 10(*bis*)(b).

[3] M.M.C. to Delanneau, 18 June 1881, MFOM Sénégal I 64(c); see also: M.M.C. to Canard [Governor of Senegal], Instructions, 16 Sept. 1881, MFOM Sénégal I 66(a).

[4] Canard to M.M.C., 23 Oct. 1881; same to same, 5 Nov. 1881, MFOM Sénégal I 66(b). A copy of the treaty is printed in Ministère de la Marine, *Sénégal et Niger, la France dans l'Afrique occidentale* (Paris, 1884), pp. 406–14.

Clearly, the reason for the Government's rejection of the Nango treaty was not, as it later maintained, the discrepancy between its French and Arab texts. A discrepancy did exist; the protectorate clause which Gallieni considered so important did not appear in the Arab version.[1] But this fact was not mentioned in any of the Ministry's criticisms. What made the treaty unacceptable was not that the Tokolors had deceived Gallieni but the fact that Gallieni had failed to deceive the Tokolors effectively enough. The envoy's passionate arguments in favour of ratification did not convince the Colonial Department. Michaux remained apprehensive about the supply of arms, and he was not reassured on the question of Bafoulabé and Kita. He was afraid lest the mutual declaration of peace and friendship alienate the animist states which had recently accepted French protectorate. He was particularly opposed to the guarantee of free communications between Futa and Segu which would enable Abdul-Bubakar to join forces with the Sultan. The only solution, he concluded, was 'to take immediate measures against Abdul-Bubakar, who must somehow or other [be made to] disappear and adopt an openly anti-Tokolor policy'.[2]

The belligerence of the Colonial Department was in no sense a reaction to Tokolor hostility. So far, Ahmadu had conscientiously kept the peace and had made no attempt to oppose the French advance. He did not interfere with the forts, and even when the French invaded Beledugu he confined himself to diplomatic protests. Fear of the potential threat of Muslim resistance may have exerted some influence on the Government's attitude, but the decisive factor was the nature of its Sudanese policy. Having accepted the creation of a political empire on the Niger, it had to accept the corollary of a military confrontation with Ahmadu. Confrontation, of course, had to be postponed until the French were strong enough to make victory certain, and for the moment the expediency of maintaining good relations with the

---

[1] The official reason for the rejection was given in Ministère de la Marine, *Sénégal et Niger*, p. 339, which also printed a French translation of the Arab text. According to it, the Arabic version read: 'Les traitants et marchands français pourront commercer dans tous les pays du Chef des croyants, à l'intérieur et sur les bords du fleuve, partout où s'étend son autorité depuis les sources du Niger jusqu'à Tombouctou, à moins qu'il ne leur ordonne de s'arrêter pour des motifs dont il sera seul juge.' This was a reasonably accurate translation of the original. I am grateful to Dr J. M. A. Bakhiet, formerly of St John's College, Cambridge, for the translation of this and other Arabic documents.

[2] Direction des Colonies, Note pour le Ministre, 31 Oct. 1881, MFOM Sénégal III 10 (*bis*) (b).

Tokolors was accepted. But by 1881 the traditional conflict in French policy between commercial and political expansion had been resolved, and with it the ultimate fate of the Tokolor empire had been decided. Paris and the local authorities in Senegal were now at one in their belief that genuine accommodation with Ahmadu was impossible and that war with him was inevitable. Only the time and the place remained to be determined.

4

The Occupation of the Niger, 1880-3

By the time the Treaty of Nango was signed, the final confrontation with the Tokolors seemed near; even as Gallieni waited for negotiations to open, the Ministry of Marine ordered the military advance to begin. Having recovered from his Parliamentary ordeal, Jauréguiberry authorised the construction of an advance post at Kita, and before he left office in September 1880 he ordered Brière to occupy the Upper Senegal as far as the new fort. The new Minister, Admiral Cloué, issued similar instructions to the head of the Upper Senegal Military Command. Cloué too saw Kita as a base for expansion to the Niger and was ready to sanction military action when necessary. To maintain the prestige on which security depended, the ambush of the Gallieni expedition had to be avenged, and the *Commandant-Supérieur* was therefore ordered to inflict a heavy punishment upon those responsible for the outrage. Brière's instructions, even more strongly worded, dealt almost exclusively with the punitive expedition into Beledugu. The *Commandant-Supérieur* was to destroy Dio, raze the fortifications of Goubanko, and prepare the way for the occupation of the Niger by imposing a French protectorate on Bamako.[1]

But the military advance still had to be paid for. The Ministry's plans went far beyond the restricted programme of surveying approved by Parliament in July, and they were bound to cost more than the allocated 1,300,000 fr. To solve this financial problem, Cloué reintroduced the Senegal–Niger Railway project and asked for an immediate credit of 8,500,000 fr. Security rather than facility for trade was now his principal argument. The newly built fort at Bafoulabé, he told the Chamber, was necessary for the protection of the topographic surveys which Parliament had approved. But because of transportation difficulties the fort was extremely difficult to provision and could not hold

[1] M.M.C. to Brière, 4 Sept. 1880, MFOM Sénégal I 63 (b); M.M.C. to Borgnis-Desbordes, Instructions, 4 Oct. 1880, MFOM Sénégal IV 73 (a); Brière to Borgnis-Desbordes, Instructions, 23 Nov. 1880, *ibid.*

out until the surveys had been completed. Only a railway could guarantee its safety; without it Bafoulabé would have to be evacuated, and the consequent loss of prestige might well provoke a general uprising among warlike peoples poised to attack at the first sign of French weakness. Such arguments were as effective in Parliament as they had been in the Ministry. For all their caution, neither the Budget Commission nor the Chambers dared accept responsibility for a decision which might endanger the security of Senegal itself.[1] Accordingly, they dropped their demands for more information and approved the construction of the Railway as far as Bafoulabé.

Parliament, however, did not capitulate without a struggle. The Budget Commission was severely critical of the decision to build Kita and forced Legros to promise its evacuation if it were decided not to extend the line beyond Bafoulabé. More pertinently, it obliged Cloué to make a firm declaration about the strictly peaceful nature of his plans and published his assurances in its report.[2] In the Chamber the project's evident lack of preparation and the Ministry's obvious attempt to rush it through came under heavy fire. Cloué himself, sadly deficient in Parliamentary expertise, suspected of anti-republican sympathies and the most unpopular of Ferry's Ministers,[3] did not get a friendly hearing. The vote on his Bill, 315 to 120 with over 50 abstentions, could not have reassured him.[4] Worse still his opponents in the Senate, much to his dismay, managed to delay its final approval until the end of February 1881.[5]

---

[1] Cloué, Projet de Loi, 13 Nov. 1880, *J.O. Doc. Parl. Chambre*, no. 2972, pp. 11206–7; Blandin, Rapport, 21 Dec. 1880, *ibid*. no. 3216, p. 13146: 'Il serait certainement dangereux de laisser ainsi le poste de Bafoulabé sans appui; mieux vaudrait l'abandonner. Nous ne saurions nous résoudre à ce parti; car…ce serait compromettre l'avenir.'

[2] Procès-Verbaux de la Commission du Budget, séance du 17 décembre 1880, AN C 3176.

[3] Cloué had provoked the anger of the Republicans both by his opposition to them when Governor of Martinique in 1873 and by his allegedly active intervention in the elections of 1877 when he was *préfet maritime* of Cherbourg. His appointment as Minister of Marine was violently attacked by the Deputy from Cherbourg, La Vieille, and by Georges Périn. Defending him, Ferry lamely explained (to the hilarity of the Chamber): 'Messieurs, les marins sont des hommes rudes par profession; leur commandement est impérieux; il est parfois brutal…Il ne faut donc pas chercher en eux les finesses parlementaires. Il ne faut pas leur demander des talents oratoires.' See: Débats Parlementaires, Chambre, séance du 25 novembre 1880, cited in Robiquet, *op. cit*. VI, 1–10.

[4] *J.O. Déb. Parl. Chambre*, séance du 27 décembre 1880, pp. 12978–80.

[5] The delay was caused by the passage of some minor amendments to the conventions governing the construction of the Dakar–Saint-Louis Railway, which Cloué had submitted together with his proposals for the line to Bafoulabé. The Minister then had to resubmit the amended project to the Chamber, which made further changes, and this enabled the opponents of the Sudan Railway in the Senate to have the Bill sent back to the Finance Commission. The Senate finally agreed to consider the Bafoulabé line separately and

The extent of Parliament's opposition forced the Ministry to trim its sails and cancel its plans for a punitive campaign against Beledugu. Brière's aggressiveness had already caused some anxiety in Paris,[1] and his instructions to the expeditionary column now became a potential source of political embarrassment. As the Director of Colonies pointed out, they violated the Minister's solemn pledges and could gravely compromise his Parliamentary position if they were allowed to stand. Cloué took the warning to heart and immediately countermanded the orders, reproaching his Governor for misinterpreting the Ministry's intentions.[2]

Brière could not ignore such an explicit command and was forced to order the *Commandant-Supérieur* not to advance beyond Kita. But he complained with some justice about the unfairness of the reproof, and he continued to argue in favour of sterner measures on the grounds of security.[3] This time, however, his appeals made no impact. His relations with Cloué had never been close, and the Minister, one of the most senior Admirals in the French navy, was not a man to tolerate insubordination. Accordingly, he again forbade all military action in Beledugu, sharply reprimanded the Governor for questioning his instructions and took steps to have him replaced by a naval officer who might be more amenable to his control. On 11 March Brière de l'Isle, to his great chagrin, was recalled.[4] His summary dismissal ended his Senegalese career on an undeservedly anti-climatic note, but it was to have little

voted the Estimates on 24 February. The delay greatly embarrassed Cloué because he had undertaken to sign the contracts for the delivery of material to the Upper Senegal by the 20th.

[1] When giving its half-hearted approval to the Governor's plans for a punitive expedition against Abdul-Bubakar in December, the Ministry ordered him to act with caution lest prolonged hostilities compromise the colony's economic development. After Cloué's declarations to the Budget Commission, the expedition itself was postponed. M.M.C. to Brière, 4 Dec. 1880; same to same, 30 Dec. 1880, MFOM Sénégal I 63(b).

[2] Michaux, Note pour le Ministre, 3 Jan. 1881, MFOM Sénégal I 99(a), Correspondance Générale; M.M.C. to Brière, 4 Jan. 1881, MFOM Sénégal I 63(b).

[3] Brière to Borgnis-Desbordes, 17 Jan. 1881 (Conf.), MFOM Sénégal IV 73(b); same to same, 25 Jan. 1881, cited in Borgnis-Desbordes, Rapport...1880–1, 6 July 1881, pp. 81–2, MFOM Sénégal IV 73(*bis*); Brière to M.M.C., 23 Jan. 1881; same to same, 23 Feb. 1881, MFOM Sénégal I 63(a).

[4] M.M.C. to Brière, 19 Feb. 1881, MFOM Sénégal I 63(b); Cloué, Rapport au Président de la République, 4 Mar. 1881, MFOM Dossier Administratif, Delanneau. Brière tried to save face by maintaining that the decision corresponded with his innermost desire to return to France after his recent promotion to Brigadier-General. But he was in fact both shocked and hurt by the suddenness of his replacement. The almost immediate arrival of his successor, he claimed, had forced him to hand over command without having the time even to prepare a decent set of notes. See: Brière to M.M.C., 8 Apr. 1881, MFOM Dossier Administratif, Brière de L'Isle; same to same, 23 Apr. 1881, MFOM Sénégal I 63(a).

effect upon the course of Sudanese expansion. For the focus of local initiative was no longer centred on Saint-Louis; by now the Niger empire had found a new champion in the head of the Upper Senegal Military Command, Lieutenant-Colonel Gustave Borgnis-Desbordes.

BORGNIS-DESBORDES AND THE ADVANCE TO THE NIGER

The appointment of Desbordes as *Commandant-Supérieur du Haut-Fleuve* formally opened the era of military expansion in the Western Sudan. Jauréguiberry's creation of the Upper Senegal Command presented him with a highly attractive and influential military posting. Although he remained subordinate to the Governor of Senegal, he was responsible for all aspects of the Government's Sudanese policy, exploration and railway-construction as well as defence. The new battalion of *tirailleurs sénégalais* gave him a sizeable force to command; the Minister's decision to occupy Kita, quite apart from the abortive Beledugu campaign, provided ample opportunity for the exercise of his military skill and initiative. Governor Brière was equally generous. In order to avoid complications with the leader of the topographic mission, he soon managed to have Desbordes promoted to the rank of Lieutenant-Colonel. In order to allow him the widest possible latitude, the Governor also gave him the powers of a *commandant d'arrondissement*, making him in effect Lieutenant-Governor of the Upper Senegal.[1]

Desbordes was just the man to take advantage of these opportunities. Like Brière, he was by background a typical Marine officer. A graduate of the Ecole Polytechnique and of the Ecole d'Application at Metz, he had served his colonial apprenticeship as an Artillery Captain in Indochina and had later acquired administrative experience in the *inspection générale de l'armée*. As a career officer, he too could be expected to favour strictly military solutions to the problems which would confront him. Not content with the Governor's already far-reaching proposals, he soon announced his intention to capture the Tokolor stronghold of Murgula, march on Bamako, demand full rights to a piece of land near the town and start immediately on the construction of a fort. When the Ministry's loss of nerve and Brière's new orders compelled him to abandon his plans, he complained bitterly about such unwarranted

---

[1] Same to same, 8 Nov. 1880 (Conf.), *ibid.*; Brière to Derrien, Instructions, 11 Nov. 1880, MFOM Sénégal IV 74 (a). The leader of the mission, Major Derrien, had seniority and resented the appointment of a junior over his head. See also: Brière to Desbordes, Instructions, 23 Nov. 1880, MFOM Sénégal IV 73 (a).

interference with his military freedom of action and refused to accept responsibility for the consequences.[1]

His disappointment, however, did not prevent him from exploiting the independence which he still retained. Although the outbreak of a typhoid epidemic in Saint-Louis had completely disrupted the organisation of the expeditionary force, he insisted on pushing forward to Kita as quickly as possible. Two weeks after Brière had ordered him to stop at the fort, he destroyed the town of Goubanko, fifteen miles beyond it. Still unsatisfied, he then prepared to attack Murgula, in spite of the Governor's repeated instructions to the contrary.[2] Brière got wind of the scheme and intervened to block it; but he took no disciplinary action. Indeed, he covered up for the Commander over the destruction of Goubanko and managed to save him from the Minister's displeasure.[3] Once Brière had been recalled, Desbordes became still more difficult to control; for hitherto only the Governor's personal authority had been able to keep him in check. After Brière's departure, moreover, Desbordes, as the man on the spot, became the Government's chief Sudanese expert and its most important local adviser on Sudanese policy. It was in this capacity that he returned to Paris in the summer of 1881.

The difficulties of the first campaign had made the Ministry even more cautious, and its plans for the coming year were correspondingly modest. The preparation of adequate storage facilities at Saint-Louis, the establishment of a new and more suitable railhead at Kayes (the sister-town of Médine), navigational improvements to the Senegal, the completion of topographic surveys and some progress in railway-construction were all it hoped to achieve. Military operations were to be limited to the provisioning of the forts. Once more, there was to be no advance beyond Kita.[4] But Desbordes's plans were altogether more ambitious. In his final report he had reaffirmed his belief in the need for strong military action in the Western Sudan. 'The peaceful conquest of the Niger', he declared, 'is an illusion.' The Sudan was not an Eldorado as he had been led to believe and would never become economically viable until France had established her undisputed political mastery over it. Ideally, therefore, the next campaign should aim at the immediate occupa-

1 Desbordes to Brière, 25 Jan. 1881; same to same, 2 Feb. 1881; same to same, 8 Feb. 1881, MFOM Sénégal IV 73 (b).
2 Same to same, 20 Feb. 1881; Brière to Desbordes, 17 Jan. 1881, *ibid.*; Brière to M.M.C., 8 Apr. 1881, MFOM Sénégal I 63 (a).
3 Same to same, 23 Feb. 1881; same to same, 8 Apr. 1881, *ibid.*
4 M.M.C. to Gov. Sen., 19 May 1881, MFOM Missions 50, Borgnis-Desbordes 1881–2.

tion of Beledugu, the construction of a fort at Bamako and the capture of Segu itself. If the Ministry were too timid to risk the political repercussions of a new colonial war, then Segu might be spared; but at the very least Bamako would have to be taken before the end of the next dry season.[1] And as a direct result of his personal intervention in Paris, the Ministry came round to his way of thinking. Although Director Michaux rejected the immediate occupation of Bamako and continued to stress the importance of consolidation, he agreed to a compromise plan for building a new fort half-way between Kita and the Niger. His recommendation was accepted by the Minister, who in turn authorised Desbordes to use force against those who threatened the security of his column.[2]

Once more, however, circumstances beyond the policy-makers' control forced them to change their plans. Conditions in Senegal had been deteriorating throughout the summer; the colony had hardly recovered from the typhoid epidemic when it was swept by a still more virulent outbreak of yellow fever. In July the Governor had been compelled to order the suspension of all preparations for the next campaign in order to reduce the risk of contagion, and by September the Ministry too saw that a full-scale expedition would be quite suicidal. Once more the programme was cut back to provisioning and maintenance, and, since no reinforcements could be sent from France, action beyond Kita was again postponed.[3]

Desbordes was dismayed; after a whole year in a potentially brilliant command he had virtually nothing to show for his efforts. But he was determined not to waste another campaign. By passing rapidly through the infected regions on the Lower Senegal, his expeditionary column escaped the worst ravages of the epidemic and reached Kita intact. Paris had confirmed his responsibility for the control of military operations on the *Haut-Fleuve*, and when the Governor of Senegal formally

[1] Desbordes, Rapport...1880–1, 6 July 1881, MFOM Sénégal IV 73 (*bis*). See also: Desbordes to Brière, 9 Apr. 1881, MFOM Sénégal IV 73 (b).

[2] Desbordes, Note pour le Ministre, August 1881, cited in Desbordes, Rapport...1881–2, n.d., MFOM Missions 50, Borgnis-Desbordes 1881–2; Michaux, Rapport au Ministre de la Marine, 20 Aug. 1881 (Approved), MFOM Sénégal IV 75 (a); M.M.C. to Desbordes, Instructions, 3 Sept. 1881, *ibid.* See also: Michaux, Note, 25 Dec. 1881, *ibid.*

[3] Deville [Gov. Sen. *par intérim*] to M.M.C., 23 Aug. 1881, MFOM Sénégal I 99 (a), Correspondance du Gouverneur. Marginal note by Minister: 'Evidemment il n'est pas possible dans ces conditions de songer à rien faire. Nous perdrions du monde inutilement'; Michaux, Rapport au Ministre, 9 Sept. 1881 (Approved, 13 Sept. 1881), MFOM Sénégal IV 75 (a); M.M.C. to Gov. Sen., Instructions, 16 Sept. 1881, MFOM Sénégal I 66 (a); M.M.C. to Desbordes, Instructions supplémentaires, 19 Sept. 1881, MFOM Sénégal IV 75 (a).

ordered him not to advance beyond the fort he flatly refused to comply. Instead, he organised a small flying column and set out for the Niger. By a series of forced marches he reached the river in ten days, crossed it, and attacked the warriors of the Mandinka chieftain Samori who were besieging the town of Keniéra.[1] His rapid campaign, he explained on his return, had been an 'offensive reconnaissance' designed to test the dispositions of Samori, whose rapidly growing military power was becoming dangerous to the French. Besides, his advance had been a necessary tonic for his troops, whose morale would have been sapped by another period of enforced inactivity at Kita. He had an equally ready excuse for the actual skirmishes at Keniéra, blaming the whole affair on the Commandant of Kita, who had rashly promised to help the town.[2] But the Governor had a more convincing explanation for the campaign. Desbordes, he told Paris, 'has found what he was looking for: *des coups de fusil*'.[3]

Neither Paris nor Saint-Louis was pleased. The Governor reprimanded Desbordes for disobeying orders and deliberately provoking hostilities, and the Under-Secretary seriously considered the possibility of dismissing him.[4] But nothing more was done; indeed the Governor himself was the first to point out that Desbordes's presence on the Upper Senegal was absolutely vital for the success of the Government's plans. And when the Commander in turn submitted his resignation, it was the Governor who recommended its rejection;[5] for by now an alarming breakdown of authority in Saint-Louis had made Desbordes indispensable. Brière's replacement, Rear-Admiral Delanneau, had died of yellow fever only four months after his appointment. His successor, Colonel Canard, was an inept administrator who failed to impose any semblance of order on the chaos which the epidemic created.[6] Unable to

---

[1] Desbordes to Gov. Sen., 18 Jan. 1882; Gov. Sen. to Desbordes, 28 Jan. 1882; Desbordes to Gov. Sen., 11 Feb. 1882; same to same, 6 Mar. 1882, MFOM Sénégal IV 75 (b).

[2] Desbordes, Rapport, 20 Mar. 1882, *ibid*. The Commandant of Kita sent a Native Lieutenant, Alakamessa, to intercede with Samori on behalf of Keniéra. According to Desbordes, Alakamessa was arrested but managed to escape. Desbordes added that it was still essential to punish the insult lest failure to do so be taken as a sign of weakness.

[3] Gov. Sen. to M.M.C., 21 Mar. 1882, MFOM Sénégal I 66 (b).

[4] Gov. Sen. to Desbordes, 15 Mar. 1882, MFOM Sénégal IV 75 (b); Gov. Sen. to M.M.C., 21 Mar. 1882, MFOM Sénégal I 66 (b); *ibid*. minute by Under-Secretary for Colonies: 'Si, comme le dit le Gouverneur, le Lt. Colonel Desbordes cherche des faits de guerre au lieu de calmer les populations qui l'entourent...il perd complètement de vue l'objet de sa mission. Il faut donc le rappeler énergiquement à l'ordre et même le remplacer s'il n'obéit pas.'

[5] *Ibid.*; same to same, 1 June 1882, MFOM Sénégal I 99 (a), Correspondance du Gouverneur.

[6] The most glaring illustration of the colony's disorganisation was the failure to transmit the detailed breakdown of costs for the 1879 campaign. These, Canard explained, had

cope with the difficulties confronting him and egged on by the commercial opponents of the Railway, Canard soon turned from a half-hearted supporter into a violent critic of the Government's policies. In November 1881 he complained about the 'reckless and disreputable' measures which he had been forced to authorise in order to enable the expeditionary column to move upstream. Four months later he declared himself openly against the Ministry's plans for the Upper Senegal and refused to accept further responsibility for their execution. Neither reminders of his duty nor appeals to his self-interest persuaded him to change his mind, and in May he was replaced.[1] After his dismissal, Paris simply could not afford to lose Desbordes as well.

By the spring of 1882, moreover, the prospects for expansion were definitely beginning to improve. The Government's railway estimates, optimistically inaccurate to begin with, had been rendered completely meaningless by the epidemic; by January 1882 not one metre of track had actually been laid. Accordingly, the Ministry was forced to ask for a new credit of 7,500,000 fr., twice as high as its initial forecast.[2] But by accepting the project without the information it had originally considered essential, Parliament had in effect surrendered control over its cost. In March it approved the Ministry's request with hardly a murmur of opposition; only the Railway's most implacable enemies were willing to waste the millions already spent by refusing to vote the funds necessary for its completion.[3]

This easy solution to the Colonial Department's immediate financial problems revived its flagging spirits. Much more important, Admiral Jauréguiberry again became Minister of Marine, and he soon dispelled the Department's hesitations. In April he warned Canard of his personal determination to secure 'the greatest possible extension of French influence in the Upper Niger Basin', and he demanded the Governor's full co-operation. After Canard's dismissal he ordered the new Governor,

---

been lost in one of the frequent moves of personnel during the epidemic. M.M.C. to Canard, 10 Feb. 1882, MFOM Sénégal I 66(c); Canard to M.M.C., 23 Mar. 1882, MFOM Sénégal I 66(b).

[1] Canard to M.M.C., 8 Oct. 1881, MFOM Sénégal I 66(b); same to same, 22 Oct. 1881, MFOM Sénégal I 99(a), Correspondance du Gouverneur; same to same, 6 Nov. 1881; same to same, 7 Nov. 1881; same to same, 20 Mar. 1882, MFOM Sénégal I 66(b); M.M.C. to Canard, 4 Apr. 1882, MFOM Dossier Administratif, Canard; Canard to M.M.C. 22 Apr. 1882, MFOM Sénégal I 66(b).

[2] Rouvier, Projet de Loi, 16 Jan. 1882, *J.O. Doc. Parl. Chambre*, no. 291, pp. 163–4.

[3] *J.O. Déb. Parl. Chambre*, séance du 13 mars 1882, pp. 312–15; *J.O. Déb. Parl. Sénat*, séance du 31 mars 1882, pp. 345–51. The vote in the Chamber was 363 to 17, in the Senate, 178 to 60.

Captain Vallon, to devote all his energies to 'this great enterprise...
destined to carry our flag, our civilisation and our trade into the heart
of West Africa', and assured him of the Ministry's complete support.[1]

Desbordes could now expect a more favourable reception for his
proposals. The difficulties he had so far encountered had failed to
weaken his commitment to a rapid military advance. In January 1882
he had again called for the immediate occupation of Bamako, warning
that another delay would be fatal because both Ahmadu and Samori
were preparing to march on the town. The success of his campaign
across the Niger increased his confidence in the feasibility of his bold
plan.[2] Paris, it is true, remained to be convinced. Despite his enthusiasm,
Jauréguiberry had doubts about the wisdom of concentrating on
military expansion when only serious progress on the Railway could
guarantee Parliament's continued financial support. Under-Secretary
Berlet was still more cautious and opposed any advance beyond Kita
before the line to Bafoulabé had been finished.[3] Railway-building was
therefore given top priority, and expansion was relegated to second
place. Although Jauréguiberry approved the declaration of a protectorate over Bamako, he postponed the construction of forts beyond
Kita and ordered the expeditionary column to avoid military complications at all costs.[4] But this time the Commander's task of persuasion was
much less arduous. The Ministry's most influential advisers were now
fully behind him. The head of the *Bureau du Haut-Fleuve*, Lieutenant-
Colonel Bourdiaux, was a brother-officer and a reliable ally.[5] The new
Director of Colonies, Paul Dislère, was a close friend, and it was
Dislère who assured the Minister that the credits approved by Parliament could legitimately be used to pay for a military campaign. Even
the more prudent Legros insisted that only a fort could make the Bamako
protectorate effective.[6] And in the summer Desbordes himself again

[1] Jauréguiberry to Canard, 4 Apr. 1882, MFOM Dossier Administratif, Canard; Jauréguiberry to Vallon, Instructions, 12 May 1882, MFOM Sénégal I 67(a).
[2] Desbordes to Canard, 18 Jan. 1882, MFOM Sénégal IV 75(b); Desbordes, Rapport,
20 Mar. 1882, *ibid.*
[3] Berlet, marginal note on Canard to M.M.C., 20 Mar. 1882, MFOM Sénégal I 66(b).
[4] Colonial Department, Rapport au Ministre, 22 Apr. 1882 (Approved), MFOM Sénégal
IV 77(a); Jauréguiberry to Vallon, Instructions, 12 May 1882, MFOM Sénégal I 67(a);
same to same, 19 June 1882, MFOM Missions 50, Borgnis-Desbordes 1881–2.
[5] See: Bourdiaux, Note pour le 1er bureau, 30 Nov. 1880, MFOM Sénégal IV 73(a); *idem*,
Note pour le sous-secrétaire, 29 Apr. 1882, MFOM Sénégal I 99(a), Correspondance du
Gouverneur.
[6] Dislère, Note pour le Ministre, 30 Aug. 1882, MFOM Sénégal I 99(a), Correspondance
Générale; Legros, Note pour la direction des colonies, 17 Aug. 1882, MFOM Sénégal
IV 77(a).

returned to Paris in order to press his case. In conversations with Jauré-guiberry he admitted that the restriction of the campaign to railway-construction would make military action unnecessary; but he warned the Minister that it would also confirm the prevalent impression of French weakness and destroy any hope of reaching the Niger peacefully by giving Ahmadu and Samori more time to prepare their opposition.[1] Once more, the Commander's personal intervention turned out to be decisive. At the end of their talks, Jauréguiberry cancelled his previous instructions and ordered him to occupy Bamako.[2]

Desbordes could at last carry out the policies he had so fervently advocated for the past two years. The pre-eminence of his position in Senegal was now undisputed. Jauréguiberry had not consulted Vallon about the new programme and had confirmed the autonomy of the Upper Senegal Command by separating its administrative services from Saint-Louis.[3] Although Desbordes remained nominally sub-ordinate to the Governor, in practice he made all his own decisions. As soon as he returned, he insolently demanded and received Vallon's personal recognition of his complete freedom of action. At the same time, he browbeat the unfortunate man into reducing the garrison strength of Senegal in order to provide reinforcements for the expedi-tionary column.[4] Offended by the Ministry's cavalier treatment and dispirited by the impossible administrative burdens which he had to bear, Vallon soon followed Canard back to France.[5] His replacement, René Servatius, was an unlikely candidate for the post; his scandalous administration of justice in Martinique had led to his dismissal from the Attorney-Generalship of that colony only two weeks before. But he could at least be relied on to carry out his instructions energetically

---

[1] This conversation was recounted by Desbordes in his report on the 1882–3 campaign: Desbordes, Rapport...1882–3, 16 Feb. 1882, Cap. I, MFOM Missions 50, Borgnis-Desbordes 1882–3.

[2] Decision ministérielle, 21 Aug. 1882, MFOM Sénégal IV 77(a); M.M.C. to Desbordes, Instructions, n.d. (rec'd 2 Oct. 1882), cited in Desbordes, Rapport...1882–3, 16 Feb. 1883, Cap. I, MFOM Missions 50, Borgnis-Desbordes 1882–3.

[3] Règlement ministériel, 13 Sept. 1882, MFOM Sénégal I 99(b), Correspondance du Gouverneur; M.M.C. to Vallon, 5 Sept. 1882, MFOM Missions 50, Borgnis-Desbordes 1882–3; Vallon to M.M.C., 1 Nov. 1882, MFOM Sénégal I 67(b).

[4] Desbordes to Vallon, 18 Oct. 1882; Vallon to Desbordes, 19 Oct. 1882; Desbordes to Vallon, 19 Oct. 1882; Vallon to Desbordes, n.d., MFOM Sénégal IV 77(b).

[5] Vallon to M.M.C., 1 Sept. 1882; same to same, 4 Sept. 1882; same to same, 13 Sept. 1882; same to same, 19 Sept. 1882, MFOM Sénégal I 99(a), Correspondance du Gouver-neur; same to same, 8 Oct. 1882, cited in evidence to the Board of Inquiry, 9 Jan. 1883, MFOM Dossier Administratif, Vallon; same to same, 20 Oct. 1882, *ibid.*; same to same, 1 Nov. 1882, MFOM Sénégal I 67(b).

if only to save his career, and Desbordes was assured of his full support.[1]

Secure in his political independence, the Commander now concentrated on the military aspects of his campaign. When logistical difficulties forced him to prolong his stay at Kita, he took advantage of the delay to march on Murgula, expel its Tokolor garrison and destroy its fortifications. Once his supplies arrived, he resumed his advance, captured the Bambara town of Daba in Beledugu, and finally reached Bamako in February 1883. He immediately set to work on the construction of a fort and was easily able to repel an attack by Samori's forces in April. He then took the offensive, led a short but successful punitive expedition along the left bank of the Niger, and confirmed French influence in Beledugu by negotiating new treaties of protectorate.[2]

Desbordes had every reason to be pleased with the results of his efforts. By occupying Bamako he had achieved the principal objective of the Government's West African policy and had made at least part of Faidherbe's dream come true. As he declared at the ceremony marking the occasion, the shots which his troops fired in salute to the *tricolore* would be heard far beyond the banks of the Niger. His own name too was to be carried along by their echo. His brilliant military feats made him the toast of Paris; the *Avenir de la Marine et des Colonies* devoted its front page to an account of his career; Prime Minister Ferry himself proclaimed his accomplishments to the Chamber. And, to crown his satisfaction, the Minister of Marine sent him his warmest congratulations and announced his promotion to the rank of Colonel.[3]

[1] M.M.C. to Servatius, 20 Oct. 1882, MFOM Dossier Administratif, Servatius; Servatius to M.M.C., 7 Dec. 1882, MFOM Sénégal I 68(b); Servatius to Desbordes, 25 Jan. 1883, MFOM Sénégal IV 77(b): 'Vous me parlez pour la première fois de résistances inattendues: brisez-les, vous êtes là pour cela! Vous serez soutenu par moi, par le Ministre et par le Parlement.'

[2] Desbordes, Rapport...1882-3, 23 Mar. 1883, Cap. IV, MFOM Missions 50, Borgnis-Desbordes 1882-3; *idem*, Rapport, 27 Apr. 1883, MFOM Sénégal IV 77(b); Desbordes to Bayol, 31 Mar. 1883, cited Desbordes, Rapport...1882-3, n.d., Cap. VI, MFOM Missions 50, Borgnis-Desbordes 1882-3.

[3] Desbordes, Discours à Bamako, 5 Feb. 1883, MFOM Sénégal IV 77(b); *L'Avenir de la Marine et des Colonies*, 7 Apr. 1883; *J.O. Déb. Parl. Chambre*, séance du 3 juillet 1883, p. 1562 [speech by Ferry]; M.M.C. to Gov. Sen., 4 Apr. 1883, MFOM Sénégal I 63(b).

The Occupation of the Niger, 1880–3

The growing influence of the Military over Sudanese policy inevitably hardened French attitudes towards the Tokolor empire. Although Brière and the Ministry both foresaw the empire's eventual subjection to French rule, they did at least appreciate the importance of avoiding an immediate confrontation. The Colonial Department was anxious not to arouse opposition by launching a campaign of conquest against Parliament's express wishes. Its aim was to establish French hegemony over the Tokolor empire, not necessarily to liquidate it: 'one does not wipe out a nation', Cloué remarked in July 1881.[1] The peaceful extension of influence until French control of the Niger deprived Ahmadu of his means to resist was better suited to its purpose. Brière himself was determined not to jeopardise the safety of Gallieni and his companions at Nango, and he too committed himself to the maintenance of the alliance until the French were solidly established on the Niger.[2]

But the views of Desbordes were much more uncompromising. From the moment he arrived he advocated and prepared for all-out war with Ahmadu. As early as January 1881 he was calling on Paris to authorise a pre-emptive attack which might catch the Tokolors unawares.[3] Gallieni's safety was of no concern to him. 'The lives of a few officers' were of secondary importance compared with the political advantages to be gained by the capture of Murgula and Bamako. Any possibility of negotiating with the Tokolors was angrily rejected. No words were too harsh for Gallieni's treaty, the terms of which would force them to evacuate Bafoulabé and Kita and so leave the field clear for their English rivals. Full of righteous indignation, Desbordes condemned the envoy's 'odious' attempts to deceive the Tokolors, claiming that his own proposals would have made such shameful hypocrisy unnecessary.[4]

In fact, his plans were no less deceitful. His opposition to the Treaty of Nango was based not on a scrupulous regard for the rules of diplomatic behaviour but on his conviction that the crafty Sultan would

---

[1] Cloué, marginal note on Gov. Sen. to M.M.C., 23 June 1881, MFOM Sénégal I 64(b).
[2] Brière to Desbordes, 25 Jan. 1881, cited in Desbordes, Rapport...1880–1, MFOM Sénégal IV 73(bis); idem, Notes...laissées à mon successeur, 14 Apr. 1881, MFOM Sénégal I 64(a): '...nous devons rechercher quant à présent et jusqu'à une solide occupation du Niger l'alliance de l'état Toucouleur. Cet état implanté dans le pays de Ségou est destiné à disparaître; nous pouvons suivant les intérêts de notre entreprise sur le Soudan, précipiter ou retarder cette disparition.'
[3] Desbordes to Brière, 25 Jan. 1881, MFOM Sénégal IV 73(b).
[4] Same to same, 1 Apr. 1881, cited in Desbordes, Rapport...1880–1, 6 July 1881, MFOM Sénégal IV 73(bis); see also: ibid. pp. 437–8, 478–9.

easily see through the young Captain's clumsy efforts at duplicity. Once the caution of his superiors had prevented him from attacking in strength, he too adopted the policies of subversion which the despised Gallieni was advocating. After Brière had forbidden him to march on Murgula, he sent a French envoy to proclaim the peacefulness of his intentions and then despatched a Native Interpreter to reconnoitre the town's fortifications and negotiate secret alliances with the surrounding Malinké population. His orders to the Commandant of the new fort at Kita were exactly the same as those which Brière had issued to the Commandant of Bafoulabé in November 1879.[1] For all his bluster, Desbordes was no more anxious than Brière to declare war before he felt certain of its outcome. The difficulties of the first campaign convinced him that 1,200 troops at least were needed to ensure victory, and since the Ministry seemed unlikely to provide them straight away, he accepted the expediency of maintaining a show of friendship towards the Sultan while working secretly to undermine his authority.[2] Throughout the second campaign he continued to sign treaties with Ahmadu's subjects and tried to wean the Tokolors of Kaarta away from their allegiance to Segu. Since the acquiescence of Murgula was essential for the safe passage of the Keniéra expedition, he renewed his friendly overtures; but even as he acknowledged the town's assistance he stressed how easily he could have captured it.[3] At the end of the year he proved his point.

After the occupation of Bamako, Desbordes's attitude did become more moderate. Recognising the vulnerability of French communications in the Sudan, he too called for a resumption of negotiations with Ahmadu. But his intentions remained the same. He continued to press for the subversion of Kaarta and the conclusion of new anti-Tokolor offensive alliances with the Bambaras of Beledugu. It was not enough for the French merely to avoid conflict, he claimed; they would also have to oblige Ahmadu to remain at peace. They would have to convince the Sultan of his own weakness, and they could only do this by destroying his strength.[4]

---

[1] Desbordes to Mahmadu Alfa, 4 May 1881; Desbordes to Monségur, 8 May 1881, cited *ibid.* See above: p. 74.
[2] Desbordes, Rapport...1880–1, 6 July 1881, pp. 507–27, MFOM Sénégal IV 73(*bis*); Desbordes to Brière, 9 Apr. 1881, MFOM Sénégal IV 73(b).
[3] Desbordes, Rapport, 20 Mar. 1882, MFOM Sénégal IV 75(b); *idem*, Rapport...1881–2, n.d., Cap. IV, MFOM Missions 50, Borgnis-Desbordes 1881–2.
[4] Desbordes, Rapport...1882–3, 14 July 1883, Cap. XX, MFOM Missions 50, Borgnis-Desbordes 1882–3.

The Military View of Islam

The commander's views were understandable enough. Desbordes had a personal reason for seeking action. His future career was bound to depend on the success with which he conducted his campaigns, and from the first he set out to make the most of his command.[1] Moreover, he was not a soldier-administrator like Brière or a fledgling diplomat like Gallieni but a field-commander on active service, and potential threats to security could loom still larger on the trail between Bafoulabé and the Niger than they did in the administrative offices of Saint-Louis. Like his contemporaries, Desbordes was obsessed by the threat of Muslim resistance. He knew that Ahmadu was actively seeking to oppose the French advance. When the Nango treaty failed to guarantee the territorial integrity of the empire, the Sultan took more practical steps to protect himself. At the end of 1881 the Tokolors closed the markets of Guidimaka and cut off trade between Koniakary and Médine, thus making it still more difficult for the French to supply their expeditionary columns. The Commander also considered Murgula a serious potential threat to Kita and a refuge for deserters from the *tirailleurs*.[2] To a degree, therefore, his policies can be seen as strictly military solutions to the problems of security which he perceived.

But they were much more than this. If the desire to prevent the extension of French influence was a prominent feature of Tokolor foreign policy, the determination to avoid war was a still more significant one. Ahmadu never sought to oppose the French advance by force. After the destruction of Goubanko he had merely expressed his shock that his new-found allies should demonstrate their friendship by sending an army to invade his lands.[3] After the capture of Murgula he took no stronger measures. Even the occupation of Bamako, a threat to the very existence of the Tokolor empire, failed to provoke any violent reaction.[4] And Desbordes knew perfectly well that Ahmadu would not fight. In

[1] Desbordes was never modest in describing the success of his efforts, and his attempts to present his campaigns in the best possible light at times reached ridiculous proportions. Among the results of his first campaign, for example, he included: '[la] mise en liberté de la mission Gallieni [et le] traité avec Ahmadou...inacceptable dans la forme et dans le fond, mais capable de nous permettre de gagner du temps'. Desbordes, Rapport... 1880–1, 6 July 1881, p.2, MFOM Sénégal IV 73 (*bis*).
[2] Desbordes to Gov. Sen., 11 Dec. 1881, MFOM Sénégal IV 75 (b); Piétri to Desbordes, 19 Dec. 1882, cited in Desbordes, Rapport...1882–3, 20 Mar. 1883, Cap. IV, MFOM Missions 50, Borgnis-Desbordes 1882–3; Desbordes to Gov. Sen., 24 Dec. 1882 [Copy], MFOM Sénégal I 99 (b), Correspondance Générale.
[3] Ahmadu to Brière, n.d. [rec'd 12 May 1881], MFOM Sénégal IV 73 (c).
[4] The Sultan, Desbordes maintained, knew that the appearance of French gunboats on the Niger would spell the end of his independence. See: Desbordes, Rapport...1882–3, 14 July 1883, Cap. XX, MFOM Missions 50, Borgnis-Desbordes 1882–3.

December 1881 he declared that the Tokolors were too weak to risk an all-out attack on his column. Once he had taken Murgula, he again predicted that Tokolor anger was more likely to turn into sullen resignation than violent hostility.[1] The Keniéra expedition itself was proof enough of his faith in the Sultan's peaceful intentions.

In fact, the most serious threat to French security came not from the ramshackle *jihadi* state of Ahmadu but from the expanding military empire of Samori. Its founder was not a Tokolor cleric but the scion of a Mande trading family which had renounced Islam after settling in the Upper Niger basin during the early eighteenth century. Samori's youth was distinguished not by his learning or religious zeal but by his abilities of leadership and organisation. Seeking wider outlets for his energies, he became a trader; and by 1850, when only twenty years old, he had developed an extended network of commercial relations stretching as far as Freetown in Sierra Leone. After the capture of his mother by the chief of Konyan in 1851, he abandoned trade for service in the army of her captor and gradually rose to become his war-chief. Over the next twenty years he served various local rulers in the same capacity until his military prestige had won him a sufficient following to challenge and overcome all his former masters. By the time Desbordes ran into his forces at Keniéra, Samori had already become the dominant power on the right bank of the Niger from the frontiers of Sierra Leone and Liberia to the marchlands of the Tokolor empire.[2]

Religion was undoubtedly an important factor in Samori's attempts at state-formation. He himself had adopted Islam as an essential tool for his trading activities, and there is no reason to doubt the sincerity of his conversion. In his youth he had come under the influence of a local *marabout*, Konyan-Morifin; and a Qadiriyya cleric, Alfa Uthman, was later to become his chief spiritual adviser. He built mosques in the territories he conquered and made some attempt to enforce religious observances. He set up Koranic schools under the guidance of the

[1] Desbordes to Gov. Sen., n.d. [10–15 Dec. 1881], cited in Desbordes, Rapport...1881–2, n.d., Cap. II, MFOM Missions 50, Borgnis-Desbordes 1881–2; Desbordes to Gov. Sen., 24 Dec. 1882 [Copy], MFOM Sénégal I 99(b), Correspondance Générale.

[2] The definitive study of Samori has been undertaken by M. Yves Person. Until the publication of his work, the standard accounts remain: E. Péroz, *Au Soudan français* (Paris, 1891 ed.), pp. 375–418; and L. G. Binger, *Du Niger au Golfe de Guinée* (Paris, 1892), I, 144–53. For an African account see: A. Kouroubari, 'Histoire de l'imam Samori', *Bulletin de l'I.F.A.N.*, série B, xxi (1959), 544–71. Samori's antecedents and early career are described in Y. Person, 'Les ancêtres de Samori', *Cahiers d'études africaines*, no. 13 (1963), pp.125–56; and *idem*, 'La jeunesse de Samori', *Revue française d'histoire d'outre-mer*, xlviii (1962), 151–80.

Qadiriyya, established a judicial system based on Koranic principles, and appointed *cadis* to each of the empire's provinces. To confirm the religious character of his state, he himself took the title of *imam*.[1]

But for Samori the propagation of Islam was less an end in itself than a means for adding to the cohesion of an empire whose basic strength lay in its complex and efficient military organisation. Samori's territories were divided into ten provinces, eight under the command of a governor assisted by a war-chief and two central districts under the *imam*'s personal control. Each outer province maintained an army corps of four to five thousand men composed of a highly trained professional force of two or three hundred *sofas* supplemented by a levy of ten per cent of the able-bodied male population; in times of war the conscription rate could be raised to fifty per cent. The corps were organised down to squad level, each unit commanded by a mounted *sofa-kun* who was generally armed with a musket. The two central provinces maintained an elite contingent of some five hundred *sofas* who were recruited by Samori and provided most of the senior officers for the provincial armies. The *imam* also had a small personal bodyguard which by 1887 was armed with repeating rifles. The armies, which in peace-time spent six months in training and six working on the land, were well-disciplined, tactically proficient, able to make good use of cavalry, and adept at laying ambushes. Military organisation was deliberately adapted to territorial expansion. Campaigns were generally waged by four army corps acting in concert, three forming a constantly advancing arc with the fourth held in reserve. Military expenditure was met by revenue drawn from taxation, generally paid in agricultural produce, from the goldfields of Buré, and from trade. Slave trading was an important feature of the empire's economy. Captives were sold in Futa Jallon and the proceeds used to purchase weapons from the Europeans on the coast. The need to maintain the army's stock of firearms thus provided an additional incentive for expansion.[2]

Samori's empire was clearly a force to be reckoned with, and Desbordes himself appreciated the *imam*'s military strength.[3] But he played down its significance. He was unconcerned by the attack on

---

[1] See: A. Le Chatelier, *L'Islam en Afrique occidentale* (Paris, 1899), pp. 225–52.
[2] For a useful account, based on published works, of Samori's military organisation, see: M. Legassick, 'Firearms, Horses and Samorian Army Organization', *Journal of African History*, VII (1966), 95–115.
[3] Desbordes, Rapport...1880–1, 6 July 1881, pp. 484–5, MFOM Sénégal IV 73 (*bis*); *idem*, Rapport, 20 Mar. 1882, MFOM Sénégal IV 75 (b).

Bamako, for he was convinced that Samori was essentially a military adventurer who was bound to co-operate once he had been taught the power of French arms. The Commander was confident that his campaigns on the Niger had dealt the *imam*'s prestige a grave blow and that this would induce him to abandon his struggle against the French. Indeed, Samori might even become an ally against the Tokolors. His advance was already threatening their empire, and the Commander was quite prepared to see him capture Segu.[1]

As far as Desbordes was concerned, Ahmadu was and would continue to be the real enemy. The Sultan might be weak, but he still personified the force of Muslim fanaticism with which France could never compromise. He might be conciliatory, but he was still a despot whose power was based on the ruthless oppression of his subjects and who could never accept French principles of justice and humanity.[2] There could be no place for him in the Sudanese empire which France hoped to create, and because of his very presence this empire would have to be created by conquest. War, Desbordes maintained, was the inescapable consequence of the French advance to the Niger.[3] But none of this was original. Desbordes was merely restating, in their simplest and most forceful terms, the propositions which Faidherbe had expounded over twenty years before.

THE SUDAN AND FRENCH WEST AFRICAN POLICY, 1880–3

Meanwhile, the Ministries in Paris were beginning to consider the relevance of Sudanese expansion for their policies in West Africa as a whole.[4] As in the past, the extension of French influence on the Upper Niger was their first priority, and to it interests elsewhere in West Africa were often subordinated. On the coast, the policy-makers showed

---

[1] *Idem*, Rapport, 27 Apr. 1883, MFOM Sénégal IV 77(b); Desbordes to Bayol, Instructions supplémentaires, 10 Apr. 1883, cited in Desbordes, Rapport...1882–3, n.d., Cap. VI, MFOM Missions 50, Borgnis-Desbordes, 1882–3; 'Il faudrait...les [the chiefs of Beledugu] décider à entrer activement en lutte avec nous contre Samory, mais en ayant bien soin de faire ressortir que nous ne nous opposons en rien aux projets de ce chef contre Ségou.'

[2] Desbordes, Rapport...1882–3, 14 July 1883, Cap. XX, MFOM Sénégal IV 77(b).

[3] Desbordes, Rapport...1880–1, 6 July 1881, p.509, MFOM Sénégal IV 73 (*bis*): '...il faut admettre tout d'abord que la guerre est la conséquence forcée de notre marche en avant ... [et] qu'il faut l'accepter ou renoncer à aller sur le Niger en laissant les Anglais arriver avant nous....'

[4] For a fuller discussion on French West African policies during this period, see: C. W. Newbury and A. S. Kanya-Forstner, 'French Policy and the Origins of the Scramble for West Africa', *Journal of African History*, no. 2, x (1969),

little of the energy and resolution which were becoming apparent in the drive towards the Niger. The Ministry of Marine remained as suspicious as ever about the activities of the coastal traders and as reluctant to assume political commitments on their behalf.[1] The Ministry of Foreign Affairs was no less anxious to preserve the Anglo-French entente which formed the basis of French foreign policy at the time, and it refused to allow minor territorial or commercial disputes on the coast to complicate its task. To facilitate good relations, it hoped to remove the sources of friction by negotiating a general agreement involving some form of territorial exchange. French claims on the coast continued to be seen as bargaining counters in the broad negotiations which the Quai d'Orsay sought diligently to arrange until the fall of the Conservative Government in 1880 destroyed any hope of a comprehensive settlement.[2] But the maintenance of Anglo-French amity was not the only objective. What France hoped to secure from the exchange was the Gambia, and her reasons were the same as they had been a decade before. Once the advance into the Sudan began, control over this alternative route became all the more desirable. The Ministry of Marine, most directly concerned with Sudanese policy, was particularly insistent on this point. As late as 1881, when all hope of an exchange had disappeared, it was still prepared to offer sweeping concessions on the coast in return for unchallenged control over the Senegambian Triangle.[3]

The Ministry of Marine was less preoccupied than the Quai d'Orsay with the promotion of Anglo-French relations. The danger of British penetration into the Upper Niger had been a subject of increasing concern at the Rue Royale ever since Brière's first reports about it in 1877.[4] By 1881 Jauréguiberry, now out of office, was proclaiming to the Senate:

We have [in Africa]...implacable rivals who are constantly challenging the influence we already exercise in Senegal. They seek to hinder us in every way

---

[1] E.g. Jauréguiberry to M.A.E., 5 July 1879; Cloué to M.A.E., 23 Apr. 1881, cited in Hargreaves, *Prelude to the Partition of West Africa*, pp. 213–14, 239.

[2] See: *ibid*. pp. 198–200, 234–7.

[3] Bases du négociation à engager avec l'Angleterre, n.d., MFOM Afrique VI 27(a), also cited in Hargreaves, *op. cit.* pp. 249–50. The Ministry of Marine was prepared to offer French rights in Kotonou, Grand Bassam, Assinie and Dabou, concessions in Newfoundland, and a renunciation of French claims between the Scarcies and the northern frontier of Gabon in return for the Gambia, concessions in the Leeward Islands, and a renunciation of British claims between the Scarcies and the northern limits of Senegal.

[4] Michaux to M.A.E., 19 Jan. 1878, AEMD Afrique 49; same to same, 22 Mar. 1878, *ibid*.: '...depuis que les Anglais de Sierra Leone et de la Gambie font des efforts pour nouer des relations avec le Ségou...notre attention est plus vivement appelée sur nos rapports avec les indigènes dans le haut-Sénégal'.

they can. They wish to reach the Niger before us, and from what I have learned they have already sent out an expedition of 200 men...from Bathurst...[1]

These fears were much exaggerated. Although Administrator Gouldsbury of the Gambia, to whom Jauréguiberry was referring, did manage to sign a rather suspect treaty of trade and friendship with Futa Jallon in March 1881, his report was extremely pessimistic about the economic potential of the interior and confirmed the British Government's intention not to waste money on its development.[2] But the fears of the French were no less real. As soon as news of Gouldsbury's activities reached Paris, a mission was despatched to assert French claims to Futa Jallon, and in July its rulers signed a treaty of protectorate. 'The prestige of France in the northern [*sic*] Sudan is growing', declared the French envoy; 'we are definitely stealing a march on the English.'[3]

The policy-makers at the Rue Royale were not concerned solely with the defence of the Upper Niger. They never forgot the possibility that the Sudan itself might become the nucleus of a still more extensive African empire. Although the massacre of the Flatters expedition in February 1881 had destroyed the possibility of a union between Algeria and Senegal across the Sahara, Faidherbe's vision of a specifically West African empire could still be realised. The military advance into the Senegal–Niger valley was laying one of the bases of this new domain; the steady growth of French trade on the Lower Niger—where the *Compagnie française de l'Afrique équatoriale* and the *Compagnie du Sénégal* had fifty-five trading stations by 1883[4]—seemed to be laying the other. When Jauréguiberry returned to the Ministry of Marine in 1882, he built on both of them. A month after approving the occupation of Bamako, he authorised the construction of gunboats to patrol the Niger as far as Bussa and show the flag at Timbuktu.[5] Then in January 1883 he called on the Quai d'Orsay to ratify a treaty which the consular agent Mattei had signed with King Ahmadu of Loko on the Benué. He also recommended the negotiation of further treaties to ensure unrestricted commercial access to the Lower Niger and to establish French

1 *J.O. Déb. Parl. Sénat*, séance du 17 février 1881, p. 107.
2 For the Gouldsbury mission, see: Hargreaves, *op. cit.* pp. 265–7.
3 Bayol to Bareste [French Consul, Freetown], 17 July 1881, AEMD Afrique 50. See also: Hargreaves, *op. cit.* pp. 267–71.
4 Cavalié, Rapport, 29 Aug. 1883, AEMD Afrique 86. For French activities on the Lower Niger, see: Hargreaves, *op. cit.* pp. 275–8; le cdt. Mattei, *Bas-Niger, Bénoué, Dahomey* (Grenoble, 1890), pp. 50 ff.
5 Dislère, Rapport au Ministre, 30 Sept. 1882 (Approved), MFOM Sénégal IV 77 (a).

political as well as commercial influence along the Benué. Five days later he ordered the Commandant of the South Atlantic Naval Division to sign treaties with the chiefs of Bonny and Calabar.[1]

Only when French initiatives on the Upper and Lower Niger are considered together can their significance be fully appreciated. For it then becomes clear that the long-term objective of the Ministry of Marine was to create a West African empire by extending French political control into the interior.[2] Admittedly, this was not the only element in its policy. Despite his dislike for the traders, Jauréguiberry had never shirked his responsibility for the defence of French trade and had long sought to prevent the extension of British influence into the Southern Rivers district of Senegal. As Anglo-French rivalry intensified after the failure to reach a comprehensive agreement, so did the Rue Royale's determination to protect French interests on the coast. Its representatives were uncompromising in their assertion of French claims during the discussions about the Sierra Leone boundary in 1881.[3] When the Colonial Department was transferred to the Ministry of Commerce at the end of the year, the protection of coastal trade became for a short time the dominant feature of West African policy.[4] On his return to office in February 1882, Jauréguiberry continued to show considerable firmness in his handling of coastal affairs. In April he and the Minister of Commerce, Maurice Rouvier, persuaded the Foreign Ministry to declare a protectorate over Porto-Novo. In September he rejected any idea of concessions to Great Britain on the eastern frontier

[1] Jauréguiberry to M.A.E., 25 Jan. 1883; Jauréguiberry to *Commandant de la division navale de l'Atlantique du Sud*, 30 Jan. 1883, cited and annotated in: J. Stengers, 'L'Impérialisme Colonial de la Fin du XIXᵉ siècle; Mythe ou Réalité?', *Journal of African History*, III (1962), 477–9.

[2] For other interpretations of French African policy at this time, see, *inter alia*: R. E. Robinson and J. Gallagher, *Africa and the Victorians* (London, 1961), pp. 163–7; Stengers, 'L'Imperialisme Colonial de la Fin du XIXᵉ Siècle', [review of *Africa and the Victorians*], *loc. cit.* pp. 471–91; C. W. Newbury, 'Victorians, Republicans and the Partition of Africa' [review of *Africa and the Victorians*], *Journal of African History*, III (1962), 493–501; Hargreaves, *op. cit.* pp. 253 ff.; H. Brunschwig, 'Les Origines du Partage de l'Afrique Occidentale' [review of *Prelude to the Partition of West Africa*], *Journal of African History*, v (1964), 121–5.

[3] These negotiations were all that remained of the original proposals for a comprehensive boundary settlement. The minutes of the discussions are to be found in MFOM Afrique VI 27(a) and AEMD Afrique 57. See also: Hargreaves, *op. cit.* pp. 247–52.

[4] The Colonial Department remained attached to the Ministry of Commerce until the fall of the Gambetta Ministry in January 1882, when it was returned to the Ministry of Marine. Gambetta's Minister of Commerce, Maurice Rouvier, had a special interest in West African trade; he was the Deputy from the *Bouches-du-Rhône* and the spokesman for the Marseilles merchants. For his policies, see: Hargreaves, *op. cit.* pp. 279–82; *idem*, 'Towards a History of the Partition of Africa', *Journal of African History*, I (1960), 103–6.

of the Ivory Coast.[1] In January 1883, as part of his new policy in the Gulf of Guinea, he urged the Quai d'Orsay to make the Porto-Novo protectorate effective by sending a garrison, and to extend the protectorate along the Slave Coast. 'Under our flag', he maintained, 'French trade...will be able to compete more effectively with its British rival.'[2]

But the defence of French coastal trade was not Jauréguiberry's main concern. What interested him more was the prospect of tapping the supposedly vast trade of the interior. The treaties along the Benué were supposedly to give France political control over 'a route to Lake Chad and the rich markets of Bornu and Adamawa'. The treaties with Bonny and Calabar were designed to give French trade on the Niger, 'and also on the Benué where it is now intending to concentrate all its efforts', an independent outlet to the sea. Meanwhile, French gunboats operating from Bamako were to establish French influence along the whole course of the Upper Niger and to forestall any British move upstream beyond the rapids of Bussa towards Timbuktu.[3] Faidherbe's old plan for a two-pronged advance into the Sudan was now part of official French policy.

And it had become so largely through the efforts of the Ministry of Marine. Both in the Western Sudan and on the Guinea Coast, Jauréguiberry and his advisers were the ones who took the initiative and pressed the Foreign Ministry for action. Only in the extension of French influence along the Congo did the Quai d'Orsay take the lead, and the ratification of the Brazza treaty in November 1882, for all its diplomatic repercussions, was not of major significance for the immediate development of French African policy. Both Jauréguiberry and the Foreign Minister himself warned their agents not to overestimate the importance of 'an area where our interests are as yet relatively weak'.[4]

Even here, the desire to exploit the riches of the African interior was

---

[1] Newbury, *The Western Slave Coast and its Rulers*, p. 107; Hargreaves, *op. cit.* pp. 294–7, 287–8.

[2] Jauréguiberry to M.A.E., 19 Jan. 1883, cited in Stengers, 'L'Impérialisme Colonial de la Fin du XIXᵉ Siècle', *loc. cit.* p. 478.

[3] Jauréguiberry to M.A.E., 25 Jan. 1883, AEMD Afrique 86; Jauréguiberry to *Commandant de la division navale*, 30 Jan. 1883, cited in Stengers, 'L'Impérialisme Colonial de la Fin du XIXᵉ Siècle', *loc. cit.* p. 479; Dislère, Rapport au Ministre, 30 Sept. 1882 (Approved), MFOM Sénégal IV 77(a).

[4] Projet d'instructions, encl. in Jauréguiberry to M.A.E., 22 Nov. 1882, cited in: H. Brunschwig, *L'avènement de l'Afrique noire* (Paris, 1963), pp. 163–4; M.A.E. to Brazza, February 1883, cited in: C. Coquery-Vidrovitch, 'Les idées économiques de Brazza et les premières tentatives de compagnies de colonisation au Congo français, 1885–1898', *Cahiers d'études africaines*, no. 17 (1965), p. 57.

apparent. Prime Minister Duclerc was forced to submit the Brazza treaty to Parliament by the pressures of public opinion which the explorer and his friends had been able to generate. But the harnessing of popular support for particular schemes of African expansion was not a new phenomenon. Many of Brazza's supporters in 1882 had been the champions of the Trans-Sahara Railway in 1879,[1] and Parliament responded to their propaganda for the same reasons that it had three years before: because it saw the Congo as yet another route into the Sudanese interior.[2] Rouvier reported on the treaty to the Chamber: 'France', he declared,

closer to Africa than most other nations, more directly interested than they in the future of this continent because of her possessions in Algeria, Senegal, Gabon and her numerous trading posts on the West African coast, would gravely misjudge her own most certain interests if she allowed herself to be overtaken in the movement which is drawing the civilised world towards these still mysterious regions.

He had delivered the same speech about the Trans-Sahara Railway in 1879. Not even the details of the text had been altered.[3]

Certainly, Jauréguiberry's initiatives did not amount to a well-conceived, carefully elaborated and detailed imperialist plan. The Minister never declared his policies on the Upper and Lower Niger to be part of a single grand design. But the design itself was too well known and his initiatives resembled it too closely for the relationship to have been purely coincidental. Faidherbe had been the prophet of the new empire in the 1860s, and his were the prophecies which Jauréguiberry had been seeking to fulfil since 1879. Soleillet had talked of a French Chad in 1876, and his speech had been noted by the Colonial Department.[4] Rouvier had said much the same in 1879 and again in

---

[1] Most notably the Paris Geographical Society, Georges Périn and Paul Bert. For details of the publicity campaign, see: Stengers, 'L'Impérialisme Colonial de la Fin du XIXᵉ Siècle', *loc. cit.* pp. 474–7; Brunschwig, *L'avènement de l'Afrique noire*, pp. 153–4.

[2] E.g. Xavier Blanc, Rapport, *J.O. Déb. Parl. Sénat*, séance du 28 novembre 1882, pp. 1089–91: 'Mieux placée qu'aucune autre nation pour pénétrer dans ces immenses et fertiles contrées, la France s'est déjà acheminée vers le Soudan par les deux grandes voies de l'Algérie et du Sénégal. Les découvertes récentes de Monsieur Savorgnan de Brazza lui ouvrent une nouvelle voie par le Bassin du Congo.'

[3] Rouvier, Rapport, 21 Nov. 1882, *J.O. Doc. Parl. Chambre*, no. 1406, pp. 2447–8. See above: pp. 62–3.

[4] Soleillet, Speech delivered on 3 Jan. 1876 [newspaper clipping], MFOM Missions 15, Soleillet 1876–9: 'Par ses possessions de l'Algérie et du Sénégal, la France devrait voir toute l'Afrique occidentale, de Tripoli au lac Tschad, du lac Tschad au Bénin, du Bénin au Cap Vert, du Cap Vert au Sénégal, du Sénégal à Tombouctou, de Tombouctou au Maroc, ouverte à son commerce, à ses mœurs et à sa civilisation.'

1882, and his words carried still more weight. The creation of a West African empire embracing much more than the Senegal–Niger valley was an unmistakeable if ill-defined objective of French African policy by the early 1880s, and this objective was to influence the course of French expansion until the end of the century.

THE BALANCE-SHEET OF THE FIRST CAMPAIGNS

By 1883, the basic principles of French expansion in the Western Sudan had also been irrevocably determined. Despite its lip-service to trade, the Ministry of Marine was now firmly committed to the extension of political and military domination. It saw the Railway in strategic rather than economic terms, less as a vehicle for trade than as a means for enhancing security by improving communications with the frontier, and even this objective was subordinate to the establishment of effective political occupation.[1] Indeed, railway-construction soon became little more than a convenient disguise for the mounting costs of military expansion. According to the Ministry's original estimates, its railway programme was to cost 12,000,000 fr., of which only 1,300,000 fr. were set aside for the completion of topographic surveys and the construction of the fort at Kita. Yet by 1883 Parliament had voted funds totalling 16,000,000 fr., and of the 13,500,000 fr. actually spent only 7,000,000 fr. had been devoted to the Railway. The rest had gone on surveys, diplomatic missions and military construction. The forts themselves had cost not 300,000 fr. but 3,000,000 fr. The route to the Niger was now secured by forts at Médine, Bafoulabé, Badumbé, Kita, and Bamako; meanwhile the Railway had progressed precisely seventeen kilometres.[2]

What is more, the Chambers accepted the full-scale military occupation of the Senegal–Niger valley with no more than a whisper of dissent. Although the Ministry's inadequate preparations, its inability to control costs, and its unwillingness to divulge sufficient information were often sharply criticised, its basic objectives were not questioned. Opposition to colonial entanglements was certainly a potent political force at the time; the heated debates on the Tunisian expedition and the refusal to participate in the Suez campaign were proof enough of that.

[1] See: Bourdiaux's evidence to the Board of Inquiry, 4 Jan. 1883, MFOM Dossier Administratif, Vallon.
[2] Peyron, Rapport, 31 Dec. 1883, *J.O.* 4 Feb. 1884, pp. 585–622.

The Balance-Sheet of the First Campaigns

But it had no effect on Sudanese policy. Virtually nobody in the Chamber voiced any doubts about the future economic importance of the Western Sudan or the strategic need to reach the Niger before the British. Even the staunchest and most articulate of the anti-colonialists, Clemenceau, felt obliged to proclaim himself a partisan of Sudanese expansion in principle at least.[1]

There were good reasons for the Sudan's relative immunity from criticism. Parliamentary anti-colonialism may not have been as significant a factor in the politics of the 1880s as it appeared.[2] Opposition to colonial expansion, moreover, was based on fairly definite considerations. The disasters of 1870–1 had taught France a terrible lesson about the importance of maintaining her military strength in Europe and had left her citizens determined never again to allow the pursuit of colonial ambitions to interfere with the needs of continental defence. Ferry learned this to his cost when he committed 40,000 troops, many of them metropolitan conscripts, to an arduous summer campaign in Tunisia. Less than a year later Freycinet learned the same lesson in Egypt.[3] The seamy *affairisme* associated with the Emperor's colonial ventures left Frenchmen no less determined never again to permit the prostitution of the State to private financial interests. Nobody had forgotten the connection between the Mexican expedition and Jecker, and when the treaty of Bardo inflated the value of the Tunisian bonds, the analogy was all too clear.[4]

Sudanese policy raised no such issues. Military commitments here were borne by the 'Marines' and by African contingents recruited on the spot. Because the metropolitan Army was not involved, the nation's capacity to defend itself from European aggression was in no way weakened. Nor was there any question of the State pandering to the speculators. The avowed objective was to serve the national interest by opening new territories for the benefit of French trade in general, and

---

[1] *J.O. Déb. Parl. Chambre*, séance du 3 juillet 1883, pp. 1570–1.

[2] It has been suggested that the opposition to Ferry's expansionist policies was due as much to the antagonism of the Right towards his laicisation programme and the disillusionment of the Left with his gradualism on matters of constitutional reform as to any genuine anti-colonialism. See: T. F. Power, *Jules Ferry and the Renaissance of French Imperialism* (New York, 1944).

[3] E.g. *J.O. Déb. Parl. Chambre*, séance du 29 juillet 1882 [speech by Clemenceau]: 'Nous avons le devoir de ne pas risquer légèrement l'armée...dans des aventures dont personne ne peut prévoir la fin et qui pourraient nous conduire à des désastres, à la ruine de la patrie.' Clemenceau was one of the most effective opponents of the Suez campaign.

[4] See: Ganiage, *op. cit.* pp. 668–99. The epithet: 'Les Jeckers de la Tunisie' was used by the monarchist Deputy Lenglé during the debate of 12 April 1881.

this was a goal whose legitimacy even Clemenceau accepted.[1] When the Ministry introduced the argument of security, its battle was as good as won. Originally, Parliament had approved the construction of forts as essential for the protection of the railway surveys; but it was soon persuaded to approve the Railway as essential for the security of the forts. By doing so it effectively surrendered its control over the enterprise. The Chamber may have rejected the Government's Senegal–Niger Railway project in 1880, but nobody challenged the Ministry in 1882 when it confidently announced that the Kayes–Bafoulabé line would eventually be extended to the Niger.[2] It may have declared itself against military expansion, but it dared not challenge the need for a military presence on the Upper Senegal.

This same concern for security also assured the victory of the Military. Once the advance had begun, Desbordes and his men were all too easily pictured as loyal servants of the Republic, steadfastly upholding its honour on distant and dangerous fields. It was impossible for a Deputy from the safety of his seat in the Chamber to attack 'these heroic sons of France...who astonish [us] by their courage, by their daring and by the range of their abilities'.[3] Like Faidherbe and Brière before him, the Commander appreciated the political strength of his position and took full advantage of it. He made the Niger plan his own, and by relentless pressure he overcame the hesitations of his metropolitan superiors. In three years he was able to win his complete independence from Saint-Louis and to have himself recognised as the principal agent of French expansion on the Upper Senegal. He more than anyone was responsible for the military occupation of the Niger and the establishment of the Military's primacy in the Western Sudan.

But his victory was expensive. From the start, both railway-construction and the military advance were constantly hampered by the combined effects of natural calamities and inadequate planning. As early as September 1880, Brière had warned that the late start to the campaign would place the whole operation at the mercy of the elements, and his pessimism was entirely justified.[4] The expeditionary column reached Saint-Louis at the height of a typhoid epidemic which soon

---

[1] *J.O. Déb. Parl. Chambre*, séance du 8 novembre 1881, p. 1971: 'Je ne vois pas là l'institution de grands débouchés pour notre commerce, la création de comptoirs ou d'établissements industriels, rien, en un mot, qui ressemble à la légitime exploitation des ressources du sol tunisien.'
[2] *Ibid. Sénat*, séance du 31 mars 1882, p. 350 [speech by Berlet].
[3] *Ibid. Chambre*, séance du 3 juillet 1883, p. 1562 [speech by Ferry].
[4] Brière to M.M.C., 24 Sept. 1880, MFOM Sénégal I 63 (a).

put thirty per cent of its European force out of action. By the end of the campaign disease had taken the lives of fifty-nine Europeans; another sixty were ill.[1] The fall in the water level of the Senegal and the growing hostility of Abdul-Bubakar in Futa disrupted communications with the Sudan and made the transport of men, material and supplies much more difficult than the planners had expected. When Desbordes finally reached Bafoulabé in January 1881, he had only two days' provisions left.[2] The Commander's own rash advance to Kita strained these shaky supply lines to the breaking point. By February his provisions were again exhausted, and he was having to consider the possibility of a retreat. Although he managed to hold out, his position remained critical throughout the following months.[3]

The yellow-fever epidemic of 1881 created exactly the same problems. Once more Saint-Louis was paralysed, the departure of the column delayed and the provisioning of the forts disrupted. In October Governor Canard warned Paris that Kita and Bafoulabé might have to be evacuated lest their garrisons starve, and even Desbordes predicted disaster. Two months later the Commander was still at Kayes, without money and without supplies.[4] Yet he again insisted on pressing forward. Certainly, his expedition to Keniéra was no mean feat, but his passage through a hundred and fifty miles of hostile territory with not much more than an armed reconnaissance party was almost suicidally reckless. As Governor Canard rightly pointed out, 'only the Colonel's lucky star...and...his iron determination' averted a major catastrophe.[5]

The Railway fared much worse still. Essential materials were either delivered late or were not delivered at all. Transportation and storage facilities proved completely inadequate, and as a result there was a thirty per cent wastage of stock during the first campaign.[6] The administrative personnel in Senegal were notoriously incompetent. The

---

[1] Desbordes, Rapport, 14 Dec. 1880; *idem*, Rapport, 24 Dec. 1880; *idem*, Rapport, 14 June 1881, MFOM Sénégal I 99(a), Correspondance du Gouverneur.

[2] Brière to M.M.C., 24 Nov. 1880; same to same, 23 Feb. 1881; same to same, 8 Mar. 1881, MFOM Sénégal I 63(a); Desbordes to Brière, 18 Jan. 1881, MFOM Sénégal IV 73(b).

[3] Same to same, 24 Feb. 1881, *ibid.*; Delanneau to M.M.C., 23 Apr. 1881, MFOM Sénégal I 64(b): '...les ressources du pays sont nulles; d'où il résulte qu'une retraite sur Bafoulabé, nécessitée par la faim, *est dans les occurrences possibles.*'

[4] Canard to Desbordes, Instructions, 23 Oct. 1881, MFOM Sénégal IV 75 (a); Canard to M.M.C., 6 Nov. 1881, MFOM Sénégal I 66(b); Desbordes to Canard, 6 Oct. 1881, MFOM Sénégal I 99(a), Correspondance du Gouverneur; same to same, 6 Dec. 1881; same to same, 11 Dec. 1881, MFOM Sénégal IV 75(b).

[5] Canard to M.M.C., 21 Mar. 1882, MFOM Sénégal I 66(b).

[6] Leroy, Rapport, 9 June 1883, *J.O. Doc. Parl. Chambre*, no. 1964, p. 934.

most elementary rules of budgetary procedure were disregarded; detailed accounts of expenditure were poorly kept, and even these were at times mislaid. The Moroccan workers recruited to work on the Railway were not supplied with enough tools, and the administrator in charge of them could hardly speak any Arabic. By December 1882 only four kilometres of track had been laid.[1]

The Ministry was now forced to take stock of the situation. Although Desbordes was moving rapidly on the Niger, the rest of its programme was in ruins. Railway-building was clearly an expensive farce, and military expansion had destroyed any immediate hope of making the Sudan pay for itself. In 1881 Governor Delanneau had been forced to lift his restrictions on the arms traffic, 'because it is the only branch of commerce which can profitably be carried on at the moment'. A year later the exasperated Vallon condemned the enterprise *in toto* and categorically declared that the Sudan would never become profitable.[2] Incensed by the Governor's attitude, Jauréguiberry set up an official Board of Inquiry to refute his allegations, and the Board dutifully concluded that the Ministry's plans were by no means impracticable. But it still had to admit that the poor quality of administrative personnel, the late delivery of material, the high costs of transportation and the unsuitable location of Kayes (constantly in danger of flooding) all presented serious obstacles to their successful completion.[3] Unfortunately, it was too late now for the Ministry to remedy these deficiencies; once the occupation of Bamako had been sanctioned, non-military considerations became secondary.

But the subordination of railway-building to military expansion was itself unwise. First of all, it completely upset the Ministry's financial calculations. In April 1883, the new Minister, Charles Brun, had to tell Parliament that the total cost of the operation would be 24,000,000 fr., twice the original estimate. He could no longer rely on the old argument of security, for Bafoulabé had after all managed to survive without its railway. There was only one justification which he could offer.

---

1 Brière, Notes…laissées à mon successeur, 14 Apr. 1881, MFOM Sénégal I 64(a); Vallon to M.M.C., 23 July 1882, MFOM Sénégal I 67(b); Desbordes, Rapport…1881–2, n.d., Caps. II, X, MFOM Missions 50, Borgnis-Desbordes 1881–2; Peyron, Rapport, 31 Dec. 1881, *J.O.* 4 Feb. 1884, p. 592.
2 Delanneau to M.M.C., 23 June 1881, MFOM Sénégal I 64(b); Vallon to M.M.C., 1 Nov. 1882, MFOM Sénégal I 67(b).
3 Jauréguiberry to Admiral Courbet [President of the Board of Inquiry], 28 Dec. 1882; Rapport de la Commission d'Enquête…, 24–27 Jan. 1883, MFOM Dossier Administratif, Vallon. The proceedings of the Commission are also to be found *ibid.*

Parliament, he claimed, had already approved an expenditure of 16,000,000 fr. on the project. Failure to approve the 8,000,000 fr. still required would force him to abandon the whole scheme and so lose everything. No matter how badly costs had been miscalculated in the past, it would still be cheaper to finish the line as far as Bafoulabé· Thereafter, he promised, its extension to the Niger could be undertaken by private enterprise.[1] This time, however, Parliament was much less obliging. Although the Budget Commission eventually gave its assent, it roundly condemned the Ministry's previous failings, demanded a much clearer indication of future expenditure, and rejected any idea of extending the line beyond Bafoulabé.[2] The Commission's report gave the Government's opponents new heart, for it was difficult to see what possible use there could be for a railway running 'from an entirely desolate plain, Kayes, across a complete wilderness to an absolute desert, Bafoulabé'.[3] The Government's financial mismanagement was widely and bitterly criticised. In the Chamber a motion to adjourn the debate for a week was defeated by only 241 votes to 216; another calling for a full investigation of the Railway's finances by 286 to 182, and this only after Ferry himself had spoken against it. In the end the Ministry's demand for 4,677,000 fr. as a first instalment was approved by 273 votes to 101 with 126 abstentions.[4] The financing of the Government's projects could no longer be taken for granted.

In the Sudan, the emphasis on military expansion created a permanently precarious situation which could at any moment become critical. Desbordes's rush to the Niger left France in tenuous control along an over-extended line of forts deprived of an efficient system of communications and supply. These vulnerable positions were soon exposed to the consequences of the Commander's aggressiveness. The skirmishes at Keniéra and on the Niger did not destroy Samori's prestige. His army remained intact; his empire remained united; and his will to fight was in no way sapped. The *imam* did not come to terms with the French as Desbordes had hoped; instead he continued to resist, and he

[1] Brun, Projet de Loi, 26 Apr. 1883, *J.O. Doc. Parl. Chambre*, no. 1855, pp. 689–90. The Minister's revised estimates, based on the assumption that the line would be completed to Bafoulabé by the end of the next campaign, were of course no more accurate than the original ones.

[2] Procès-Verbaux de la Commission du Budget, séance du 1er juin 1883; séance du 6 juin 1883, AN C3304, pp. 88–98, 116–33; Leroy, Rapport, 9 June 1883, *J.O. Doc. Parl. Chambre*, no. 1964, pp. 929–36.

[3] *J.O. Déb. Parl. Sénat*, séance du 1er août 1883, pp. 1183–4 [speech by Lambert de Sainte-Croix].

[4] *Ibid. Chambre*, séance du 3 juillet 1883, pp. 1561–73.

even carried the war into European territory. By 1885 his *sofas* had reached the outskirts of Bafoulabé.

Others, however, would have to deal with these problems. As Desbordes realised, the occupation of Bamako marked the end of a definite stage in Sudanese expansion. There could be no further advance until his gains had been consolidated by the completion of the Railway. In the near future at least, the rôle of the Military would have to be restricted to the provisioning of the forts and the relief of their garrisons.[1] This was not a rôle which the Commander was prepared to play. At the end of the campaign, Saint-Louis was again hit by a typhoid epidemic which quickly struck down Governor Servatius. Acting on instructions from Paris to prevent the spread of infection, his temporary replacement, Le Boucher, quarantined Desbordes and his men on the Ile de Todd.[2] But housing facilities on the island proved inadequate, and the Commander used this alleged maltreatment of his men as the pretext for his immediate resignation. The tactic succeeded admirably. Determined not to lose his most experienced Sudanese agent, the Minister reprimanded the unfortunate Le Boucher, refused to accept Desbordes's resignation and ordered him back to Paris, where his services would be of great value to the Colonial Department.[3] Desbordes was only too glad to obey.

[1] Desbordes to Gov. Sen., 24 Dec. 1882, MFOM Sénégal I 99(b), Correspondance Générale.

[2] M.M.C. to Gov. Sen., 5 May 1883, MFOM Sénégal I 99(b), Correspondance Générale: 'Ce qu'il importe avant tout d'éviter à Saint-Louis, c'est une agglomération d'hommes sujette à contracter ou à porter l'épidémie; il convient même, autant que possible, ne pas laisser ce personnel pénétrer à Saint-Louis.' Desbordes himself reported that typhoid had broken out among his troops. Desbordes to Gov. Sen., 17 May 1883; same to same, 19 June 1883, MFOM Sénégal I 99(b), Correspondance du Gouverneur.

[3] Same to same, 23 June 1883, *ibid.*; M.M.C. to Le Boucher, 8 July 1883, MFOM Sénégal I 99(b), Correspondance Générale; M.M.C. to Desbordes, 16 July 1883, MFOM Sénégal IV 79(c).

5

The Problems of Occupation, 1883-6

As Desbordes had predicted, the occupation of Bamako put an end to further expansion. Before leaving the Sudan, even he stressed the importance of consolidating the existing position. Only in the south, where the goldfields of Buré still lay beyond French influence, did he see any scope for continued activity and suggest the construction of new forts at Niagassola and Siguiri.[1] Paris was still more cautious. Recent embarrassments in the Chamber had forced the Ministry to realise that Parliament's continued financial support depended upon a convincing demonstration of the railway programme's feasibility. Accordingly, railway-construction was again accorded top priority. Desbordes's proposals for expansion into Buré were rejected. The size of the expeditionary column was reduced; its duties were restricted to the provisioning of the forts, and its sphere of operations was strictly limited to the immediate environs of Bamako. Its new Commander was ordered 'not to seek a quarrel with anyone or to meddle in anybody's affairs'.[2] But the Ministry soon found out that consolidation was a much more difficult undertaking than conquest.

UNCERTAINTIES ON THE UPPER SENEGAL

Parliament gave the Rue Royale its first rude shock. Anxious to settle the Sudan's financial position, the Ministry decided to ask for the second instalment of the new credit when the Extraordinary Estimates were submitted in July 1883. But this placed its demand on an entirely different footing. The first instalment had been covered by a budgetary surplus available on the Public Works Estimates for 1881;[3] the second would have to be considered as part of a general demand for

[1] Desbordes to Gov. Sen., 24 Dec. 1882, cited in Desbordes, Rapport...1882-3, 14 July 1883, Cap. XX, MFOM Sénégal IV 77(b).
[2] Dislère, Rapport au Ministre, 21 Aug. 1883, MFOM Sénégal IV 79(a); M.M.C. to Gov. Sen., 3 Sept. 1883; same to same, 4 Sept. 1883, MFOM Sénégal IV 79(bis)(a).
[3] Leroy, Rapport, 11 Mar. 1884, *J.O. Doc. Parl. Chambre*, no. 2694, p. 575.

265,000,000 fr. which could only be met by floating a State Loan. When submitting this highly unpopular proposal, the Minister of Finance himself admitted that the whole procedure for granting extraordinary credits would have to be tightened up in future.[1] The Sudan credit was an obvious place to begin. Although the Budget Commission gave its assent, the Chamber did not feel bound by its approval for the first instalment and rejected the credit by 234 votes to 197.[2] Fortunately for the Government, it was restored in the Senate. General Faidherbe, now a *sénateur inammovible*, warned each of his colleagues of the catastrophic effects which the abandonment of the Sudan would have on French prestige throughout Africa, and the Senate Finance Commission took him at his word. Admiral Peyron, the new Minister of Marine, added his own *caveat* that a rejection of his demand would force him to repudiate his contracts and repatriate his personnel, a more expensive operation than completing the work in progress. The Senate accepted his assurances that the money would only be used to pay off outstanding debts, and the Chamber did not press the issue.[3] But this brought the Minister small comfort. The Budget Commission had by now lost all its enthusiasm for the enterprise. Many of its members called for a full Parliamentary investigation, and even the Railway's most loyal supporters talked ominously of a *crédit de liquidation*. Before approving the credit, it demanded a firm pledge that ninety kilometres of track would be laid by the beginning of June, and it specifically reserved its decision on any future requests, whether the Railway were completed or not. The Chamber passed the Bill only after further assurances that no new work would be undertaken without its prior consent.[4]

The situation in the colony was equally alarming. Desbordes's successful attempts to secure his independence from Senegal by systematically attacking its Governors and the effects of disease had together wrought havoc with the Saint-Louis administration. Since Brière had been recalled, two Governors had died of fever and two others had

---

[1] Tirard, Projet de Loi, 31 July 1883, *ibid.* no. 2226, p. 1317.

[2] Leroy, Rapport, 17 Nov. 1883, *ibid.* no. 2393, pp. 1618–20; *J.O. Déb. Parl. Chambre*, séance du 17 décembre 1883, pp. 2872–9.

[3] Faidherbe, Circular Letter, 28 Dec. 1883, cited in Faidherbe, *Le Sénégal*, pp. 6–10; Rapport de la Commission des Finances, 12 Jan. 1884, *J.O. Doc. Parl. Sénat*, no. 3, pp. 1–3; *J.O. Déb. Parl. Sénat*, séance du 22 janvier 1884, pp. 88–9.

[4] Procès-Verbaux de la Commission du Budget, séance du 28 janvier 1884, AN C3304, p. 982 [Rouvier's remarks]; Procès-Verbaux de la Commission Spéciale, séance du 11 février 1884, AN C3316; *ibid.* séance du 15 février; Leroy, Rapport, 11 Mar. 1884, *J.O. Doc. Parl. Chambre*, no. 2694, pp. 574–7; *J.O. Déb. Parl. Chambre*, séance du 31 mars 1884, p. 971.

resigned in disgust. After the quarantine incident they were followed by Le Boucher, who refused to carry on even until his replacement, Governor Seignac, arrived. The Ministry had to send Colonel Bourdiaux of the Upper Senegal Bureau to take charge in the interim; but Bourdiaux's support for military expansion and his strong advocacy of the Railway had already alienated the Saint-Louis traders whose co-operation was essential for the provisioning of the Sudanese garrisons.[1] In the Sudan itself, the gap left by the departure of Desbordes proved even more difficult to fill. His successor, Lieutenant-Colonel Boilève, was a man of great experience and demonstrated ability; but his years of service in Senegal had sapped his strength, and he asked to be relieved even before the campaign began. Paris refused to hear of it, and Boilève had to carry on as best he could; but he was clearly in no fit state to follow his predecessor's example.[2]

In the circumstances, the new *Commandant-Supérieur* gave a creditable account of himself. By following his instructions to avoid all complications, he managed to keep the political situation relatively calm and was thus able to provision the forts and devote proper attention to railway-building. But his progress was hindered at every turn by chronic deficiencies in planning and lack of support from Senegal. The administration remained as ineffectual as ever; transport services were still disorganised and storage facilities inadequate; money and supplies continued to arrive late. Natural disasters also played their part. Although the campaign was not for once disrupted by an epidemic, a severe fire at Kayes in May destroyed most of the railway stores and with them any hope of completing the promised ninety kilometres of track.[3]

But the Ministry was no longer interested in the fate of the Railway. In February Admiral Peyron had told the Budget Commission that his only reason for continuing the work was to avoid wasting all the money which had already been spent on it.[4] Peyron's sole concern was

---

[1] See: M.M.C. to Gasconi, 4 Aug. 1883, MFOM Sénégal I 70(c). For the rôle of the traders in the provisioning of the expeditionary force, see: Vallon, Note, n.d., MFOM Dossier Administratif, Vallon.

[2] Dislère, Rapport au Ministre, 22 Aug. 1883, MFOM Sénégal IV 79(a); Gov. Sen. to M.M.C., 7 Oct. 1883, MFOM Sénégal I 99(b), Correspondance du Gouverneur; M.M.C. to Gov. Sen., 19 Nov. 1883, MFOM Sénégal I 70(b).

[3] Bourdiaux to M.M.C., n.d. [October 1883]; same to same, 19 Feb. 1884, MFOM Sénégal IV 70(a); Seignac to M.M.C., 8 June 1884, MFOM Sénégal I 99(b), Correspondance Générale; Boilève, Rapport...1883–4, 8 Aug. 1884, Caps. I, IV, MFOM Sénégal IV 79(*bis*)(a).

[4] Procès-Verbaux de la Commission du Budget, séance du 1er février 1884, AN C3304, p. 997.

to guarantee continued financial support for the military occupation of the Sudan. He was careful to draw a clear distinction between the two issues and told the Senate in April that no decision on the future of the Railway could affect the permanence of French military control along the Kayes–Bamako line. In June he asked for a supplementary credit of 1,800,000 fr. to pay for the maintenance of the forts, claiming that their abandonment 'would deal our prestige on the African continent a fatal blow'. In order to secure Parliament's approval, he was quite prepared to make concessions on the Railway, and when the Budget Commission demanded the indefinite suspension of all work on it he readily agreed.[1] This in turn was enough for the Chamber. Its mounting opposition had been directed against the high costs of Sudanese policy and unsatisfactory progress of railway-building, not against the principle of military occupation. In July 1884 the Budget Commission approved the supplementary credit, declaring that the occupation of the Sudan 'is today an accomplished fact which nobody, even among those most hostile to certain aspects of Sudanese policy, is prepared to question'. A month later it transferred the 1885 Estimates to the Ordinary Budget as a further sign of the occupation's permanent character.[2] And its decision was not seriously challenged by anyone in the Chamber.[3]

Parliament's approval for military occupation, however, did not put an end to the Ministry's troubles. Despite its unimportance, the Railway had been the financial cover under which the costs of military expansion had always been hidden. Its abandonment deprived the Rue Royale of the only justification for the extravagant expenditure which its military operations had so far entailed. Although the Budget Commission accepted the need for a yearly campaign to provision the forts, it was determined to reduce costs, and it used the suspension of railway-construction as an excuse to cut the 1885 Estimates in half, from 3,110,000 fr. to 1,600,000 fr.[4] But military costs could not be controlled.

[1] Projet de Loi, 1 Apr. 1884, *J.O. Doc. Parl. Sénat*, no. 106, p. 208; Projet de Loi, 10 June 1884, *J.O. Doc. Parl. Chambre*, no. 2850, p. 980; Procès-Verbaux de la Commission du Budget, séance du 3 juillet 1884; séance du 18 juillet 1884, AN C3305, pp. 226–8, 299.

[2] De Lanessan, Rapport, 18 July 1884, *J.O. Doc. Parl. Chambre*, no. 3004, p. 1324; *idem*, Rapport, 14 Aug. 1884, *ibid.* no. 3087, p. 1525.

[3] *J.O. Déb. Parl. Chambre*, séance du 30 juillet 1884, p. 1925. Only Périn objected, and he too reserved his criticisms until a general debate could be held on the issue. Despite his advocacy of the Trans-Sahara Railway, Périn, a partisan of peaceful expansion, was an implacable opponent of military occupation in the Sudan.

[4] De Lannessan, Rapport, 14 Aug. 1884, *J.O. Doc. Parl. Chambre*, no. 3087, p. 1518. When credits already on the Ordinary Budget were added, the total Estimate rose to some 2,000,000 fr.

116

The provisioning of the forts in 1883 had already created a deficit of 350,000 fr. By February 1885 the Ministry had to admit that the 1884 campaign had produced a further deficit of 1,100,000 fr., and in June it had to announce that the 1885 estimates would also have to be increased by 800,000 fr.[1]

Without money, there could be no thought of further expansion. Even Desbordes, who drafted the instructions for the next campaign, recognised the impossibility of continuing the advance. The objective as he saw it could only be 'to maintain our existing position using... the very limited resources available on the Budget, and...to lose as little prestige as possible...while avoiding...all military complications'. His proposals were accepted, and for added emphasis the expeditionary column was again forbidden to operate beyond the Bamako region.[2] It was difficult enough merely to maintain the existing position. The transportation problem remained acute, and the provisioning service remained inadequate. The start of the campaign was again delayed, and the column was unable to leave Kayes before the end of December. The renewed agitation of Abdul-Bubakar in Futa kept the area around Bakel in a constant state of turmoil. The populations around Médine, Bafoulabé, Kita and Bamako were all unco-operative and refused to supply either provisions or labour. The Tokolor authorities in Kaarta maintained their trade ban and so aggravated the problem of supply. The forts themselves were unable to provide adequate protection for caravans, and in conditions of insecurity trade continued to decline. The suppression of the railway credits brought construction to a halt. Using the materials already at hand, the engineers were able to add only four kilometres to the existing track.[3]

Without money, there could be no thought of a more active policy towards Ahmadu or Samori. 'We must be extremely careful to avoid war', declared the Ministry of Marine in November 1883; 'the number of troops at Commandant Boilève's disposal makes it impossible to

[1] Projet de Loi, 4 Nov. 1884, *ibid.* no. 3177, p. 1940; Projet de Loi, 17 Nov. 1884, *ibid.* no. 3229, pp. 2031–2; Projet de Loi, 5 Feb. 1885, *ibid.* no. 3511, pp. 109–10; Projet de Loi, 29 June 1885, *ibid.* no. 3922, p. 1077.

[2] Desbordes to Under-Secretary, 5 Apr. 1884; Desbordes, Note pour M. Pérard, 2 Sept. 1884; M.M.C. to Combes, Draft Instructions, n.d. [4 Sept. 1884], MFOM Sénégal IV 81 (a). Because of the restricted nature of the next campaign, Desbordes himself asked to be transferred to a regiment on active service and was posted to Indochina at the end of the year.

[3] Combes to Gov. Sen., 3 Oct. 1884, MFOM Sénégal IV 81 (c); Combes, Rapport... 1884–5, n.d., Caps. I, III, MFOM Sénégal IV 81 (b); Chief Engineer's Report, 15 Oct. 1886, *ibid.*

adopt any other course of action.' Ahmadu was still regarded as a potentially dangerous enemy, but for the moment Paris was content to foment unrest in his empire while outwardly maintaining a show of friendship towards him. It was just as anxious not to provoke an open conflict with Samori, and it ordered the Governor to sound out the possibility of negotiating a treaty with him.[1] Reports that Bambara rebellion and *talibé* desertions were further undermining the Sultan's position and that the *imam* might be ready to make common cause with the French against him seemed to confirm the wisdom of the Government's policy.[2] As the Sudan's financial future grew more uncertain, vigorous military action became still more impracticable. Desbordes himself pointed out that the French lacked the troops to exploit the Sultan's difficulties and would have to remain on cordial terms with him even at the risk of alienating their Bambara allies. Paris agreed and ordered Boilève's successor, Major Combes, to avoid hostilities with either Muslim power. Instead, the new Commander was to 'proclaim our wish to live in peace with everyone and our intention to maintain [our forts] exclusively in the interests of trade'.[3]

But the policy-makers did not reckon with the new *Commandant-Supérieur*. Unlike Boilève, Combes was not satisfied with the restricted and professionally unattractive programme laid down in his instructions. Desbordes had revealed the opportunities which the Sudan offered to the ambitious officer, and Combes was determined not to waste them. In true military fashion he argued the case for conquest. The Government's policy of non-involvement, he claimed, was a potential threat to security. French power had so far rested upon demonstrated military superiority. If the prestige of their arms were allowed to wane, the French would lose the initiative, and their warlike opponents would grow bold enough to attack them. On the other hand, a decisive victory over the Muslim states would make the French masters of the Sudan and all its trade; and victory was within their grasp. The Tokolor empire was crumbling, and Samori's attention had been diverted east-

---

[1] Under-Secretary to Gov. Sen., 5 Nov. 1883, MFOM Sénégal I 70(b).
[2] Bourdiaux to M.M.C., 9 Nov. 1883, MFOM Sénégal I 70(a); Seignac to M.M.C., 9 May 1884, MFOM Sénégal I 71(b); Boilève, Rapport...1883–4, 8 Aug. 1884, Cap. II, MFOM Sénégal IV 79(*bis*)(a). The Ministry, however, did recognise the danger of allowing Samori to capture Segu and so unite the two empires under his leadership, and it ordered the local authorities to prevent this eventuality at all costs.
[3] Desbordes, Note pour M. Pérard, 2 Sept. 1884, MFOM Sénégal IV 81(a); M.M.C. to Gov. Sen., 4 Nov. 1884, MFOM Sénégal I 72(b); M.M.C. to Combes, 5 Nov. 1884, cited in Combes, Rapport...1884–5, n.d., Cap. III, MFOM Sénégal IV 81(b).

ward to the kingdom of Sikasso. Indeed, action could no longer be delayed. Ahmadu had just sent a most insulting letter, and this affront to French honour had to be punished. Accordingly, Combes requested permission to lead a punitive expedition against him, and Governor Seignac gave the plan his full support.[1]

The argument was well phrased. For all its determination to avoid conflict, the Government had always been ready to sanction the use of force when security was directly threatened. Contingency plans drawn up in April 1884 had provided for limited military action if Ahmadu made any preparations to attack Bamako or if he moved to Nioro on the exposed flank of the French supply lines.[2] Thus, when Peyron received the Commander's proposals, he prudently ordered his Under-Secretary to reply as non-committally as possible. Combes was authorised to act energetically if the occasion arose, but only if he were certain of victory. If he ran into difficulties he was not to expect reinforcements from France.[3]

The Commander needed no more prompting, but at the last moment he changed his plans. In November he decided not to reply to Ahmadu's letter, and even when the Sultan moved to Nioro he made no attempt to stop him.[4] Instead, he advanced south against Samori. In February 1885 he had a fort built at Niagassola, and in March he led an offensive reconnaissance through Buré and Kangaba on the left bank of the Niger. To consolidate these gains he ordered the construction of another small fort at Nafadié. In the interests of prestige, he later explained, he had decided to protect his allies there against the raids of the *sofas* and to confirm French influence on the Left Bank. Because the *imam* was already at war with Sikasso in the east and had left only a small force in Buré, the operation involved no military risk. Since he was confident of victory, he considered his action quite in keeping with the spirit of the Ministry's instructions.[5]

This optimism was sadly misplaced. Although Combes was no less ambitious than Desbordes, he was neither as talented nor as lucky. It

---

[1] Combes to Gov. Sen., 1 Nov. 1884, MFOM Sénégal IV 81(c); Gov. Sen. to M.M.C., 16 Nov. 1884, MFOM Sénégal IV 81(d).

[2] Bourdiaux to M.M.C., 23 Mar. 1884, MFOM Sénégal IV 99(b), Correspondance du Gouverneur; Under-Secretary to Gov. Sen., 19 Apr. 1884, MFOM Sénégal I 71(c).

[3] Peyron to Faure, Note, 17 Nov. 1884, MFOM Sénégal IV 81(d); M.M.C. to Gov. Sen., n.d. [Draft], MFOM Sénégal IV 86.

[4] Combes to Gov. Sen., 26 Nov. 1884; same to same, 29 Nov. 1884; same to same, 1 Apr. 1885, MFOM Sénégal IV 81(c).

[5] Combes, Rapport...1884–5, n.d., Cap. III, MFOM Sénégal IV 81(b).

was a mistake for him to have built Niagassola in the first place, for the surrounding population was unco-operative and the fort extremely difficult to provision. Nafadié proved completely untenable. Without supplies or ammunition, its small garrison could not hold out against the *sofas* and had to be rescued by a flying column from Niagassola. When the onset of the rains forced the expeditionary column to return to its base, Niagassola was also besieged. During the summer, the *imam* restored control over the left bank of the Niger, and the *sofas* advanced to the gates of Bafoulabé.[1] By the time Combes returned to Senegal, moreover, his troops were too exhausted to deal with Abdul-Bubakar. Combes's absurd attack against Samori, the Governor pointed out, seriously undermined French security on the Upper Senegal and had almost ended in a disaster of incalculable proportions.[2]

FRENCH PRIORITIES IN WEST AFRICA, 1883–5

The failure of the Railway and the shortcomings of the Military in the Western Sudan were not the only problems which beset French policy-makers after 1883. Their more ambitious schemes for the creation of a West African empire fared no better. Although the occupation of Bamako was followed by a period of consolidation on the Upper Senegal, Jauréguiberry's plans for continued expansion along the Niger remained in force, and in October 1883 his order to build a gunboat was confirmed.[3] Here at least the Ministry was prepared to adopt a more adventurous policy. Although the Colonial Department would have been satisfied merely to show the flag at Segu, General Faidherbe, whom it consulted for detailed advice, recommended an immediate attempt to reach Timbuktu. He saw no reason why the gunboat should encounter any opposition if its mission were strictly peaceful and its commander promised Ahmadu not to interfere with his subjects. But if the Sultan tried to bar their way, they could always challenge his authority over the river and threaten to secure their passage by force. Even this was to cautious for Desbordes, who considered it foolish to make declarations of non-interference while at the same time offering support to the rebels in Beledugu. He thought it wiser to promise the Sultan not to interfere with those of his subjects who actually recognised

[1] *Ibid.* I am grateful to Professor Person for this information about the effectiveness of Samori's counter-offensive.
[2] Gov. Sen. to M.M.C., 28 July 1885, MFOM Sénégal I 73(a).
[3] M.M.C. to Gov. Sen., 9 Oct. 1883, MFOM Sénégal I 70(b).

his authority, thus leaving the French free to help the Bambaras. Desbordes's proposal became the basis for Commandant Delanneau's instructions in January 1884.[1] In April the Colonel even drafted plans for an overland expedition to Timbuktu which could be sent if the gunboat's journey were successful.[2]

The journey was doomed from the start. To reach Timbuktu before the dry season made navigation on the Niger impossible, the gunboat had to leave Bamako by May at the very latest. But its transportation overland was slow and its assembly was not completed until September. Timbuktu was now out of the question. Not even a shorter trip to Sansanding could be attempted; for the gunboat *Niger* was unseaworthy and its Master, Captain Froger, came down with fever. In November the ailing Froger was replaced by Lieutenant Davoust, and by the following April the *Niger* had been patched up. But Davoust then quarrelled with Delanneau and refused to serve under his command. It was September 1885 before the dispute was settled and the *Niger* finally set off downstream.[3]

In the meantime, however, the Ministry's hopes had been revived by the arrival at Saint-Louis of a Muslim traveller claiming to be an envoy from Timbuktu's Grand Council. This *soi-disant* ambassador, *al-hajj* Abd el-Kader, brought with him a request for protection against the Tokolor state of Macina and an offer to establish exclusive commercial relations with the French. The Senegalese authorities hoped at first to send him back with the gunboat, and when this proved impossible they persuaded him to continue his journey to France.[4] Both the Colonial Department and the Quai d'Orsay were eager to seize this opportunity for establishing relations with Timbuktu, and they decided to open negotiations even though Abd el-Kader had no authority to sign a treaty.[5] The Ambassador was royally treated, introduced to the leading personalities of the day, presented with lavish gifts and finally returned to Saint-Louis with instructions to await the arrival of a mission which was

[1] Faidherbe, Draft Instructions, enclosing letters to Ahmadu, n.d. [December 1883]; Desbordes, Note pour le sous-secrétaire, 2 Jan. 1884, MFOM Sénégal IV 82(a); M.M.C. to Delanneau, Instructions, 5 Jan. 1884, cited in Delanneau, Rapport, 24 Sept. 1884, *ibid.*

[2] Desbordes, Rapport, 28 Apr. 1884, MFOM Sénégal III 11 (*bis*). See also: Under-Secretary to Gov. Sen., 19 Apr. 1884, MFOM Sénégal I 71 (c).

[3] Combes, Rapport...1884–5, n.d., Cap. VIII (le Voyage du *Niger*); Delanneau to Frey [*Commandant-Supérieur*], 30 Nov. 1885, MFOM Sénégal IV 84 (c).

[4] Gov. Sen. to M.M.C., 24 Sept. 1884; same to same, 8 Oct. 1884; same to same, 23 Oct. 1884, MFOM Sénégal IV 82 (b).

[5] M.M.C. to M.A.E., 1 Dec. 1884; M.A.E. to M.M.C., 6 Dec. 1884; same to same, 20 Dec. 1884; M.M.C. to M.A.E., 24 Dec. 1884; M.A.E. to M.M.C., 30 Dec. 1884, *ibid.*

to escort him back to Timbuktu. The leader of the mission, the interpreter Angeli, was given a draft treaty of peace, friendship and trade, with orders to present it to the Grand Council if its terms seemed acceptable.[1]

Unfortunately, the whole scheme was much too fanciful to have the slightest chance of success. The French had no information whatsoever about the ambassador's status except for his letter of introduction, which could well have been forged. Nor did his conduct inspire any confidence. After his return to Saint-Louis his main concern was to get out of town as quickly as possible, and he refused to wait for his escort.[2] Angeli's credentials were even more dubious. Despite his extravagant claims to linguistic prowess, the interpreter had only the most elementary grasp of Arabic and no knowledge at all of the Timbuktu dialect. During the negotiations in Paris the Foreign Ministry had been forced to call in Consul-General Féraud to act as interpreter.[3] Angeli too was unwilling to put himself to the test, and he constantly delayed his departure on the grounds of ill health. In April 1885 the Under-Secretary finally cancelled the mission in disgust.[4] Undeterred, the Upper Senegal Bureau quickly drafted plans for a three-man expedition to investigate commercial prospects and secure political concessions; but this project was no less fantastic. By 1885 the funds available for colonial missions were so limited that Senegal could not even be reimbursed for the expenses which Abd el-Kader had incurred in Saint-Louis.[5]

French setbacks on the Lower Niger were much more alarming. Jauréguiberry's ambitious schemes for challenging British influence here had quickly come to grief. A French warship did call at Bonny in March 1883 but failed to sign a treaty; Consul Mattei had no more luck at Brass River in August, nor were his efforts up-river any more success-

[1] Faure to Council of Timbuktu, encl. in Faure to M.A.E., 19 Jan. 1885, *ibid.*; M.A.E. to M.M.C., 10 Feb. 1885, MFOM Sénégal IV 82 (c).

[2] Abd el-Kader to M.A.E., 10 Mar. 1885, MFOM Sénégal IV 82 (b). When Abd el-Kader reappeared in Senegal in 1886, both the Governor and the *Commandant-Supérieur* reported that he was probably an impostor who had not been to Timbuktu for years. Gov. Sen. to M.M.C., 12 Feb. 1886; same to same, 27 Feb. 1886, MFOM Sénégal I 73 (b); Frey to Gov. Sen., 7 May 1886, MFOM Sénégal IV 84 (b); Gov. Sen. to M.M.C., 14 May 1886, MFOM Sénégal I 74 (b); same to same, 14 Nov. 1886, MFOM Sénégal IV 85 (c).

[3] Angeli to Under-Secretary, 12 Mar. 1885, MFOM Sénégal IV 82 (c); Féraud to M.A.E., 8 Mar. 1886, Ministère des Affaires Etrangères, Correspondance Politique [henceforth AE] Maroc 50. See also: Abd el-Kader to M.A.E., 18 Mar. 1885, MFOM Sénégal IV 82 (b): 'Méfiez-vous de lui [Angeli]. Il ne comprend pas notre langue ni l'arabe.' Angeli, in fact, was the official whose linguistic deficiencies Desbordes had noted in 1882. See above: p. 110.

[4] Faure to Angeli, 15 Apr. 1885, MFOM Sénégal IV 82 (c).

[5] Pérard, Note pour M. Goldscheider, 24 Apr. 1885, MFOM Sénégal IV 82 (c); M.M.C. to Gov. Sen., 27 Aug. 1885, MFOM Missions 17, Abd-el-Kader.

ful. The Emirate of Nupe refused him permission to trade, and although he managed to sign a commercial treaty with Ibi on the Benué, he was unable to secure any political advantages.[1] Worse still, the initiatives which Jauréguiberry had set in motion finally goaded the British Government into action. In October 1883 Abo and Idah on the Niger were shelled by British gunboats for co-operating too closely with the French. In May 1884 'Too Late' Hewett finally set out on his famous treaty-making expedition, and together with Vice-Consul McIntosh he established a chain of protectorates from the Oil Rivers to the Benué.[2] Meanwhile, the French companies were finding the going even more difficult. Neither the *C.F.A.E.* nor the *Compagnie du Sénégal* could hope to match the financial resources of Sir George Goldie's National African Company with its nominal capital of £1,000,000, and when Goldie decided to drive them off the river by undercutting their prices, neither could survive for long. The *Compagnie du Sénégal* sold out its Niger interests in June, and the *C.F.A.E.* followed suit in October.[3]

By 1884 the whole French position in West Africa seemed to be under attack. The Sierra Leone Boundary Agreement of June 1882 had brought no relaxation of tensions along the frontier nor any relief to the constant unrest which menaced French influence in the Southern Rivers. Governor Bourdiaux was convinced that the nefarious activities of British agents were responsible for all the trouble. 'Only a blind man', he reported, 'could fail to see in the complications which daily arise the workings of British gold and of British intrigues.' The incursion of Samori into the Southern Rivers, he claimed, was merely the preliminary stage in a colossal British plot to ruin French trade on the coast, break up their treaties with Futa Jallon, undermine their influence on the Upper Niger and cut off any trade with Algeria. Reports that an embassy from Ahmadu had arrived in Freetown confirmed his worst fears.[4] The Colonial Department was equally alarmed. 'The progressively more critical situation which British attacks on our influence have created along the coast', the Under-Secretary for Colonies, Félix

---

[1] Cdt. Bories to M.M.C. [Copy], May 1883, AEMD Afrique 86; Mattei, *Bas-Niger, Bénoué, Dahomey*, pp. 56–9; Hargreaves, *Prelude to the Partition of West Africa*, pp. 310–12.

[2] Mattei, *op. cit.* pp. 60–1; Analyse sommaire, 19 Jan. 1884, MFOM Afrique VI 38(e); Hargreaves, *op. cit.* pp. 313–15, 328–9; Robinson and Gallagher, *Africa and the Victorians*, pp. 171–2, 175.

[3] For the activities of Goldie, see: J. E. Flint, *Sir George Goldie and the Making of Modern Nigeria* (London, 1960), pp. 34–87. For the fate of the companies, see: Mattei, *op. cit.* pp. 61–3.

[4] Bourdiaux to M.M.C., 8 Jan. 1884 [based on reports from the French Consul in Sierra Leone]; same to same, 10 Mar. 1884, MFOM Sénégal I 70(a). See also: Hargreaves, *op. cit.* pp. 290–4.

Faure, warned the Quai d'Orsay, 'cannot be allowed to continue without creating the most serious difficulties for us'.[1] Even the tenuous boundary agreement was destroyed in February 1884 by the refusal of the French Chamber to ratify it.[2] Although the demarcation was generally respected in practice, the situation remained unsettled and the Colonial Department's fears continued to grow.[3]

The failure of Jauréguiberry's imperialist schemes and the growing danger of British expansion forced the policy-makers in Paris to undertake a fundamental reassessment of their West African priorities. For the Ministry of Foreign Affairs the task was relatively easy. The Quai d'Orsay had never been very confident about the possibility of supplanting Britain on the Lower Niger and hesitated to use trading concerns of doubtful strength as instruments of official policy. It approved Jauréguiberry's plans for Mattei's treaty-making expedition and accepted his successor's offer to increase the frequency of naval patrols in the Delta region, but it refused to commit itself financially and gave Mattei only 3,000 fr. to buy presents for the local chiefs.[4] When the Consul's efforts failed to produce results, it immediately ordered him to abandon his political activities and concentrate exclusively on securing freedom for French trade and navigation. Mattei's frantic reports about British plans to expand east towards Lake Chad and west towards the Upper Niger were ignored; and, despite his desperate appeals for financial assistance, no attempt was made to rescue the companies on whose presence French claims on the Lower Niger rested.[5]

[1] Faure to M.A.E., 4 Feb. 1884, AEMD Afrique 84.

[2] Dureau de Vaulcomte, Rapport, 7 Feb. 1884, *J.O. Doc. Parl. Chambre*, no. 2608, pp. 78–80. The Treaty Commission's unfavourable report most probably reflected the views of the Deputy from Senegal, Gasconi, who was unalterably opposed to the agreement. Detailed examination of the treaty had been entrusted to a subcommission of three, of whom Gasconi was one. The minutes of the Treaty Commission are to be found in AN C3393, Dossier 2071. See also: Gasconi to M.M.C., 26 Oct. 1883, MFOM Afrique VI 34(a).

[3] E.g. Faure to Seignac, Instructions, 31 Mar. 1884, MFOM Sénégal I 71(a): '...il est incontestable que nous n'avons cessé de rencontrer, de la part de l'Angleterre, sur cette partie de la côte d'Afrique comme sur tous les autres points du globe où nous exerçons une légitime influence, les marques d'un esprit d'envahissement des plus nuisibles à nos intérêts. En vous signalant la situation, je ne puis donc que vous recommander d'apporter la plus grande vigilance pour déjouer des intrigues dont la réussite aurait, non seulement pour notre colonie du Sénégal mais encore pour nos possessions algériennes, les plus fâcheuses conséquences.'

[4] M.A.E. to Mattei, 6 Mar. 1883; M.M.C. to M.A.E., 18 June 1883; M.A.E. to M.M.C., 25 June 1883; Mattei, Reçus, 29 June 1883, AEMD Afrique 86.

[5] M.A.E. to M.M.C., 5 Oct. 1883, *ibid.*; same to same, 21 Nov. 1883; same to same, 22 Nov. 1883, MFOM Afrique IV 12(b); Mattei to M.A.E., 5 Nov. 1883; M.A.E. to Mattei, 25 Apr. 1884; Mattei to M.A.E., 6 May 1884; same to same, 13 Oct. 1884, AEMD Afrique 86.

The Rue Royale, however, was much more disturbed. The Colonial Department was convinced that Britain was using all measures fair and foul to drive French trade off the Lower Niger and extend her control into the Central Sudan. Under-Secretary Faure accepted the fact that the strength of their rivals and their readiness to use force made it impossible to answer their violence in kind. But he was somewhat less pessimistic about the success of a diplomatic initiative. The only solution to their difficulties, he told Ferry (now Foreign Minister as well as *Président du Conseil*) in February 1884, was to begin negotiations with London on the neutralisation of the Lower Niger and the guarantee of equal treatment for French trade there. Even if the negotiations failed, the French could at least gain the moral satisfaction of having tried to establish the peaceful conditions essential for commercial development.[1]

Faure's proposals aroused no enthusiasm at the Quai d'Orsay. The French were so weak on the Lower Niger that Ferry doubted whether the protection of their immediate interests there warranted the concessions which they would inevitably be asked to make elsewhere in West Africa. In any case, he told the Under-Secretary, it might be wiser to raise the issue at the international conference which would shortly be held to discuss the question of the Congo. By now the Prime Minister was no longer concerned about the future of French trade in the Delta. His attention was fixed on the one area of West Africa where French influence was firmly established: the Western Sudan. 'For the moment', he wrote in a cancelled passage of his draft reply, 'we must concentrate above all on strengthening our ties with the Upper Niger Basin, either from Senegal itself or from the Southern Rivers and Futa Jallon.'[2]

With the approach of the Berlin West Africa Conference, Ferry's priorities hardened. Diplomatically, his position seemed strong. Germany had now joined in the scramble for African territory and appeared eager to work in concert with France against Britain. During conversations with the French Ambassador, Baron de Courcel, in the spring of 1884, Bismarck denounced the Gladstone Government, spoke of a common European interest in Egypt, raised the possibility of German support for France in Morocco and hinted vaguely at his wish to conclude a Franco-German colonial *entente*, directed against England. At

[1] Analyse sommaire, 19 Jan. 1884; Faure to M.A.E., 12 Feb. 1884, MFOM Afrique VI 38(e).
[2] Ferry to M.M.C., 11 June 1884 [Draft], AEMD Afrique 86.

the London Conference in July, the German delegates backed the French in their refusal to allow the diversion of Egyptian debt revenues to meet the costs of defence and administration. In August the Chancellor again assured Courcel of his continued co-operation and promised to support any Egyptian initiative which the French might care to take.[1]

Bismarck was equally forthcoming on West African questions. He supported the French in their opposition to the Anglo-Portuguese Treaty of February 1884 relative to the Congo. In April he suggested an agreement between Germany and France on the rules to be observed by European powers in the unclaimed regions of the globe. In August he called more specifically for a joint statement of their intention to guarantee freedom of trade in all territories which they might occupy on the West African coast, and to reject territorial claims by other Powers which did not satisfy these conditions. In order not to interfere with French commercial policies in Senegal, the scope of the declaration was to be restricted to the southern half of the continent. Once France and Germany had agreed on these points, they were to invite the assent of other nations and summon an international conference to draw up the necessary regulations.[2]

The French response to these overtures was extremely cautious. Both Ferry and his ambassador were profoundly suspicious about Bismarck's intentions. The real purpose of the Chancellor's diplomacy, Courcel maintained, was 'to make us forget Alsace and . . . separate us completely from England'.[3] Neither eventuality was acceptable. The Lost Provinces were unforgettable, and no French Government could risk an open breach with Great Britain; as Courcel told the German Foreign Minister, 'not even the support of Germany and her allies could protect us against all the difficulties which England might create in all parts of the world if she were moved by feelings of real hostility towards us'.[4] Much to Bismarck's surprise, therefore, the French did not take up his offer of support for an Egyptian initiative, and in November Courcel told the Chancellor that France, because of her interests in Egypt, had to remain on good terms with the occupying Power, whoever it might

[1] Courcel [Ambassador, Berlin] to Ferry, 25 Apr. 1884; same to same, 14 May 1884; same to same, 11 Aug. 1884, *D.D.F.* v, nos. 249, 270, 361.

[2] Same to same, 22 Apr. 1884; same to same, 11 Aug. 1884; same to same, 17 Aug. 1884; same to same, 30 Aug. 1884, *ibid.* nos. 244, 361, 372, 383.

[3] Same to same, 27 Dec. 1884, *ibid.* no. 500. See also: same to same, 25 Apr. 1884, *ibid.* no. 247.

[4] Same to same, 17 Aug. 1884, *ibid.* no. 372.

be. 'If it is England', he added, 'we must necessarily reach agreement with her...and she in turn will need our co-operation.'[1]

If Ferry was not prepared to risk an Anglo-French crisis over Egypt, he was still less likely to do so on the Niger. He thought that some advantage might be gained here through diplomatic pressure, and he was certainly willing to make the effort. He had agreed with the Germans upon an internationally controlled system of free trade and navigation for the Congo, and in August he suggested its extension to the Niger as one of the points for discussion at the forthcoming conference. But he was careful not to push things too far. He too could see that Bismarck was merely seeking to embroil him with the British, and he was too astute to play the Chancellor's game. As he told Courcel, he had no intention of turning the Conference into a *machine à guerre* against England.[2] When the Powers assembled at Berlin in November, Ferry authorised the French *chargé d'affaires* to act in concert with the Germans on issues of mutual interest but warned him not to interpret such an *entente* as 'a demonstration directed against other Powers or as the inauguration of a new political system'. If at all possible, any direct challenge to the legitimate claims of a third party was to be avoided. There was no reason for the Prime Minister to take a stronger line. His principal objective was to protect French interests on the Upper Niger, and to this end he was quite ready to sacrifice non-existent claims in the Delta. Certainly, he was not going to give the British any more than he could help, and he ordered the *chargé* not to discuss any questions of territorial sovereignty. But in his instructions to Ambassador Courcel he accepted the possibility that the Niger might be divided into a number of sections 'over which the authorities empowered to ensure freedom of navigation will progressively extend their influence as trade... develops'.[3]

The British on the other hand were much more determined. Britain

---

[1] Same to same, 29 Nov. 1884, *ibid*. no. 471. This does not mean, of course, that the French regarded the Egyptian question as unimportant. Ferry himself considered a permanent British occupation 'the greatest danger' which France could face and saw the attempt to prevent it as 'the overriding consideration' of his foreign policy. But he also recognised the fact that the old Dual Control was 'dead and buried', and he had no ambition to return to the *status quo*. His objective was to make the Egyptian question an international one, and it was primarily for this reason that he disregarded Germany's call for an independent French initiative. See: Ferry to Decrais [Ambassador, Rome], 17 Apr. 1884, *ibid*. no. 239; Courcel to Ferry, 25/26 Aug. 1884; same to same, 30 Aug. 1884, *ibid*. nos. 377, 385.

[2] Ferry, Note, n.d. [22–24 Aug. 1884], *ibid*. no. 376.

[3] Ferry to Raindre, Instructions, 8 Nov. 1884, *ibid*. no. 446; Ferry to Courcel, Instructions, 8 Nov. 1884, AEMD Afrique 109.

too had suffered many reverses in Africa during the previous year. Both France and Germany had been able to stake out claims between Lagos and the Gold Coast. Their combined assault had knocked down the diplomatic barrage which she had tried to erect at the mouth of the Congo. Their opposition had prevented her from settling Egyptian finances to her own satisfaction. And, in an unsuccessful bid to secure German co-operation over Egypt, she had given way both at Angra Pequena and in the Cameroons. But on the Lower Niger she had important trading interests which had to be protected; here she had her political treaties and her commercial monopoly; and here she stood firm. When Lord Granville agreed to send delegates to the conference, he asserted his Government's claims to exclusive influence on the Lower Niger. Britain's legitimately acquired rights, he declared, could not be made a subject for discussion, and there could be no question of international supervision over navigation. In his opening address, Ambassador Malet accepted the principle of free navigation, but he again rejected any proposal for an international control commission.[1]

Ferry made only a token gesture of opposition. He ordered Courcel to press for a commission, but he foresaw the possibility of dropping this demand for the sake of an agreement. In this case the Ambassador was to secure recognition for French control over the navigation of the Upper Niger.[2] Accordingly, Courcel did not oppose the British claims, and the Conference duly recognised the two Powers as guarantors of free navigation on their respective branches of the river. Ferry himself was perfectly satisfied with the outcome. 'I should have no regrets over the triumph of British influence on the Lower Niger', he had told Courcel just one week before, 'because we should then remain in sole control on the Upper Niger.'[3]

But the Prime Minister's colleagues at the Rue Royale were much less pleased. By now the Minister of Marine and his Colonial Under-Secretary were no longer very optimistic about the Sudan's future prospects. Admiral Peyron, Jauréguiberry's former Chief of Naval Staff, was not passionately interested in African affairs. From the start he had his doubts about his Ministry's Niger policies, and the Parlia-

---

[1] Protocol I, 15 Nov. 1884, *Documents Diplomatiques* [*Livre Jaune*], *Affaires du Congo et de l'Afrique Occidentale*, p. 63. For British policies towards the Lower Niger, see: Robinson and Gallagher, *Africa and the Victorians*, pp. 175–80.

[2] Ferry to Courcel, 17 Nov. 1884, AE Allemagne 59; same to same, 30 Nov. 1884 [Copy], MFOM Afrique VI 43.

[3] Protocol IV, 1 Dec. 1884, *Livre Jaune, Affaires du Congo...*, p. 122; Annexe au protocole, 13 Dec. 1884, *ibid.* pp. 167–9, 174–5; Ferry to Courcel, 5 Dec. 1884, AE Allemagne 60.

mentary embarrassments which they caused him had done nothing to restore his confidence.[1] Under-Secretary Faure, on whom much of the responsibility for the direction of colonial policy now devolved, was also becoming disillusioned. As a businessman and the representative of the merchants of Le Havre, he was primarily interested in the commercial development of the colonies, and he could derive little satisfaction from the present state of Sudanese trade.[2] Both men accepted the occupation of the Sudan as an accomplished fact, and neither of them ever contemplated a withdrawal; but by 1884 the Ministry's African priorities were beginning to change. Although Faure was alarmed by the threat of British expansion into the Western Sudan, he now seemed to accept the inevitability of British competition on the Upper Niger.[3] On the other hand, his interest in the prospects for French trade on the Lower Niger was rapidly growing. Throughout the summer, he repeatedly urged the Quai d'Orsay to help the French companies in their unequal battle against Goldie.[4] By November, his earlier proposal to neutralise the Niger had become the keystone of his African policy. When Ferry told him of British claims to exclusive control over the Lower Niger, he strongly urged their rejection and called on the Prime Minister to secure equal treatment for French trade. To obtain this concession he was even ready to abandon the French monopoly over the navigation of the Upper Niger.[5]

Ferry dismissed this suggestion out of hand. He had made up his mind and was not going to change it merely to satisfy the whims of an Under-Secretary for Colonies.[6] As far as he was concerned, the signature

[1] Minute by Peyron on Bourdiaux to M.M.C., 9 Nov. 1883, MFOM Sénégal I 70(a): 'Reste à savoir si, après avoir fait tous les sacrifices que demande le Gouverneur, nous recueillerons le fruit de nos dépenses. J'en doute fort.'

[2] There are no reliable figures on the extent of Sudanese trade during this period. In November 1884, the Ministry of Marine and Colonies gave the total commercial movement for the year as 18,206,000 fr. But this figure was based on estimates made by Combes when arguing the case for a continued military advance. See: *J.O.* 29 Nov. 1884, pp. 6271–3; Combes to Gov. Sen., 1 Nov. 1884, MFOM Sénégal IV 81(c).

[3] Réponse au Rapport de Dureau de Vaulcomte, n.d., MFOM Afrique VI 38(a): '...quels que soient nos droits antérieurs et notre vif désir de nous réserver la route commerciale du Niger, d'ouvrir à notre commerce des débouchés vers le Soudan, nous ne pouvons avoir la prétention d'empêcher les Anglais de se frayer une autre voie vers le même but. C'est là une concurrence inévitable qu'il nous faudra subir comme ailleurs...'

[4] Faure to M.A.E., 12 Feb. 1884; same to same, 9 May 1884; same to same, 11 June 1884, AEMD Afrique 86.

[5] Minute by Faure on Ferry to Courcel, 17 Nov. 1884 [Copy], MFOM Afrique VI 43: 'Mieux vaut abandonner le monopole de la navigation du Haut-Niger en obtenir l'égalité de traitement sur le Bas-Fleuve.' Faure to Ferry, 12 Dec. 1884, AEMD Afrique 109.

[6] Minutes by Ferry on Faure to Ferry, 12 Dec. 1884: On neutralisation: 'Mais ce n'est pas dans le programme de la conférence.' On the abandonment of the French monopoly:

of the Berlin Act put an end to the matter. And he had logic as well as seniority on his side. The position on the Upper Niger may not have been all one could have desired, but it was at least based on a strong military presence and was relatively immune from a serious foreign challenge. The French had never been able to establish themselves firmly on the Lower Niger, and once the companies had sold out they had no interests left to protect. But the Colonial Department, incensed by Ferry's off-hand treatment, was not in a mood to appreciate the logic of the situation or to accept its responsibility for Sudanese affairs gracefully.

THE UPPER SENEGAL CRISIS OF 1885–6

Ferry's decision to concentrate upon the development of the Upper Niger could not have come at a more inopportune time for the Ministry of Marine. Security was deteriorating; plans for sending a gunboat to Timbuktu were coming unstuck; Sudanese finances were in a shambles; and there was cause for alarm over the growth of Parliamentary hostility to the whole Sudanese enterprise. Then at the end of March, a month after the signature of the Berlin Act, the Ferry Government itself was destroyed by the storm over the retreat from Lang-Son. In the confusion which followed, the whole cause of colonial expansion was discredited. Heavy Opportunist losses and Right-wing victories at the 1885 elections gave the new Chamber a distinctly anti-colonialist complexion. When Parliament reassembled, the combined opposition of the Right and the Extreme Left almost forced through the liquidation of the Tonkin expedition.

Sudanese credits had already been similarly hit. In February, the Budget Commission refused to report on the Supplementary Estimates and demanded an accurate breakdown of the increased cost, something which neither the Under-Secretary nor the head of the Upper Senegal Bureau was able to supply. The Commission eventually approved the supplementary credit of 1,100,000 fr. because it was urgent, but it publicly condemned the Ministry's book-keeping methods as criminally negligent.[1] After a violent debate, the Chamber also gave its assent; but in

'Mais c'est aussi en vertu des situations...analogue[s] que nous avons consenti à ce que l'Angleterre exerçât sur le Bas-Niger les droits qui nous sont reconnus sur le Haut-Niger.'
[1] Procès-Verbaux de la Commission du Budget, séance du 21 mars; séance du 23 mars 1885, AN C3305, pp. 718–24, 726–7; de Lanessan, Rapport, 2 Apr. 1885, *J.O. Doc. Parl. Chambre*, no. 3684, pp. 447–8; 'Votre commission exprime le regret que l'administration des colonies n'ait pas établi ses budgets avec la rigueur et la clarté nécessaires au contrôle

the heat of the argument the new Under-Secretary, Armand Rousseau, was forced to admit that his Department no longer exercised effective control over Sudanese expenditure. Paris, he exclaimed, had given the Sudanese authorities the strictest possible instructions to keep expenses down; but, when funds ran short anyway, it could hardly tell them: 'We can't give you any more; go and live off the land.'[1]

Hoping to avoid further trouble, the Ministry kept its estimates for 1886 artificially low, but the Budget Commission quickly saw through the manœuvre and again condemned the Ministry's deplorable attempts to mislead the Chamber. Only the rush of business before the Dissolution enabled the Sudan credit to pass without opposition.[2] In a final attempt to save himself further embarrassment, the Minister of Marine then submitted a *crédit de liquidation* of 1,480,000 fr. This sum, he claimed, would be enough for him to pay off all outstanding debts and regularise the Sudan's financial position. The Upper Senegal Bureau could then be wound up, the special budgetary Chapter for Sudanese credits abolished, and future costs distributed among the relevant Chapters of the regular Colonial Budget. But the Commission again refused to co-operate until it had been given more information, and its report was not presented until August. Thus the Bill could not be debated before the Dissolution and had to be resubmitted to a potentially much more hostile Chamber in November.[3]

Once more, the Sudan's financial difficulties made further expansion impossible. In any case, the Radically orientated Brisson Ministry which replaced Ferry's Government after Lang-Son was unlikely to adopt an energetic Sudanese policy. Although Brisson fought hard to save Tonkin, he was at best a lukewarm partisan of African expansion. His Minister of Marine, Admiral Galiber, had troubles enough over his

---

des dépenses; elle se plaint de ce que le Parlement n'ait pas été suffisamment renseigné sur les dépenses réelles occasionnées par l'occupation du Haut-Sénégal, et elle exprime la crainte justifiée que la comptabilité de ces dépenses n'ait pas été tenue avec le soin qu'exigent nos lois financières et les intérêts du pays.'

[1] *J.O. Déb. Parl. Chambre*, séance du 28 mai 1885, pp. 931–6. A demand for a full investigation was defeated by 269 votes to 138, and the supplementary credit approved by 268 votes to 81.

[2] Projet de Loi, 23 Mar. 1885, *J.O. Doc. Parl. Chambre*, no. 3635; de Lanessan, Rapport, 22 June 1885, *ibid.* no. 3887, pp. 987, 1000; *J.O. Déb. Parl. Chambre*, séance du 9 juillet 1885, p. 1385. In the rush to finish the Budget debate before the dissolution of Parliament, the Chamber approved the credits without discussion.

[3] Projet de Loi, 29 June 1885, *J.O. Doc. Parl. Chambre*, no. 3920, pp. 1074–5; Procès-Verbaux de la Commission du Budget, séance du 3 août 1885, AN C3306, pp. 422–4; de Lanessan, Rapport, 4 Aug. 1885, *J.O. Doc. Parl. Chambre*, no. 4087, p. 1470. Parliament was dissolved two days later on the 6th.

naval Estimates.[1] Under-Secretary Rousseau was more resolute, but he lost his seat at the elections. Nobody was appointed to replace him, and for the next three months the Colonial Department was again demoted to the status of a Directorate.[2] In the Sudan, Galiber's sole preoccupation was 'to maintain the existing position *within the limits of the Budget*'. He refused to take any long-term decisions until the new Parliament had made its views on the Sudan clear. The objectives of the next campaign were again limited to provisioning and maintenance. There were to be no new conquests, no new protectorates, no new forts. Under no circumstances was the expeditionary column to cross the Niger.[3]

As always, the local authorities advocated more robust policies. According to Governor Seignac, the only way to make the Sudan commercially profitable was to enforce law and order and provide effective protection for those who accepted French rule. When the Ministry rejected his requests for new forts and troop reinforcements, he refused to accept responsibility for the success of the campaign.[4] The new *Commandant-Supérieur*, Lieutenant-Colonel Frey, called even more vigorously for action. Although he had not volunteered for Sudanese service, he was determined to make the most of his posting. Even before he left France, he issued dire warnings about the danger of the Samorian advance to French security, requested permission to drive the *sofas* back across the Niger, and asked for at least a thousand men with which to do the job. After his arrival, he renewed his appeals for increased forces and refused to hold himself responsible for the consequences if his demands were not met.[5]

Having learned its lesson from Combes, the Government rejected his requests and ordered him to keep strictly to his instructions.[6] But

---

[1] Procès-Verbaux de la Commission du Budget, séance du 20 mai 1885, AN C3306, p. 143: 'M. le Rapporteur [Gerville-Réache] a pu constater que l'état actuel de notre marine comparé aux marines étrangères présente...une regrettable infériorité. D'après lui, on serait encore aux anciens errements, et le Département de la Marine ne ferait pas d'efforts suffisants dans le sens du progrès.'

[2] Berge, *op. cit.* pp. 37–8. The Director of Colonies was a M. Portier. For Rousseau's attitude on Sudanese policy see: H. Frey, *Campagne dans le Haut-Sénégal et le Haut-Niger 1885–86* (Paris, 1888), pp. 41, 49, and below: p. 134.

[3] M.M.C. to Gov. Sen., 4 July 1885, MFOM Sénégal I 73(b); same to same, Instructions, 4 Oct. 1885, MFOM Sénégal IV 84(a).

[4] Seignac to M.M.C., 28 May 1885; same to same, 28 July 1885, MFOM Sénégal I 73(a); same to same, 29 Oct. 1885, MFOM Sénégal I 99(b), Correspondance Générale.

[5] Frey to Gov. Sen., 10 Sept. 1885; same to same, 25 Nov. 1885; same to same, 12 Dec. 1885; same to same, 14 Dec. 1885; same to same, 24 Dec. 1885, MFOM Sénégal IV 84(b).

[6] Under-Secretary to Gov. Sen., n.d. [1 Feb. 1886?], MFOM Sénégal I 73(b).

the critical situation in the Sudan could not be ignored. Samori's incursion into the Bakhoy Valley posed an intolerable threat to French security, and even Paris accepted the need to drive his forces out.[1] Accordingly, Frey ordered his *commandants de poste* to intercept all caravans bound for the *imam* and organised a two-pronged attack on the *sofa* headquarters at Galé. The *sofas* retreated but were surprised and routed on 17 January 1886. Elated by his easy victory, Frey immediately asked for permission to pursue them across the Niger and deal Samori's prestige a fatal blow.[2]

Yet the Commander soon changed his mind. On 4 February he announced the suspension of all military operations and the arrival of an ambassador from Samori with an offer to make peace and retire across the Niger. Frey was confident that his recent victory had finally persuaded the *imam* to give up his struggle against the French, and he asked for permission to negotiate the terms of a cease-fire.[3] Permission was granted, and in March an embassy led by Captain Tournier met Samori at Keniéba-Koura. Despite strong pressure from anti-French elements in his entourage, Samori agreed to withdraw from the left bank of the Niger and even declared himself ready to accept a nominal French protectorate; but he refused to abandon all his claims, and in the end Tournier had to recognise his nominal authority over the provinces of Buré and Kangaba. The Ambassador was most dissatisfied with the arrangement, but he felt obliged to accept it because he had been ordered to conclude his negotiations as quickly as possible.[4]

Frey had good reason to make a hasty peace on his eastern frontier, for he had received alarming reports about the outbreak of a widespread rebellion on the Upper Senegal. The rebel leader, *al-hajj* Mahmadu Lamine, was a former disciple of Umar and an unsuccessful claimant to his temporal legacy. After his release from imprisonment in Segu, he had offered to help the French against Ahmadu, but his overtures were curtly rejected. Mahmadu Lamine then embarked upon an independent career as a religious leader, using the prestige which he had acquired from the pilgrimage to rally support among the populations of the Upper Senegal. Frey realised the danger but was unable to deal with it

[1] M.M.C. to Gov. Sen., 4 Aug. 1885, MFOM Sénégal IV 84 (*bis*).
[2] Seignac to M.M.C., 12 Jan. 1886, MFOM Sénégal I 73 (a); Frey to Gov. Sen., 22 Jan. 1886, MFOM Sénégal IV 84 (b).
[3] Same to same, 4 Feb. 1884, *ibid.* In November 1885, Samori had already written to the Commandant of Niagassola asking for peace. Samori to Péroz, November 1885, MFOM Sénégal IV 85 (b).
[4] Tournier, Rapport, 6 July 1886, *ibid.*

before the start of his campaign against Samori, and the Médine garrison proved completely unable to curb the *marabout*'s rising influence. With an ease that underlined the ineffectiveness of French control along the Senegal, Mahmadu Lamine drove the aged Umar Penda, Bubakar Saada's brother and successor, out of Bondu and established his influence over the province of Guoy as well. By February he was burning villages in the vicinity of Bakel.[1] As soon as Frey learned of these developments, he sent a small expeditionary column to quell the uprising; but his main force could not return to Kayes until the beginning of April. In the meantime, a company of *tirailleurs* had been ambushed and driven back to Bakel with heavy casualties and the loss of its cannon. Mahmadu Lamine at once cut the telegraph lines and besieged the fort itself. His attacks were beaten off, and Frey was later able to drive him south to the Gambian border. But the Commander's victory was not decisive, and the rainy season gave Mahmadu Lamine time to recoup much of his strength.[2] To make matters worse, Frey then led a punitive expedition through Guidimaka in reprisal for the assistance which the province had given to the rebels, and he thus provoked a potentially more serious crisis with Ahmadu.

Relations with the Sultan had also been deteriorating over the previous year. Combes's attack on Samori had averted the immediate threat of a confrontation, and the Ministry's anxiety to avoid complications gave the empire a further reprieve. By 1885 Paris was convinced that an alliance with Ahmadu against Samori was both feasible and desirable, and it ordered Frey to negotiate a new treaty on these terms.[3] But Paris did not intend the agreement to be anything more than temporary; it was willing to negotiate only because it lacked the means to take more decisive measures. 'If we had the money to pay for a military campaign', wrote Under-Secretary Rousseau in June 1885, 'it would be puerile to treat with Ahmadu.' The Ministry's policy was still to break up the Tokolor empire by promoting dissension within its ranks.[4] As always, the military commanders were anxious to hasten the

---

[1] Gov. Sen. to M.M.C., 12 Dec. 1885, MFOM Sénégal I 73 (a); Frey to Gov. Sen., 7 Feb. 1886; same to same, 28 Feb. 1886, MFOM Sénégal IV 84 (b). For Mahmadu Lamine's career, see: Frey, *op. cit.* pp. 252 ff.; Brière to M.M.C., 1 Aug. 1879, MFOM Sénégal I 63 (a).

[2] Gov. Sen. to M.M.C., 14 Mar. 1886, MFOM Sénégal I 73 (a); Frey, Rapport, 22 June 1886, MFOM Sénégal IV 85 (a).

[3] M.M.C. to Gov. Sen., Instructions, 4 Oct. 1885, MFOM Sénégal IV 84 (a); same to same, 4 Nov. 1885, MFOM Sénégal I 73 (b).

[4] Minute by Rousseau on Seignac to M.M.C., 28 May 1885, MFOM Sénégal I 73 (a); M.M.C. to Seignac, 4 July 1885, MFOM Sénégal I 73 (b): 'Quant [à Ahmadu], étant

process of disruption. Before Combes left the Sudan, he warned of the imminent danger of a Tokolor attack and called for military action to avert it. By January Frey was convinced that war could break out any day, and he was enchanted by the prospect. His campaign in Guidimaka was deliberately designed to precipitate a conflict, and in May he urged the Ministry to occupy southern Kaarta, hoping to provoke Ahmadu into a premature attack.[1]

The Sultan on the other hand remained anxious to avoid a clash. As in the past, the problem of internal unrest was his major preoccupation. In 1884, the need to deal with the rebellion in Beledugu had forced him to transfer his military headquarters to Nyamina. When he moved to Nioro at the end of the year, it was not to menace the French but to overthrow his brother Muntaga and reassert his authority over Kaarta. His siege of the city lasted for six months and left him too weak to force his way back through Beledugu, for the French had cut off his reinforcements from Futa and had again incited rebellion among the Bambaras. When the gunboat returned to Bamako in November 1885, Delanneau reported that Segu was also on the point of revolt.[2] Thus Ahmadu had good reason not to complicate matters with the French. He knew that their gunboat could pose a serious threat to Segu, and when Combes asked him to help it on its proposed journey to Timbuktu, he angrily refused. But he did not specifically prohibit the voyage, and he made no attempt to interfere with it. On its first trip the *Niger* reached Diafarabé, well beyond the frontier of Ahmadu's empire, and returned to Bamako without encountering any opposition.[3]

By the end of 1885, however, the Sultan's attitude was also beginning to harden. During the *Niger*'s voyage, Delanneau persuaded Nyamina to sign a treaty with the French and expel its Tokolor garrison.[4] In

donné son caractère rusé et trompeux, nous aurions bien des chances de faire un marché de dupes avec lui. Nous avons d'ailleurs tant d'intérêt sous tous les rapports de voir s'écrouler ce qui reste de son autorité qu'il serait déraisonnable de la soutenir…Le meilleur moyen de ruiner la puissance des Toucouleurs [consiste] à la diviser…'

[1] Combes, Rapport…1884–5, n.d., Cap. VII, MFOM Sénégal IV 81(b); Gov. Sen. to M.M.C., 14 Jan 1886; same to same, 14 Feb. 1886, MFOM Sénégal I 73(a); Frey to Gov. Sen., 10 May 1886, MFOM Sénégal IV 84(b).

[2] Delanneau to Frey, 30 Nov. 1885, MFOM Sénégal IV 84(c). See also: Combes to Gov. Sen., 1 Apr. 1885, MFOM Sénégal IV 81(c); Gov. Sen. to M.M.C. 11 Apr. 1885, MFOM Sénégal I 73(a).

[3] Ahmadu to Combes, rec'd. 22 Sept. 1884, MFOM Sénégal IV 82(a); Delanneau, Rapport complémentaire, n.d., *ibid.*

[4] Houry [*Commandant-Supérieur par intérim*] to Gov. Sen., 24 Sept. 1885, MFOM Sénégal IV 84(b). Determined not to prejudice chances of an agreement with Ahmadu, however, the Ministry of Marine refused to ratify the treaty.

retaliation, Ahmadu imposed another trade ban and sent troops to occupy the caravan routes. According to the Senegalese authorities, he also tried to conclude anti-French alliances with Abdul-Bubakar in Futa and Lat Dyor of Cayor. Although he was still prepared to negotiate with the French as well, he now demanded the evacuation of all forts between Bafoulabé and the Niger as the precondition for any agreement.[1] After Frey's expedition through Guidimaka, he broke off the talks completely and tightened his restrictions on trade. Frey himself was all for re-opening the caravan routes by force, and for a time the outbreak of hostilities seemed imminent. In his final report, the Commander urged Paris to declare war at the start of the next campaign and confidently predicted that Ahmadu would be too weak to put up much of a resistance.[2]

His proposal was curtly rejected. By now the Ministry was profoundly disillusioned by the whole enterprise. When Galiber learned of Combes's escapades in August 1885, he spoke gloomily of 'a setback whose consequences will be very difficult to overcome'.[3] In December Captain Monteil, fresh from a survey of the Bafoulabé–Bamako route, underlined the blunder which had been committed by subordinating railway-construction to the military advance. All their difficulties, he claimed, stemmed from the absence of an efficient system of communications and the consequent impossibility of maintaining security along an over-extended line of forts. Until communications were improved, the Sudan could never become a profitable field for private enterprise, and the total cost of its occupation would continue to fall on the State. Inspector Legros accepted the validity of these criticisms.[4] Pérard, the head of the Upper Senegal Bureau, was alarmed by the Sudan's continued political instability; unless the position could be consolidated, he warned, it might be wiser to withdraw from the Sudan altogether and save the 4,000,000 fr. a year which it cost. By April 1886 even the new

[1] Gov. Sen. to M.M.C., 29 Nov. 1885; same to same, 29 Dec. 1885, MFOM Sénégal I 73 (a); Frey to Gov. Sen., 12 Dec. 1885; same to same, 14 Dec. 1885, MFOM Sénégal IV 84 (b).
[2] Gov. Sen. to M.M.C., 28 June 1886, MFOM Sénégal I 74 (b); Frey, Rapport, 22 June 1886, MFOM Sénégal IV 85 (a).
[3] M.M.C. to Gov. Sen., 4 Aug. 1885, MFOM Sénégal I 73 (b).
[4] Monteil, Rapport, 2 Dec. 1885, MFOM Missions 109, Monteil 1884–5; Legros, Note pour la direction des colonies, 28 Jan. 1886, MFOM Sénégal IV 83. To solve the transportation problem, Monteil strongly advocated the construction of a monorail between Bafoulabé and Bamako. But Legros rejected this far-fetched scheme as too costly and vulnerable, and urged the construction of a hard-surface road instead.

Minister of Marine, Admiral Aube, was talking of 'a crisis whose end is not yet in sight'.[1]

The traditional bases of French policy towards the Muslim states of the Western Sudan also came under critical examination. Alliances with the animists, Monteil pointed out, alienated the only powers in the Sudan capable of maintaining the political stability on which commercial development was bound to rest. Captain Rodier of the Minister's military staff condemned the excessive reliance on military expeditions, urged the maintenance of friendly relations with Ahmadu and Samori, and even suggested a renegotiation of the Nango treaty on the basis of its Arab text.[2] The results of Frey's campaign confirmed the Ministry's belief that diplomacy was preferable to war. 'We must give up these costly and useless offensive campaigns as quickly as possible', wrote Admiral Aube in May 1886; it was not the objective of French policy to establish undisputed mastery over a desert, he warned the new Governor of Senegal.[3] Peace, prudence and economy were again to be the watchwords. There were to be no further attempts at territorial expansion, no more military campaigns, and no conflicts with the Muslims.

The same strictures applied to the extension of French influence along the Niger. Disillusioned by the total failure of the attempt to reach Timbuktu, Admiral Galiber had already ordered the gunboat to to be dismantled and shipped back to France; not even news of its successful journey beyond Segu persuaded him to change his mind.[4] Only the arrival of Admiral Aube, Faidherbe's brother-in-law, saved the *Niger* from immediate destruction. In response to reports of growing tension with Ahmadu, to the urgent entreaties of Seignac and Frey, and possibly to the pressure of Faidherbe himself, he allowed its dismantling to be postponed.[5] Nevertheless, the gunboat's movements were severely restricted, and in June Aube personally rejected Frey's request for permission to send it to Nyamina.[6]

[1] Pérard, Note pour le sous-secrétaire, April 1886, MFOM Sénégal IV 84(a); M.M.C. to Gov. Sen., Instructions, 5 Apr. 1886, MFOM Sénégal I 74(a).
[2] Rodier, Note, March 1886, MFOM Sénégal IV 86.
[3] Minute by Aube on Gov. Sen. to M.M.C., 14 May 1886, MFOM Sénégal IV 74(b); M.M.C. to Gov. Sen., Instructions, 5 Apr. 1886, MFOM Sénégal I 74(a).
[4] M.M.C. to Gov. Sen., Instructions, 4 Oct. 1885, MFOM Sénégal IV 84(a); same to same, 1 Dec. 1885, MFOM Sénégal I 73(b).
[5] Gov. Sen. to M.M.C., 14 Jan. 1886, with minute by Aube, MFOM Sénégal I 73(a); de Montholon, Note, 5 Jan. 1886, AEMD Afrique 85, reporting Faidherbe's opinion that any decision to dismantle the gunboat would be disastrous.
[6] Minute by Aube on Frey to Gov. Sen., 28 May 1886, MFOM Sénégal IV 84(b).

The Problems of Occupation, 1883–6

It was the Quai d'Orsay not the Rue Royale which rescued Sudanese policy from complete disintegration. In the critical months after Lang-Son Charles de Freycinet, first as Brisson's Foreign Minister and then as *Président du Conseil*, was the Sudan's most influential and effective champion. Of all French statesmen he was the most firmly committed to the creation of a Sudanese empire, and he at least remained unshakeably convinced that the future of France in Africa lay on the Upper Niger. His priorities were those of Ferry. He had no desire to renew the French challenge on the Lower Niger, and he flatly rejected all appeals for any new initiatives there. Plans for an expedition from Porto Novo into the Middle Niger were just as curtly dismissed, for the French possessions on the Slave Coast were considered much too weak to provide a suitable base.[1] Like Ferry, Freycinet thought it more important to concentrate on the development of French influence in the Western Sudan. But his efforts were blocked at every turn by the sullen inertia and petty obstructionism of the Ministry of Marine.

The declaration of a British protectorate over the 'Niger Districts' in June 1885 began the controversy. Anxious not to be outdone, Freycinet immediately broached the possibility of declaring a French protectorate over the Upper Niger; but the Ministry of Marine refused to co-operate. The Colonial Department had never accepted Ferry's decision to abandon the Lower Niger; despite the signature of the Berlin Act, it was still determined to prevent the establishment of monopoly British control, and it again urged the Foreign Minister to secure the neutralisation of the river while there was still time.[2] At that, its reply was not transmitted, and for the next two months the Department kept completely silent on the question. Only in September did Rousseau condescend to answer the Quai d'Orsay's urgent appeals for a prompt decision. Reluctantly accepting the British protectorate as a *fait accompli*, he now agreed to the declaration of a French protectorate over the Upper Niger as far as Burrum.[3]

[1] Minute by Freycinet on Rousseau to M.A.E., 16 Sept. 1885, AEMD Afrique 85; Viard to M.A.E., 12 Feb. 1886; same to same, 26 Mar. 1886, *ibid.*; Note, 15 Apr. 1886, AEMD Afrique 86. Viard was reluctantly given 20,000 fr. for a mission towards the Middle Niger and Sokoto; but the Quai d'Orsay's approval was quickly withdrawn when the explorer failed to raise the 80,000 fr. which he still required.

[2] M.A.E. to M.M.C., 25 June 1885, AEMD Afrique 86; Goldscheider, Note, 17 July 1885; Colonial Department to M.A.E., July 1885 [Draft], MFOM Afrique IV 12(b). The argument was based on the fact that the Berlin Act had not yet been ratified by Parliament.

[3] M.A.E. to M.M.C., 27 July 1885; same to same, 13 Aug. 1885; Rousseau to M.A.E., *ibid.*

Freycinet was understandably upset by the delay; but he could at least proceed with his plans, and he now asked for more information about the exact state of French influence in the provinces of Buré and Kangaba. Alarmed by reports of a British advance into the Upper Niger and of attempts by Sierra Leone to establish relations with Samori, the Foreign Minister repeatedly called for a prompt reply.[1] But his desperate appeals were again ignored; in the aftermath of the retreat from Nafadié, nobody at the Rue Royale knew what the position on the Niger was; not even the relevant treaties could be found.[2] It was December before Admiral Galiber finally informed the Quai d'Orsay that the situation in Buré was again well in hand and that Frey had been ordered to reassert French authority over the territories lost to Samori at the end of the last campaign. The Minister of Marine made no apology for the delay; instead he reminded his colleague that the need for a declaration of French rights would never have arisen if his Department's policy towards the Lower Niger had been approved in the first place.[3]

Ignoring the remark, the Quai d'Orsay drafted a declaration of protectorate over the Upper Niger basin as far as Macina, and Freycinet asked the Colonial Department to establish French influence, if only temporarily, over the Right Bank.[4] Once more, however, the Rue Royale balked. Aube's Under-Secretary for Colonies, Amédée de La Porte, objected to the proposed wording as too restrictive—mention of Macina could be interpreted as a renunciation of claims to Timbuktu—and asked for the limits of the protectorate to be redefined as the Algerian Sudan in the north and the states of Samori in the south. But he was not prepared to back these claims on the ground, and he adamantly refused to permit any show of force across the Niger.[5] Although Freycinet was not pleased, he was somewhat placated by news that Samori had signed a treaty, and in May his officials drew up a draft protectorate over the vast quadrilateral bounded by Cape Blanc, the frontiers of Gwandu, Kong and the sea. The Prime Minister

---

[1] M.A.E. to M.M.C., 14 Oct. 1885; same to same, 31 Oct. 1885; same to same, 10 Nov. 1885; same to same, 9 Dec. 1885, *ibid.*

[2] Note pour le chef du service du Haut-Fleuve, 22 Oct. 1885, *ibid.*

[3] M.M.C. to M.A.E., 17 Dec. 1885, AEMD Afrique 86.

[4] Note, 23 Dec. 1885, *ibid.*; Freycinet to M.M.C., 9 Feb. 1886, MFOM Sénégal IV 84(a). The terms of the proposed declaration were: 'Le protectorat français comprend, notamment, les pays qui s'étendent, entre le Bakhounou au Nord, la rivière Tankisso au Sud, le Fouladougou à l'Ouest, et la limite du Macina à l'Est.'

[5] De La Porte to M.A.E., 1 Mar. 1886, AEMD Afrique 122.

next asked for copies of all treaties which could support this extensive claim.[1]

He should have known better. Despite the Colonial Department's increasingly peremptory demands, the Senegalese administration remained as lax as ever in its transmission of diplomatic documents; in August 1886 de La Porte was still calling for the originals of the 1860 convention with Umar and the Mage treaty.[2] Because of the disruption of communications along the Senegal, the forwarding of the recent treaty with Samori was also delayed, and without it the Colonial Department refused to reply. By September the Quai d'Orsay was reduced to making private appeals for information, because 'the silence ...which has so far met our *innumerable* demands...does not encourage us to use official channels'.[3] Worse still, when de La Porte finally did send a copy of the Samori treaty, he recommended its rejection. The recognition of the *imam*'s nominal claims to the Left Bank, he claimed, robbed the arrangement of much of its value; since the Senegalese authorities were confident that Samori would accept a French protectorate during the coming campaign, he thought it wiser to delay ratification; the publication of the agreement as it stood would merely prompt the British to establish a protectorate of their own.[4]

This was the final exasperation. Freycinet, usually calm and self-controlled, could merely exclaim: '*Parbleu!*' His *direction politique* banished the offending document to its archives before preparing a reply, a mistake which it only discovered two months later.[5] Without the Samori treaty the Quai d'Orsay was forced to modify its proposed notification drastically. When Britain asked for a statement about the extent of French claims on the Upper Niger, it could do no more than draft a vague declaration about the rights of both Powers as recognised at Berlin, and announce that Colonel Frey had reached agreement with

[1] *Ibid.*, minute by Freycinet: 'C'est renoncer expressément à la rive droite du Niger'; M.M.C. to M.A.E., 13 May 1886; M.A.E. to M.M.C., 1 June 1886, MFOM Sénégal IV 84 (d); Projet de Notification, 27 May 1886; M.A.E. to M.M.C., 22 June 1886, AEMD Afrique 122.
[2] De La Porte to Gov. Sen., 24 July 1886; same to same, 4 Aug. 1886, MFOM Sénégal I 74 (c). See also: M.M.C. to Gov. Sen., 29 Nov. 1884, MFOM Sénégal I 72 (b).
[3] Nisard to Révoil [*chef de cabinet du sous-secrétaire*], 1 Sept. 1886, AEMD Afrique 85.
[4] De La Porte to M.A.E., 14 Sept. 1886, AEMD Afrique 122. De La Porte's conclusions were based on a note drafted by Desbordes who had recently returned to the Colonial Department. Desbordes condemned the treaty as 'absolutely disastrous' and warned that French authority over the left bank of the Niger, so shamefully surrendered, would have to be re-established during the next campaign. Desbordes, Notes..., 10 Sept. 1886, MFOM Sénégal IV 87 (d).
[5] Minute by Freycinet on de La Porte to M.A.E., 14 Sept. 1886; Minutes by the *direction politique* on same to same, 6 Nov. 1886, AEMD Afrique 122.

Samori on a treaty whose detailed terms had yet to be settled. The Colonial Department accepted this draft as sufficiently imprecise not to reveal the true extent of French weakness on the right bank of the Niger, and on 13 October, fifteen months after his original suggestion, Freycinet officially notified the Powers.[1] The protectorate which he had once hoped to declare over the whole of the Western Sudan had now been reduced to a nebulous claim of influence over both banks of the Niger. Even this was based largely on bluff and on the hope that the next treaty with Samori would prove more successful than the last.

But at least a protectorate had been declared, and with it the diplomatic fate of the Sudan was settled. Although the Colonial Department never became fully reconciled to the loss of French influence in the Niger Delta, it too had to accept its inevitability. French priorities in West Africa were no longer in doubt. Even in Parliament the future of the Sudan was assured. Despite its severe condemnations of the Ministry's financial mismanagement, the Budget Commission never questioned the permanent character of military occupation. For all their hostility, the Sudan's critics in the Chamber never raised an effective cry for its evacuation. The Commission's delaying tactics over the *crédit de liquidation* were themselves a blessing in disguise. In December 1885 the new Parliament, anxious to clear up the backlog of Bills left over from the previous session, approved the credit without a discussion or a division.[2] Thereafter, the Sudan question lapsed into a decent obscurity where it was to remain for the next six years.

There were glimmers of hope in the colony as well. Although Ahmadu had moved on to the flank of the Kayes–Bamako line, he was too weak to cause the French any trouble, and the Guidimaka crisis soon passed. Samori too had agreed to withdraw his troops from French territory and seemed willing to co-operate. Only the activities of Mahmadu Lamine presented an immediate threat to French security, and he was the least formidable of the three. Even the decline in the quality of military leadership which had contributed so much to the deterioration of French influence since the departure of Desbordes was not irreparable. Frey, of course, was not reappointed. Instead, the Ministry of Marine chose Lieutenant-Colonel Joseph Gallieni, and its choice was soon proved right.

---

[1] Projet de Notification [Draft], 1 Oct. 1886; de La Porte to M.A.E., 5 Oct. 1886; Projet de Notification (bonne minute), 13 Oct. 1886, *ibid.*

[2] *J.O. Déb. Parl. Chambre*, séance du 29 décembre 1885, p. 408. The credits were rushed through the Senate on the same day. *Ibid. Sénat*, séance du 29 décembre 1885, p. 1414.

6

The Consolidation of the Sudan and the New African Policy

By the autumn of 1886 the Sudan's prospects were beginning to show definite signs of improvement. The anti-colonialist tide of the previous year had ebbed, and Sudanese credits were no longer the subject for acrimonious debate. The new *rapporteur* for the Colonial Budget, the Algerian Deputy Eugène Etienne, was a strong advocate of African expansion, and he gladly approved the Ministry's Estimates for 1887. The Chamber seemed equally well disposed, and it accepted the *rapporteur*'s recommendation to proceed with the construction of the Railway using the materials already available in the Sudan.[1]

After the declaration of the Upper Niger protectorate, the Government also adopted a more resolute approach to the Sudanese problem. Although Freycinet no longer concerned himself directly with Sudanese affairs, he continued to urge his colleagues at the Rue Royale to concentrate on the extension of French influence along the Upper Niger.[2] Admiral Aube himself was temperamentally inclined to take the offensive, and for all his pessimism about the Sudan he was unwilling to remain entirely on the defensive there. 'If even in Europe force is the only sanction for our rights [and] for the treaties which enshrine them', he minuted on one of the Prime Minister's letters,

it is evident that in the territories where we wish to establish our influence—it is force—a force *relatively* very weak in appearance—but sufficient because of its *continuity*—its *constancy*—which alone can render effective the *rights* which we expect to secure from our treaties.[3]

[1] Etienne, Rapport, 28 Oct. 1886, *J.O. Doc. Parl. Chambre*, no. 1201, pp. 1033-5; *J.O. Déb. Parl. Chambre*, séance du 22 janvier 1887, p. 117.
[2] Freycinet to M.M.C., 9 Nov. 1886, MFOM Sénégal IV 88(c); same to same, 6 Dec. 1886, MFOM Sénégal IV 87(a).
[3] Minute by Aube on Freycinet to M.M.C., 22 June 1886, MFOM Sénégal IV 84(a). Aube was the leader of the *Jeune Ecole* of naval strategists whose conception of the *guerre de course* dominated French naval thinking in the 1880s.

The Consolidation of the Sudan and the New African Policy

Even the cautious de La Porte recognised the need for a more determined effort at consolidation. Equally significant changes were taking place in the lower echelons of the Colonial Department. Desbordes had left Paris in 1884 to serve as General Brière's artillery commander in Indochina, and there the two men had cemented the close personal relationship which they had first formed in the Sudan.[1] By 1886 both had returned to Paris, the senior to become Deputy Inspector-General of the *infanterie de marine* and the junior, now promoted to the rank of Brigadier-General, to resume his post as the Colonial Department's Sudanese expert. From these key positions they quickly made their influence felt. Together with Faidherbe, they secured the command of the next campaign for Brière's former subordinate, Joseph Gallieni.[2] Desbordes even drafted the new Commander's instructions.

As the Brigadier appreciated, the most urgent task was to repair the damage which had been caused over the past two years. Frey's campaign in particular had left the Sudan in a sorry state. His expeditions against Samori and Mahmadu Lamine had forced him to neglect the maintenance of his lines of communication and had prevented him from provisioning the forts adequately. His devastation of Guidimaka had cut off a valuable source of supply for the expeditionary column, and his failure to crush the rebellion of Mahmadu Lamine left the most pressing problem of security unsolved. French influence along the Upper Senegal had to be restored, if necessary by force; but Desbordes advised against any further military action. It was more important, he claimed, to supply and repair the forts, and it was essential not to place an additional strain on the transportation services. The new *Commandant-Supérieur* would have to follow 'an astute and prudent policy, exempt from any weakness but absolutely free from any aggressive intent'. Only when communications had been improved could further ex-

---

[1] E.g. Brière to Peyron, 19 Mar. 1885 [typed copy], Faure Papers. After the retreat from Lang-Son, for whose disproportionate political consequences his own exaggerated reports about its military significance were largely responsible, Brière appointed Desbordes to replace Colonel Herbinger, the officer who ordered the retreat, and to conduct the official investigation. Desbordes loyally absolved his chief of all responsibility and placed the entire blame on the unfortunate Herbinger, whom he accused of being drunk during the action. The subsequent court-martial, however, acquitted Herbinger of all charges. See: Brière to Minister of War, 28 Mar. 1885, *D.D.F.* v, no. 367; A. Brébion (ed.), *Dictionnaire de bio-bibliographie générale, ancienne et moderne, de l'Indochine française* (Paris, 1935), p. 192. I am grateful for this reference to M. François Berge.

[2] Gallieni to Etienne, 16 Jan. 1888, BN n.a.fr. 24327, Etienne Papers; Gallieni to Archinard, 5 Aug. 1888, Archinard Papers.

pansion be contemplated.[1] Under-Secretary de La Porte, ready now to shoulder his responsibilities, accepted Desbordes's proposals. 'Our Sudanese policy', he told Gallieni in his instructions,

must be firm, prudent and peaceful. Firm because the natives would grow bolder if we were weak..., prudent because a military setback might provoke a general rebellion against us, peaceful because...it is time to think of the organisation and development of these vast lands...In future we must not deliberately seek military action, but we must be ready to use force against those who attack us.

Accordingly, he ordered the *Commandant-Supérieur* to crush the insurrection of Mahmadu Lamine but to offer clemency to those rebels who renewed their allegiance to the French. Having dealt with Mahmadu Lamine, Gallieni was also to provision and repair the forts and resume work on the Railway.[2] De La Porte had every confidence in the Commander's ability to carry out his duties successfully, and the latter fully justified the Under-Secretary's faith in him.

GALLIENI'S SUCCESSFUL CAMPAIGNS

Joseph Gallieni had matured considerably since his days as an impetuous and belligerent young Captain on the Upper Senegal. The intervening years had tempered his boldness with prudence, farsightedness and self-control. He was intelligent enough to realise that the problems confronting him had their origins in the reckless and ill-prepared adventures of his predecessors, and he showed no desire to follow them on dangerous forays beyond the line of forts. He saw that peace was essential for the growth of trade, and the economic development of the Sudan was his most cherished objective.[3]

But first he had to deal with Mahmadu Lamine. The rainy season had given the *marabout* time to reorganise his forces, regain his prestige and consolidate his power on the southern flank of the French lines. During the summer, his agents had murdered Umar Penda of Bondu, and in September his troops attacked Sénoudébou. Accordingly, Gallieni sent reconnaissance parties into Bondu and Bambuk and

[1] Desbordes, Notes pour servir...aux instructions pour la campagne de 1886–7, 10 Sept. 1886, MFOM Sénégal IV 87(d).
[2] De La Porte to Gov. Sen., Instructions, 20 Oct. 1886, MFOM Sénégal IV 87(*bis*).
[3] Gallieni to Etienne, 16 Jan. 1888, BN n.a.fr. 24327, Etienne Papers: 'J'ai vu...qu'une campagne comme celle menée avec si grand tapage par mon prédécesseur serait absolumment mortelle pour l'œuvre du Soudan, et j'ai désiré remettre celle-ci dans le droit chemin, car je persiste à croire que l'avenir appartient à notre futur Empire Soudanien...'

drafted plans for an all-out assault on Mahmadu Lamine's headquarters at Diana. As soon as his preparations were complete, he led his columns south and took the town by storm on Christmas Day 1886. Although Mahmadu Lamine himself managed to escape into the Gambia, French influence was successfully re-established over Diakha province.[1]

Having coped with the immediate threat to security, the Commander organised his provisioning column and set out for Bamako. On the way, he carried out essential repairs at Badumbé, Kita and Koundou, and after a short stay on the Niger he returned to Kayes by way of Niagassola. During the whole of the ten-week campaign, his column of 500 men did not suffer a single casualty.[2] Progress on the Railway was equally impressive. Without funds, the civilian engineers had found it difficult even to maintain the existing track; but Gallieni soon discovered that their stocks contained sufficient material to complete the line as far as Bafoulabé. Once he had persuaded the local chiefs to provide labour, work proceeded rapidly; by the summer of 1887 the Railway had reached kilometre 94.[3] Gallieni was even able to introduce some semblance of order into the Sudan's chaotic book-keeping arrangements. His orders to keep a strict account of all expenses incurred by his columns were taken to heart, and his administrative service managed to draw up a detailed reckoning of the costs of the provisioning column by 10 May, four days after its return.[4]

Under the Commander's energetic direction, the Sudan's commercial position also improved. Before he set out against Mahmadu Lamine, Gallieni promised the merchants of Bakel to help their trade with the peoples of the Upper Falémé once the *marabout* had been neutralised. On their advance south, his columns left the fertile lands through which they passed untouched and limited their punitive measures to the destruction of Diana. To reverse the commercial current which was developing between Bambuk and the Gambia, Gallieni recommended

---

[1] Combes, Rapport, 5 Oct. 1886, MFOM Sénégal IV 87 *(bis)*(b); Gallieni to Gov. Sen., 8 Dec. 1886, MFOM Senegal IV 87(b); Gallieni, Rapport, 15 Feb. 1887, MFOM Sénégal IV 87 *(bis)*(b); J. S. Gallieni, *Deux campagnes au Soudan français, 1886–1888* (Paris, 1891), pp. 19–137.

[2] Gallieni, Rapport, 30 May 1887, MFOM Sénégal IV 87 *(bis)*(c); Gallieni to Gov. Sen., 31 May 1887, MFOM Sénégal IV 87 *(bis)*(b); Gallieni, *Deux campagnes*, pp. 154–90.

[3] Engineer's report, 17 July 1885; Engineer's report, 15 Oct. 1886, MFOM Sénégal IV 81(b); Gallieni to Gov. Sen., 9 May 1887, MFOM Sénégal IV 87(b).

[4] Gallieni, Order no. 6, 2 Dec. 1886; Inventories, 16 Feb. 1887, 10 May 1887, MFOM Sénégal IV 87 *(bis)*(b); Roux Rapport, 5 May 1887, MFOM Sénégal IV 87 *(bis)*(c). The *chef du service* attributed these excellent results to 'la direction et...l'influence incontestées exercées par le commandement, l'impulsion énergique imprimée dès le début des opérations...'

145

the establishment of a major trading centre at Bafoulabé and sent missions to encourage the populations of the south to seek their markets at the French forts. His efforts were successful; by May he could report that the chiefs of Bambuk had guaranteed protection for French caravans and had agreed to stop trading with the Gambia.[1]

The Commander was pleased by the highly satisfactory results of his first campaign and anxious to continue his work of consolidation. His plans for the coming year stressed the need for an efficient supply system and called for the completion of the Railway to Bafoulabé. The construction of a post at Siguiri was his only proposed addition to the established system of fortifications. The Colonial Department was equally pleased by his progress and accepted his recommendations as the basis for its new instructions.[2]

Once more, however, military action had to be taken before a peaceful programme could be implemented. After his flight, Mahmadu Lamine had again recouped his losses and in July had captured Mete-bulu in Ouli province. This time Gallieni was determined to finish with him once and for all. Although the *marabout* sued for peace, Gallieni persuaded the Colonial Department to reject the overture and sent two companies of *tirailleurs* to reinforce Captain Fortin, who had remained in the south after the capture of Diana. On 8 December French troops took the *marabout*'s stronghold at Toubakouta; the following day Mahmadu Lamine himself was killed. With his death the insurrection collapsed, and effective French control was extended to the borders of the Gambia.[3]

The rest of the campaign could now proceed without complications. By the beginning of April the forts had been provisioned and Siguiri built. At the end of May the Railway at last reached Bafoulabé.[4] Trade also continued its steady improvement. After the death of Mahmadu Lamine, Bubakar Saada's son, Usman Gassi, was recognised as ruler of

---

[1] Gallieni to Gov. Sen., 11 Dec. 1886, MFOM Sénégal IV 87(b); Gallieni, Rapport, 15 Feb. 1887, MFOM Sénégal IV 87(*bis*)(b); Reichemberg, Rapport, 25 Feb. 1887, MFOM Missions 18, Gallieni 1886–7; Gallieni to Gov. Sen., 4 Apr. 1887; same to same, 31 May 1887, *ibid.*

[2] Gallieni, Note, 24 Sept. 1887, MFOM Sénégal IV 90(a); M.M.C. to Gov. Sen., Instructions, 12 Oct. 1887, MFOM Sénégal IV 90(*bis*)(a).

[3] Monségur [*Commandant-Supérieur, p.i.*] to Gov. Sen., 17 July 1887; same to same, 24 July 1887, MFOM Sénégal IV 90(b); Gallieni to Under-Secretary, 28 July 1887, MFOM Sénégal IV 91(a); Gallieni, Note, 24 Sept. 1887, MFOM Sénégal IV 90(a); Gallieni, *Deux campagnes*, pp. 323–71.

[4] Gallieni to Gov. Sen., 27 Jan. 1888; same to same, 4 Apr. 1888, MFOM Sénégal IV 90(b); Gov. Sen. to M.M.C., 31 May 1888, MFOM Sénégal IV 90(*bis*)(c).

Bondu on condition that his people traded exclusively with the French. Commercial surveys were carried out along the Falémé; the villages which Frey had burned in 1886 were rebuilt, and monthly fairs were organised. Further east, commercial expeditions were sent into Bele-dugu, the Bakhoy valley and Buré. These efforts again produced results, and in May Gallieni was able to report that Médine was a thriving commercial centre with a population of 7,000, increasing daily.[1]

FRANCO-MUSLIM RELATIONS, 1886–8

Gallieni's work of consolidation would not have been possible without a settlement of the outstanding issues between the French and the two most powerful empires of the Western Sudan. Frey's campaign had left relations with Ahmadu and Samori in a state of flux, and the resolution of the uncertainty on favourable terms was the Colonial Department's main political objective. Towards Ahmadu, Gallieni was ordered to maintain an attitude of dignified reserve, of firmness tempered with conciliation. Negotiations could be reopened only if the Sultan took the initiative, and his demands for the evacuation of the forts were to be rejected outright. But, if Ahmadu agreed to this condition, his overtures were to be cautiously accepted. The renegotiation of the treaty with Samori was a more urgent priority, and de La Porte there-fore drafted plans for a new diplomatic mission which was to secure the renunciation of the *imam*'s residual rights over Buré and Kangaba. In order to placate the Quai d'Orsay, the Under-Secretary also ordered the mission to establish a nominal protectorate over Samori's empire, or at least to persuade him not to enter into relations with foreign powers.[2]

Samori proved ready to co-operate. By now he was openly at war with King Tiéba of Sikasso on his eastern frontier. His preparations for an invasion were well under way, and he was anxious to secure European military assistance against his formidable African adversary. The French mission which arrived at his capital, Bissandugu, in February 1887 was therefore given a friendly reception. Samori at first refused to surrender his rights to Buré; but when the French Ambassador, Captain Péroz,

---

[1] Gallieni to Gov. Sen., 17 Apr. 1888, MFOM Sénégal IV 90(b); Gallieni, Rapport no. 2, 10 May 1888, MFOM Sénégal IV 90(*bis*)(b); Gallieni to Gov. Sen., 11 May 1888, MFOM Sénégal IV 90(*bis*)(c); same to same, 18 May 1888, MFOM Sénégal IV 90(*bis*)(b); Gallieni, *Deux campagnes*, pp. 573–603.

[2] De La Porte to Gov. Sen., Instructions, 20 Oct. 1886, MFOM Sénégal IV 87(*bis*).

threatened to break off the talks unless his conditions were accepted, the *imam* became more transigent and agreed to sign a new treaty. By its terms he placed all his existing territories and future possessions under French protectorate, gave up his claims on the left bank of the Niger and guaranteed his protection for French trade. In turn, the French undertook not to sent troops across the Niger so long as the treaty was respected.[1]

Negotiations with Ahmadu were equally uncomplicated. Having overcome his brother Muntaga and reaffirmed his authority in Kaarta, the Sultan was anxious to return to Segu. But the way back was blocked by the Bambaras, and his own *talibés* were reluctant to leave Nioro, much closer than Segu to their homelands in Futa and the religious capital of the empire as well.[2] Before he could risk the passage through Beledugu, Ahmadu had to replenish his arsenals, and he could only do so by persuading the French to cancel their prohibition on the sale of arms. He had already offered to lift his own trade ban if the French agreed; when they refused he reopened commercial relations anyway.[3] As soon as Gallieni announced his peaceful intentions, the Sultan proclaimed his own desire for good relations and suggested a new round of negotiations based on the Treaty of Nango. Gallieni rejected the overture but removed his ban on the sale of munitions as a sign of good faith. When Ahmadu accepted the gesture and helped the French in their campaign against Mahmadu Lamine, the Commander decided to make proposals of his own and sent him a draft treaty. In addition to a protectorate, the French were to be given full navigational rights to the Niger and guarantees for the safety of their trade. In return they promised never to invade the Tokolor empire nor construct fortified posts on its territory, and to pay an annual rent which could be adjusted as the volume of trade increased.[4] Although Gallieni was willing to modify these terms if necessary, the Sultan accepted the draft in full

[1] Péroz to Gallieni, 18 Feb. 1887; same to same, 24 Feb. 1887, no. 167; same to same, 24 Feb. 1887, no. 172, MFOM Sénégal III 11(g); Gallieni to Samori, 10 Mar. 1887, MFOM Sénégal IV 88(c). The treaty is printed in: E. Rouard de Card, *Les traités de protectorat conclus par la France en Afrique, 1870–1895* (Paris, 1897), pp. 230–1.
[2] De La Porte to Gov. Sen., Instructions, 20 Oct. 1886, MFOM Sénégal IV 87(*bis*): 'Nioro est devenu...un grand centre de fanatisme religieux; il est considéré comme la Mecque du Soudan occidental...'
[3] Gallieni, *Deux campagnes*, p. 33; Gov. Sen. to M.M.C., 13 Sept. 1886, MFOM Sénégal I 76(a).
[4] Gallieni to Ahmadu, 28 Nov. 1886; Ahmadu to Gallieni, 4 Jan. 1887; Gallieni to Ahmadu, 6 Feb. 1887; Ahmadu to Gallieni, 7 Mar. 1887; Projet de Traité, n.d., MFOM Sénégal IV 88(b).

and affixed his seal to it on 12 May 1887.[1] Except for minor disputes over Ahmadu's continued encouragement of Tokolor emigration from Futa, the two sides remained on good terms throughout the following year.[2]

But the establishment of friendly relations with the Muslim states was not the symptom of any fundamental change in French attitudes towards them. For Paris the purpose of the treaties was merely to guarantee the political stability essential for consolidation and commercial development, and to protect the Sudan from European rivals. Its traditional views about the threat of Islam to French security remained unaltered. Although Ahmadu's demonstrations of goodwill were not ignored, the Colonial Department remained suspicious of his sincerity and alarmed by the possibility that his more fanatical *talibés* might force him to declare war. It therefore continued to promote dissension within the Tokolor empire and ordered Gallieni to supply the Bambaras with more weapons.[3] The Commander agreed completely. He too saw the treaties as nothing more than a method of forestalling the spread of British influence and did not consider them binding on his own freedom of action.[4] He was still convinced that 'the disciples of Islam never lay down their arms and only conclude truces...which they have the right to break whenever they wish'; as always he saw the pagan Bambaras as the true allies of the French.[5] Gallieni was confident that the Tokolor empire would break up when Ahmadu died; in the meantime he was content to keep it as unstable as possible. Seeing that

[1] Gallieni to Ahmadu, 5 Apr. 1887, *ibid.* The treaty is printed in Rouard de Card, *op. cit.* pp. 227–9. The Quai d'Orsay was at first reluctant to accept the treaty because Ahmadu had not personally signed it (his seal had been affixed by his envoys). Gallieni was therefore asked to secure the Sultan's actual signature, and this he managed to do with no difficulty whatsoever at the start of the next campaign.
[2] Gallieni to Gov. Sen., 7 Feb. 1887; same to same, 19 May 1887, MFOM Sénégal IV 87(b); Gallieni, Note, 24 Sept. 1887, MFOM Sénégal IV 90(a); Gallieni to Gov. Sen., 24 Mar. 1888, MFOM Sénégal IV 90(b); Gallieni, Rapport, 10 May 1888, MFOM Sénégal IV 90(bis)(b).
[3] De La Porte to Gov. Sen., Instructions, 20 Oct. 1886, MFOM Sénégal IV 87(bis); M.M.C. to Gov. Sen., Instructions, 12 Oct. 1887, MFOM Sénégal IV 90(bis)(a).
[4] Gallieni, Note, 24 Sept. 1887, MFOM Sénégal IV 90(a): 'Suivant moi, c'est par nos traités de protectorat que nous devons combattre les entreprises des nations rivales. Ces documents, ainsi qu'il est facile de constater...n'engagent en rien notre liberté d'action ...Ils ont seulement pour objet d'étendre au loin les limites de notre futur domaine commercial et de fermer aux tentatives étrangères toutes ces contrées nigériennes.'
[5] Gallieni to Under-Secretary, 30 July 1887, MFOM Sénégal IV 90(a); same to same, 12 Sept. 1887, MFOM Sénégal IV 86: 'Notre devoir consiste toujours, dans nos possessions soudaniennes, à soutenir les faibles contre les forts, sinon ostensiblement, du moins secrètement, au moyen de conseils, de prêts d'armes, de munitions etc.' See above: pp. 75, 80.

the Sultan's enforced stay at Nioro contributed to the empire's weakness, he used his network of secret agents to inflame *talibé* feelings against any move back to Segu, encouraged the Bambaras in their resistance, and ordered the construction of an anchorage for the gunboat at Nyamina.[1] His plan succeeded. The Tokolor army became prey to growing dissension, and the Bambaras cut all communications between Nioro and Segu, thus splitting the empire in two.

French policies towards Samori were just as hostile. The Colonial Department still regarded him as 'our old enemy'[2] and Gallieni himself was convinced that he had no intention of honouring any treaty. Reports about the extent of British influence at Bissandugu confirmed his suspicions and led him to adopt a policy of active subversion. Even as Péroz was conducting his negotiations, the Commander was secretly encouraging the *imam*'s subjects on the right bank of the Niger to desert across the river. After Samori had moved against Sikasso, the new fort at Siguiri was turned into a base for inciting rebellion in his Niger provinces.[3] Although the *imam* repeatedly called on his European protectors to help him in his war against Tiéba, his appeals were consistently rejected. Instead, the king of Sikasso was promised a supply of arms, and in June 1888 his envoys signed a treaty accepting French protectorate.[4] It mattered little that the French were now allied to both participants in the conflict; their attempts to weaken Samori were richly rewarded. European support for Tiéba eliminated any possibility of his defeat, while Samori's obstinate siege of Sikasso cost him the flower of his army.[5] By August 1888 the *imam* had had enough. Abandoning the struggle, he returned to Bissandugu with his forces shattered and his prestige in ruins.

---

[1] Gallieni to Gov. Sen., 17 Apr. 1887, MFOM Sénégal IV 90(b); Gallieni, Rapport, 10 May 1887, MFOM Sénégal IV 90(*bis*)(b).

[2] M.M.C. to Gov. Sen., Instructions, 12 Oct. 1887, MFOM Sénégal IV 90(*bis*).

[3] Gallieni to Gov. Sen., 3 Feb. 1887; same to same, 11 Mar. 1887; same to same, 31 Mar. 1887, MFOM Sénégal IV 87(b); same to same, 17 Apr. 1888, MFOM Sénégal IV 90(b); same to same, 30 Apr. 1888, MFOM Sénégal VI 18(b).

[4] Gallieni, Rapport, 10 May 1888, MFOM Senegal IV 90(*bis*)(b); *Commandant-Supérieur* (*p.i.*) to Gov. Sen., 9 June 1888, MFOM Sénégal IV 90(b). The treaty with Tiéba is printed in Rouard de Card, *op. cit.* pp. 229–30.

[5] Binger, *Du Niger au Golfe de Guinée*, I, 69–108. According to Binger, Samori lost 1,000 men, twenty per cent of his force, during the first six months of the siege. Among the casualties were three of his best generals, Fabou, Malinkamori and Lankafali.

The Consolidation of the Sudan and the New African Policy

The declaration of a French protectorate over the Upper Niger and Gallieni's successful campaigns encouraged the policy-makers to reconsider their plans for a more extensive West African empire. Despite its emphasis on consolidation, the Ministry of Marine was not unalterably opposed to further expansion. Although Admiral Aube had forbidden Frey to send the gunboat to Nyamina in May 1886, he ordered his Under-Secretary to draw up plans for a new expedition to Timbuktu four months later.[1] This time the gunboat reached its destination; on 1 July 1887 Lieutenant Caron left Bamako on the *Niger*, and on 18 August he dropped anchor at Koriumé, Timbuktu's river port. Unfortunately, the political results of the mission were negligible. Caron's diplomatic task was to sign treaties with Tijani of Macina and with the Grand Council of Timbuktu; but Tijani refused to negotiate unless the French paid him duties on their trade or to let the gunboat pass until a treaty had been signed. Although Caron pressed on regardless, the populations along the river would not sell him fuel or provisions, and the Council of Timbuktu, forewarned by Tijani, refused to meet him. The approach of the dry season forced Caron to return to his base with nothing concrete to show for his efforts.[2] Disappointed, the Ministry next sent the gunboats to explore the tributaries of the Niger running southeast into the territories of Samori; but this expedition was no more successful.[3]

The difficulties of expansion along the Niger intensified the Government's interest in the possibility of extending French influence into the south. Fears of British expansion from Sierra Leone had plagued the policy-makers throughout the 1880s, and by early 1886 both the Ministry of Marine and the Quai d'Orsay had committed themselves to the defence of French rights in Futa Jallon.[4] The campaigns against Mahmadu Lamine also drew Gallieni's attention to the economic

---

[1] Aube to de La Porte, 12 Sept. 1886, MFOM Sénégal IV 87(d); de La Porte to Gov. Sen., Instructions, 20 Oct. 1886, MFOM Sénégal IV 87(bis).

[2] Caron, Rapport, 31 Oct. 1887; Gov. Sen. to M.M.C., 5 Oct. 1887; *Commandant-Supérieur* (p.i.) to Gov. Sen., 4 Nov. 1887, MFOM Sénégal XII 114(a).

[3] Davoust to Gallieni, 22 Apr. 1888; Gallieni to Davoust, Instructions, 18 May 1888, MFOM Sénégal IV 90(c); Archinard to Gov. Sen., 16 Oct. 1888; same to same, 30 Oct. 1888, MFOM Sénégal IV 93(d). Davoust did not set out until October 1888 when the water level of the Niger was already falling, and he was unable to proceed beyond Nyamina.

[4] M.M.C. to M.A.E., 17 Dec. 1885, AEMD Afrique 86; M.A.E. to M.M.C., 8 Feb. 1886, AEMD Afrique 122.

potential of the lands between the Senegal–Niger valley and the Southern Rivers. To bring these regions within the orbit of French influence, he sent missions to establish a chain of protectorates along the northern frontiers of the Gambia and Futa Jallon, and signed a treaty of protectorate with Aguibou, Ahmadu's brother and ruler of Dinguiray.[1] The success of these initiatives breathed new life into the old concept of a Senegambian Triangle. As early as February 1887 Gallieni confidently predicted that the Sudan and the Southern Rivers would soon become part of 'the same Colonial Empire, entirely under our own influence'. To guard against the danger of British expansion, he called for the strengthening of French influence over Futa Jallon, the establishment of direct communications between the Upper Niger and the Mellacourie, and the construction of Siguiri as a base for expeditions into the Niger Bend or even towards the Ivory Coast.[2]

These proposals made a considerable impression on de La Porte's successor as Under-Secretary for Colonies, Eugène Etienne. A close friend and disciple of Gambetta and an intimate of Ferry and Rouvier, Etienne was already a prominent figure in Republican politics and a fervent advocate of a more active colonial policy. As Deputy from Oran, he had a special interest in North African affairs. He had played his part in the establishment of the Tunisian protectorate and since the early 1880s had pressed for the extension of French influence into Morocco. As *rapporteur* of the Colonial Budget, he had shown his support for Sudanese expansion as well. On becoming Under-Secretary in June 1887, he too began to think in terms of a larger West African empire, and finding Gallieni's proposals most attractive, he gave them his full support.[3]

The impetus of French expansion into the south was maintained during Gallieni's second campaign. At the end of March 1888, Lieutenant Plat signed a new treaty of protectorate with Futa Jallon, and Captain Audéoud completed an overland journey from Siguiri to

---

[1] Gallieni to Gov. Sen., 3 Feb. 1887, MFOM Sénégal IV 87(b); same to same, 19 May 1887, MFOM Sénégal IV 86; Gallieni, Rapport, 22 June 1887, MFOM Sénégal IV 87(e).

[2] Gallieni, Rapport, 15 Feb. 1887, MFOM Sénégal IV 87(*bis*)(b); Gallieni to Gov. Sen., 20 May 1887, MFOM Sénégal IV 87(b); Gallieni, Rapport, 24 Sept. 1887, MFOM Sénégal IV 90(a).

[3] Etienne to Gov. Sen., 16 Nov. 1887, MFOM Sénégal IV 90(a); Gallieni to Etienne, 16 Jan. 1888, BN n.a.fr. 24327, Etienne Papers. For Etienne's rôle in the development of French policy towards Tunisia and Morocco, see: Ganiage, *Les origines du protectorat français en Tunisie*, pp. 639, 657, 695; Miège, *Le Maroc et l'Europe*, IV, 42, 235–8.

Benty, thus opening the road from the Niger to the Atlantic.[1] These new successes confirmed the Commander's belief in the wisdom of the new policy. His campaigns had shown him that the Senegal was not a viable outlet for Sudanese trade. The Southern Rivers, on the other hand, were closer to the Upper Niger basin and separated from it by easier and richer terrain. In his final report, therefore, he strongly urged the Colonial Department to direct the Sudan's trade towards the customs posts on the South Atlantic coast and to create a thriving commercial empire centred around Timbo, the capital of Futa Jallon.[2]

Etienne's departure from the Colonial Department in December 1887 and the return of the more cautious de La Porte in February 1888 prevented these plans from being carried out immediately. Although de La Porte recognised the commercial importance of the south, he refused to authorise the construction of a fort at Timbo and ordered the new *Commandant-Supérieur*, Major Archinard, to assure the *almamys* that the French had no intention of extending their political control over them.[3] The local authorities too were critical. Both Archinard and Governor Clément-Thomas of Senegal opposed the ratification of the Plat treaty, which merely aroused the *almamys'* suspicions without adding to the safeguards already provided by the Bayol treaty; both dismissed any possibility of taking military action.[4] But when Etienne again took charge of colonial policy in March 1889, he overrode their objections. British designs on Futa Jallon, he told the Quai d'Orsay in May, made it dangerous to rely exclusively on the Bayol treaty, the terms of which had never been fully implemented. The only way to guarantee the future of the projected Upper Niger empire, he added, was to ratify the Plat treaty, build a fort at Timbo, and install a Resident.[5]

While Gallieni and Etienne were pressing for the occupation of Futa Jallon, developments elsewhere along the coast added a further dimension to the new West African empire. During the early 1880s, the protection of French interests on the Ivory Coast remained low on the list of African priorities, and Paris was content to leave the care of the old forts in the hands of the La Rochelle trader, Verdier. At the

---

[1] Gallieni to Gov. Sen., 3 Apr. 1888, MFOM Sénégal IV 90(b); Gallieni, *Deux campagnes*, pp. 449–551, 553–69. The treaty with Futa Jallon is printed in Rouard de Card, *op. cit.* pp. 207–8.

[2] Gallieni, Rapport, 10 May 1888, MFOM Sénégal IV 90(*bis*)(b).

[3] De La Porte to Archinard, Instructions, 19 Oct. 1888, MFOM Sénégal IV 93(a).

[4] Archinard to Clément-Thomas, 1 Mar. 1889, MFOM Sénégal IV 93(c); Clément-Thomas to *Colonies*, 8 Mar. 1889, same to same, 7 Apr. 1889, MFOM Sénégal I 80(b).

[5] Etienne to M.A.E., 14 May 1889, AEMD Afrique 122.

end of 1886, however, Jean Bayol, now Lieutenant-Governor of the Southern Rivers, sent a strong force of *tirailleurs* to quell a local disturbance and re-establish effective occupation. The immediate reason for Bayol's intervention was the need to restore security, but his long-term objective was to develop the Ivory Coast as another base for penetration into the Sudan. Bayol was convinced that the colony's future lay in the interior. He was confident that relations could be established with the important entrepôt of Kong, and he was determined to open up the whole of the Niger Bend to French trade.[1] Others felt the same, and none more strongly than Faidherbe's *officier d'ordonnance*, Captain Louis-Gustave Binger.

In December 1886 Binger, armed with a letter of support from Faidherbe and a promise of 10,000 fr. in merchandise from Verdier, asked the Ministry of Marine for permission to explore the regions lying between the Upper Niger and the Ivory Coast. The Rue Royale's response was unenthusiastic. Although Admiral Aube was inclined to approve the scheme, de La Porte testily reminded him that the necessary funds were not available.[2] But the Quai d'Orsay's reactions were much more favourable. The Ministry of Foreign Affairs had never been completely satisfied with its vague declaration of protectorate over the Upper Niger. It remained apprehensive about the threat of British rivalry, and its fears were heightened by rumours that a British agent had reached Timbuktu from the direction of Sokoto.[3] Anxious to base French claims in the Niger Bend on a more solid foundation than the dubious treaty with Samori, it welcomed Binger's proposals and promised to give the explorer financial support.[4] When informed of its decision, Aube decided to give the mission 17,500 fr. The Quai d'Orsay agreed to contribute a similar amount.[5]

Still lukewarm to the idea, de La Porte merely instructed Binger to report on his mission when he returned; but the Foreign Ministry

---

[1] For the history of the Ivory Coast and the policies of Bayol, see: Atger, *La France en Côte d'Ivoire*, pp. 94–126.

[2] Binger, Projet d'exploration, encl. in Binger to Aube, 19 Dec. 1886, with minute by Aube; same to same, 3 Jan. 1887; de La Porte to Aube, 5 Jan. 1887, MFOM Missions 12, Binger. See also: Faidherbe to de La Porte, 27 Dec. 1886 [Copy], AEMD Afrique 85.

[3] M.A.E. to M.M.C., 6 Dec. 1886, MFOM Sénégal IV 87(a); Note pour le Ministre [des Affaires Etrangères], 24 Jan. 1887, AEMD Afrique 85.

[4] Binger to M.A.E., 7 Jan. 1887; Note pour le Ministre, 24 Jan. 1887, AEMD Afrique 85; M.A.E. to M.M.C., 27 Jan. 1887, MFOM Missions 12, Binger. To help his case, Binger told the Foreign Ministry that the Colonial Department had agreed to contribute 20,000 fr. towards the cost of his mission.

[5] M.M.C. to M.A.E., 28 Jan. 1887; M.A.E. to M.M.C., 31 Jan. 1887, *ibid.*

took the expedition much more seriously and ordered the explorer to sign treaties assuring France a privileged political and economic position in all the lands through which he passed. Thus equipped with diplomatic powers, Binger left Médine in May 1888, met Samori at Sikasso, visited Kong, tried unsuccessfully to sign a treaty with Wagadugu, travelled through Gurunsi, Mamprusi, Salaga, Kintapo and Bonduku, and then returned to Kong. There he met one of Verdier's agents, Treich-Laplène, who had already signed a treaty with the town and with Bonduku as well. Together, the two explorers returned to Grand Bassam, establishing protectorates over Djimini and Anno on the way.[1]

Binger's exploration was to have a profound effect upon the development of French African policy. During Etienne's first administration, both he and Gallieni had seen the Senegambian Triangle as the foundation for the Niger empire. Like Faidherbe, they were disturbed by the British presence on the Gambia, and they too advocated a territorial exchange as the solution to the problem. Thus when Britain offered to negotiate a general settlement of outstanding territorial disputes in 1887, they both urged the Government to secure the Gambia, if necessary by ceding the Ivory Coast. Somewhat reluctantly, therefore, the Foreign Ministry told the British ambassador of its willingness to consider the question of the Gambia together with that of Assinie and Grand Bassam, and asked for more information.[2] But the British Government did not agree to frontier negotiations until March 1889, and by then Binger's expedition had completely altered the situation. The chain of treaties he and Treich established between Kong and the sea convinced Etienne, who was again Under-Secretary, that the Ivory Coast was too valuable to be given away. Accordingly, he now rejected any suggestion of an exchange involving Assinie and Grand Bassam, and he further demonstrated his new interest in the coast by appointing Bayol as the Colonial Department's representative on the Boundary Commission.[3]

[1] De La Porte to Binger, Instructions, 15 Feb. 1887 [Copy]; M.A.E. to Binger, Instructions, 18 Feb. 1887, AEMD Afrique 85. The mission is described in Binger, *Du Niger au Golfe de Guinée*, 2 vols.

[2] Etienne to M.A.E., 10 Dec. 1887, AEMD Afrique 86; Gallieni, Note, 20 Jan. 1888, MFOM Afrique VI 66(b); M.A.E. to M.M.C., 13 Jan. 1888, MFOM Afrique VI 66(a); Note pour le Ministre, 4 Mar. 1889, AEMD Afrique 128.

[3] Etienne to M.A.E., 25 Apr. 1889, MFOM Afrique VI 73(a). Etienne specifically claimed that the new importance of the Ivory Coast derived from the successful expeditions of Binger and Treich.

The Consolidation of the Sudan and the New African Policy

During the discussions which followed, the protection of the embryonic Niger empire was the French delegates' dominant concern. A British offer which amounted to an exchange of the Gambia for French possessions between Sierra Leone and Gabon was rejected outright. The Commissioners then agreed to settle the frontier between the Ivory and Gold Coasts as far north as the ninth parallel, taking into account the treaties of both sides in the area. At British insistence, the northern frontier of Sierra Leone was also discussed. After some debate, the French agreed to recognise British claims to Lokko, Tambakha, Lembo and Sulimana, all technically part of Samori's empire, in return for the recognition of French rights in Futa Jallon and the Upper Niger basin. As an added concession, the French were guaranteed possession of a practicable road between the Sudan and the Mellacourie, running south of the mountains of Futa Jallon.[1] Both Etienne and the Quai d'Orsay were pleased with the outcome. French claims to Futa Jallon and the Upper Niger basin, the nucleus of the new empire, had been recognised by the only Power in a position to challenge them; the route from the Niger to the Atlantic had been guaranteed; communications between the Sudan and the Ivory Coast had been ensured. The British remained in Gambia, but they no longer posed a serious threat to French plans.[2] Secure in their position on the Upper Niger, the policy-makers in Paris now set their sights still further afield.

THE DEVELOPMENT OF THE CHAD PLAN

The satisfactory diplomatic settlement of the Niger empire's frontiers was quickly followed by a marked accentuation of French activity throughout West Africa. Etienne himself insisted vehemently upon the need not only to defend but also to extend French rights in the continent.[3] He was determined to establish French preponderance over the whole of the Niger Bend, and in February 1890 he authorised the Sudanese Military to launch their long-awaited assault on Segu. Hoping to take advantage of the impression created by its capture, he sent

---

[1] The minutes of the Boundary Commission are to be found *ibid*. For the text of the treaty, see: E. Hertslet, *The Map of Africa by Treaty*, 3rd ed. (London, 1909), II, 729–36.

[2] Résumé de la situation...avant et après...10 août 1889, n.d.; Etienne to M.A.E., 14 Aug. 1889, AEMD Afrique 128.

[3] E.g. Etienne to M.A.E., 25 Oct. 1889, MFOM Afrique VI 80(a): 'Notre situation actuelle en Afrique ne nous permet pas seulement de maintenir nos droits acquis, mais nous fait un devoir de revendiquer à notre tour une large extension de notre zône d'action.'

diplomatic missions into Macina, Yatenga and Mossi, and ordered the gunboats to proceed down the Niger as far beyond Timbuktu as their resources allowed.[1] To confirm French influence on the Ivory Coast and guarantee its communications with the Upper Niger, he called on the Quai d'Orsay to make a formal notification of their treaties with Kong, Djimini and Anno.[2] On the Slave Coast he reversed the policy of restricted occupation which had been in force since the early 1880s. In April 1889 he reinforced the garrison of Kotonou; in August he sent Bayol to annex Avrekete and Godomey and to negotiate a new customs agreement with King Glele of Dahomey. When the talks fell through, the Under-Secretary sent further reinforcements and ordered the arrest of Fon customs officials. By March 1890 Kotonou was under attack, and although a major war with Dahomey was for the moment avoided, Etienne made his intentions perfectly plain. 'If after the defeats inflicted on the king of Dahomey we do not receive complete satisfaction', he told the Chamber at the height of the crisis,

if our treaties...and our protectorate over Porto Novo are not...recognised and respected, we shall have to take more energetic measures. We are determined, not to undertake a conquest but to teach our adversary such a lesson that the question will be settled once and for all. We shall then ask Parliament to make...a vigorous and decisive effort. We are convinced that wherever French interests are at stake, they must be protected, that wherever the flag flies, none must touch it.[3]

Three weeks later, the publication by *Le Temps* of a supplement devoted to the Binger mission gave the Under-Secretary an unexpected opportunity for elaborating his views. With the supplement, *Le Temps* printed a map showing all the territories north-west of a line drawn from the Black Volta to Burrum as a 'zone of French influence'. When a copy reached Berlin, the German Government immediately protested against the apparent violation of the Anglo-German Neutrality Agreement of 1887 and asked for more precise information about the eastern

[1] Etienne to Gov. Sen., 15 Apr. 1890; same to same, 16 July 1890, MFOM Sénégal I 80 (c). The missions were sent out in order to forestall the German explorer Krause who was rumoured to be heading for Gurunsi, Mossi and Timbuktu. None of them was successful. Nothing came of the plans for Timbuktu either, because the gunboats were not in a fit state to undertake such a long journey.

[2] Etienne to M.A.E., 15 Nov. 1889; M.A.E. to Etienne, 29 Dec. 1889, AEMD Afrique 122. The Foreign Ministry at first considered such notification unnecessary but later changed its mind. See below: p. 158.

[3] *J.O. Déb. Parl. Chambre*, séance du 8 mars 1890, p. 487. For developments on the coast during this period, see: Newbury, *The Western Slave Coast and its Rulers*, pp. 127–30.

limits of the French sphere.[1] This demand aroused great anxiety at the Quai d'Orsay. Desbuissons, the Ministry's geographer, saw it as proof of secret German designs on Wagadugu and Timbuktu, and he urged the immediate negotiation of new treaties to protect French rights in the Niger Bend. Although he accepted the Burrum line as an accurate representation of French aspirations, he added ruefully that they had no diplomatic substance without treaties to support them. Accordingly, he suggested a cautiously worded reply which would not reveal the actual weakness of the French position. Ribot, the Foreign Minister, was equally concerned.[2] But Etienne was much more upset by the rumoured advance of a British expedition on Bissandugu. The German Note did not disturb him in the least, for he was confident that his recent measures in the Sudan would forestall any possible German designs on Mossi or Timbuktu. The Binger map, he claimed, was an unofficial document which required no official explanation. Indeed, the incident could even be turned to advantage by using it to draw a clear distinction between those territories actually under a French protectorate and those within her sphere of influence. Although title to the first had to be solidly based on treaties, claims to the second could be justified on the generally accepted theory of 'Hinterland': that a protecting Power automatically had the right to consider regions adjacent to its protectorate as a legitimate zone for further expansion. Since the extent of the zone depended on the size and importance of the existing protectorate, their vast Niger empire gave the French every right to claim the lands north of the Black Volta.[3] Ribot accepted the argument. In response to Etienne's appeals, he had already notified the British Government of the Binger treaties. He now informed the Germans as well, adding that the French sphere in the Niger Bend ran as far as the intersection of the Niger with the northern frontier of the kingdom of Gwandu.[4]

Although Etienne had so far taken most of the initiative, the Quai d'Orsay itself did not remain idle, and it soon extended French claims

[1] *Le Temps*, Supplement, March 1890 [Copy in AEMD Afrique 123]; German Note, 28 Mar. 1890, encl. in M.A.E. to Etienne, 29 May 1890, MFOM Afrique VI 84(a). For the Anglo-German Agreement of 1887, see: Hertslet, *The Map of Africa by Treaty*, III, 890.

[2] Desbuissons, Note, 18 Apr. 1890, AEMD Afrique 123; Ribot to Etienne, 29 May 1890, MFOM Afrique 84(a).

[3] Etienne to M.A.E., 29 May 1890 (Urgent); same to same, 18 June 1890, AEMD Afrique 123.

[4] Ribot to Etienne, 12 June 1890, *ibid.*; Ribot to Herbette [Ambassador, Berlin], 1 July 1890, AE Allemagne 97.

east to Lake Chad. In the summer of 1890 Lord Salisbury, seeking to protect the head-waters of the Nile, concluded an agreement with Germany ceding Heligoland in return for the renunciation of German claims to Uganda, the cession of the 'Witu strip' and the recognition of a British protectorate over Zanzibar.[1] Salisbury, however, did not inform the French, who, as a party to the Joint Declaration of 1862 guaranteeing Zanzibar's independence, had a right to be consulted about any change in the island's status. When they protested he apologised, and Ribot, not one to let the opportunity slip, immediately raised the question of compensation. The major concession which the Foreign Minister hoped to secure was the modification of the Anglo-Tunisian Perpetual Treaty so that it would expire in 1896 at the same time as the Italo-Tunisian Treaty, or earlier if France reached agreement with the Italians. But he also wanted Britain to recognise the French protectorate over Madagascar, and he was particularly anxious to delimit the respective spheres of the two Powers in West Africa as far east as Lake Chad.[2]

Although the Tunisian question figured most prominently in the subsequent negotiations,[3] the Quai d'Orsay never forgot the importance of securing a favourable West African settlement. Ribot became more insistent on this point when he learned that the Anglo-German Agreement contained a guarantee of mutually free access to Lake Chad. He now ordered Ambassador Waddington to press for a delimitation along a line drawn between the Lower Niger and the lake so as to give France part of its shoreline and all the territory to the north. Accordingly, Waddington demanded recognition of French rights of access both to Timbuktu and to Chad, and when Salisbury raised no objections Ribot ordered him to secure the widest possible concessions around the lake.[4] But Waddington was reluctant to complicate negotiations, already in

---

[1] For the significance of this agreement, see: Robinson and Gallagher, *Africa and the Victorians*, pp. 290–300.

[2] Waddington [Ambassador, London] to Ribot, 21 June 1890; Ribot to Waddington, 24 June 1890; same to same, 25 June 1890, *D.D.F.* VIII, nos. 91, 93, 95; same to same, 28 June 1890, AE Angleterre 850.

[3] This was the only point on which the French were asking for a real concession and on which the British seemed reluctant to give way. Neither Ribot nor Waddington expected any difficulties over Madagascar or Chad. Waddington to Ribot, 14 July 1890, *D.D.F.* VIII, no. 113; Ribot to Waddington, 17 July 1890, AE Angleterre 851.

[4] Ribot to Waddington, 10 July 1890; Waddington to Ribot, 11 July 1890; M.A.E. to Waddington, Draft despatch, n.d.; Ribot to Waddington, 24 July 1890; same to same, 24 July 1890; same to same, 25 July 1890, *ibid*. Ribot wanted recognition for a French sphere right round the lake or, failing that, the extension of the delimitation line to its eastern shore.

danger of breaking up over Tunisia, by pressing claims to territories which he considered manifestly unimportant. He was convinced that Britain would never accept French control over the whole of Lake Chad and thought that a recognition of French influence on its north-west shore was the most he could hope for.[1] Nor did he object when Salisbury insisted that any delimitation must take into account the rights of the Niger Company in Sokoto. By now all hope of British concessions in Tunisia had disappeared, and after a last-minute attempt to gain a marginal advantage at Chad, the French accepted what their Ambassador described as the best terms they could get.[2] On 5 August the two sides exchanged formal declarations. The French Government recognised the British protectorate over Zanzibar. In return Britain recognised the protectorate over Madagascar and a French sphere of influence running south from her Mediterranean possessions to a line between Say on the Niger and Barruwa on Lake Chad, 'drawn in such a manner as to comprise within the sphere of action of the Niger Company all that fairly belongs to the Kingdom of Sokoto'. The details were to be determined by Commissioners meeting in Paris who would also discuss respective spheres of influence in the Niger Bend.[3]

Having got what it could from the British, the Quai d'Orsay next turned its attention to the Germans. On 1 July Ribot had instructed Ambassador Herbette to raise the question of compensation with Berlin. This time the Foreign Minister's most important objective was to provide the Congo with guaranteed access to the south-east corner of Lake Chad, thus ensuring the possibility of free communications with the Sudan. When the German Foreign Ministry agreed in principle to an exchange of Notes on the general issues raised by the Anglo-German Treaty, he immediately ordered Herbette to press for a delimitation along the Chari, giving Bornu and Adamawa to the Germans and Baghirmi to the French.[4] Herbette, however, was less fortunate than Waddington. Although he was confident of an agreement if the Germans were given access to Chad, he quickly discovered that

[1] Waddington to Ribot, 27 July 1890; same to same, 29 July 1890, *ibid.*; same to same, 26 July 1890, *D.D.F.* VIII, no. 132. Waddington thought it much wiser to concentrate on the delimitation of the Niger Bend rather than to 'chercher à accaparer le lac Tchad, où nous n'aurons pas de longtemps le moindre moyen d'action'.

[2] Waddington to Ribot, 30 July 1890; Ribot to Waddington, n.d. [1 Aug. 1890], AE Angleterre 851; Waddington to Ribot, 1 Aug. 1890, *D.D.F.* VIII, no. 136.

[3] For the text of the Agreement, see: Hertslet, *op. cit.* II, 570–2.

[4] Ribot to Herbette, 1 July 1890; same to same, 16 July 1890; same to same, 25 July 1890, AE Allemagne 97; Herbette to Ribot, 19 Aug. 1890; Ribot to Herbette, 21 Aug. 1890, *D.D.F.* VIII, nos. 154, 156.

Berlin had no intention of making any material concessions. When serious discussions began in August, Baron Marschall declined to offer anything more than a recognition of the Madagascar protectorate. He refused point-blank to consider any guarantee of French access to Lake Chad, and he soon called for the talks themselves to be adjourned *sine die*.[1] Paris reluctantly agreed. When the discussions were reopened in October they dealt exclusively with the protectorate over Madagascar, which the German Government recognised by an exchange of Notes in November.[2]

Nevertheless, the French were well pleased by the outcome of their diplomatic efforts. Ambassador Waddington for one was perfectly satisfied with his part in the affair. In return for minimal concessions in Zanzibar, where French rights were practically speaking non-existent, he had secured recognition for the Madagascar protectorate, a vast extension of French influence beyond the Niger, and, most important of all, a favourable position for any future delimitation in the Niger Bend.[3] The Ambassador was not at all disturbed by Salisbury's famous remark about 'very light land'. He did protest as a matter of form, but in private he dismissed the Prime Minister's speech as a clever manœuvre to gain the British Parliament's approval for the Agreement and as further evidence of Salisbury's penchant for the *bon mot*.[4]

The Quai d'Orsay was equally happy. The long-feared British advance up the Niger had been halted at Say, well beyond the limits of Etienne's 'Hinterland' claim. French influence had been recognised over the vast tracts of land running south from Algeria and the Sahara to Chad. In the process, a more urgent and more vital need had been satisfied: France could no longer be challenged in the Sahara, and no Power could ever take her from behind in Algeria. Most important of all, she had secured the possibility of a territorial union between North Africa, the Sudan, the Guinea coast and the Congo, and had thus laid the diplomatic foundations for the vast African empire which her

[1] Herbette to Ribot, 13 Aug. 1890; same to same, 27 Aug. 1890; *ibid.* nos. 146, 164.
[2] Herbette to Ribot, 16 Oct. 1890; Ribot to Herbette, 4 Nov. 1890; Herbette to Ribot, 11 Nov. 1890, *ibid.* nos. 186, 198, 207.
[3] Waddington to Ribot, 1 Aug. 1890, *ibid.* no. 136.
[4] Waddington to Salisbury, 13 Aug. 1890, cited in Lady G. Cecil, *Life of Robert, Marquis of Salisbury* (London, 1932), IV, 324; Waddington to Ribot, 12 Aug. 1890; same to same, 13 Aug. 1890, AE Angleterre 852. Salisbury had said: 'Anyone who looks at the map and merely measures the degrees will perhaps be of the opinion that France has laid claim to a very considerable stretch of territory. But it is necessary to judge land not only by its extent but also by its value. This land is what agriculturalists would call "very light land"; that is to say, it is the desert of Sahara.'

policy-makers had dreamed of for so long. 'Without any great effort', ran its considerations on the Agreement,

without any real sacrifice, without the expense of exploration...without a single treaty, we have secured the recognition by Britain (the only Power whose rivalry we need fear...) that Algeria and Senegal will in the near future form a single domain; we have demanded and we have been given exclusive influence over the lands between Biskra and our possessions on the West African coast by way of Timbuktu, and we have joined to the Senegal 2,500 kilometres of the Niger which thus becomes, for most of its course, a French river...Today the Government can tell the nation that this vast African empire is no longer a dream, a distant ideal...but a reality.[1]

THE CHAD PLAN AND PUBLIC OPINION

The policy-makers were not the only ones with such dreams. By the summer of 1890 French public opinion was also beginning to exhibit the symptoms of the African fever which had gripped it a decade before. The failure of the Trans-Sahara and Senegal–Niger Railways, the repercussions of the Tonkin campaign, political instability after the fall of Ferry, and growing concern over France's economic difficulties, had dampened the colonialist enthusiasm of the late 1870s. But the vision of an African empire never faded completely from the public mind. In 1885 Paul Leroy-Beaulieu could still write:

I count myself among those who believe that the future of France lies...in Africa, and that with Algeria joined to Senegal, we shall one day dominate and civilise the whole north-western portion of this continent, that is to say all the territory between Tripoli and the Atlantic, between the Mediterranean in the north and the Gambia and the Equator in the south, including the whole course of the Niger and its affluents and the lands bordering Lake Chad.[2]

As the years passed, the number of these faithful increased. In 1888 the debate over the Trans-Sahara Railway was reopened in the columns of

[1] Considérations sur le projet d'arrangement franco-anglais, 13 Aug. 1890, AEMD Afrique 129. The emphasis on the defence of the Algerian frontier, while undoubtedly important, is not evidence of an exclusive preoccupation with Mediterranean strategy. On this point, the Ministry's considerations echoed the views of François Deloncle, who believed that the special position of Algeria and Tunisia provided a much more solid foundation for the claim to Lake Chad than Etienne's dubious hinterland theory. Deloncle was a leading exponent of expansion towards Chad, and his views were well known in official circles. See: *Le Siècle*, 22 July 1890, citing an interview given by Deloncle to *L'Indépendance Belge*.
[2] P. Leroy-Beaulieu, *De la colonisation chez les peuples modernes*, 3rd ed. (Paris, 1885), p. 447.

The Chad Plan and Public Opinion

the *Revue française de l'étranger et des colonies*.[1] In March 1890 the *Congrès colonial national* passed a resolution calling for the construction of a strategic railway system in the Sahara, and for a simultaneous advance into the Sudan from Senegal and the Congo.[2] In July an inter-ministerial commission was set up to re-examine the Trans-Sahara Railway question, and in August it cautiously recommended the construction of a line from Biskra to the Niger Bend.[3] By the end of October the French Ambassador in Madrid, Paul Cambon, was calling for the occupation of the Tuat oasis, claiming that this 'first stage in the march on Timbuktu' would satisfy the Algerian interests, Parliament, the Press and public opinion alike.[4]

A new generation of colonialists led this revived campaign for an African empire, and most prominent among them was François Deloncle, a former member of Freycinet's *cabinet* and now Republican Deputy for Castellane in the *Basses Alpes*. Closely connected with the Colonial Department through his cousin Jean-Louis, Etienne's principal collaborator on African affairs, François became one of the most articulate and energetic supporters of the Under-Secretary's African policies. Under his direction, the important Parisian daily *Le Siècle* became the new empire's chief propaganda organ. After 1889 the paper regularly carried articles about the importance of bringing the African interior under French sway. Deloncle's editorials all urged the Government to be resolute in its defence of French interests against foreign encroachment; by January 1890 he was warning his countrymen of British designs on Lake Chad and of the urgent need to keep their rivals from expanding north of the fourteenth parallel.[5] In Parliament he was the most frequent spokesman for the cause of African expansion; it was Deloncle's question about the Dahomey crisis in March 1890 which gave Etienne his first clear opportunity for publicly declaring his determination to uphold French rights on the continent.[6]

[1] *Revue francaise de l'étranger et des colonies*, VII (1888), 41–9, 120–6, 243–9. The debate was sparked off by a letter from Faidherbe (15 Dec. 1887) supporting expansion towards Timbuktu from the Sudan but discounting any possibility of an advance south from Algeria.

[2] Cited in le général Philebert and G. Rolland, *La France en Afrique et le Transsaharien* (Paris, 1890), p. 95. These years saw the publication of several books and pamphlets about the Trans-Sahara Railway. Rolland and Philebert were among those who advocated a line running to Lake Chad.

[3] Projet de Loi, 16 July 1890, no. 841; Picard to *Président du Conseil*, Rapport de la Commission, 20 Aug. 1890, MFOM Afrique XII 21 (b).

[4] Cambon to M.A.E., 28 Oct. 1890, cited in Miège, *op. cit.* IV, 251.

[5] E.g. *Le Siècle*, 24 Oct. 1889, 4 Dec. 1889, 3 Jan. 1890, 14 Jan. 1890, 21 Jan. 1890.

[6] See above: p. 157.

The Under-Secretary himself was active in the attempt to marshal public support for his new policies. His statement on the Dahomey crisis in March had created a favourable impression in Parliament. The continuation of the crisis gave him the chance to state his intentions even more specifically. 'If you drop a perpendicular from the frontier of Tunisia through Lake Chad to the Congo', he told the Chamber in May, 'then you could say that the major portion of the territories bounded by this perpendicular and the sea...is either French or is destined to come under French influence.' Here at last was a clear formulation of the objective which Jauréguiberry had vaguely perceived a decade before. A member of the Government had now publicly declared the creation of an empire embracing most of North-West Africa to be a definite aim of official policy; and if Etienne's phrasing was extravagant enough to raise a laugh of incredulity from the Right, the reaction of most Deputies was one of surprised delight.[1]

Etienne's speech was still fresh in the minds of his colleagues when news of the Anglo-German negotiations was made public in June. Deloncle was the first to react, questioning the Government about its views on the apparent violation of the 1862 Joint Declaration. Ribot's answer, a judicious mixture of firmness and prudence, satisfied Deloncle, and three days later the Foreign Minister was able to smother a much more unfriendly intervention by the former Prime Minister, Brisson. But the publication of the full text of the Anglo-German Agreement provoked another storm. An interpellation on the Government's African policy by the Boulangist Deputy Laur was now postponed by the disturbingly close margin of 212 votes to 174.[2] Throughout the summer indignation against British African policy ran high, and the need to satisfy public opinion became an important reason for Ribot's insistence on a favourable conclusion to the Anglo-French talks.[3] The publication of the Anglo-French Agreement did little to assuage his critics. Salisbury's wounding remarks about the Sahara were keenly felt. When Parliament reassembled, Ribot was again taken to task for his apparent failure to safeguard French rights. The young Deputy

[1] *J.O. Déb. Parl. Chambre*, séance du 10 mai 1890, p. 750; *Le Siècle*, 12 May 1890.

[2] *Annales de la Chambre, Débats Parlementaires*, séances du 20 juin, 23 juin, 10 juillet 1890, pp. 529–32, 536, 845.

[3] Ribot to Waddington, 20 June 1890, D.D.F. VIII, no. 90; same to same, 25 June 1890, AE Angleterre 850; same to same, 10 July 1890, AE Angleterre 851; same to same, 15 July 1890, D.D.F. VIII, no. 116. Meanwhile, Deloncle conducted his own private newspaper war against British African policy. See: *Le Siècle*, 10 July, 22 July, 23 July, 24 July, 25 July, 30 July, 10 Aug. 1890.

from Ariège, Théophile Delcassé, even accused him of giving away the best parts of West Africa, erecting an impassable barrier between the Congo and the Sudan, and so forever destroying Etienne's dream of a Chad empire.[1]

But too much should not be read into these criticisms. Delcassé's opposition to the Anglo-French Agreement was only a minor point in a much wider assault on the Government's general policy towards Great Britain. His principal target was Ribot's pusillanimous handling of the Egyptian question, and in particular his acceptance of British proposals for the conversion of the Egyptian Debt without a prior British commitment on the date of evacuation. Had it not been for this demonstration of the Foreign Minister's weakness, Delcassé claimed, Britain might have thought twice before presenting him with a *fait accompli* over Zanzibar. And Delcassé was Ribot's only opponent who could properly be described as a colonialist. The Foreign Minister's two other critics were Gustave de Lamarzelle and the Marquis de La Ferronays, whose protestations of support for colonial expansion were taken even less seriously than they were made. The majority of the colonialist Deputies supported the Government in the vote on Laur's interpellation; those who opposed it did so in the company of such erstwhile 'imperialists' as Clemenceau and Pelletan. Ribot justified the Agreement by using the arguments which his officials had drawn up, and his speech was generally well received. Deloncle himself fully approved the Minister's policy; when Delcassé claimed that the Say–Barruwa line destroyed the 'Chad Plan', it was Deloncle who shouted 'No!'[2]

Nevertheless, the opposition to Ribot's African policy is not without significance. Whatever its sincerity, it did reflect certain changes which had been taking place in French public opinion since 1885. After the furore over the Tonkin expedition had died down, the cause of colonial expansion gradually regained its respectability. Right-wing nationalists in particular began to focus their attention not only on the German danger in Europe but also on the menace of British expansion elsewhere in the world. The continued British presence in Egypt began in some measure to replace the ever-detested German occupation of Alsace-Lorraine as the favourite target for their wrath. By the early

[1] *Annales de la Chambre, Débats Parlementaires*, séances du 4 novembre, 6 novembre 1890, pp. 213–14, 225.
[2] *Ibid*. See also: *Le Siècle*, 12 Aug., 5 Nov. 1890.

1890s there was evidence that substantial sections of right-wing opinion had come to accept the extension of French power overseas as a legitimate subject for their concern.[1] The debates on the Anglo-French Agreement helped to illustrate these new political alignments on colonial questions. As in 1885 the Right and the Left united on a colonial issue to attack the Centre. But five years before they had brought down Ferry for being too aggressive in Indochina; they now hounded Ribot for not being aggressive enough in Africa.

At the same time, developments no less significant were taking place outside Parliament. In 1889 a group of private individuals united by the common vision of an African empire had formed the *Syndicat français du Haut Bénito* in order to finance an exploration of the territories between the Congo and Lake Chad.[2] By the time the Deputies reassembled after the summer recess of 1890, the *Syndicat* had transformed itself into the *Comité de l'Afrique française*, pledged to the realisation of Etienne's Chad Plan. 'We are witnessing an event unique in the history of the world', declared its manifesto:

the partition of a...continent by certain civilised nations of Europe. In this partition France has the right to a major share because of her...efforts to develop her possessions in Algeria, Tunisia, Senegal and the Congo. The Anglo-French convention has already confirmed the union, across the Sahara, of Senegal and Algeria. The same document gives us a foothold north of Lake Chad which we shall reach from the Congo by way of Baghirmi. The extension of our influence from the Congo must complete the union, across the Sudan, of the French Congo, Senegal, Algeria and Tunisia.[3]

The cause of African empire now had an organised and effective pressure group, and with its creation the foundations of the *parti colonial* were laid.

THE NATURE OF THE NEW AFRICAN POLICY

The new African policy of 1890, like its forerunner of 1879–80, evolved in a climate of opinion broadly favourable to its expansionist objective. But once more public opinion was not a decisive factor. The policy was formulated in the *bureaux* of the Rue Royale and the Quai d'Orsay by

---

[1] When the *Groupe colonial de la Chambre* was formed in 1892, nineteen of its ninety-odd members belonged to various factions of the Right. See: Brunschwig, *Mythes et réalités*, pp. 111–16.

[2] *Bulletin du Comité de l'Afrique française* [henceforth B.C.A.F.], January 1891, September 1891 [giving list of subscribers].

[3] *Ibid.* January 1891.

men who were moved by the same considerations which had led their predecessors along the same imperialist path a decade before. The objectives of Etienne, Ribot and their advisers were not different from those of Freycinet and Jauréguiberry. Their aim too was to create an empire based on the control of the African interior and to secure vast tracts of land not for immediate gain but for long-term development. They too considered it the function of the State to take the political measures necessary for the protection of the future commercial interests of the Nation. 'The Government of the Republic', the Foreign Ministry declared,

did not think it sufficient to restrict its work to the French Sudan properly speaking...It felt that it had a duty to extend its activities further into Central Africa, and it took as its objective the western shore of Lake Chad...This great interior lake, so little explored, so little known, may well hold some surprises in store for the future of civilisation in Africa. It might become the focal point of the continent's major trade routes. Its affluents, most notably the Chari, link it to the basin of the Congo. There is here a reservoir for the future which our policy cannot afford to neglect.[1]

Etienne's speeches echoed the same theme. 'We have [in our proposed Chad empire]', he proclaimed in May 1890,.

a vast domain which will be ours to colonise and make profitable. I believe that at present, given the expansionist movement being generated throughout the whole world, when foreign markets are being closed to us and when we ourselves intend to become masters of our own markets once more; I believe that it is prudent to think of the future and to reserve for the trade and industry of France the outlets which are provided in her colonies and by her colonies.[2]

This was the end towards which the policies of both Departments were directed. Etienne, in 1890 at least, fully supported the Quai d'Orsay's diplomatic efforts to extend French influence. When consulted about the negotiations in Berlin, he wholeheartedly approved the attempt to secure access to Lake Chad for the Congo, and at the same time he declared his satisfaction with the Anglo-French Agreement of 5 August. The Foreign Ministry, he assured Ribot, was quite right to stress the importance of uniting the Congo with the Sudan and North Africa; 'for this union, which a few years ago would have been dismissed as an extravagant dream, is fully justified today. Thanks to the Anglo-French

---

[1] Considérations sur le projet d'arrangement franco-anglais, 13 Aug. 1890, AEMD Afrique 129.
[2] *J.O. Déb. Parl. Chambre*, séance du 10 mai 1890, p. 750.

accord we have gained a footing on Lake Chad, while from the Ubangi, whose right bank is French, we are advancing towards what Lord Salisbury has called the "Algerian Hinterland".'[1]

But this apparently cordial agreement over the objectives of the new African policy could not disguise the abysmal state of relations between the Colonial Department and the Quai d'Orsay in 1890. In March 1889 Etienne had been reappointed Colonial Under-Secretary by Presidential Decree, just like any other Minister, and he guarded his new status jealously. Apparently unaware of his sensitivity on this issue, the Quai d'Orsay was quick to give offence; during the negotiations over the Sierra Leone frontier later in the year, it consulted the Ministry of Marine (no longer responsible for the Colonial Department) about the strategic implications of the proposed delimitation. When he found out, Etienne interpreted the incident as a deliberate slight and a veiled criticism of his new autonomy.[2] Despite Foreign Minister Spuller's attempts to soothe his ruffled feelings,[3] the Under-Secretary remained in a huff, and he used the expedition against Segu to pay back the insult in kind. The Foreign Ministry first learned of the capture of Segu from newspaper reports, and when it complained Etienne testily replied that he had already informed the Cabinet. There was no point, he added, in communicating directly with the Quai d'Orsay when all the available details had already been published in the Press.[4] In retaliation, the Foreign Ministry kept the Colonial Department almost completely in the dark over the progress of its diplomatic negotiations. Only once was Etienne consulted about the Franco-German talks; he was not even informed of the Anglo-French Agreement until a week after its signature.[5]

This failure to seek his advice on 'so eminently a colonial subject'[6] was the last straw for the Under-Secretary. Leaving Ribot to his Notes,

[1] Etienne to M.A.E., 3 Sept. 1890, MFOM Afrique VI 84(a).
[2] Etienne to M.A.E., 4 July 1889; M.A.E. to Etienne, 11 July 1889; Etienne to M.A.E., 25 July 1889; same to same, 14 Aug. 1889, AEMD Afrique 128.
[3] As a concession, Spuller allowed the Colonial Department's representative, Jean Bayol, to sign the Agreement.
[4] *Directeur politique* to Etienne, 30 May 1890; Etienne to M.A.E., n.d. [Draft], MFOM Sénégal I 90(c).
[5] M.A.E. to Etienne, 29 July 1890, MFOM Afrique VI 84(a); same to same, 12 Aug. 1890, MFOM Afrique VI 82(c).
[6] See: E. Etienne, *Les compagnies de colonisation* (1897), cited in: [*La Dépêche Coloniale* (ed.)], *Eugène Etienne, son œuvre coloniale, algérienne et politique, 1881–1906* (Paris, 1907), II, 19 n. 2: '...[l'arrangement franco-anglais] conclu, malgré son caractère éminemment colonial, en dehors de toute entente avec le soussecrétariat des colonies, qui n'en eut connaissance qu'après sa signature'.

he mounted his own offensive on Lake Chad, relying for support not on his official colleagues but on the unofficial partisans of his Chad Plan. The members of the *Syndicat français du Haut-Bénito* were natural allies, and he had already assured them of his sympathy with their aims.[1] In the summer of 1890 a new initiative by the *Syndicat* gave him the chance to break completely with the Quai d'Orsay. On 19 July the publicist and future Secretary-General of the *Comité de l'Afrique française*, Henri-Hippolyte Percher (Harry Alis as he was commonly known), approached Etienne unofficially about the possibility of a new attempt to challenge Britain on the Lower Niger. The clauses relating to Chad in the recently published Anglo-German Agreement, he claimed, posed a serious danger to French plans for uniting the Congo with North-West Africa. Speed was essential if Britain and Germany were to be forestalled. The *Syndicat*'s explorer, Paul Crampel, was already moving towards Lake Chad from the Congo. The new plan was to send another mission under Lieutenant Mizon (one of Brazza's old companions in the Congo) up the Niger and the Benué. For the benefit of the Royal Niger Company, the expedition could masquerade as a strictly scientific and commercial venture. Once past the Delta, however, it was to move up the Benué towards Chad and then split up, Mizon going to Kuka, the capital of Bornu, and his second-in-command to Massenya, capital of Baghirmi. Both were to sign political treaties which could be used as the basis for negotiations. If successful, the mission would give France a much stronger hand in any discussions about the future of this vital area. If questioned, it could stick to its cover story. If this were broken, then the mission itself, being unofficial, could easily be disavowed. The major share of the cost, Alis added, would be borne by the *Compagnie française de l'Afrique centrale*, an offshoot of the *Syndicat* headed by Léon Tharel (himself a close friend of François Deloncle).[2] All they needed was the Under-Secretary's blessing and a financial contribution of 50,000 fr. At the same time, Alis suggested a third expedition to move on Chad from the Sudan. In February 1890 Commandant Monteil had drafted plans for such a mission, and Alis drew Etienne's attention to them.[3]

The Under-Secretary approved both projects, and on 12 August he obtained the sanction of the *Conseil des Ministres*. In September, he

---

[1] See: H. Alis [Henri-Hippolyte Percher], *A la conquête du Tchad* (Paris, 1891), p. 125.

[2] Abdul-Lahi [Ahmadu's son Abdallahi] to Archinard, 31 Dec. 1897, Archinard Papers: 'M. Deloncle est l'ami intime de M. Tharel...'

[3] Alis to Etienne, 19 July 1890, MFOM Missions 6, Mizon. See also: Monteil, Projet de mission, 21 Feb. 1890, AN 66 AP 4, Monteil Papers; Alis, *op. cit.* p. 164.

instructed Monteil to proceed by way of Sikasso and Say along the delimitation line to Barruwa and thence to Bornu and Kanem. The explorer was to establish a chain of protectorates along the route. In October, Mizon arrived in the Niger Delta. Although his instructions were verbal, there can be little doubt that they were based on the programme outlined by Alis.[1] But Etienne presented the expedition to his ministerial colleagues as a strictly unofficial and non-political enterprise; the Quai d'Orsay, which refused to contribute to its costs, was not informed of its real purpose.[2]

These initiatives added the final touches to the new African policy and completed the parallel with the old. As in the past, the policy-makers, building first upon the development of French influence in the Western Sudan, had extended their claims down the Niger and east towards Chad, and had eventually incorporated the Lower-Niger–Benué complex into their grand African design. If Etienne's precise objectives on the Benué remain obscure,[3] his general purposes were clear enough. The *Syndicat français* and the *Compagnie française de l'Afrique centrale* were to replace the companies which had sold out to Goldie in 1884. The return of French traders to the lower Niger was to restore the French presence which the Colonial Department had tried so hard to maintain in the early 1880s. Where Jauréguiberry had once had his Mattei, Etienne now had his Mizon.

---

[1] Etienne to Monteil, Instructions, 15 Sept. 1890, MFOM Missions 4, Monteil. The nature of Mizon's instructions can be seen from: Note, n.d. [with postscript dated 13 Feb. 1896], MFOM Missions 6, Mizon; Mizon to Under-Secretary, 12 May 1893, BN n.a.fr. 10726, Mizon Papers; Under-Secretary to M.A.E., 14 Dec. 1893, MFOM Afrique VI 106(g).

[2] Etienne to M.A.E., 19 Aug. 1890; same to same, 5 Nov. 1890, MFOM Missions 6, Mizon.

[3] The obscurity in Etienne's policy lies in the fact that he fully approved the Foreign Ministry's plans to recognise German influence in Bornu and Adamawa in return for French access to Lake Chad. The most probable explanation is that the Under-Secretary intended to use the political rights secured by Mizon as bargaining counters in any future negotiations. Alis seems to have envisaged this possibility in his original proposal. This too was the policy of the Colonial Department three years later when Mizon's second expedition to the Benué created a similar situation. At the end of 1893, the Department recommended the ratification of the explorer's treaties with Muri and Adamawa, although the area had already been promised to the Germans during negotiations which were then in progress at Berlin. French rights on the Benué, it claimed, could still be used to extort concessions from the British. See: Under-Secretary to M.A.E., 14 Dec. 1893 [drafted by Deloncle], MFOM Afrique VI 106(g): Deloncle, Note, 29 Sept. 1894, AEMD Afrique 131.

The Consolidation of the Sudan and the New African Policy

It was within the context of this wider African policy that policies in the Western Sudan came to be determined. The Sudan had to be integrated into the larger scheme and transformed from the unproductive desert to which the military advance had reduced it into a profitable sector of the new empire. Under Gallieni the colony had begun to move in the right direction, and Paris was determined to maintain its progress. Henceforth, economic development was to be the guiding principle. Etienne did not intend to claim his empire by right of conquest; his authorisation for the assault on Segu was an uncharacteristic decision forced on him by his local authorities.[1] In general, his policy was to send small treaty-making expeditions far beyond the frontiers of military occupation in order to establish diplomatic claims which could later be made effective by the gradual and peaceful expansion of trade. The explorations of Binger and Monteil appealed to him much more than the activities of the Sudanese military commanders.

But it was not enough merely to halt the march of conquest. If the Sudan were to become profitable, its trade had to find an easy outlet to the sea, and this the Under-Secretary sought on the coast of the Southern Rivers. If French energies were to be directed towards the south, then there was little reason to maintain the established axis of advance along the Kayes–Bamako line. 'It will be necessary to rebuild the line of forts which now links the Senegal with the Niger', Etienne told the Quai d'Orsay when outlining his plans for Futa Jallon in May 1889; 'as it stands...this line would no longer be relevant to the new political and economic situation resulting from the establishment of our influence at Timbo.'[2] By the end of the year the Under-Secretary had become convinced of the need for a critical re-examination of traditional objectives in the Sudan, and he therefore set up a Departmental Commission to advise on the future course of French policy on the Upper Niger. The Commission was given wide terms of reference. It was to decide whether annual military columns were necessary, whether the number of forts was too large, whether the Railway should be extended beyond Bafoulabé or abandoned in favour of an alternative line from the Southern Rivers, and whether French influence

[1] For details of this incident, see below: pp. 179–81.
[2] Etienne to M.A.E., 14 May 1889, AEMD Afrique 122.

should be extended north towards Timbuktu or south into Futa Jallon.[1]

The Under-Secretary's decision augured ill for the Military. His two main concerns were to reduce the excessive costs of military occupation in order to satisfy Parliament's demands for greater economies and to justify continued expenditure by tangible commercial results. His choice of Commissioners was equally disquieting. Only Bourdiaux and one or two Saint-Louis merchants who made their profits from supplying the expeditionary columns identified themselves clearly as partisans of the Military. Admiral Vallon, now Deputy from Senegal, was a long-standing enemy of military expansion. His colleague François Deloncle had as his watchword: *Pas de politique militaire aux colonies!* Etienne's *chef de cabinet*, Jacques Haussmann, fully shared the Under-Secretary's views. The Commission's Sudanese military expert was Gallieni, whose radical views had led Etienne to convene it in the first place.[2]

Predictably, the Commissioners recommended sweeping changes. Prompted by Gallieni, they did accept the traditional view that military occupation was the only guarantee for security, and they recommended the formation of a new battalion of *tirailleurs soudanais*. They even called for the establishment of the Sudan as an autonomous entity under the military and administrative control of the *Commandant-Supérieur*. But they also declared that 'the period of military conquest must now be considered as closed'. They recommended major cuts in the number of European troops serving in the Sudan and their replacement by African levies. They called for the evacuation of Koundou, Bamako and Siguiri, the reduction of Médine, Badumbé, Kita and Niagassola to storage depots or telegraph stations, and the establishment of Bafoulabé as the colony's political capital and military headquarters. They decided against the extension of the Railway and in favour of its replacement by a narrow-gauge line. Although they made no specific recommendation about the future direction of the French advance, Gallieni submitted a special report calling once more for the occupation of Futa Jallon.[3]

---

[1] Etienne to Minister of Commerce and Colonies, 19 Dec. 1889; Procès-Verbaux de la Commission, séance du 15 janvier 1890, MFOM Soudan VII 1 (a).

[2] The Commission consisted of Vallon and Deloncle, Deputies; Haussmann, Dubard and Billecoq from the Colonial Department; and Le Cesne, Buhan, Chaumet and Maurel representing the Senegalese traders. Bourdiaux, Carnavant and Gallieni represented the Military. For the views of Deloncle, see: *Le Siècle*, 7 Mar. 1890; for Haussmann, see: Haussmann, Note, 30 Dec. 1889, MFOM Soudan VII 1 (a).

[3] Rapport de la Commission, 22 Jan. 1890; Gallieni, Rapport, 29 Jan. 1890, *ibid*. The report was drafted by a subcommission consisting of Vallon (President), Bourdiaux, Carnavant, Gallieni and Billecoq.

Yet the final victory belonged to the Military. Although the Commission's report as a whole was approved, only its administrative proposals were implemented. In May 1890, steps were taken to create the new battalion of *tirailleurs*. In August, Etienne confirmed the Sudan's autonomy. From 1 January 1891, the *Commandant-Supérieur* was to become the head of a separate colony with its own local budget. He was to remain politically subordinate to the Governor of Senegal, but he would in future have the right to correspond directly with the Under-Secretary for Colonies.[1] The Commission's other proposals were shelved. Its recommendations for Bafoulabé did not secure the *Commandant-Supérieur*'s approval and were never followed up. Its plans for cutting back on railway-construction met with his strong opposition and were dropped.[2] No forts were abandoned; no troops were withdrawn, and the era of military expansion did not come to an end. The policy-makers in Paris had made one fatal miscalculation. They had recognised the deficiencies of the existing system, and the modifications which they proposed were both courageous and correct. But they had forgotten that the execution of Sudanese policy depended on the active co-operation of the local military commanders. Although they grasped the need for radical changes, they did not consult the *Commandant-Supérieur* about them. Apparently, they considered Gallieni to be sufficiently representative of Sudanese military opinion. They soon discovered that the views of Gallieni were not those of Archinard.

[1] Projet de dépêche, 10 May 1890, MFOM Sénégal XVI 66(a); Decree, 18 Aug. 1890, MFOM Soudan VII 1(a).
[2] Archinard, Rapport, 5 Mar. 1890, MFOM Soudan VII 1(a); Archinard to Gov. Sen., 10 Mar. 1890, MFOM Sénégal IV 95(b).

7

The 'Total Conquest' of the Sudan, 1888-93

With the appointment of Louis Archinard as *Commandant-Supérieur* in 1888, the Sudanese Military came into their own. Under his leadership, they shrugged off the last restraints of metropolitan control, completed the conquest of the western portions of the Sudan and created a military empire worthy of comparison with Algeria in the heyday of the *Armée d'Afrique*. Archinard himself had long been designated as a future *Commandant-Supérieur*. A graduate, albeit an undistinguished one, of the Ecole Polytechnique,[1] he too had gained his first colonial experience as an Artillery Captain in Indochina. In 1880 he went to the Sudan to take charge of military construction and quickly became a leading member of the *clique Desbordes*.[2] This friendship with the Colonel was to serve him well throughout the rest of his career. He was also closely connected with the head of the Upper Senegal Bureau, Colonel Bourdiaux, who tried hard to have him appointed as Desbordes's immediate successor in 1883.[3] When Brière and Desbordes returned to Paris from Tonkin, Archinard's Sudanese future was assured. Desbordes's backing for Brière's protégé, Gallieni, won Archinard the patronage of the Inspector-General of the *infanterie de marine* and the support of Gallieni as well. In 1887 the latter promised to put Archinard's name forward as his successor and to inform him as soon as he decided to relinquish the command. 'Desbordes was too kind to me in 1886', he told Archinard, 'for me not to do the same for you.'[4] True to his word, Gallieni persuaded Under-Secretary de La Porte to press for Archinard's nomination as his successor, and as soon as the post officially fell vacant Archinard was duly appointed.[5]

Throughout the summer of 1888 Gallieni showered the new Com-

---

[1] Archinard graduated 137th in a class of 141. His class list can be found in the Archinard Papers.
[2] See: *Le Moniteur des Colonies*, 15 Aug. 1883.
[3] Bourdiaux to M.M.C., 7 Oct. 1883, MFOM Sénégal I 99 (a), Correspondance du Gouverneur.
[4] Gallieni to Archinard, 5 Sept. 1887; same to same, 5 Aug. 1888, Archinard Papers.
[5] De La Porte, Note pour le Ministre, 16 Apr. 1888, MFOM Missions 40, Archinard.

mander with information and advice. He minced no words about the best way to deal with the empires of Ahmadu and Samori. 'Our policy in the Sudan', he declared, 'must be neither pro-Tokolor nor pro-Samori but exclusively French, and we must look on all these chiefs as people to be ruined and made to disappear before very long.' He opposed an immediate attack on Ahmadu; but he did point out how easily the isolated Tokolor fortress of Koundian could be captured if the Sultan attempted to conscript new recruits in Futa. Samori was a much more serious danger and was to be annihilated with the help of Tiéba. Tiéba himself was not a problem. The French could use him as an ally against Samori, and once the *imam* had been crushed they could easily get rid of him.[1]

Gallieni's suggestions for dealing with possible opposition from the Colonial Department were equally outspoken. Despite his wide powers of initiative, he remained resentful of the Ministry's imagined lack of sympathy and irritated by his nominal subordination to Saint-Louis. 'What has discouraged me [most]', he confided to Etienne in January 1888, 'is the fear of being taken for a vulgar careerist. My God, one would think from the Ministry's...sceptical smiles [whenever I recommend my officers for decorations] that our stay in the Sudan was a perpetual holiday.'[2] One could not afford to have any faith in the Colonial Department, he warned Archinard; de La Porte was unreliable and his permanent officials even worse. It was much better to pretend that they did not exist. 'If you follow my example', he wrote,

you won't pay any more attention to the missives of M. Billecoq & Co. than you think necessary. The *Commandant-Supérieur*...can alone decide what measures have to be taken, especially on matters affecting the political situation. Everything I accomplished during these two campaigns was done in spite of the Ministry which was always afraid to commit itself, to say nothing of Saint-Louis which panicked at the hint of any action...Everything was done on my own initiative, despite the objections of Saint-Louis and the criticisms of everybody. And I advise you to do the same.[3]

Archinard proved a willing pupil.

[1] Gallieni to Archinard, 3 Aug. 1888; same to same, 25 Sept. 1888; same to same, 17 Oct. 1888, Archinard Papers.
[2] Gallieni to Etienne, 16 Jan. 1888, BN n.a.fr. 24327, Etienne Papers.
[3] Gallieni to Archinard, 25 Sept. 1888; same to same, 17 Oct. 1888, Archinard Papers.

The 'Total Conquest' of the Sudan, 1888–93

THE DESTRUCTION OF THE
TOKOLOR EMPIRE

It was fortunate that de La Porte knew nothing of this advice. The consolidation of the Sudan was the Under-Secretary's overriding concern and the maintenance of peace his first priority. 'The sole aim of our policy', he told the new Commander in October 1888, 'must be the consolidation of our influence, the extension of our trade and the improvement of agricultural production in the vast territories under our control. Our victories have sufficiently demonstrated our power; it is time now to reap the benefits from the sacrifices we have been forced to make in the past.' Archinard was ordered to avoid all complications with the Muslims. He was not to persist in Gallieni's efforts to undermine Samori's power on the right bank of the Niger, and he was to remain strictly neutral in the conflict between the *imam* and Tiéba. He was not to disturb the cordiality of French relations with Ahmadu nor take any further action at Nyamina. Tokolor attempts to interfere with French trade or to encourage emigration from Futa were not to be used as a pretext for hostilities. Only if Ahmadu proved completely intractable and an open breach became inevitable could the Commander act more forcefully and march on Koundian. But this eventuality was neither hoped for nor expected.[1]

At first, Archinard complied with his instructions. He congratulated Tiéba on his victories, but he refused to give the king more concrete support. At the same time, he assured Samori of his friendship and promised not to help his rebellious subjects in any way. When the *imam*, weakened by his campaign against Tiéba, made new overtures, the Commander sent another embassy to him, and in February 1889 an additional treaty was signed. Its terms confirmed the protectorate and recognised French rule over the left bank of the Niger from the Tankisso river to its source. Both parties undertook to remain on their own side of the frontier and to encourage each other's trade.[2] Archinard's policy toward the Tokolors was equally prudent. Although he warned the Governor of Senegal that the Sultan was not friendly, he was confident that the Bambaras would soon be strong enough to overthrow their masters without active assistance from the French. Accordingly, he

[1] De La Porte to Archinard, Instructions, 19 Oct. 1888, MFOM Sénégal IV 93 (a).
[2] Archinard to Gov. Sen., 4 Dec. 1888, MFOM Sénégal IV 93 (c). The text of the treaty is printed in Rouard de Card, *Les traités de protectorat*, pp. 231–2.

agreed to leave Nyamina alone and promised to give the rebels no more than moral support.[1]

Then, without warning, Archinard informed Saint-Louis that his troops had captured Koundian. The fortress, he claimed, had been heavily reinforced during the rainy season and had compelled the surrounding populations to renounce their allegiance to the French. Because of the urgent need to restore security, he had immediately formed a small expeditionary column and had taken the town by storm on 18 February. He apologised for not having consulted his superiors; but the success of the whole operation, he explained, had depended upon the maintenance of the strictest secrecy.[2]

Archinard had learned his lessons all too well. It is doubtful whether Koundian actually presented a serious threat to French security. Gallieni himself was most surprised by first reports that the fortress had been defended by 3,000 heavily armed warriors; when he had left the year before, its garrison had consisted of no more than 300 poor devils wishing above all to remain forgotten.[3] But all this was irrelevant to Archinard. Like his predecessors, he was firmly committed to the destruction of the Tokolor empire, and by 1889 conditions were ripe for him to put a more aggressive policy into effect. The defeat of Mahmadu Lamine and the completion of the Railway to Bafoulabé had greatly improved both the security and the efficiency of the French supply lines. The treaties with Samori protected the south-east frontier and left them free to concentrate on the Tokolors. The progressive deterioration of Ahmadu's influence in Kaarta lessened the danger of a Tokolor counter-attack on their northern flank.[4] The capture of Koundian set the stage for the final assault on Segu; for it demolished the bases of Franco-Tokolor co-operation which Gallieni had laid in 1887. Although Archinard assured the Sultan that he considered Koundian an independent town and that the expedition had in no way

[1] Archinard to Gov. Sen., 4 Nov. 1888; same to same, 3 Jan. 1889, MFOM Sénégal IV 93(c).
[2] Same to same, 21 Feb. 1889; same to same, 26 Feb. 1889, *ibid.*
[3] Gallieni to Archinard, 22 June 1889, Archinard Papers. In his final report, Archinard himself admitted that the garrison of Koundian numbered 300. See: L. Archinard, *Le Soudan français en 1888–9* (Paris, 1890), pp. 27–8.
[4] Archinard to Desbordes, 24 Oct. 1889, cited in J. Méniaud, *Les pionniers du Soudan, avant, avec et après Archinard* (Paris, 1931), I, 436; 'Je vous assure bien...que les choses ont bien changé depuis...[1883], et qu'il n'y aurait plus à craindre, par une marche sur Ségou, de galvaniser tout ce monde du Kaarta et de risquer de voir notre ligne de ravitaillement attaquée. Chacun a peur aujourd'hui et espère qu'on le laissera personnellement tranquille s'il ne s'occupe pas de son voisin.'

been directed against the territorial integrity of the Tokolor empire, the argument was unconvincing and Ahmadu was not convinced. The Sultan immediately cut off all trade with Médine; according to Archinard, he would have declared war had his soldiers at Nioro and Koniakary not refused to fight.[1] The Commander also prepared for war. In order to prevent a concentration of Tokolor power, he now sent a small force to occupy Nyamina, and at the end of the campaign he sent Lieutenant Marchand to reconnoitre the fortifications of Segu in preparation for an attack.[2]

Archinard had a particular and personal interest in seeking to hasten the final confrontation. Despite the efforts of Gallieni and de La Porte, his appointment to the Sudan had not been accompanied by his promotion to the rank of Lieutenant-Colonel.[3] The only way to remedy the situation was through some brilliant demonstration of his military ability. The attack on Koundian had itself been timed to coincide with the drafting of the promotion lists at the Rue Royale. On the same day that he informed the Governor, Archinard cabled Brière an account of the engagement, asking him to bring it to the attention of the Ministry. Unfortunately, Brière was just too late; the Minister had made his final choices for the *tableau d'avancement* the day before, and Archinard had not been one of them. Brière promised to exert all his influence to secure the Commander's well-deserved promotion, and Desbordes, seeking to calm his irate protégé, also assured him that everything possible was being done for him in Paris.[4] But Archinard was not likely to remain idle while others worked on his behalf, and in the summer he returned to France in order to press his plans for an immediate expedition against Segu on the Ministry.[5]

The situation on his return was tense. Archinard had undertaken the Koundian operation entirely on his own initiative; not even Desbordes

[1] Gov. Sen. to Under-Secretary, 8 Mar. 1889, MFOM Sénégal I 80(b); Archinard to Gov. Sen., 15 Mar. 1889, MFOM Sénégal IV 93(c).
[2] Archinard to Underberg [Commandant, Bamako], 2 July 1889, cited in Méniaud, *op. cit.* I, 413.
[3] Gallieni to Archinard, 3 Aug. 1888, Archinard Papers; de La Porte, Note pour le Ministre, 16 Apr. 1888, MFOM Missions 40, Archinard.
[4] Brière to Minister of Marine, 23 Feb. 1889 [Copy], AEMD Afrique 122; Brière to unnamed intermediary, 26 Feb. 1889; Desbordes to Archinard, n.d. [Spring, 1889], Archinard Papers.
[5] Archinard to Colonna de Giovellina [*Commandant-Supérieur, p.i.*], n.d., cited in Méniaud, *op. cit.* I, 427: 'J'ai caressé certains projets que je serais désolé de ne pas mettre en exécution, et pour lesquels même j'aurais renoncé à mon voyage en France s'il ne me fallait pas justement aller en France pour les faire accepter et obtenir quelque matériel et quelques troupes.'

had been given advance warning, and the Colonel was more than a little concerned about the political repercussions of the unauthorised action.[1] In March 1889, moreover, Etienne had again become Under-Secretary, and he was not a man to be trifled with. As Desbordes feared, the Under-Secretary took a dim view of the business and formally ordered Archinard 'to obtain my specific instructions before undertaking any [future] military operation'. Such authorisation would not be lightly given, for Etienne was determined to keep the costs of military expansion within bounds.[2] The Commander therefore justified his plans on the grounds of economy. Tokolor hostility, he claimed, had so far been the greatest single obstacle to commercial development and the efficient collection of taxes, and the major reason for the high costs of military occupation. As long as the Tokolors continued to threaten security, there could be no question of any substantial reduction in expenditure. Once their power had been broken, however, the French could reap the benefits of all their past sacrifices. Médine, Bafoulabé, Badumbé and Koundou could be evacuated completely, and the garrison of Bamako could be halved. Trade would prosper, and the Sudan would cease to be a burden on the Treasury. These objectives could even be achieved without a declaration of war. The capture of Segu would not lead to general hostilities, for Ahmadu himself was a coward and would not fight unless directly attacked.[3] Etienne did not remain unmoved by the argument. According to Archinard at least, the Under-Secretary assured him of his confidence and promised his approval for all necessary military action. Certainly, the Commander was allowed to take two 95 mm siege guns back with him to the Sudan.[4]

Armed with his cannons and the Under-Secretary's assurances, Archinard made his final preparations. In November Marchand submitted a gloomy report about the strength of Segu's defences; but the Commander was unperturbed, for he was confident that the walls would be unable to withstand the fire of his heavy artillery.[5] In order not to arouse Tokolor suspicions, he sent cordial messages to Ahmadu,

[1] Desbordes to Archinard, n.d. [Spring 1889], Archinard Papers: 'Je crois que la chute de Koundian par les armes a été une chose regrettable...parce qu'à la moindre complication la France abandonnera ce pays.'
[2] Etienne to Archinard, Instructions, n.d., cited in Archinard to Gov. Sen., 9 Jan. 1890, MFOM Sénégal IV 95 (b). Etienne had already reprimanded the Commander for exceeding the Budget. See: Etienne to Gov. Sen., 17 Apr. 1889, MFOM Sénégal I 80(c).
[3] Archinard, Note, 19 Aug. 1889, MFOM Sénégal IV 93 (a).
[4] Archinard to Gov. Sen., 9 Jan. 1890, MFOM Sénégal IV 95 (b).
[5] Marchand to Archinard, 3 Nov. 1889; Archinard to Marchand, 4 Dec. 1889, cited in Méniaud, *op. cit.* 1, 438–40, 440–1.

pledging never to invade his empire. He asked the Sultan to accept the Senegal as a frontier and to recognise French influence over the town of Saboné north of Koundou; but he also gave assurances that none of their differences was important enough to lead to war. As late as 16 January he was still professing his desire for peace and friendship.[1]

By then, however, the last stage of his plan had been activated. A week before, he had warned the Governor that a Tokolor attack on the French supply lines was imminent. The Sultan, he claimed, was actively conspiring with Samori and was mobilising his troops in Kaarta. In the interests of security, Archinard asked for permission to take whatever action he deemed necessary, including an attack on Segu. This was not a request for specific orders, he claimed; all he wanted was recognition of his freedom of action. Two weeks later, he wrote directly to Etienne, assuring him that the capture of Segu would ruin Ahmadu's prestige without provoking serious unrest and would enable the French to collect 100,000 fr. a year in taxes from Beledugu. After the capture of Segu, he added, the French would be able to concentrate on the development of the more profitable regions in the south and on the extension of their influence into Futa Jallon. Not even a direct order was needed; a simple *faites pour le mieux* from the Under-Secretary would do.[2]

Archinard's demands placed Etienne in a dilemma. Although he may have given the Commander some assurances of his support, he was by no means a committed partisan of military expansion. His own Sudan Commission had just called for an end to the era of conquest, and he had approved its report. His closest military adviser on Sudanese affairs, Gallieni, was against an attack on Segu, confident that the city would fall to the French of its own accord as soon as Ahmadu died.[3] But, on the other hand, its capture would undoubtedly boost French prestige and improve prospects for expansion into the Niger Bend. If Archinard's assessments were correct, it might even result in substantial economies. To help him make up his mind, Etienne asked Saint-Louis for its opinion; but by then the Governor had been care-

[1] Archinard to Ahmadu, 6 Dec. 1889; same to same, 28 Dec. 1889, cited in Archinard to Gov. Sen., 9 Jan. 1890, MFOM Sénégal IV 95 (b); Archinard to Ahmadu, 16 Jan. 1890, cited in Méniaud, *op. cit.* I, 442.

[2] Archinard to Gov. Sen., 9 Jan. 1890; Archinard to Etienne, 20 Jan. 1890, MFOM Sénégal IV 95 (b).

[3] Rapport de la Souscommission, 22 Jan. 1890, MFOM Soudan VII 1 (a): 'La pénétration doit toujours être pacifique; l'emploi des armes n'est justifié que pour la défense des intérêts engagés et pour le...châtiment d'une aggression.' Gallieni, Rapport, 29 Jan. 1890, *ibid.*

fully prompted to give the right answer. Throughout February, Archinard sent back a series of alarming reports about the increasingly critical situation in the Sudan. He now claimed that a close *entente* existed between Ahmadu, Samori and Abdul-Bubakar, and that diversionary attacks would be mounted in Futa while the Sultan himself moved against Nyamina. Indeed, Ahmadu had just rejected the Senegal frontier, and this was equivalent to a declaration of war. Governor Clément-Thomas dutifully passed on this information, adding his own opinion that the capture of Segu was both feasible and essential.[1] His reply was enough to dispel the Under-Secretary's doubts, and on 27 February Etienne ordered him to 'cable Archinard the agreed formula: *faites pour le mieux*'.[2]

Having secured the Colonial Department's approval, Archinard could drop the pretence that his expedition was urgent. He had always intended to launch his attack towards the end of March when the water level of the Niger would be low enough to permit an easy passage; so he spent the next few weeks completing the revictualling of the forts. The bogey of Abdul-Bubakar had also served its purpose and could be forgotten. Although unrest did break out in Futa, the Commander made no attempt to suppress it. Instead he kept his column together and moved east. On 6 April, according to plan, his troops arrived before the Tokolor capital. After prolonged shelling, the walls were breached and the city was stormed. The French suffered no casualties; the Tokolor defenders had fled as soon as the bombardment began.[3] Archinard did not even bother to justify the attack by inventing any new act of Tokolor aggression. Segu had been taken, he told Ahmadu, because the Sultan had refused to accept the Senegal frontier or to recognise French claims to Saboné.[4]

Despite the confident predictions of the local authorities, the capture of Segu made the continuation of the conflict inevitable. When justifying the operation, Archinard and Clément-Thomas had both argued strongly against an invasion of Kaarta. But as soon as Segu had fallen

---

[1] Archinard to Gov. Sen., 13 Feb. 1890; same to same, 25 Feb. 1890, MFOM Sénégal IV 95(b); Gov. Sen. to Etienne, 25 Feb. 1890, MFOM Sénégal I 80(b); same to same, 26 Feb. 1890, MFOM Télégrammes Afrique, Sénégal, 1889, II, Arrivée no. 243.

[2] Etienne to Gov. Sen., 27 Feb. 1890, MFOM Télégrammes Afrique, Sénégal, 1890, Départ no. 28.

[3] Archinard to Gov. Sen., 1 Mar. 1890; same to same, 12 Apr. 1890, MFOM Sénégal IV 95(b). See also: Archinard, Rapport...1889–90, cited in Méniaud, *op. cit.* I, 445–66.

[4] Archinard to Ahmadu, n.d., cited in Archinard to Gov. Sen., 12 Apr. 1890, MFOM Sénégal IV 95(b).

they changed their tune. The Governor now claimed that Kaarta too would have to be taken and Ahmadu's power completely broken if Médine were to have any future as a trading centre.[1] Archinard too was determined to complete the conquest. With scarcely a pause for breath, he reorganised his column and led it north against Oussébougou, Ahmadu's fortress on the eastern frontier of Kaarta. By its capture he hoped to clear the way for his Bambara allies to harass the Tokolors as far as the gates of Nioro. 'Oussébougou after Segu', he told Desbordes in May 1890, 'will, I am sure, give us the whole of Kaarta soon.'[2] Even Ahmadu was finally stung into action. At the end of May his troops attacked the Railway at Talaari; on 3 June they fought a heavy engagement with the French at Kalé; three days later tentative attacks were launched against Kayes. Archinard now had his excuse for invading Kaarta, and on 16 June he captured Koniakary.[3]

With the outbreak of war, all hope of reducing Sudanese expenditure vanished; there could be no question now of any cuts in garrison strengths. The costs of occupation continued to rise. In 1888 the Sudanese estimates had been exceeded by 925,000 fr.; in 1889 the figure was 1,405,000 fr.; in 1890 it was to be 1,200,000 fr.[4] But the Commander himself could feel satisfied. His capture of Segu reinforced the efforts of his patrons to obtain his promotion to Lieutenant-Colonel. Brière, Desbordes, Etienne and Paul Dislère all urged the Minister of Marine to recognise his services, and on 27 April their persistence was finally rewarded.[5] Archinard's tenure of the command was also safe. In May he had warned the Governor that any decision to replace him should be kept secret because Ahmadu had declared him to be the only Frenchman whom he feared.[6] But it was an unnecessary precaution. By approving the Segu expedition, Etienne had effectively placed himself at the mercy of the Military, and he had to accept the consequences. The decisions of the Sudan Commission were set aside; the incensed protests of Vallon and his prophecies of disaster were ignored.[7] Archinard was duly reappointed. He was not given new instructions, for, as he later

---

[1] Archinard to Gov. Sen., 9 Jan. 1890 (Conf.), MFOM Sénégal IV 95 (b); Gov. Sen. to Etienne, 25 Feb. 1890; same to same, 4 May 1890, MFOM Sénégal I 80(b).

[2] Archinard to Desbordes, 4 May 1890, cited in Méniaud, *op. cit.* 1, 523–4.

[3] Archinard, Rapport...1889–90, cited *ibid.* pp. 488–514.

[4] Picanon to Etienne, 1 Sept. 1890, MFOM Soudan XIX 2: *J.O. Déb. 'arl. Chambre*, séance du 30 novembre 1891, p. 2357.

[5] Desbordes to Archinard, 2 Apr. 1890, Archinard Papers.

[6] Archinard to Gov. Sen., 22 May 1890, MFOM Sénégal IV 95 (b).

[7] Vallon to Etienne, 22 Mar. 1890, MFOM Sénégal IV 95 (c).

pointed out, 'the next campaign could only be the continuation of the previous one'.[1]

After the Commander's return, events followed their predictable course. Ahmadu had tried unsuccessfully to retake Koniakary during the rainy season, and this was ample reason for the inevitable attack on Nioro. In December, Archinard formed his expeditionary column, set out for the Sultan's capital, and after a series of skirmishes occupied it on New Year's Day 1891. Ahmadu and a small band of followers fled eastward across the desert towards Macina. The campaign cost the French five killed and fifty-three wounded; Tokolor losses were estimated at three thousand killed or captured.[2] It was an easy victory and not an unexpected one. The crucial battles in the war were political, not military; they had been fought and won in Paris, not in the Sudan, and it was his victory over the Colonial Department which Archinard now set out to exploit. For the overthrow of the Tokolor empire did not satisfy the Commander's military ambitions; within a week of capturing Nioro, he was calling for an immediate campaign against Samori.

THE WAR AGAINST SAMORI

Although Archinard had chosen to deal with Ahmadu first, he had not forgotten Samori. Despite his losses at Sikasso, the *imam* was still the most formidable African power in the Western Sudan and the most dangerous threat to French security. The treaty of 1889 had not been observed by either party. Both sides continued to raid across the Niger, and when the *sofas* refused to evacuate the lands south of the Tankisso, Archinard drove them out. In May 1889 Samori repudiated the agreement and sent back his copy of it. As far as Archinard was concerned this too amounted to a declaration of war.[3] Anxious not to fight on two fronts, the Commander took no immediate action in the south-east; but he made the necessary preparations. In April 1890 Tiéba's ambassadors were invited to witness the capture of Segu. After its fall, Archinard sent an embassy to Sikasso with instructions to persuade Tiéba to join the French in an invasion of Samori's empire during the next campaign. In order to gain his support, Captain Quiquandon and a force of 3,000 Bambaras from Segu helped him in his siege of Kinian, a well-defended

---

[1] Archinard, Rapport...1890–1, Cap. I, *J.O.* 10 Oct. 1891, p. 4863.
[2] *Ibid.* Cap. II, 11 Oct., 14 Oct. 1891, pp. 4882–6, 4928.
[3] Archinard to Gov. Sen., 13 Apr. 1889, MFOM Sénégal IV 93 (c); Archinard, Rapport...
1890–1, Cap. IV, *J.O.* 19 Oct. 1891, pp. 5026 ff.

town hostile to Sikasso.[1] Archinard prepared the political ground just as carefully. In November 1890 he warned both Etienne and the Governor that Samori was strengthening his connections with the British in Sierra Leone, who were supplying him with modern weapons. As long as this situation persisted, he claimed, the French could never hope for a lasting peace.[2] As soon as he had dealt with Ahmadu, he intensified his agitation. On 9 January he told Etienne that a campaign against the *imam* would have to be launched as soon as possible. In February he told the Governor that Samori was actively supporting anti-French rebels in the newly conquered province of Segu. In March he reported the discovery of further correspondence between Ahmadu and Samori which provided conclusive proof of the *imam*'s hostile intentions.[3] In April, as soon as he had suppressed the Segu rebellion, Archinard reformed his expeditionary column and moved south. He did not wait for the Ministry's approval.

Indeed, his proposed campaign ran dead against the wishes of his superiors. Etienne was alarmed by the heavy losses suffered during the rebellion in Segu and apprehensive about the political repercussions of continued military operations in the Sudan.[4] The new Governor of Senegal, De Lamothe, was equally concerned. Both men gave Archinard strict instructions not to launch a new campaign, and Etienne sent Captain Péroz to negotiate yet another treaty with the *imam*.[5] But the Commander was not to be diverted from his objective. Public opinion in France, he told the Governor, could not be allowed to interfere with the maintenance of security in the Sudan. The Péroz mission itself was useless because a Samorian embassy was already on its way to Siguiri.[6]

[1] Quiquandon, Rapport, 8 July 1891, MFOM Sénégal IV 96(b). Despite the help from Segu, however, Kinian held out until 8 March, and Archinard was thus deprived of Tiéba's active support.

[2] Archinard to Etienne, 4 Nov. 1890; Archinard to Gov. Sen., 4 Nov. 1890, MFOM Sénégal IV 95(b); same to same, 1 Dec. 1890, MFOM Soudan I 1(c).

[3] Archinard to Etienne, 9 Jan. 1891, MFOM Soudan I 1(a); Archinard to Gov. Sen., 14 Feb. 1891, cited in Archinard, Rapport...1890–1, Cap. III, *J.O.* 16 Oct. 1891, p. 4959; same to same, 14 Mar. 1891, MFOM Soudan I 1(c).

[4] Etienne to Gov. Sen., 11 Mar. 1891, MFOM Sénégal I 91(b): 'Affaire Diana [Diéna]... impressionne vivement et défavorablement gouvernement et opinion publique...Opinion redoute prolongation indéfinie état guerre Soudan. Dites Archinard que ma confiance en lui est absolue mais il est indispensable que je puisse rassurer opinion et gouvernement.' The attack on the rebel town of Diéna (24 February) had cost the French over 100 casualties, among them eight officers wounded.

[5] Gov. Sen. to Etienne, 6 Apr. 1891, MFOM Sénégal I 91(a); Etienne to Gov. Sen., 22 Nov. 1891, MFOM Sénégal I 91(b).

[6] Archinard to Gov. Sen., 17 Mar. 1891, MFOM Soudan I 1(c); Gov. Sen. to Etienne, 28 Mar. 1891, MFOM Sénégal I 91(a).

Less than a week after this announcement, Archinard crossed the Niger and attacked Kankan. A flying column was immediately sent against Bissandugu and burned the town on 9 April. Leaving a small garrison at Kankan, Archinard then returned with his main force to Siguiri.

There was great consternation at Saint-Louis. De Lamothe had been given no warning of the operation; Archinard had told him that the purpose of his column was to provision the French fort at Kouroussa. Both the Governor and his *Commandant-Supérieur des Troupes* considered the Kankan garrison completely inadequate for the defence of the territory which had just been occupied.[1] Etienne himself was enraged. He denounced the campaign as 'an absolute violation of [my] instructions' and reprimanded the Commander for not keeping him fully informed. Determined not to accept the *fait accompli*, he ordered the Governor to investigate the possibility of evacuating Kankan and resuming relations with Samori.[2] But Archinard treated the whole furore with sovereign indifference. Choosing to ignore the less convenient wording of the Under-Secretary's reprimand, he replied that the campaign had not been a violation of the Samori treaty because the *imam* had already repudiated it. He offered no justification for his action beyond the claim that Samori had been supplied with modern weapons and had always shown himself hostile. He dismissed the charge of deliberately failing to inform his superiors with the off-hand comment that he did not generally bother to report such petty military incidents. To set the Governor's mind at rest, he assured him that Samori had put up very little resistance and that the French occupation force was in full command of the situation.[3]

Archinard could afford to remain calm. Despite his concern about the military situation, Governor De Lamothe rejected any suggestion of evacuating Kankan as potentially disastrous for security.[4] Etienne too was powerless; he could not halt the operation in midstream. Archinard's unauthorised advance, he told the Quai d'Orsay, confronted the Colonial Department with a *fait accompli* 'which I [greatly] regret, but which makes the continuation of the conflict inevitable'.[5] The Under-Secretary could not even exercise his powers of recall, because Archi-

---

[1] Same to same, 13 Apr. 1891; same to same, 15 Apr. 1891, *ibid.*
[2] Etienne to Gov. Sen., 14 Apr. 1891; same to same, 19 Apr. 1891, MFOM Sénégal I 91 (b).
[3] Archinard to Gov. Sen., 19 Apr. 1891 [Copy], Archinard Papers; same to same, 20 Apr. 1891, MFOM Soudan I 1 (c).
[4] Gov. Sen. to Etienne, 15 Apr. 1891; same to same, 16 Apr. 1891, MFOM Sénégal I 91 (a).
[5] Etienne to M.A.E., 27 Apr. 1891, AEMD Afrique 123.

nard had already contracted a bout of blackwater fever which made it impossible for him to carry on in his command. Indeed, the alarming state of his health finally dissuaded Etienne from taking sterner disciplinary action against him.[1] And to crown the Commander's success, his military feats in Kaarta and on the Niger earned him a recommendation for promotion to the rank of Colonel.[2]

After Archinard's departure, Etienne tried hard to reassert his control over Sudanese policy. He gave the new *Commandant-Supérieur* strict orders to keep him fully informed of all developments and to take no action without the Department's prior consent. The events of the last campaign were not to be repeated; the organisation of the new territories, not the pursuit of Samori, was to be the objective. But he had to admit that the campaign could not be broken off completely, and he could do no more than insist on extreme prudence in the conduct of all military operations.[3] Poor Etienne was now truly a prisoner of his military commanders. Archinard's campaign had thrown the Sudan question back into the Parliamentary arena, and in December 1891 the Under-Secretary was forced to give a solemn pledge not to authorise further expeditions without the approval of the Chambers.[4] Accordingly, he issued new instructions restricting military action to the defence of Kankan and vetoed plans for a campaign to cut off Samori's arms supply from Sierra Leone.[5] But Archinard's successor, his friend and classmate Gustave Humbert, was just as intractable. He told the Governor that he had accepted the command only after approving the policies laid down in his instructions and threatened to resign if these were changed. De Lamothe passed on the ultimatum, adding that any decision not to carry out the original programme would be disastrous for French prestige. And Etienne had to give in. He quickly assured his local authorities that the new instructions were merely intended to underline the importance of avoiding any risk of defeat, and he reaffirmed his approval for continued operations against Samori provided success

[1] Gov. Sen. to Etienne, 13 Apr. 1891, MFOM Sénégal I 91(a); Etienne to Gov. Sen., 19 Apr. 1891, MFOM Sénégal I 91(b): 'En présence d'une attitude aussi blâmable je n'aurais pas hésité à proposer à ses égards une mesure de rigueur, si je n'avais pris en considération l'état alarmant de sa santé...'

[2] The recommendation was most probably the work of Desbordes, who was by then permanent Inspector-General of the *artillerie de marine*.

[3] Etienne to Humbert, Instructions, 16 Sept. 1891, MFOM Soudan I 2(a).

[4] See below: p. 204.

[5] Etienne to Gov. Sen., 25 Nov. 1891; same to same, 4 Dec. 1891, MFOM Télégrammes Afrique, Sénégal, 1891, Départ, nos. 91, 94.

were certain and the costs of occupation were not increased.[1] Humbert's defiance of Paris, more forthright than Archinard's, was just as effective.[2]

The Commander soon discovered, however, that victory over Samori did not automatically follow easy triumphs over the Colonial Department. Archinard's assessment of the military situation had been wildly optimistic; Samori's initial lack of resistance had not been a sign of his weakness but part of a deliberately conceived strategy. The campaigns of the 1880s had taught the *imam* the folly of committing his troops to set-piece engagements where the full superiority of French discipline and fire-power could be brought to bear. Accordingly, he resorted to guerrilla tactics, enticing the French away from their bases, harassing their supply lines, systematically destroying their local sources of provisions in the wake of his retreat, and ambushing their columns whenever the conditions of the ground were favourable. His *sofas*, now reported to possess 8,000 repeating rifles, used their modern weapons with devastating effect. After a particularly bloody engagement in the marshes of Diamanko, Humbert was forced to admit that they were by far the strongest military force which the French had so far encountered in the Sudan. 'Samori's troops fight exactly like Europeans', wrote the embattled Colonel, 'with less discipline perhaps, but with much greater determination.'[3]

To deal with this formidable opposition, Humbert had to rely exclusively on his own resources. Before returning to France, Archinard had sent Lieutenant Marchand to carry on the work of Quiquandon and persuade King Tiéba to attack from the north-east. But Marchand was no diplomat and soon antagonised their ally by insisting that he march during the rainy season. Rightly suspecting that the French wanted to weaken his own forces as well as to secure his help against their common enemy, Tiéba refused to advance beyond Tengréla. Renewed protestations of French goodwill and the recall of Marchand failed to calm his

---

[1] Humbert to Gov. Sen., 8 Dec. 1891, MFOM Soudan I 2 (d); Gov. Sen. to Etienne, 11 Dec. 1891, MFOM Sénégal I 91 (a); Etienne to Gov. Sen., 12 Dec. 1891, MFOM Télégrammes Afrique, Sénégal, 1891, Départ no. 96.

[2] According to Humbert, his frankness aroused considerable alarm on the part of Archinard. See Archinard to Humbert, 23 Jan. 1892, cited by Humbert in *Le Soir*, 30 July 1897: 'Tu as agi carrément et correctement...mais j'aurais tremblé si j'avais su cela plus tôt...et peut-être t'aurais-je conseillé de ne tenir aucun compte des nouvelles instructions et de marcher sans offrir de te démettre du commandement. C'est ce que j'ai fait moi-même dans deux circonstances...'

[3] Humbert to Gov. Sen., 12 Jan. 1892, MFOM Soudan I 2(d). See also: Humbert, Rapport ...1891–2, Part II, *J.O.* 10 Mar. 1893, p. 1249.

fears, and by the end of March the king was openly hostile.[1] Unable to rely on Sikasso, Humbert had to reinforce his column by reducing his garrison strengths in the occupied territories to a minimum. He then found that his expeditionary force of 1,300 men was much too large to be efficiently supplied, especially in the face of the *imam*'s scorched-earth policy. The inevitable happened. Although Humbert managed to chase Samori as far as Kerouané, the exhaustion of his supplies then forced him to return to Bissandugu, leaving small and precarious advance posts at Kerouané and Sanankoro. To make matters worse, the reduction of the garrisons in the north compromised security and left the French unable to deal effectively with new rebellions in Segu and Sansanding. Humbert's campaign was clearly a failure. Even before its start, yellow fever had taken the lives of thirteen officers and sixty-seven men; by its end another twenty Europeans had been lost and the costs of occupation increased by 1,500,000 fr. Governor De Lamothe spoke disparagingly of 'a partial success... a glorious adventure which led [the Commander] to lose sight completely of the complications which might arise in other parts of the territory'.[2]

Naturally disappointed by his failure to emulate the brilliant feats of his predecessor, Humbert began to look for scapegoats. The Governor of Senegal, he claimed, had failed to provide adequate transport facilities or to authorise a diversionary campaign in the Mellacourie in order to cut off the *imam*'s arms supply. The Under-Secretary too had done nothing about the sale of arms from Sierra Leone. Both men had treated him with an utter lack of sympathy; Etienne had sent him only one message of congratulations throughout the whole campaign; De Lamothe had not even bothered to acknowledge his despatches.[3] Overwhelmed by his sense of personal injustice, the unfortunate Commander soon lost what little remained of his self-control. 'I was wrong to expose myself to disaster and dishonour', he raved; 'I was lucky to escape. I have done more than my duty. I shall leave here unafraid, with a clear conscience, and determined...to sacrifice my position and my

---

[1] Gaëtan Bonnier to Archinard, 2 Nov. 1891; same to same, 19 Jan. 1892, Archinard Papers; Péroz, Rapport, 9 Jan. 1892, MFOM Soudan III 1; Humbert to Gov. Sen., 31 Mar. 1892, MFOM Soudan I 2(d).

[2] Humbert to Gov. Sen., 10 Nov. 1891; Humbert to Etienne, 29 Dec. 1891, MFOM Soudan I 2(b); Humbert, Rapport...1891–2, *J.O.* 10 Mar. 1893, 2 July 1893, pp. 1249ff., 3382; Gov. Sen. to Under-Secretary, 6 Apr. 1892, MFOM Sénégal I 91(a).

[3] Humbert to Gov. Sen., 17 Mar. 1892; same to same, 25 Mar. 1892; same to same, 29 Mar. 1892, MFOM Soudan I 2(d).

life in order to make the truth known.'¹ After a time his resentment against Paris and Saint-Louis diminished; but his sense of grievance remained acute, and he next trained his guns on the real author of his misfortunes, Archinard. The cause of all his difficulties, he now claimed, had been the decision to attack Samori in the first place. After the capture of Nioro, his predecessor should have organised and consolidated his new conquests; instead, he rashly began another military advance which doomed his own campaign to failure.² Although the accusation was not without its validity, its immediate effect was to give Archinard the opportunity to stake a new claim to the Sudan Command.

ARCHINARD'S LAST CAMPAIGN

Although Archinard had willingly approved Humbert as his successor, he never regarded his colleague as anything more than a temporary replacement. Before surrendering the command, he had already put himself at the disposal of the Colonial Department 'should it wish me to complete the work which Colonel Humbert will continue'.³ As long as Etienne remained in control, his chances of reappointment were small; but the ministerial reshuffle of February 1892 greatly improved his prospects. The Colonial Department was now returned to the Ministry of Marine, where Brière and Desbordes, as the Inspectors-General of the *infanterie* and *artillerie de marine*, could exert a still more direct influence on Sudanese policy. Better still, Etienne's replacement, Emile Jamais, lacked the necessary strength of personality to keep the Military in check. By March he was having talks with Archinard, and in June the former Commander, with Desbordes's full approval, officially submitted his request to lead the next campaign. Humbert, he claimed, had blamed him for the unsatisfactory situation in the Sudan, and he was anxious to disprove the charge.⁴

Jamais was reluctant to approve the request. Parliament's continued opposition to the spiralling costs of military occupation had forced him to renew Etienne's declaration that the era of military expansion had come to an end. As the Sudan's critics pointed out, Archinard's appoint-

---

¹ Same to same, 10 Apr. 1892; same to same, 12 Apr. 1892, *ibid.*
² Humbert to Gov. Sen., 2 May 1892, *ibid.* See also: Humbert Rapport...1891–2, *J.O.* 2 July 1893, p. 3382.   ³ Archinard to Gov. Sen., 15 May 1891, MFOM Soudan I 1 (c).
⁴ *Le Siècle*, 17 Mar. 1892; Archinard to Jamais, 15 June 1892, MFOM Soudan I 2(f). See also: *Le Siècle*, 11 Nov. 1893 [Jamais's obituary]: 'Pour gouverner et administrer, il ne suffit pas de savoir parler; il faut encore...savoir agir. M. Emile Jamais avait d'autres qualités mais il n'en avait pas celle-là.'

ment would make nonsense of this pledge, and indeed the Under-Secretary moved heaven and earth to secure the nomination of the more reliable Gallieni. But Brière de l'Isle categorically refused to give his consent and held out for Desbordes's protégé.[1] In the end, Jamais gave in to the pressure of the Generals, and in August Archinard's reappointment was formally confirmed. But the Under-Secretary did not surrender unconditionally. Having failed to prevent Archinard's return, he looked for more subtle ways to bridle the commander's known ambitions.

Although the reorganisation of 1890 had greatly increased the Military's influence in the Sudan, the Commanders remained unsatisfied with the arrangement and continued to object to their notional dependence on Saint-Louis. In 1891 Archinard himself had called for the complete separation of the Sudan from Senegal. The following year Humbert demanded full political autonomy from the Governor. Even De Lamothe, while opposing the suggestion in principle, was not averse to a reform which might relieve him of responsibility for an area where he could no longer exercise effective control.[2] During the summer, the Governor returned to Paris for discussions on the issue, and on 27 August a new Decree reorganising the Sudan was promulgated. Superficially, its terms gave the Military as much as they could have hoped for. Although Bakel and Bondu were detached to Senegal, the rest of the colony was placed under the full political and military authority of the *Commandant-Supérieur*. The last traces of his subordination to the Governor were eradicated; in future he could correspond directly with Paris and only send copies of his despatches to Saint-Louis. But the real purpose of the reorganisation was to make the *Commandant-Supérieur*'s functions administrative rather than military. In future, military operations were to be conducted by a subordinate commander. By giving Archinard gubernatorial status, Jamais could forbid him to lead any campaign in person and at the same time forestall any opposition to the move.[3]

The Under-Secretary's instructions confirmed his intentions.[4] He warned Archinard that the new system was in no way designed to prolong 'the era of military action'; its sole aim was to prepare the

[1] Etienne Bonnier to Archinard, 3 July 1892, Archinard Papers. For the attitude of the Chamber and Jamais's declarations, see below: p. 204.
[2] Archinard, Rapport...1890–1, Cap. V, *J.O.* 28 Oct. 1891, p. 5189; Humbert to Under-Secretary, 18 Mar. 1892, MFOM Soudan I 2 (b); De Lamothe to Under-Secretary, 21 Apr. 1892; same to same, 28 May 1892, MFOM Sénégal I 91 (a).
[3] Decree, 27 Aug. 1892, MFOM Soudan VII 1 (c).
[4] Jamais to Archinard, Instructions, 12 Sept. 1892, MFOM Soudan I 4 (a).

way for the eventual creation of a completely civilian administration. Once more, consolidation, commercial development and the reduction of expenditure were to be the Commander's principal objectives. He was at all times to remember the prohibition against his personal involvement in military operations; if exceptional circumstances forced him to assume direct command of a column, he was immediately to inform the Colonial Department and obtain its permission. In conclusion, Jamais expressed his confidence that Archinard would now devote himself to the organisation of 'a sound and enlightened administration, capable of securing the pacification of [your] territory and the solid establishment of French civilising influence there'. It was a fond hope.

The struggle against Samori allowed Archinard to demonstrate his own intentions. Although Jamais was forced to allow the campaign to continue, he insisted that its objective must be to cut the *imam*'s communications with Sierra Leone, not to pursue him into unknown territories whose occupation could only weaken French control over the rest of the colony. If the conditions were right, Archinard could even negotiate a new agreement with him. But the Commander ignored the Under-Secretary's cautious plans. The only way to maintain security, he told his military commander, Colonel Combes, was to attack him, defeat him, and pursue him as far east as possible. Archinard set no limit on the advance, but he foresaw the occupation of Guéliba, 100 km. east of Sanankoro. In the west, he ordered Combes to occupy Farana on the main caravan route from Sierra Leone, to attack Samori's lieutenant, Bilali, pursuing him if necessary into English territory, and to occupy Bilali's headquarters at Erimakono. Archinard admitted the possibility of complications with the British and gave orders for all their nationals to be treated with courtesy. But any British attempt to drive the French out of their occupied positions was to be resisted, in the last resort by force.[1] He could rely on his military commander to carry out his orders to the full. Taking charge of the main column, Combes chased Samori well beyond Guéliba to the banks of the Baoulé river. At the same time, Commandant Briquelot moved south from Kouroussa, occupied Farana, and in February 1893 captured Erimakono as well.[2]

When it came to the test, Paris was completely unable to control its determined *Commandant-Supérieur*. Although Archinard sent Jamais a

---

[1] Archinard to Combes, 19 Nov. 1892 (Conf.), MFOM Soudan V 1 (c).
[2] Archinard to Under-Secretary, 24 Mar. 1893, MFOM Télégrammes Afrique, Soudan, 1893, Arrivée no. 11; Briquelot to British Commander, Falaba, 14 Feb. 1893 [Copy], AEMD Afrique 131.

copy of his instructions to Combes, the Under-Secretary made no comment on them. When Archinard informed the Department of the full extent of the advance, the new Under-Secretary, Théophile Delcassé, merely sent Combes his congratulations.[1] The drive towards Sierra Leone was a potentially more serious affair. The Boundary Commission set up under the terms of the Anglo-French Agreement of August 1890 had discussed the northern frontier of Sierra Leone, and in June 1891 it had confirmed French rights to the road between the Niger and the Mellacourie. But the Commissioners appointed to carry out the frontier survey soon quarrelled, and the French delegates refused to proceed. The British party carried on alone, completing the survey as far as Farana, and placed Erimakono in the British sphere. Anxious to avoid diplomatic complications, Jamais ordered Archinard not to occupy the village until the dispute had been settled; but the *Commandant-Supérieur* refused to be put off. Erimakono, he claimed, was on the Niger–Mellacourie road and could not be abandoned simply on the unconfirmed assertions of the British surveyors. Only the Boundary Commission itself could decide the question of ownership; in the meantime, it would do no harm to take effective possession of the town. Accordingly he made no attempt to halt Briquelot.[2]

The Commander's uncompromising attitude almost provoked a major international crisis. The British Government protested hotly at the seizure of Erimakono, and in March the Lieutenant-Governor of the Southern Rivers reported that a strong column under Captain Lendy was moving on the town. Although an actual clash was averted, tempers on both sides ran high, and the situation remained tense throughout the spring. The French were left in possession of Erimakono, but the British occupied Kaliere, thus cutting the road to Benty. In turn, Archinard ordered Briquelot to continue his pursuit of the *sofas* and to occupy Wassu and Walia, also on the Benty road. As a reprisal for Sierra Leone's participation in the arms trade, he instructed Briquelot to intercept all caravans to or from the British colony. For added effect, Colonel Combes threatened to burn the British fort at Falaba if the *sofas* were allowed to take refuge there and claimed the whole northern

---

[1] Archinard to Jamais, 26 Nov. 1892, MFOM Soudan I 4(b); Delcassé to Archinard, 27 Mar. 1893, MFOM Télégrammes Afrique, Soudan, 1893, Départ no. 15.

[2] Jamais to Archinard, 5 Jan. 1893, *ibid.* Départ no. 1; Archinard to Under-Secretary, 7 Jan. 1893 [Copy]; same to same, 21 Jan. 1893 [Copy], AEMD Afrique 131. The proceedings of the Boundary Commission can be found in AEMD Afrique 129. See also: C. Fyfe, *A History of Sierra Leone* (Oxford, 1962), pp. 50–2, 504.

part of Sulimana province, indisputably British, by right of conquest.[1] And in the end the Military had their way. Archinard's firm stand had the support of the Quai d'Orsay—which rejected British protests on the grounds that a frontier could not be violated until it had been delimited—and of Under-Secretary Delcassé as well.[2] Although the coming of the rains took much of the heat out of the situation and allowed negotiations to proceed on a less unfriendly basis, both Archinard and Combes continued to press for the retention of Erimakono, warning that its surrender would have disastrous consequences for French prestige in the south. As a result, the French Commissioners stood firm on the issue, and the British, failing to match their intransigence, finally agreed to recognise their claim.[3]

Diplomacy was not the only sphere in which Archinard made his influence felt. Although he had been content to leave the conduct of the Samori campaign to Combes, he was not a man to while away all his time on unexciting administrative duties at Kayes. Ever since the capture of Segu, he had been planning a further advance down the Niger towards Timbuktu. Immediately after the fall of Ahmadu's capital, he had sent Mademba Si, one of the Military's most trusted Native Agents, on an abortive mission to establish relations with Macina. After the capture of Nioro, he had installed Mademba Si as *fama* of the newly created kingdom of Sansanding, with orders to prepare the way for the continued extension of French influence. 'I think the conquest of Macina will soon become necessary', he wrote in his instructions, 'and it is with the thought that you will one day reign at Bandiagara and give us the Niger as far as Timbuktu, and Timbuktu itself, that I have made you king of Sansanding.'[4] The diversion of his

[1] Lieutenant-Governor, *Rivières du Sud* to Under-Secretary, 11 Mar. 1893, MFOM Télégrammes Afrique, Konakry, 1893, Arrivée no. 12; Archinard to Under-Secretary, 22 Mar. 1893; same to same, 24 Mar. 1893; same to same, 13 Apr. 1893, MFOM Télégrammes Afrique, Soudan, 1893, Arrivée nos. 12, 11, 23; Bouvier [Commandant, Farana] to Lendy, 20 Apr. 1893; Combes to Lendy, 12 May 1893; same to same, 24 May 1893 [Copies], AEMD Afrique 131.

[2] Note, 1 Mar. 1893; M.A.E. to Under-Secretary, 8 Mar. 1893; Haussmann to *directeur politique*, M.A.E., 10 Apr. 1893, AEMD Afrique 131; Delcassé to M.A.E., 29 Apr. 1893, AEMD Afrique 124.

[3] Combes, Rapport au sous-secrétaire, 7 Aug. 1893, MFOM Soudan I 4(b); Archinard, Note, 26 Oct. 1893, AEMD Afrique 131; Phipps [British *chargé*, Paris] to Hanotaux, 25 Dec. 1893, *ibid*. The agreement was later made formal by the Anglo-French Convention of 21 January 1895.

[4] Archinard to Mademba Si, Instructions, 7 Mar. 1891, cited in Archinard, Rapport... 1890–1, Cap. III, *J.O.* 17 Oct. 1891, p. 4998. See also: Archinard to Etienne, 9 Jan. 1891, MFOM Soudan I 1(a).

advance towards Samori prevented him from putting his plans into immediate execution, and the difficulties of the Humbert campaign kept the French still more firmly tied down in the south. Paris too was opposed to any action in the north; for Parliament's mounting opposition to the continued state of war in the Sudan made it essential to avoid all military complications with Macina.[1] But by the end of 1892 the prospects for a new advance were much more favourable. Combes was dealing effectively with Samori, while on the Niger itself the situation was relatively calm for the first time in three years. The presence of Ahmadu in Macina was a more than adequate pretext for action, and Archinard did not hesitate to exploit it. Forming his own expeditionary column, he set out from Segu in March 1893, ostensibly to deal with unrest in the neighbouring region of Minianka. As soon as the rebel centres had been taken, he invaded Macina. On 12 April, Jenné was taken after heavy fighting; on the 17th Mopti fell without a struggle; and with the capture of Bandiagara on the 29th, the conquest was complete. Ahmadu and his followers again fled eastward, and Archinard installed his brother Aguibou as Sultan.[2]

Once more, Archinard had acted in violation of his instructions. Under-Secretary Jamais had specifically forbidden him to take command of an expedition, and Delcassé too had ordered him on no account to extend the sphere of military operations. But the Commander remained as unperturbed as ever. He gave the Colonial Department no warning whatsoever of his plans; only after the fall of Jenné did he inform Paris of his campaign, assuring his superiors that the whole operation was simply an attempt to consolidate French influence in Segu and Sansanding.[3] And once more his insubordination seemed to go unpunished. Whatever Delcassé might have felt in private, he gave no official hint of his displeasure. He had not been in office long enough to risk an open breach with his military commanders, and he was not anxious to make a public issue of his inability to control them. Therefore, he merely recognised the Commander's responsibility for security and let

[1] Etienne to Humbert, Instructions, 16 Sept. 1891, MFOM Soudan I 2 (a); Etienne to Gov. Sen., 24 Nov. 1891; same to same, 4 Dec. 1891, MFOM Sénégal I 91 (b).

[2] For an account of the campaign, see: Archinard, Rapport...1892–3, cited in Méniaud, *op. cit.* II, 327–446. After his flight from Nioro, Ahmadu had quickly displaced his brother Muniru as Sultan of Macina. Muniru himself had come to power after the death of Tijani in 1887.

[3] Delcassé to Archinard, 9 Feb. 1893; same to same, 6 Apr. 1893, MFOM Télégrammes Afrique, Soudan, 1893, Départ nos. 5, 17; Archinard to Delcassé, 13 Apr. 1893, *ibid.* Arrivée no. 23.

him be the judge of the measures necessary to maintain it. Since the campaign would soon be drawing to a close, he added, a fuller discussion of the matter could be postponed until Archinard returned to Paris.[1] For the moment at least, the Commander had every reason to be satisfied with the results of his efforts.

THE SUDANESE MILITARY EMPIRE

'All I have done for [French] penetration in Africa', wrote Archinard before he returned to France in 1891, 'was to take the Sudan where General Desbordes left it and to follow his policy...I have not gone any further than my predecessors—I have worked within the same limits, and the sole purpose of [my] war has been to secure peace and establish the bases of organisation.'[2] His claim was not altogether unfounded. The destruction of the Tokolor empire and the war against Samori were the solutions to the problems of security which the Military had been advocating since the era of expansion had begun. The fear of Muslim resistance and the determination to crush it had dominated Sudanese military thinking for almost half a century. Archinard shared the same fear and set out to achieve the same objective. In the organisation of his conquests, the Commander's guiding principle was to prevent the Tokolors from ever becoming an effective political force again. After the capture of Segu, the Tokolors were deported to Futa, where they could be kept under stricter control. The *commandants de poste* along the Senegal were ordered to exercise 'the greatest possible rigour' in their surveillance and were assured of the Commander's full support for any measures which they deemed necessary to maintain security and crush resistance.[3] The outbreak of a rebellion in Futa prevented Archinard from adopting the same policy after the capture of Nioro; but the lot of the Kaarta Tokolors was to be just as hard. The Commandant of Nioro was instructed to extend his protection first to animists and then to Muslims who did not belong to the Tijaniyya. The Tokolors themselves were split into two groups and confined to restricted areas. They were forbidden to travel without a pass or to communicate with their countrymen on the Senegal. In order to keep them weak and to

---

[1] Delcassé to Archinard, 24 Apr. 1893, *ibid*. Départ no. 20. Nor did the Under-Secretary comment on the news when transmitting it to the Quai d'Orsay. Delcassé to M.A.E., 26 Apr. 1893, AEMD Afrique 124. But, for the Under-Secretary's real feelings, see below: p. 209.   [2] Archinard to Gov. Sen., 6 May 1891, MFOM Soudan I 1 (c).
[3] Archinard to *commandants de poste*, 2 Dec. 1890, cited in Archinard to Gov. Sen., 18 Apr. 1891, MFOM Soudan II 2.

provide a pretext for expelling troublemakers, the Commandant was ordered to provoke rather than to suppress dissension between them. Once the situation in Futa had improved, the Tokolors of Kaarta were also encouraged to return to their homelands.[1] Only in Macina did Archinard allow them to remain after first expelling the rest of their countrymen from Kaarta, thus preventing any contact between Futa and the Niger.[2]

To replace the Tokolors, Archinard installed more pliant and reliable rulers. Like Desbordes and Gallieni before him, he looked to the animist Bambaras as the true allies of the French in the Sudan, and after the capture of Segu he restored the former Diara dynasty. But loyalty rather than religion was the Commander's chief concern. In 1891 Sansanding was given to the trustworthy Mademba, himself a Tokolor and a member of the *torodbe* caste.[3] In 1893 Macina was given to Aguibou, who had proved himself equally trustworthy after his surrender of Dinguiray to the French in 1891. As far as possible, Archinard administered his conquests through such intermediaries. Only in Kaarta, where no replacement for the Tokolors could be found, did he authorise the immediate establishment of direct French control. French Residents in the subject states were instructed not to interfere with local customs and usages and to restrict their personal intervention to matters affecting the maintenance of security or the collection of revenue.[4]

But Archinard's administrative system was not the product of any firm belief in the principles of 'Indirect Rule'. On the contrary, he was convinced that a more direct form of administration would eventually have to be imposed as the populations came to realise that the French were both more equitable and more efficient than their own chiefs. His reliance on African authorities was merely a temporary expedient designed to free his European personnel from the additional burdens of administration.[5] For the system was evolved at a time when the con-

---

[1] Archinard to Commandant Nioro, Instructions, cited in Archinard, Rapport...1890–1, Cap. II, *J.O.* 14 Oct. 1891, pp. 4924–5.

[2] Archinard, Rapport...1892–3, cited in Méniaud, *op. cit.* II, 335–6.

[3] For the career of Mademba Si, see: Abd-el-Kader Mademba, 'Au Sénégal et au Soudan français; le Fama Mademba', *Bulletin du Comité des Etudes Historiques et Scientifiques de l'A.O.F.*, XIII (1930), 107–216.

[4] Archinard, Rapport...1890–1, *J.O.* 13 Oct. 1891, p. 4903: 'J'ai toujours recommandé d'ailleurs aux commandants de cercle...d'éviter de perdre leur temps en intervenant dans toutes les petites questions d'intérêt particulier...'

[5] Archinard, Rapport...1892–3, cited in Méniaud, *op. cit.* II, 339: 'Souvent, en reconnaissant l'autorité d'un Chef ou même en nommant un Chef, j'ai cherché à alléger pour nous les devoirs et les obligations que l'administration directe nous impose, alors que notre personnel européen est si réduit et a une si lourde tâche.'

quest of the Sudan was still in progress, and in the allocation of resources the needs of military expansion were always accorded top
priority. In the conquered territories, Archinard's principal objective
was to maintain sufficient order and security for his columns to concentrate on their military tasks without being distracted by 'petty
[administrative] problems'.[1] Indeed, the subject states were themselves
created specifically to serve as bases for further expansion. In 1891 the
Resident of Segu was told to regard his province as the nucleus of an
ever-growing sphere of French influence; Mademba Si at Sansanding
was given 2,000 Bambara warriors and ordered to advance north and
east towards Macina; and when Aguibou was eventually installed at
Bandiagara, he too was given tacit instructions to pave the way for the
incorporation of Timbuktu into the empire.[2]

Nor were the new rulers in any sense independent. They were
originally chosen for their loyalty, and the system was deliberately
designed to ensure their continued subservience. When Archinard
enthroned Mari Diara at Segu, he was careful to establish Bodian, a
scion of the rival Massasi clan, at Nango, and to warn them both that
their positions rested entirely on the goodwill of the French. His
appointment of Mademba Si was based on the knowledge that the
fama had no claims whatsoever to the kingdom and would thus be
completely dependent on the support of his European masters.[3] After
the conquest of Macina, he told the new Resident of Bandiagara never
to let Aguibou forget that 'we were the ones who took the country and
than gave it to the person of our choice'.[4] Aguibou himself owed his
usefulness to the fact that his co-operation with the French made him a
traitor in the eyes of the *talibés* and so deprived him of their loyalty. To
prevent dangerous concentrations of power and to enable his *commandants de cercle* to exercise their control more effectively, Archinard

---

[1] Archinard to Briquelot, Instructions, 9 Mar. 1891, cited in Archinard, Rapport...1890–1,
Cap. III, *J.O.* 18 Oct. 1891, p. 5012: 'Pour Ségou votre tâche est d'en faire un royaume fort,
riche, bien administré, bien soumis, mais bien délimité, afin de ne pas être distrait du but
principal, notre expansion en Afrique, par des questions de petite importance.'

[2] Archinard to Aguibou, Instructions, 4 May 1893; Archinard to Blachère [Resident,
Bandiagara], Instructions, 4 May 1893, cited in *B.C.A.F., Renseignements Coloniaux*,
January 1896, pp. 27–9.

[3] Gov. Sen. to Etienne, 6 Mar. 1891, MFOM Sénégal I 91 (a): 'Il [Mademba] se posera en
représentant direct de la puissance française plutôt qu'en fondateur de dynastie indigène.'
See also: Mademba to Archinard, 7 Feb. 1891, Archinard Papers: 'Il est de mon devoir
absolu de ne pas discuter, mais d'accepter tout ce qui vous croyez bon de proposer.'

[4] Archinard to Blàchere, Instructions, 4 May 1893, cited in *B.C.A.F., Renseignements
Coloniaux*, January 1896, pp. 28–9.

purposely kept the new states small. The kingdom of Sansanding was originally carved out of the province of Segu, and in 1893 its boundaries were in turn reduced. Even Kaarta was divided up between the new *cercle* of Nioro and those of Kayes, Bafoulabé and Kita. No matter how much leeway was given to the native rulers in the details of administration, the reins of power remained in the hands of the European Resident or Commandant. 'You must think of yourself as a *commandant de cercle*', Archinard told Captain Briquelot, the Resident of Segu; 'the *fama* Bodian is there to act as your intermediary so that you can govern without having to impose European ideas too quickly.'[1]

And the Europeans in charge were all military men. Archinard's objective was to turn the Sudan into an independent military preserve, protected not only against rebellion from below but also against interference from above. He deliberately excluded all civilian influence from the affairs of the colony. Acting on the advice of Brière, who had done much the same during his Governorship of Senegal, Archinard systematically purged the administrative service of its civilian personnel and replaced them with his own officers. As he admitted, the practice placed a heavy strain on his manpower; but those who remained were 'good, honest men and disciplined soldiers'.[2]

The Government's policies of expansion were similarly sacrificed on the altar of military independence. Although Archinard paid lip-service to the Chad Plan, he did not regard its execution as urgent. The menace of Islam alarmed him much more than the danger of foreign competition. Until the Muslims had been decisively defeated and French military domination effectively imposed, he could see no point in squandering resources outside the immediate theatre of operations.[3] He had no use whatsoever for the small missions of exploration favoured by the Government; he recognised only one effective instrument of expansion, and that was the military column.[4] His views prevailed.

[1] Archinard to Briquelot, Instructions, 9 Mar. 1891, cited in Archinard, Rapport...1890–1, Cap. III, *J.O.* 18 Oct. 1891, p. 5012. Bodian was appointed *fama* of Segu after the execution of Mari Diara. See below: p. 201.

[2] Archinard to Brière, n.d. [Draft], Archinard Papers. Extracts from this letter are cited in Méniaud, *op. cit.* 1, 319–20, and dated 15 Apr. 1889.

[3] Archinard to Briquelot, Instructions, 9 Mar. 1891 [Draft], MFOM Soudan I 1(a): 'Je sais bien qu'il y aurait grand intérêt à aller vite, mais nous ne manquerons cependant pas à notre devoir en proportionnant notre action à nos ressources...Nous ne devons pas être imprudents, sous prétexte que nous pourrions être devancés par d'autres puissances européennes.'

[4] Archinard, Rapport...1890–1, Cap. V, *J.O.* 28 Oct. 1891, p. 5189. See also: Binger to Archinard, 23 Nov. 1889, Archinard Papers. Archinard had complained to Desbordes

After Monteil, the only diplomatic missions to leave the Sudan were embassies bound for Tiéba; and when the French finally moved into the Niger Bend, military columns led the way.

The Government's plans for the south were just as severely affected. Archinard was not oblivious to the advantages of an advance in this direction; he had occupied Dinguiray in 1891 and had set great store by the Niger–Mellacourie road the following year. But his insistence on military expansion ruined the prospects for trade. The activities of his columns turned the suspicions of the *almamys* of Futa Jallon into active hostility and led them to make new overtures to Sierra Leone. By 1892 Etienne had been forced to abandon his plans for Timbo; only the complete exclusion of military influence from Futa Jallon and the Southern Rivers, he now maintained, would enable a commercial current to develop.[1] In the meantime, the wars against Ahmadu and Samori made it essential to maintain the traditional Senegal–Niger axis of advance. After the conquest of Macina, the Commander's next objective was the equally traditional one of Timbuktu.

As well as thwarting the Government's plans, Archinard's resolute assertion of traditional military principles brought him into violent conflict with Gallieni. Ever since his arrival in the Sudan, he had been criticising the results of Gallieni's efforts and complaining of his predecessor's failure to warn him of the difficulties which he could expect to face.[2] This growing personal animosity between the two men exacerbated their fundamental differences over policy. When Archinard received a copy of Gallieni's report to the Sudan Commission, with its proposals to abandon the Railway, evacuate the forts and avoid conflict with Ahmadu, he was alleged to have described the ex-Commander as 'a SCOUNDREL with whom I'll never shake hands again'.[3] In turn, Gallieni published his *Deux campagnes au Soudan français*, the conclusion of which was nothing more than a sustained attack on everything Archinard had achieved during his first three campaigns. He ridiculed the reports of an anti-French alliance between Ahmadu and Samori, condemned the premature attack on the Tokolors, repeated his proposals to abandon the Railway, challenged the utility of the forts,

about Binger's alleged support for the small diplomatic mission; the explorer then wrote to assure him that he too favoured the continued use of military columns.
[1] Etienne to Gov. Sen., 2 Jan. 1892 [Copy], AEMD Afrique 124.
[2] Archinard to Brière, n.d. [Draft], Archinard Papers. The relevant passages are cited in Méniaud, *op. cit.* I, 319–20.
[3] Archinard to Humbert, 8 Mar. 1890, published by Humbert in *La Politique Coloniale*, 7 Sept. 1897.

declared himself against any increase in the number of troops in the Sudan, and reaffirmed his belief in the importance of developing the south.[1] Archinard's public reaction was relatively restrained, but in private his language was much less inhibited. He now called Gallieni an unprincipled careerist seeking to curry favour with the Military's opponents, a *malhonnête homme* 'who will do much more harm than a mere scoundrel'.[2] Archinard won this battle too. He, not Gallieni, was reappointed to the Sudan in 1892. His policies, not those of his predecessor, determined the nature and the direction of the French advance. By 1893 the Government's hopes for ending the era of conquest and bringing the Sudan under civilian control had been dashed; its plans for integrating the colony into a larger West African empire had been shattered. Instead, the Sudan had been turned into an autonomous military estate, run exclusively by and for its traditional masters. The Military's victory seemed complete.

Archinard's triumph cost the Sudan as much as the victory of his patron Desbordes a decade before. Although the Commander was able to exclude civilians from the administration, his own officers were not ideal replacements. Most of them were drawn to the Sudan by the prospect of military action, and the only way to make them perform administrative duties was to demand this service as a prerequisite for participation in a campaign. According to Archinard, the system functioned adequately because the *commandants de poste* knew that their efficiency would be rewarded with an opportunity to demonstrate their 'military valour'. But he was forced to admit that it also had the disadvantage of removing capable officers from their posts just when they were becoming experienced. The only solution he could suggest was to make garrison duty more palatable by offering some form of monetary incentive.[3]

The system of Native Authorities was still less satisfactory. There was little room in it for the inculcation of French ideals of civilisation or progress, and Archinard never intended it to act as a vehicle for the *mission civilisatrice*. He was unwilling to endanger security by tampering with established local customs, however uncivilised they might be. He therefore ordered the Resident of Bandiagara to turn a blind eye to the whole question of the slave trade even if Aguibou raided the neigh-

[1] Gallieni, *Deux campagnes*, pp. 617–33.
[2] Archinard, Rapport...1890–1, Cap. III, *J.O.* 16 Oct. 1891, p. 4959; Cap. IV, *ibid.* 19 Oct. 1891, p. 5027; Archinard, Note pour M. Deloncle, 17 Oct. 1891, MFOM Soudan I 1(b).
[3] Archinard to Delcassé, 1 Sept. 1893 [Copy], Archinard Papers.

bouring province of Segu. The institution of the *razzia*, he claimed, was so deeply rooted that any attempt to eliminate it was bound to stir up unrest.[1] Freed from European restraint, the client chiefs plundered their subjects and carried on a lucrative traffic in slaves. The rule of Mademba Si at Sansanding was particularly brutal. 'It seems that you have so far tried to imitate Ahmadu in your methods of government instead of adopting French principles', Archinard admonished his nominee 'n 1893; 'all your people are afraid for their lives.'[2] But the *fama* was not deposed and no steps were taken to curb his excesses.

More seriously, Archinard's subject states failed to achieve the purpose for which they had been created. Within months of his appointment, Mari Diara of Segu began to plot against the French and was summarily executed. His successor, Bodian, was more loyal, but he proved completely incapable of maintaining order and had to be pensioned off in 1893. During every campaign after 1890, part of the expeditionary column had to be diverted to deal with unrest in Segu province. Archinard's suppression of the 1891 rebellion, when the capture of the insurgent town of Diéna cost him more casualties than the conquest of Kaarta and the campaign against Samori put together, was precisely what the system had been designed to prevent.[3]

Archinard's conquests destroyed any possibility of serious economic development. His bright talk of the Sudan's commercial prospects did not tally with Inspector Picanon's description of 'a barren and sparsely inhabited land whose population...shows neither initiative nor enterprise and whose climate is one of the worst in the world'.[4] Archinard recognised the rôle of the Senegalese merchants in the provisioning of his expeditionary columns, and he tried to gain their co-operation by lending some encouragement to their commercial activities. But he distrusted the avaricious commercial houses of Saint-Louis who sought to profit from the sacrifices of his men, and traders in the Sudan remained subject to petty restrictions.[5] For their part, the merchants

---

[1] Archinard to Blachère, Instructions, 4 May 1893 [Copy], *ibid.*
[2] Archinard to Mademba Si, Draft letter, n.d. [*ca.* May 1893], *ibid.*
[3] Archinard's losses at Diéna were 11 killed and 109 wounded. On the Nioro campaign they were 5 killed and 53 wounded, and on the campaign against Samori 4 killed and 12 wounded.   [4] Picanon to Etienne, 1 Sept. 1890, MFOM Soudan XIX 2.
[5] Archinard, Conclusion Politique, 15 Feb. 1894, MFOM Soudan II 1; 'On pouvait avoir grand souci de sauvegarder les intérêts d'une maison de commerce française, mais on ne s'en remettait pas uniquement au commerçants du soin de décider si, dans certains cas, l'intérêt de la mère-patrie qui paye du sang de ses enfants et de ses deniers l'espoir de fonder une colonie pour s'assurer dans l'avenir le rang qu'elle ambitionne parmi les nations, serait sacrifié à l'intérêt de cette maison de commerce française.'

remained implacably opposed to military rule; by 1893 Archinard was trying to persuade businessmen from his home town of Le Havre to invest in the Sudan so that he could count on the support of at least one commercial group.[1]

At the same time, Archinard's campaigns almost doubled the costs of military occupation. Hoping to keep Sudanese finances out of the public eye, the Ministry had made a determined attempt to stabilise expenditure, and after 1886 it kept its annual demands down to an average of 3,500,000 fr.[2] But the Commander's deliberately aggressive policies made nonsense of its estimates. During the three years after 1888, the Sudan Budget was exceeded by more than 3,500,000 fr. Over the next three years the Budget was exceeded by a further 6,000,000 fr., and by 1893 the costs of military occupation were running at 8,000,000 fr. a year.[3] Once more, the Government was forced to make regular appeals for supplementary credits, and as its demands rose so Parliamentary opposition to the Sudan again stirred into life.

By the time Archinard left the Sudan, his policies had incurred the enmity not only of the Sudan's traditional opponents but also of many who were sympathetic to the cause of French expansion in Africa. His failure to create the conditions of peace essential for commercial development provoked the hostility of all those who saw expansion in economic terms. His wars on the Upper Niger alienated the partisans of the new policy of peaceful expansion towards Lake Chad. His callous disregard for official policy and his deliberate disobedience of orders won him no friends in the Colonial Department. So far, he had appeared invulnerable to the attacks of his enemies; but when he returned to France in 1893, the rising tide of opposition was already undermining his defences.

THE GROWTH OF OPPOSITION TO THE MILITARY

As in the past, the financial consequences of military expansion provoked the first political repercussions in Paris. After the suppression of the special budgetary Chapter for the Sudan at the end of 1885, the colony had enjoyed a period of freedom from Parliamentary criticism.

[1] Archinard to Etienne Bonnier, 18 Sept. 1893, Archinard Papers.
[2] For 1887: 3,500,000 fr.; for 1889: 3,235,000 fr.; for 1890: 3,230,000 fr.; for 1891: 3,890,000 fr. See above: p. 142; and Etienne to Gov. Sen., 21 Oct. 1889, MFOM Sénégal I 80(c); Le Myre de Vilers, Rapport, 14 June 1890, *J.O. Doc. Parl. Chambre*, no. 665, pp. 1155, 1158–9.
[3] The Budget was exceeded by 1,300,000 fr. in 1891; 2,360,000 fr. in 1892, and 2,290,000 fr. in 1893.

Sudanese credits, hidden away in the various Chapters of the Colonial Budget, were no longer the subject for debate. But by the end of 1887 the Budget Commission was again condemning the 'sterile and costly' policy of military expansion in the Sudan. In March 1888 it called for the re-establishment of a separate Sudan Chapter in the Budget so as to permit stricter Parliamentary control over expenditure. As the financial consequences of the continued military advance became evident, the Colonial Department began to worry about the possibility of Parliamentary opposition to supplementary credits; and to satisfy the Budget Commission's demand it reintroduced the Sudan Chapter in February 1890.[1]

Once the full cost of Archinard's campaigns was made clear to the Chamber, the Ministry's Parliamentary honeymoon quickly came to an end. The credit for 1891, 3,890,000 fr., was not unreasonable and was passed without opposition. But in June 1891 Etienne had to tell the Budget Commission that the credit for 1892 would rise to 5,200,000 fr. at least. Reluctantly, the Commission gave its assent; but its decision was not unanimous, and even the majority approved the credit only because it was described as absolutely essential for the maintenance of security.[2]

When the Colonial Budget came up for debate in the autumn, the attack on Sudanese military expansion began in earnest. In October, the Radical spokesman, Camille Pelletan, accused the Government of deliberately carrying out a campaign of conquest without Parliamentary consent. In November he was joined by a *Boulangiste*, Martineau, who formally interpellated the Government on the reasons for the increased expenditure, demanded a full explanation of the war, called for an end to the policy of military expansion, and urged the Ministry to appoint a civilian Governor. More significantly, the Military's opponents now received the moral support of the Budget Commission. *Rapporteur* Delcassé expressed more than a little sympathy for those of his colleagues who had refused to approve the credit; he too asked the Government to show much greater frankness in its future dealings with Parliament

---

[1] Turquet, Rapport, 27 Oct. 1887, *J.O. Doc. Parl. Chambre*, no. 2053, p. 109; Yves Guyot, Rapport, 13 Mar. 1888, *ibid.* no. 2535, p. 384; Projet de Loi [Budget, 1891], 22 Feb. 1890, *ibid.* no. 368, p. 348.

[2] *J.O. Déb. Parl. Chambre*, séance du 28 novembre 1890, p. 2315; Projet de Loi [Budget 1892], 17 Feb. 1891, *J.O. Doc. Parl. Chambre*, no. 1203, p. 433; Procès-Verbaux de la Commission du Budget, séance du 29 juin 1891, AN C5443, p. 932; Delcassé, Rapport, 15 July 1891, *J.O. Doc. Parl. Chambre*, no. 1597, pp. 1867–8.

and demanded a firm undertaking that the Samori campaign would be wound up as quickly as possible.[1]

Etienne tried to keep his defence as general as possible, discoursing at length on the history of the Sudan since the days of Faidherbe. He justified the war on the grounds of the alleged anti-French alliance between Ahmadu and Samori and even lavished praise on Archinard. But he also assured the Chamber that he had no intention of creating his Chad empire by force, and he gave a solemn pledge not to authorise further military operations in the Sudan without first informing Parliament.[2] Pledges about the future, however, could not undo the mistakes of the past. Archinard's unauthorised campaign against Samori still had to be paid for, and in February 1892 the new Under-Secretary, Emile Jamais, was obliged to ask for a supplementary credit of 1,300,000 fr. Parliament approved his demand only after new assurances that all expansion had ceased.[3] Three weeks later, Jamais was back again, cap in hand, for an additional 360,000 fr. to pay for the troop reinforcements needed in the continued campaign against the *imam*. This time, only the energetic intervention of Etienne and Félix Faure prevented the Commission from withholding its approval.[4] In the Chamber, Martineau again led the assault, demanding the rejection of the credit as unnecessary for the maintenance of the existing position. François Deloncle, the arch-priest of African expansion, condemned the Military's single-minded preoccupation with their personal advancement and objected to any increase in their numbers. Pelletan, Déroulède, de Launay and Paul de Cassagnac joined in the chorus from the Left and from the Right. The new *rapporteur*, Emile Chautemps, warned the Under-Secretary that this time Parliament would hold him to his pledges. In reply, both Jamais and Prime Minister Loubet again declared that no further expansion was being planned. At that, a motion to adjourn the credit was defeated by only 267 votes to 228.[5]

[1] *J.O. Déb. Parl. Chambre*, séance du 24 octobre 1891, pp. 1947–8; *ibid.* séance du 30 novembre 1891, pp. 2352–68.

[2] *Ibid.* séance du 1er décembre 1891, pp. 2379–81; séance du 3 décembre 1891, pp. 2400–2; Procès-Verbaux de la Commission du Budget, séance du 3 décembre 1891, AN C 5443, pp. 747–8.

[3] Projet de Loi, 18 Feb. 1892, *J.O. Doc. Parl. Chambre*, no. 1920, p. 234; Procès-Verbaux de la Commission du Budget, séance du 11 mars 1892, séance du 16 mars 1892, AN C 5443, pp. 862–3, 882; Poincaré, Rapport, 19 Mar. 1892, *J.O. Doc. Parl. Chambre*, no. 1994, p. 338.

[4] Projet de Loi, 2 Apr. 1892, *ibid.* no. 2037, p. 754; Procès-Verbaux de la Commission du Budget, séance du 4 avril 1892, AN C 5445, pp. 22–3; Chautemps, Rapport, 5 Apr. 1892, *J.O. Doc. Parl. Chambre*, no. 2055, p. 812.

[5] *J.O. Déb. Parl. Chambre*, séance du 7 avril 1892, pp. 491–512; séance du 11 avril 1892, pp. 541–60.

The Growth of Opposition to the Military

By now, the Ministry's financial calculations were in a complete shambles. Before the end of 1892, continued operations against Samori, the rebellion in Segu and the outbreak of yellow fever had added another 2,000,000 fr. to the bill.[1] As a concession to reality, the Ministry increased its demands for 1893 to 5,730,000 fr.; but Deloncle almost persuaded the Commission to reduce the credit by a token 1,000 fr. as a sign of its determination to have the Sudan placed under civilian rule, and Chautemps again condemned the excessive costs of military expansion.[2] During the subsequent debate, Martineau attacked Archinard personally for destroying any prospect of commercial development; nobody spoke up on the Commander's behalf. In the Senate, Under-Secretary Delcassé was forced to make the same pledges about expansion which had demanded as *rapporteur* of the Colonial Budget only a year before.[3] And once more Archinard made a mockery of them. His unauthorised campaign in Macina turned out to be expensive; because of it the 1893 estimates were exceeded by almost 2,290,000 fr.[4]

Admittedly, Parliamentary opposition had little practical effect upon the course of the conquest. Governments did not remain oblivious to criticism, and their policies reflected the growing hostility of the Chambers to military expansion. But Government pledges were meaningless if they would not be enforced, and both Archinard and Humbert had shown how unenforceable they were. Despite the wishes of the Colonial Department, the pace of expansion continued to accelerate; despite the hostility of Parliament, its costs continued to be met. The Sudan's opponents could not erode the solid bloc of support on which the Republican Ministries of the day relied. No matter how vehemently military policies were condemned, few were actually prepared to risk the consequences of refusing credits which were always described as essential for military defence. The argument of security was as effective in the 1890s as it had been a decade before.

Nevertheless, the attitude of Parliament was not insignificant. Its

---

[1] Projet de Loi, 10 May 1893, *J.O. Doc. Parl. Chambre*, no. 2733, pp. 840–1. Fortunately for the Ministry, its demand was presented towards the end of the Parliament. The Budget Commission, rushed to complete its business, approved the credit without debate at its last session on 20 May. The Chamber voted it, again without debate, on 12 June.

[2] Procès-Verbaux de la Commission du Budget, séance du 4 octobre 1892, AN C5445 pp. 610–11; Chautemps, Rapport, 12 July 1892 [*sic*], *J.O. Doc. Parl. Chambre*, no. 2316, pp. 1873–7.

[3] *J.O. Déb. Parl. Chambre*, séance du 6 février 1893, pp. 385–7; *J.O. Déb. Parl. Sénat*, séance du 25 mars 1893, p. 422.

[4] Projet de Loi, 9 June 1894, *J.O. Doc. Parl. Chambre*, no. 868, pp. 899–900.

attacks on Sudanese policy came at a time when the general climate for African expansion was becoming much more favourable. After Etienne's rousing speeches during the Dahomey crisis of 1890, the Chambers had become increasingly sympathetic to the Government's new policies of extending French influence in Africa. In the summer of 1892 this transformation was completed by the formation of the *Groupe colonial de la Chambre*, a collection of more than ninety Deputies drawn from all shades of the political spectrum and united by their common desire 'to maintain the power and the glory of France overseas'. In the years after its formation, the *groupe colonial* came to play a vital rôle in the development of French African policy, particularly towards the Congo. Its unqualified support would have been of inestimable value to the Sudanese Military, yet their chances of securing it were negligible. The *groupe*'s President was Etienne, whose experiences with Archinard could not have endeared the Military to him. Its second Vice-President was their implacable opponent, Admiral Vallon. Its Secretary was Martineau, their most vocal critic in the Chamber. The two most influential members of its rank and file were Delcassé and François Deloncle, whose views about military expansion were no more favourable. Despite its interest in African affairs, the *groupe* made no attempt to influence Sudanese policy. By 1893 it was being criticised not for its support of the Military but for its failure to condemn their abuses.[1]

Nor could the Military derive any comfort from the more general rise in the popularity of African expansion. The formation of the *groupe colonial* was only one symptom of the colonialist sentiments which gripped French public opinion after 1890. In the next decade or so, the *Comité de l'Afrique française* became the model for various Committees pledged to the support of French interests in Asia, in Oceania and in Morocco. In 1893, French businessmen engaged in colonial trade formed the *Union coloniale française* for the purpose of supporting 'all measures necessary to ensure the development, the prosperity and the defence of the various branches of Trade and Industry in…lands under French influence'. New periodicals were launched to act as organs of colonialist propaganda; extended lecture tours were arranged to gain the support of the general public for colonial and particularly African expansion; and annual banquets were arranged to provide a meeting

[1] *La Politique Coloniale*, 18 July 1893. For an analysis of the membership of the *groupe*, see: Brunschwig, *Mythes et réalités*, pp. 113–16.

place for the representatives of a *parti colonial* whose existence, however amorphous its composition, was an accomplished fact by the 1890s.[1] But the new colonialists had little sympathy for military expansion; they tended to express their nationalism in economic terms. In their eyes, profit and patriotism were indistinguishable. They were staunch believers in private enterprise; although welcoming official support, they were convinced that the agents of expansion should be the employees of private commercial interests rather than servants of the State. In Africa, their heroes were not Archinard or Combes but Monteil and above all Mizon, intrepid explorers who at no cost to the Exchequer spread French influence across the continent, opened it to French trade and tweaked the British lion's tail.[2] Military expansion, costly, unproductive, positively inimical to trade, was anathema to them. There was to be no place for military columns in the Chad empire as they conceived it; 'colonial expansion through trade and other peaceful means; no armed expeditions, no military policy in the colonies' was François Deloncle's imperial creed.[3] The Sudan itself was to be assimilated into the new empire by linking it to the trading posts on the coast, thus creating the commercial current which would at last make the colony profitable.

Archinard's policies gained him their undying hatred. His wars threw the Sudan into confusion, and the resistance they provoked blocked the routes to Chad from the west. 'Given the situation left by the last campaigns', complained *Le Siècle* in April 1892, 'any plan for penetration towards Chad [from the Niger] can only be a tasteless and sinister joke.'[4] After the attack on Samori, the paper urged Etienne to dismiss Archinard and reappoint Gallieni; throughout the following year it regularly attacked the Military, accusing them of having turned the Sudan into 'a slave bazaar', and criticised the annual waste of millions in the colony, 'without profit to anyone except...our brave officers'.[5] At the end of 1891 it was joined by *La Politique Coloniale*, a colonialist journal founded to champion the cause of commercial expansion in

---

[1] Despite occasional inaccuracies, the best account of the *parti colonial* remains: H. Brunschwig, 'Le parti colonial français', *Revue française d'histoire d'outre-mer*, XLVI (1959), 49–83.

[2] For the special regard in which Mizon was held by the *parti colonial*, see: *J.O. Déb. Parl. Chambre*, séance du 6 novembre 1890 [speech by Deloncle]; séance du 21 janvier 1891 [speech by d'Arenberg]; séance du 7 juin 1894 [speech by Etienne]; *B.C.A.F.*, June, July, August 1892, December 1893.

[3] *Le Siècle*, 12 May 1890.

[4] *Ibid.* 30 Apr. 1892.   [5] *Ibid.* 20 May 1891, 21 July 1891, 25 Feb. 1892.

Africa.[1] Meanwhile, individual traders also exerted all their influence against the *officiers soudanais*. In 1893 Léon Tharel, the sponsor of Mizon and now President of the *Syndicat du Soudan français*, almost managed to block Archinard's reappointment.[2]

The attitude of the new colonial groups was no more favourable. The *Comité de l'Afrique française* was the least unsympathetic to the Military, as was only fitting for an organisation which numbered Desbordes among its most prominent members. Through his efforts, both Archinard and Humbert were given enthusiastic send-offs before they left for the Sudan.[3] But even the *Comité* was at best benevolently neutral. Its first objective was to enhance the rôle of private initiative in the realisation of the Chad Plan, and it was far more concerned with the progress of Crampel and Mizon than with the advance of the Sudanese columns. Its Secretary, Harry Alis, praised the Military during his lecture tour of 1891–2; but in the *Bulletin* he stressed the importance of commercial development in the Sudan. After the Macina campaign he openly criticised Archinard and called for the abandonment of 'the policy of military conquest—and the considerable expense which it entails'.[4] The *Union coloniale* was much more uncompromisingly hostile. The publisher of *La Politique Coloniale*, Paul Cousin, had been instrumental in its formation and soon turned his journal into its unofficial newsletter.[5] By 1894, both Léon Tharel and François Deloncle had become members, and Archinard was describing it as his most dangerous enemy.[6]

More worrying for the Military was the support which their enemies received from the Colonial Department. Archinard's persistent insubordination had built up a store of resentment in Paris, particularly among those officials most directly concerned with the formulation of the new African policy. As early as 1891 Jacques Haussmann had described the Samori campaign as a glorious but useless adventure and had called for the adoption of Gallieni's plans for expansion into the

---

[1] *La Politique Coloniale*, 9 Apr. 1892: 'Partisans résolus de l'expansion coloniale, mais d'une expansion pacifique, n'entraînant que des sacrifices proportionnés aux résultats à obtenir, nous avons prévu que tout ce qu'on laissait faire d'inutile et de dangereux au Soudan empêcherait de faire ce qu'il y avait d'éminemment utile, d'immédiatement profitable, à entreprendre dans les régions voisines.'

[2] Archinard to Etienne Bonnier, 18 Sept. 1892, Archinard Papers.

[3] *B.C.A.F.*, August 1891, July 1892.

[4] *La Politique Coloniale*, 6 June 1893 [article by Alis]. For the lecture tour, see: *B.C.A.F.*, November 1891, January, March, June 1892.

[5] See: *La Politique Coloniale*, 14 Apr. 1895 [Cousin's obituary].

[6] Archinard, Conclusion Politique, 15 Feb. 1894, MFOM Soudan II 1; *idem*, Note..., 13 July 1894, AN 81 AP 6 II, Rambaud Papers.

south.[1] Jean-Louis Deloncle, a fervent partisan of his cousin's policies, was still more hostile; and Archinard suspected him of instigating many of *Le Siècle*'s attacks.[2] There was even opposition in military circles. Although Gallieni was now in Indochina and could take no further part in the campaign, Monteil, a champion of the small diplomatic mission, was among the most virulent in his denunciations of Archinard.[3] Most alarming of all was the attitude of Under-Secretary Delcassé himself. Like Etienne, he was determined to maintain effective personal control of the direction of colonial policy; but unlike his predecessor he felt no affinity whatsoever for the Military and showed no scruples in his dealings with insubordinate Sudanese Commanders. Although he did not criticise Archinard after the Macina campaign, his connections with the Military's most violent critics showed where his real sympathies lay. In July 1893, when articles denouncing Archinard were regularly appearing in *La Politique Coloniale*, he had its editor made a *Chevalier* of the Legion of Honour 'for distinguished services to the Press'. By 1894 Archinard was describing the newspaper, not entirely without justification, as 'the official journal of the Ministry of Colonies'.[4] The *Union coloniale* was treated with similar favour. At its first banquet in November 1893, Delcassé assured its members of his 'sympathy and wholehearted co-operation'. A month later, he formally became an associate member.[5]

ARCHINARD'S DISMISSAL

By the summer of 1893 the opponents of the Military among the colonialists and within the Government were strong enough to force a showdown over the future of the Sudan, and the conquest of Macina gave them the chance to do so. The suddenness of Archinard's campaign caught Paris unawares and saved him from any immediate reprisal; but there can be little doubt that Delcassé was determined from this moment on to break his troublesome Commander.[6] Both *Le Siècle* and *La*

---

[1] *La Revue Encyclopédique*, 15 June 1891 [cutting in Archinard Papers].
[2] Archinard, Conclusion Politique, 15 Feb. 1894, MFOM Soudan II 1: 'Je vis un jour venir chez moi l'un des rédacteurs du journal *Le Siècle*... Il me présentait une recommandation de M. Deloncle, mais je ne me rappelle plus si c'était M. Deloncle Député ou son cousin M. Deloncle chef de bureau à la division des affaires politiques au Soussecrétariat d'Etat.'   [3] Klobb to Archinard, 25 Nov. 1893, Archinard Papers.
[4] *La Politique Coloniale*, 18 July 1893; Archinard, Note...13 July 1894, AN 81 AP 6 II, Rambaud Papers.   [5] *La Politique Coloniale*, 21 Nov. 1893, 17 Dec. 1893.
[6] According to *La Politique Coloniale*, Delcassé even persuaded the Minister of Marine not to recall Archinard straight away; nevertheless, he decided at this time to replace Archinard with 'a less independent agent'. *La Politique Coloniale*, 15 Feb. 1894.

Politique Coloniale immediately launched a campaign for his dismissal and replacement by a civilian Governor. 'If we were the Government', declared *La Politique Coloniale*, probably echoing the Under-Secretary's sentiments, 'we should be obliged to accept the *fait accompli*; but we should remove all temptations for future Commanders to place the Government in [such a] ridiculous position. . . As for. . . Archinard. . . we like to think that he will not be seen again in the Sudan.'[1] In August, Paul Bonnetain, a minor civilian official freshly returned from the Sudan, claimed in an interview with *Le Figaro* that the Sudan had become the personal property of the *artillerie de marine*, whose officers were only interested in their own advancement.[2] *La Politique Coloniale* immediately picked up the story and used it to mount a new series of attacks on the Commander. Demands for his replacement were soon appearing daily in the most prominent sections of the colonialist Press.[3]

At first, Archinard was not unduly alarmed. In private, he claimed, Delcassé had approved the Macina operation. He was equally confident that his appointment to the Sudan by Presidential Decree gave him a measure of immunity; it would take another Decree to remove him, and President Carnot was a friend of Desbordes. As his critics grew louder, however, the Commander began to worry. Despite Delcassé's private assurances, Archinard suspected him of complicity in the Press campaign and of instigating a plot to have him replaced by a former Colonial Department official, Albert Grodet. By October Archinard was having to admit that 'the situation is difficult and takes up much of my time'.[4]

There was good reason for alarm. The most important source of Archinard's strength had always been his position as the man on the spot. As long as he remained at his post it would have been difficult for Delcassé to recall him without creating a furore. Once he had returned to Paris for his annual rest, however, it was a much simpler operation to prevent him from reassuming his command. At the end of November

---

[1] *Ibid.* 6 May 1893. See also: *Le Siècle*, 26 Apr. 1893, 1 May 1893.

[2] *Le Figaro*, 11 Aug. 1893, Bonnetain had already run afoul of Archinard over an attempt to secure provisioning concessions for a group of Parisian businessmen, which the Commander curtly rejected. A friend of Archinard later described Bonnetain as a leading figure in the anti-Military plot. Archinard to Bonnetain, 10 May 1893 [Copy]; Oswald to Archinard, 24 Nov. 1893, Archinard Papers.

[3] *La Politique Coloniale*, 12 Aug., 19 Aug., 24 Aug., 14 Sept., 19 Sept., 1893; *Le Siècle*, 17 Oct., 12 Nov. 1893.

[4] Archinard to Etienne Bonnier, 3 Sept. 1893; same to same, 4 Oct. 1893; same to same, 29 Oct. 1893, Archinard Papers. See also: Méniaud, *op. cit.* II, 454.

the inevitable happened. Notwithstanding his appointment by Presidential Decree, Archinard was dismissed, and the Sudan was placed under a civilian Governor with responsibility for internal and external defence and full control over all military activities. Officially, the reorganisation was supposed to indicate that 'the era of conquest is now definitely closed'.[1] Six months later, however, Delcassé admitted to the Budget Commission that he had ordered the change because his Department no longer exercised effective control over Sudanese operations or expenditure.[2] Needless to say, Archinard's replacement was Albert Grodet.

But this was not the end of the matter. Whether by accident or by design, Delcassé announced the change before he had informed Archinard, and the unfortunate Commander first learned of his dismissal through the newspapers. When his official notification finally arrived, Delcassé's hypocritical expressions of gratitude for 'your brilliant and solid services' merely added insult to injury. The indignant Archinard complained about the outrageous fashion in which he had been treated and sarcastically declined his nomination to the rank of *Commandeur* in the Order of the Green Dragon of Annam, a decoration which he had requested for one of his African officers.[3] Still unsatisfied, he gave an interview to a friend on the staff of *Le Figaro*, supplied a copy of his correspondence with the Under-Secretary, and gave him permission to publish it if the newspaper wished. To complete the effect, he then gave interviews to *Le Gaulois*, *l'Eclair*, and *Le Libéral*, presenting himself as a loyal and much-wronged servant of France, and gallantly wished his successor the best of luck.[4]

The resulting scandal illustrated the nature of political alignments on the Sudanese issue. The new colonialists were virtually unanimous in their support of the Under-Secretary. Their organs, *Le Siècle* and *La Politique Coloniale*, hailed Grodet's appointment as a triumph for the principles of civilian administration and peaceful expansion; after the publication of the Delcassé correspondence, they led the cry for Archinard's blood. Even Alis of the *Comité* condemned the impropriety of

[1] Rapport au Président de la République, 21 Nov. 1893, MFOM Soudan VII 1(d); note published in *Le Journal des Débats*, 25 Nov. 1893.
[2] Procès-Verbaux de la Commission du Budget, séance du 18 juin 1894, AN C5447, pp. 172–3.
[3] Delcassé to Archinard, 21 Nov. 1893; Archinard to Delcassé, 21 Nov. 1893; same to same, 23 Nov. 1893, published in *Le Figaro*, 23 Nov. 1893.
[4] *Ibid.*; *Le Gaulois*, 24 Nov. 1893; *L'Eclair*, 24 Nov. 1893; *Le Libéral*, 26 Nov. 1893.

his action.[1] Yet the Government's reaction was surprisingly mild. Although the Minister of Marine himself was supposed to have raised the issue at the *Conseil des Ministres* and formally reprimanded Archinard for his unauthorised publication of official correspondence, he took the matter no further because of the Commander's past services.[2] By then, the Dupuy Ministry was already on the point of collapse, and its fall saved Archinard from further prosecution. The new Minister of Marine, Admiral Lefèbvre, was an intimate friend of Desbordes.[3] The ex-Commander himself was posted to the *Inspection-Générale* of the *artillerie de marine* where he could continue to work in close collaboration with his patron.

The leniency of Archinard's treatment was most probably due to the continued strength of his support. The irregular circumstances of his dismissal gained him considerable sympathy. In Paris, both *Le Jour* and the influential *Le Temps* carried laudatory articles about him, and national coverage of the affair enabled him to collect a bulky dossier of favourable editorial comment.[4] His friend Alfred Rambaud, Ferry's old *chef de cabinet* and a future Minister of Education, sang his praises in the *Revue politique et littéraire*. Paul Leroy-Beaulieu, the *doyen* of colonial theorists, declared himself opposed to civilian rule. Even Etienne, at the height of the crisis, hailed the Military's achievements before an assembly of the *groupe colonial*.[5]

Much more vociferous in their support were elements on the Right of French politics. The Archinard scandal moved the Sudan question out of the relatively isolated realm of colonial affairs into the arena of civilian–military relations. The embarrassment which Archinard created for a Republican government caused him to be idolised by the militarists. The duc d'Aumale invited him to his country estate and entertained him at the *Opéra*.[6] Paul de Cassagnac, a self-proclaimed enemy of colonial expansion but an equally stout champion of the *esprit militaire*,

[1] *Le Siècle*, 23 Nov., 25 Nov., 26 Nov. 1893; *La Politique Coloniale*, 25 Nov. 1893; *ibid.* 19 Dec. 1893 [article by Alis].
[2] Rieunier to Archinard, 28 Nov. 1893 [Copy], MFOM Dossier Administratif, Archinard. See also: *Le Gaulois*, 24 Nov. 1893; *La Politique Coloniale*, 28 Nov. 1893.
[3] Lefèbvre [not the Admiral] to Archinard, 5 Dec. 1893, Archinard Papers.
[4] *Le Jour*, 25 Nov. 1893; *Le Temps*, 23 Nov., 24 Nov. 1893. Press cuttings in the Archinard Papers included: *La Sarthe* (Le Mans), 24 Nov. 1893; *Le Salut Publique* (Lyons), 25 Nov. 1893; *L'Union-Bretagne* (Nantes), 26 Nov. 1893; *Le Message* (Cognac), 26 Nov. 1893; *Le Vosgien* (Epinal), 26 Nov. 1893; *Le Petit Niçois* (Nice), 29 Nov. 1893.
[5] *Revue politique et littéraire*, 6 Jan., 17 Feb. 1894; *La Politique Coloniale*, 5 Apr. 1894 [article by Leroy-Beaulieu]; *ibid.* 25 Nov. 1893, report of a meeting of the *groupe colonial*.
[6] See: Méniaud, *op. cit.* II, 470.

glorified him in the columns of *L'Autorité*. *La Patrie* was equally fulsome in its praise, while Drumont, the proprietor of *La Libre Parole*, predictably denounced Delcassé as an accomplice in the Judaeo-Masonic plot to destroy France.[1]

As always, however, Archinard found his most powerful allies in the upper echelons of the armed services. Delcassé's actions brought the simmering hostility between the Colonial Department and the Ministry of Marine to a boil. The Department's progressive intrusion into the sphere of colonial defence had already provoked conflicts, and before accepting the post of Under-Secretary Delcassé himself had demanded the Department's physical as well as administrative separation from the Ministry of Marine.[2] Once in office, his ill-concealed dislike of the Military soon antagonised the heads of the colonial troops. His relations with Desbordes were particularly unfriendly, and when he changed one of the General's technical instructions, the latter refused to have any further dealings with the Colonial Department.[3] Desbordes interpreted Archinard's dismissal as a veiled attack on himself and reacted violently. The jubilation at the Pavillon de Flore, the new home of the Colonial Department, formed a stark contrast to the unremitting gloom at the Rue Royale across the road. There a senior official, quite probably Desbordes, described the Under-Secretary's action as treacherous and darkly predicted that the attempt to impose civilian rule was bound to end in disaster.[4] To show their displeasure, Desbordes and Brière refused permission for Commandant Quiquandon to accompany Grodet as his military adviser; even the generally sympathetic *Le Temps* condemned this as an act of pure spite.[5] Equally influential figures rallied to Archinard's support. The former Director of Colonies, Paul Dislère, who had maintained his relations with the Rue Royale, spoke to the Minister in his defence. Lieutenant-Colonel Courbebaisse, the *officier d'ordonnance* of *généralissime* Saussier, wrote personally to congratulate him; and, according to one of Archinard's associates, the publication of the letters had the approval of Saussier himself.[6]

---

[1] *L'Autorité*, 25 Nov. 1893; *La Patrie*, 25 Nov. 1893; *La Libre Parole*, 25 Nov. 1893.
[2] See: Berge, *op. cit.* pp. 57–63.
[3] Klobb to Archinard, 25 Nov. 1893, Archinard Papers.
[4] *Le Siècle*, 27 Nov. 1893.
[5] *Le Temps*, 2 Dec. 1893; See also: *La Politique Coloniale*, 30 Nov. 1893; *Le XIXᵉ Siècle*, 1 Dec. 1893.
[6] Dislère to Archinard, 30 Nov. 1892 [*sic*: 1893]; Courbebaisse to Archinard, n.d.; Klobb to Archinard, 25 Nov. 1893, Archinard Papers.

The 'Total Conquest' of the Sudan, 1888–93

In the end, neither side could claim a complete victory. Delcassé managed to reimpose central control over Sudanese affairs but at the cost of creating an irreparable breach between the civilian and military branches of colonial administration. The Military managed to save Archinard's career but not to maintain their influence over the policies of the Colonial Department. In April 1894, Archinard submitted the Political Conclusion to his report on the last campaign, denouncing the alleged treachery of his opponents in the Colonial Department and restating the case for military rule in the Sudan. But these same opponents were now in charge at the newly created Ministry of Colonies. On 25 April Jean-Louis Deloncle minuted with evident satisfaction: '[The Minister of Colonies], having read this report and seen that it was a criticism of the Government as violent as it was perfidious, has decided that it is to be filed without comment.'[1]

[1] Archinard to Minister of Colonies, 5 Apr. 1894, enclosing Archinard, Conclusion Politique, 15 Feb. 1894; and minute by J-L. Deloncle, 25 Apr. 1894, MFOM Soudan II 1.

8

The Civilian Administration of the Sudan, 1893-5

The dismissal of Archinard and the appointment of a civilian Governor gave Paris its first real opportunity to reassert control over Sudanese affairs and implement its policies of peaceful commercial development. Delcassé was determined not to waste it. In June 1893 he had assured the Budget Commission that the conquest of Macina marked the end of the exclusively military phase in the Sudan. Henceforth, he declared, the development of a sound administration, the extension of the communications network and the encouragement of trade would be his Department's sole objectives.[1] His instructions to Grodet underlined the seriousness of these intentions. 'The period of conquest and territorial expansion must be considered...at an end', he told the Governor, '[and] all your efforts must be aimed at consolidation and exploitation.' Delcassé warned him that the organisation of the Sudan would be a more difficult and a less brilliant task than its conquest; but he expressed every confidence in the Governor's ability to carry out his duties successfully.[2]

The Under-Secretary's faith in Grodet was not entirely misplaced. The new Governor had certainly had a chequered career. While serving in the Colonial Department he had run afoul of de La Porte, who at one point abolished the office of *sous-directeur des colonies* in order to get rid of him. In 1888 he had been recalled from the Governorship of Martinique for tampering with the minutes of its *Conseil Général*. In April 1893, just six months before his appointment to the Sudan, he had been dismissed from the temporary Governorship of French Guiana for using the colony's official presses to print a polemical journal supporting him against the local opposition. But Grodet had always managed to emerge from his escapades unscathed. After his recall from Guiana, Delcassé

[1] Procès-Verbaux de la Commission du Budget, séance du 9 juin 1893, AN C5447, pp. 79–80.
[2] Delcassé to Grodet, Instructions, 4 Dec. 1893, MFOM Soudan I 6(a).

kept him on full pay and even accepted his irregular request to be paid a Governor's salary for his period of office.[1] For Grodet, as Delcassé realised, was still a highly capable administrator.[2] Whatever his failings, he was at least strong enough to stand up to the Military and keep the Colonels in their place. In November 1893 all other considerations were secondary.

Unfortunately, a change of command in the Sudan was not a guarantee that its officers would come to heel. Although the dismissal of Archinard and the subsequent scandal destroyed the influence of the military party over the policies of the Colonial Department, its powers over the men on the spot remained unaffected. After Archinard's departure, the military command had fallen eventually to Etienne Bonnier, Desbordes's *officier d'ordonnance* in Indochina, Archinard's close friend, and a full member of the Sudanese military clique. Bonnier owed his loyalty to his military superiors, and it was their commands, not those of the Colonial Department, which he followed.[3]

In September, Archinard sent his friend unofficial instructions about the military policies to be followed during the next campaign. In them, he laid particular emphasis on the importance of continuing the war against Samori; at all costs, he warned, the impetus of the French advance had to be maintained and the *imam* prevented from recouping his losses. If necessary, Bonnier was to extend the military frontier in the east by constructing a new fort in the Bagoé area. He was also to occupy Yende and cut Samori's arms supply from the south, even if this entailed a temporary incursion into Liberian territory. General Desbordes sent him advice as well, and the new Commander assured them both that their orders would be carried out as far as the situation allowed.[4] Acting on these instructions, he formed an expeditionary column and advanced against Samori, occupying Bougouni on 12

---

[1] Information about Grodet's career can be found in MFOM Dossier Administratif, Grodet. Extracts from the relevant documents are published in: M. Blanchard, 'Administrateurs d'Afrique noire', *Revue d'histoire des colonies*, XL (1953), 420–7.

[2] Delcassé to Grodet, 27 Nov. 1893, MFOM Dossier Administratif, Grodet: 'En vous appelant à ces hautes fonctions [the Governorship of the Sudan] le Gouvernement de la République s'est plu à reconnaître...votre compétence en matière d'administration coloniale...'

[3] Bonnier to Grodet, 27 Dec. 1893, cited in Grodet to Under-Secretary, 21 Jan. 1894, MFOM Soudan I 6(b): 'Toutes mes actions ont été inspirées par les leçons que j'avais été à même de recevoir du General Desbordes, et des conseils que me prodiguait le Colonel Archinard.' Minute by Grodet: 'Et le Gouvernement?'

[4] Archinard to Bonnier, 3 Sept. 1893 [1]; same to same, 3 Sept. 1893 [2]; same to same, 18 Sept. 1893; Bonnier to Archinard, 22 Oct. 1893; same to same, 7 Nov. 1893, Archinard Papers.

December. But he returned almost immediately to the Niger, and by 25 December his troops were again assembled at Segu.[1]

Bonnier knew by this time that Archinard had been deprived of the command; he had received unofficial news of Grodet's imminent arrival as early as 8 December.[2] But he was determined to permit no civilian interference with his plans. On 19 December he warned Commandant Richard of the Southern Region that a civilian Governor would shortly take charge and would probably issue new instructions. These, of course, would have to be obeyed; but insofar as they dealt with military operations they were to be disregarded. The campaign was already under way, and any change of plan might compromise its success. No matter what Grodet said, therefore, Richard was to occupy Nionsomoridugu and reconnoitre the route to Kong. Having fulfilled his mission in the north, Bonnier with the main force would move in a wide arc to Kong and rejoin Richard from this direction. With luck, Samori would be caught in the pincers and destroyed. A week later, Bonnier and his column set off down the Niger, not to inspect the political situation as he had told the Colonial Department, but to capture Timbuktu.[3]

THE CAPTURE OF TIMBUKTU

Bonnier's plans were in no sense revolutionary; Timbuktu had been one of the Military's traditional objectives since the days of Faidherbe, and Archinard himself had already laid the groundwork for its occupation. After the conquest of Macina he authorised Aguibou to demand tribute from the town and ordered the Commandant of Jenné to inform any envoys from the Grand Council that the French were prepared to send a garrison if requested to do so.[4] Before leaving the Sudan, he gave the gunboats deliberately provocative instructions to escort the traders of Jenné on their journeys to Timbuktu and ordered the flotilla commander, Lieutenant Boiteux, to build as many transport barges as

[1] See: Méniaud, *op. cit.* II, 483–92.

[2] Guiard to Bonnier, 8 Dec. 1893, MFOM Soudan V 2(b).

[3] Bonnier to Richard, 19 Dec. 1893 (très confidentielle et strictement personnelle), cited in Grodet to Minister of Colonies [henceforth M.C.], 22 Apr. 1897, MFOM Soudan IV 1(b). See also: Bonnier to Under-Secretary, 28 Nov. 1893, MFOM Soudan VI 2.

[4] Archinard to Aguibou, 4 May 1893, printed in: *B.C.A.F.*, *Renseignements Coloniaux*, January 1896, pp. 27–8; Archinard to Commandant, Jenné, May 1893, cited in: Archinard, Note... (Personnelle et Confidentielle), 13 July 1894, AN 81 AP 6 II, Rambaud Papers. This note, one of three prepared by Archinard on the Timbuktu expedition, is also printed in G. Bonnier, *L'occupation de Tombouctou* (Paris, 1926), pp. 244–55.

possible in case the Government decided to authorise an expedition during the next campaign.[1] By August echoes of these preparations had reached France.[2]

By September, however, Archinard had changed his mind. General Desbordes, he now told Bonnier, was dead against any move on Timbuktu in the near future because the Military's position in Paris was too delicate for them to provoke further controversies. Reluctantly, Archinard accepted his patron's more prudent advice and agreed that it might be best to let matters ride for the time being. Accordingly, he warned Bonnier about the possible complications which might arise from his instructions to the gunboats and ordered him to watch the reckless Lieutenant Boiteux very carefully.[3] But Bonnier was not to be put off. The capture of Timbuktu was a life-long ambition which he was not prepared to abandon even at the behest of his superiors. He knew that Boiteux might do something rash and had already forbidden the gunboats to escort the Jenné traders because of the Lieutenant's 'bellicose intentions'. But his own intentions were not in doubt either. 'We must go to Timbuktu', he minuted on Archinard's letter, '...it is indispensable and it will be done.'[4]

As was to be expected, Bonnier's plans were completely contradictory to the policies of the Colonial Department. Although Delcassé realised the advantage of extending French influence over Timbuktu, he was absolutely determined to avoid any complications which might lead to a new campaign. When Colonel Combes reported the receipt of a request for French protection, the Under-Secretary ordered him to act with extreme caution and respond to the overture only if it were genuine and seriously meant. On no account was he to make any promises which might commit France to military action in defence of the town.[5] Whether the offer of submission fulfilled these conditions is also doubtful. Ever since Caron's unhappy visit in 1887, Timbuktu had been

---

[1] Archinard to Boiteux, 2 June 1893, cited in *B.C.A.F., Renseignements Coloniaux*, January 1896, pp. 33–4. Although the wording of the instructions was obscure, Archinard himself later admitted: 'Si j'ai donné ces instructions à M. Boiteux c'est avec l'arrière pensée... que s'il arrivait quelque chose nous pourrions maintenant que nous avons le Macina aller tirer vengeance ou demander réparation.' Archinard to Bonnier, 2 Sept. 1893 [1], Archinard Papers.

[2] *La Politique Coloniale*, 12 Aug. 1893: 'Est-il exact que dès à présent, tout soit préparé au Soudan pour marcher, dès le début de la campagne prochaine, sur Tombouctou?'

[3] Archinard to Bonnier, 3 Sept. 1893 [1], Archinard Papers.

[4] *Ibid.* minutes by Bonnier. See also: Bonnier, Rapport, 2 Oct. 1893, MFOM Soudan I 5 (a).

[5] Delcassé to Combes, 7 Aug. 1893, MFOM Télégrammes Afrique, Soudan, 1893, Départ no. 36.

looking to Morocco for help against the threatened French advance. In 1888 the Grand Council had asked Sultan Mulay Hasan to renew the old Moroccan protectorate.[1] After the conquest of Macina, they repeated the request and sent an embassy to Marrakech. Timbuktu's overtures to the French were probably designed to hold them off until the Sultan's reply had been received; by November even Bonnier was convinced that its ambassadors were merely seeking to gain time.[2]

But neither the advice of his superiors, the policies of Paris nor the attitude of Timbuktu could divert the Commander from his goal. His plans had been common knowledge in the Sudan for months. In November he had appointed Commandant Joffre as commander of the North-East Region with responsibility for preparing the campaign, and by the time he returned from his short campaign against Samori everything was in readiness at Segu. On 25 December Bonnier, determined to launch the expedition before the civilian Governor could interfere, placed Joffre in command of an overland column with orders to march on Timbuktu by way of Sansanding and Goundam. On the morning of the 26th, he set off with the transport barges down the Niger. That same afternoon, as he was well aware, Grodet was due to arrive at Kayes.[3]

The battle between the two men was quickly joined. On his arrival, Grodet immediately informed Bonnier that he had assumed command, and on the 27th the latter acknowledged the despatch by telegraph, promising to send a full report by letter. In this he told Grodet about the campaign against Samori which he intended to resume after he had inspected the northern frontier and gathered more information 'on the degree of confidence which we can place in the rumours of Timbuktu's submission...on the disposition of neighbouring states and so on'.

---

[1] Féraud to M.A.E., 7 June 1888; same to same, 8 June 1888 [Copies], MFOM Sénégal IV 93 (d). According to Miège, *op. cit.* III, 372, Mulay Hassan himself intended to reaffirm Moroccan sovereignty over Timbuktu and was instrumental in the failure of Caron's mission.

[2] Minister, Tangiers to M.A.E., 5 Mar. 1894 [Copy], MFOM Afrique IV 30(b); Joffre to Grodet, 4 July 1894, *ibid.*; Minister, Tangiers to M.A.E., 11 Mar. 1895 [Copy], MFOM Soudan IV 1 (a); Bonnier, Rapport, 6 Nov. 1893, cited in Archinard, Note..., 10 Dec. 1894, AN 81 AP 6 II, Rambaud Papers.

[3] Bonnier to Joffre, Instructions, 25 Dec. 1893, cited in Grodet to M.C., 21 Apr. 1894, MFOM Soudan I 6(b); Guiard to Bonnier, 23 Dec. 1893, cited in Grodet to Under-Secretary, 2 Jan. 1894, *ibid.* See also: Grall [Medical Officer to the Column] to his sister, 21 Dec. 1893, published in *La Politique Coloniale*, 21 Dec. 1893: 'Où allons-nous? Je crois être sûr Tombouctou, et la rapidité de notre allure est faite pour nous mettre loin des postes avant l'arrivée du Gouverneur civil du Soudan qui ne manquerait pas de nous arrêter.'

As Bonnier knew, even this euphemistic description of his activities would take at least two weeks to reach Kayes.[1] But the Commander underestimated the determination of his superior. Grodet was nobody's fool, and when he saw that information about the Bonnier column was being deliberately withheld from him, he quickly guessed the worst.[2] Without hesitation, he ordered Bonnier to suspend all ¦military operations and return to Segu. At the same time, he asked Paris for permission to relieve the Colonel of his command if the order were not obeyed, and the Department gave him its full support.[3]

But nothing could stop Bonnier now. He had already learned that the impetuous Boiteux, disobeying his orders, had set off independently from his anchorage at Mopti.[4] Before receiving the Governor's orders he found out that the flotilla commander had reached Timbuktu and was calling for help. This gave him a perfect excuse for continuing his advance, and on the 31st he telegraphed Grodet that he had decided to occupy Timbuktu, 'whose submission has been seriously offered'. He gave details of Boiteux's insubordination and announced his intention to rescue the gunboats, organise the new territory and then resume the campaign against Samori. 'There is no reason for alarm', he assured the Governor; '. . . this is not a new conquest but. . . simply an extension of our influence. It will not involve any additional expenditure.' When he finally received the Governor's instructions, he merely replied that his columns were actually engaged in repelling an aggression; since any retreat would be fatal for the gunboats, he refused to return.[5]

Events at Kayes were also moving rapidly towards a climax. On 2 January Grodet reported the discovery of evidence that Bonnier had been planning the expedition since November and had known of

[1] Bonnier to Grodet, 27 Dec. 1893, encl. in Grodet to Under-Secretary, 19 Jan. 1894, MFOM Soudan I 6(b). Bonnier's report reached Kayes on 14 January.

[2] Grodet to Under-Secretary, 29 Dec. 1893, MFOM Télégrammes Afrique, Soudan, 1894, Arrivée no. 1: 'Depuis mon arrivée je remarque qu'on fait autour de moi un vide absolu calculé pour entraver toute action du Gouverneur.'

[3] *Ibid.*; Lebon to Grodet, 5 Jan. 1894, *ibid.* Départ no. 1.

[4] Whether Bonnier knew of Boiteux's action before he himself left Segu is unclear. According to Nigotte, one of the survivors of Goundam, he did not; but both Joffre and Patey claimed that he did. Nevertheless, it seems quite likely from Bonnier's orders to Joffre and his first report to Grodet, neither of which mentioned Boiteux, that the flotilla commander's indiscipline did not affect the timing of the main column's departure. See: Nigotte to G. Bonnier, 1 May 1894; Joffre to G. Bonnier, 2 May 1894; Patey to G. Bonnier, 11 Nov. 1894, cited in G. Bonnier, *op. cit.* pp. 205–8, 209–12, 214–21.

[5] Boiteux to Bonnier, received 31 Dec. 1893, cited *ibid.* p. 50; Bonnier to Grodet, 31 Dec. 1893; same to same, 1 Jan. 1894, cited in Grodet to Under-Secretary, 6 Jan. 1894, MFOM Soudan I 7(a).

the Governor's imminent arrival before he left Segu. Three days later, still without news, Grodet relieved Bonnier and Joffre of their commands and ordered their replacement, Commandant Hugueny, to lead the column back to its base. The receipt of Bonnier's explanations did nothing to change his mind.[1] Once more, the Colonial Department backed the Governor's firm stand. Despite the Minister of Marine's active intervention on Bonnier's behalf, Under-Secretary Lebon authorised Grodet to send the errant Colonel back to France as soon as circumstances allowed. He then obtained Cabinet approval for his decision and on 30 January confirmed Bonnier's recall.[2]

Once more, the order came too late. On 10 January Bonnier reached Timbuktu. The following day he told Grodet that he was expecting the overland column in four or five days' time and would move out to meet it as soon as he had organised the occupation of the town. On the 12th he set off with half his force towards Goundam, apparently to reconnoitre the route and await the arrival of Joffre.[3] On the 17th a pitiful band of survivors reappeared before the walls of Timbuktu. After skirmishing with Tuareg bands three days before, Bonnier's column had bivouacked near Goundam, using the same camp-site which the enemy had just abandoned. No patrols were sent out, and only a few pickets were posted. During the night the Tuaregs attacked 'the sleeping and badly guarded column'. By stampeding the cattle which the French had captured earlier in the day, they threw the camp into utter confusion and rendered effective defence impossible. In the carnage which followed, Bonnier, ten of his officers, the Native Interpreter, two European N.C.O.s and sixty-eight *tirailleurs* lost their lives.[4] It was the worst defeat which the French had suffered in the Sudan.

News of the Timbuktu expedition and the massacre of Goundam had its inevitable political repercussions in Paris. The departure of Delcassé

[1] Grodet to Under-Secretary, 2 Jan. 1894, MFOM Soudan I 6(b); same to same, 6 Jan. 1894, MFOM Télégrammes Afrique, Soudan, 1894, Arrivée no. 5. From Bonnier's telegrams Grodet mistakenly concluded that the Commander had already reached Timbuktu.

[2] Lefèbvre to Lebon, 8 Jan. 1894, MFOM Soudan V 2(b); Lebon to Grodet, 24 Jan. 1894; same to same, 30 Jan. 1894, MFOM Télégrammes Afrique, Soudan, 1894, Départ no. 4, n.n. See also: *La Politique Coloniale*, 1 Feb. 1894.

[3] Bonnier to Grodet, 11 Jan. 1894 [1]; same to same, 11 Jan. 1894 [2], cited in Grodet to Under-Secretary, 24 Jan. 1894, *ibid*. Arrivée no. 12.

[4] Philippe [Commandant, Timbuktu] to *Commandant-Supérieur des Troupes*, Kayes, Rapport, 21 Jan. 1894, encl. in Grodet to Under-Secretary, 23 Feb. 1894, MFOM Soudan I 6(b); published in *J.O.* 15 Mar. 1894, pp. 1217–18.

had done nothing to improve relations between Military and the Colonial Department. Although the public outcry over Quiquandon eventually forced the Inspectors-General to reverse their decision and send the officer to the Sudan, military resistance to civilian control continued unabated. When the Governor of Senegal, acting with the approval of the new Under-Secretary, Maurice Lebon, ordered two officers back to France for insubordination, the military commander, General Coronnat, forbade them to leave without instructions from the Ministry of Marine. Lebon angrily raised the matter in Cabinet and got it to annul Coronnat's orders when it confirmed Bonnier's recall.[1] Although the Colonial Department felt obliged to accept Bonnier's *fait accompli* and approved the occupation of Timbuktu provided it could be maintained without risk or additional cost,[2] it made no attempt to hide its feelings about the Military. When news of Goundam was made public, Prime Minister Casimir-Périer publicly expressed his full support for Grodet.[3] On 17 February the *Agence Havas* issued a communiqué, generally assumed to be officially inspired, stating categorically that 'the capture of Timbuktu had been ordered by Colonels Archinard and Bonnier in spite of the Government's strictest instructions to the contrary.'[4] In March the original report on the disaster with its damning assessment of Bonnier's security measures was published in the *Journal Officiel*.

Public opinion also swung against the Military. First reactions to the capture of Timbuktu were mixed. The militarists were predictably ecstatic, and even *Le Siècle* admitted that France would now be able to control the whole northern portion of the Niger Bend.[5] But both *La Politique Coloniale* and *Le Temps* condemned the operation as another instance of military indiscipline. Couchard, the Deputy from Senegal, announced his intention to interpellate the Government and changed his mind only when Bonnier was recalled.[6] Reactions to Goundam were

[1] *La Politique Coloniale*, 1 Feb. 1894; Details of this incident can be found in MFOM Sénégal XVI 68.
[2] Lebon to Grodet, 13 Jan. 1894, MFOM Télégrammes Afrique, Soudan, 1894, Départ no. 2.
[3] *J.O. Déb. Parl. Chambre*, séance du 10 février 1894, pp. 171–3.
[4] *La Politique Coloniale*, 17 Feb. 1894. See also: Archinard, Note..., 13 July 1894, AN 81 AP 6 II, Rambaud Papers.
[5] Emile Berr in *Le Figaro*, 26 Jan. 1894; *Le Journal des Débats*, 27 Jan. 1894; *Le Jour*, 27 Jan. 1894; *Le Matin*, 27 Jan. 1894; *L'Autorité*, 4 Feb. 1894; *Le Siècle*, 27 Jan. 1894.
[6] *La Politique Coloniale*, 27 Jan. 1894; *Le Temps*, 30 Jan. 1894. For Couchard's views, see: *Le Matin*, 2 Feb. 1894, and Couchard, *Profession de foi aux électeurs*, cited in Archinard, Conclusion Politique, 15 Feb. 1894, MFOM Soudan II 1.

much more hostile. The most prominent sections of the Press were virtually unanimous in holding the Military responsible for the disaster.[1] Etienne and Delcassé openly criticised Bonnier's recklessness, and the latter called once more for the restoration of effective Departmental control over military agents in the colonies.[2] In the Chamber both Couchard and Boissy d'Anglas, a close friend of Etienne and a member of the *groupe colonial*, tabled interpellations, withdrawing them only when the Prime Minister asked Parliament to postpone any debate on the disaster until further information was available.[3]

The militarists fought back as gamely as they could. Officially, Archinard and his colleagues kept silent throughout the controversy, but their champions in the Press soon rallied to Bonnier's defence. As early as 10 February *La Patrie* claimed that the column was massacred while returning to Kayes on the orders of Grodet and the Colonial Department. The report of Captain Philippe, it added, had been deliberately truncated to hide this fact and so shield those who were really responsible for the disaster. Two weeks later it published several of Bonnier's letters to Archinard, none of them mentioning Timbuktu, in order to show that charges of premeditation and collusion were completely false.[4] *L'Autorité*, *L'Eclair* and *La Libre Parole* wholeheartedly accepted this version and sought to denigrate Grodet by stressing his connections with Reinach and Cornelius Herz of Panama notoriety. The absurd story that Bonnier was on his way back to Kayes even found its way into the more respectable columns of *Le Journal des Débats*, *Le Jour*, and *Le Matin*.[5] But none of these outbursts could alter the fact that the Goundam massacre had shattered the myth of the Sudanese Military's professional brilliance and had largely discredited them in the eyes of the French public.

[1] *La Politique Coloniale*, 10 Feb. 1894; *Le Siècle*, 10 Feb. 1894; *Le Figaro*, 10 Feb. 1894; *Le Temps*, 14 Feb. 1894; *La République Française*, 11 Feb. 1894, also citing the views of *Le Rappel*, *Le Radical*, *La Justice* and *La Lanterne*.

[2] Interviews with *La France Militaire*, 11/12 Feb. 1894.

[3] *J.O. Déb. Parl. Chambre*, séance du 10 février 1894, pp. 171-3.

[4] *La Patrie*, 10 Feb., 11 Feb., 25 Feb. 1894. Although Archinard strenuously denied any participation in the controversy, he alone could have given Bonnier's letters to the newspaper.

[5] *L'Eclair*, 10 Feb. 1894; *La Libre Parole*, 11 Feb. 1894; *L'Autorité*, 15 Feb. 1894; *Le Journal des Débats*, 11 Feb., 17 Feb. 1894; *Le Jour*, 12 Feb., 26 Feb. 1894; *Le Matin*, 25 Feb. 1894.

GRODET'S WAR WITH THE MILITARY

The Military's influence in the Sudan, however, was not so badly hit. Thanks to Archinard's reforms, their domination had been too securely established and their independence too firmly entrenched for the appointment of a civilian Governor to have much effect. The heavy price of military indiscipline did not deter the surviving officers from their deliberate attacks on the civilian administration. Grodet's authority was challenged not only by Bonnier but by most of the junior officers as well. When the Governor learned of the plan to resume the offensive against Samori, he ordered Commandant Richard to suspend all operations and await further instructions. Richard, however, took orders from nobody except Bonnier. Following his Commander's lead, he merely acknowledged Grodet's despatch and thereafter maintained complete silence. He did not even report the death of Lieutenant Maritz in a mistaken attack on a British force at Waïma; Grodet learned of the incident only because he had imposed censorship on all telegraphic communications and thus received a copy of Richard's report to the *Commandant-Supérieur des Troupes*.[1] Through the same channels, he also received copies of Richard's despatches to Bonnier. But he could do little with them; they were in code, and all the code-books had been carefully removed from Kayes.[2]

The Governor's reactions were much more resolute than the officers might have expected. Although he was unable to prevent military insubordination, he punished those responsible for it without mercy. When the Commandant of Siguiri sent Bonnier copies of his correspondence with Kayes, he was reprimanded and replaced. When Richard finally asked for permission to advance against Samori, his request was emphatically rejected and he too was replaced.[3] His successor, Commandant Brunet, was strictly forbidden to move beyond Nionsomoridugu or Kankan, and when Grodet learned that Lieutenant Lecerf had been killed in a skirmish on Liberian territory, he ordered Brunet to

---

[1] Grodet to Under-Secretary, 6 Jan. 1894; same to same, 11 Jan. 1894; same to same, 22 Jan. 1894, MFOM Télégrammes Afrique, Soudan, 1894, Arrivée nos. 5, 6, 11. The most detailed and accurate account of the Waïma affair is: Y. Person, 'L'aventure de Porèkèrè et le drame de Waïma', *Cahiers d'études africaines*, no. 18 (1965), pp. 248–311.

[2] Grodet to Under-Secretary, 22 Jan. 1894, MFOM Télégrammes Afrique, Soudan, 1894, Arrivée no. 11. Grodet finally obtained a code-book from Nioro at the end of the month.

[3] Same to same, 11 Jan. 1894, *ibid.* Arrivée no. 6; same to same, 2 Feb. 1894, MFOM Soudan I 6(b).

place the Commandant of Beyla under arrest for allowing his troops to violate the frontier.[1]

Conflicts between the civilian and military authorities were just as violent elsewhere in the Sudan. In October 1893 Lieutenant Hourst had been sent to explore the Niger beyond Timbuktu and negotiate treaties as far as Say. Because of Bonnier's campaign, however, his mission had to be postponed, and he was placed under Grodet's orders. Hourst was enraged by the decision and immediately began to criticise the Governor's activities. Grodet in turn complained officially about the Lieutenant's 'presumption and stupidity' and demanded his recall. Paris was at first reluctant to agree, hoping to use Hourst as a replacement for Boiteux; but Hourst himself refused to serve under Grodet and asked to be recalled. He was soon on his way back to France.[2]

Segu and Macina were the next points of friction. In February 1894 Aguibou, having previously received Bonnier's permission, attacked the town of Bossé; but he ran into difficulties and had to ask the French for help. The Resident of Bandiagara, ignoring his instructions not to become involved in the new Sultan's military adventures, rushed to his assistance. Unfortunately, the Resident took no cannons with him, and his attacks were also beaten off. Commandant Quiquandon, through whom Grodet had hoped to reassert control at Segu, then formed an expeditionary column to avenge the defeat and warned the Governor that he would order it to march on 20 June unless he received instructions to the contrary. Since the despatch did not reach Kayes until the 17th, Grodet had to give his assent or risk seeing his orders openly disregarded.[3] On 11 July the relief column under Captain Bonnacorsi duly sacked Bossé; but it suffered heavy casualties in the process, and as

[1] Same to same, 31 Mar. 1894; same to same, 2 Apr. 1894, MFOM Télégrammes Afrique, Soudan, 1894, Arrivée nos. 49, 50.

[2] Delcassé to Hourst, Instructions, 26 Oct. 1893; Lebon to Hourst, 10 Feb. 1894; Hourst to *chef de cabinet du sous-secrétaire*, 14 Feb. 1894; Grodet to Under-Secretary, 15 Feb. 1894; same to same, 20 Mar. 1894, MFOM Missions 36, Hourst 1893; Hourst to M.C., 5 Apr. 1894; Grodet to M.C., 21 Apr. 1894, MFOM Soudan III 2.

[3] Grodet to Lebon, 2 Feb. 1894, MFOM Soudan I 6(b); Grodet to M.C., 20 June 1894, MFOM Télégrammes Afrique, Soudan, 1894, Arrivée no. 71; same to same, 21 June 1894, MFOM Soudan I 6(b); same to same, 22 June 1894, MFOM Soudan V 3(a). Quiquandon was regarded as trustworthy by the Colonial Department; he was alleged to have joined Monteil in attacking Archinard in 1893. But his views on expansion were in fact similar to those of Archinard. See: F. Quiquandon, 'Dans la boucle du Niger (1890–1)', *Bulletin de la Société de Géographie Commerciale de Bordeaux*, no. 20, 19 Oct. 1891, p. 471: 'Si nous voulons voir notre influence s'établir sérieusement, notre commerce s'étendre réellement et dans la boucle du Niger et au lac Tchad, ce serait courir à des déboires de penser que nous arriverons jamais à ce résultat autrement que par la force.'

compensation Bonnacorsi pillaged the town of Kombori. He was given thirty days' detention for his pains.[1] By the end of July Quiquandon too was on his way home, having already been placed under arrest for insubordination.[2]

The commandants of Timbuktu gave the Governor even more trouble. Despite his complicity in the expedition, Joffre had not been dismissed; and when he avenged Bonnier's death by routing the Tuaregs responsible for the massacre, he was even promoted to Lieutenant-Colonel.[3] But this was not enough to satisfy him. In April he called for a new campaign against the Tuaregs and urged the construction of new forts to improve security. Grodet opposed the plan as unnecessary and expensive, and he ordered Joffre not to attack the Irregentanem or the Kel Temoulai, two Tuareg clans which had not been directly implicated in the Goundam massacre. By then, however, Joffre had already attacked the Irregentanem, and two months after receiving his new orders he reported that he had dealt with the Kel Temoulai as well.[4]

Grodet was understandably relieved when Joffre returned to France in July. The Commandant of Timbuktu, he claimed, had allowed himself to be dominated by officers in his entourage who were determined to distinguish themselves at all costs.[5] Although the Governor was confident that Joffre's replacement, Lieutenant-Colonel Ebener, would obey his orders more scrupulously, his hopes were quickly dashed. Within a week of his arrival, Ebener was advocating new campaigns against the Irregentanem and the Kel Antassar. Grodet formally prohibited any new offensive, and Paris issued dire warnings about the measures it would take against 'any officer who, without prior and specific instructions, takes up arms for any reason other than to repel an aggression'.[6] But Ebener refused to co-operate. In October he sent a highly sarcastic circular to his *commandants de poste* telling them that the

---

[1] Grodet to M.C., n.d. [21 July 1894], MFOM Soudan I 6(b); Bonnacorsi, Rapport, 27 July 1894; Grodet to M.C. 28 Aug. 1894, MFOM Soudan V 3(a). In the attack on Bossé the French lost 9 killed and 149 wounded.

[2] M.C. to Grodet, 25 July 1894, MFOM Télégrammes Afrique, Soudan, 1894, Départ no. 49; Grodet to M.C., 3 Aug. 1894, *ibid.* Arrivée no. 82.

[3] Lebon to Grodet, 8 Feb. 1894; same to same, 10 Feb. 1894; same to same, 27 Feb. 1894; same to same, 3 Mar. 1894, *ibid.* Départ nos. 7, 9, 16, 18.

[4] Grodet to M.C., 14 Apr. 1894; same to same, 19 Apr. 1894, *ibid.* Arrivée nos. 53, 55; Grodet to Joffre, 27 Apr. 1894; Joffre to Grodet, 28 Apr. 1894; same to same, 25 June 1894, cited in Grodet to M.C., 22 July 1894, MFOM Soudan I 6(b). [5] *Ibid.*

[6] Ebener to Grodet, 15 July 1894; Grodet to Ebener, 4 Aug. 1894, cited in Grodet to M.C., 7 Aug. 1894, *ibid.*; Delcassé to Grodet, 11 Aug. 1894, MFOM Télégrammes Afrique, Soudan, 1894, Départ no. 50.

Ministry's instructions henceforth made it illegal to punish raiders or to protect loyal tribesmen. In December he refused to accept any further responsibility for the consequences of the Government's inaction, and in January Grodet asked to have him replaced by a civilian.[1]

THE FAILURE OF THE CIVILIAN EXPERIMENT

By the beginning of 1895 it was clear that the attempt to establish a viable civilian administration in the Sudan had failed. Part of the responsibility for the failure of the civilian experiment lay with Grodet himself. Nobody could describe him as a sympathetic personality or an easy man to work with. His deep-seated hostility towards the Military and his clumsy efforts to bludgeon them into submission certainly contributed to the unending squabbles which marred his Governorship. His single-minded determination to bring his unruly officers to heel took him on frequent and extended inspection tours away from Kayes, thus depriving the central administration of effective leadership. His preoccupations with military indiscipline led him to neglect his other duties and created a deep rift with the neighbouring colony of Senegal. In September 1894 Governor de Lamothe complained that he had received no information whatsoever from the Sudan for more than eight months, and when he authorised a punitive campaign along the northern frontier of Futa Jallon, Grodet treated the incident as an invasion of the Sudan. 'Frontier violations...in Europe', the Minister of Colonies later declared, 'have never led to diplomatic correspondence as complicated or passionate as [this affair] produced.'[2]

But Grodet had not been chosen for his tact. His principal task was to reimpose civilian control over the military arm, and his attempts to assert his authority usually had the Government's full approval. After Delcassé had become Minister of Colonies in May 1894, the Governor could rely completely on the Ministry's support.[3] Nor should one forget

---

[1] Ebener, ordre no. 150, 17 Oct. 1894, Archives Historiques de l'Armée (Section Outre-Mer) [henceforth Arch. Guerre], A.O.F. Soudan 4; Ebener to Grodet, 17 Dec. 1894, cited in Grodet to M.C., 16 Jan. 1895, MFOM Soudan I 7(a).

[2] De Lamothe to M.C., 4 Sept. 1894, MFOM Sénégal I 95(a); *J.O. Déb. Parl. Sénat*, séance du 17 juin 1895, p. 627 [speech by Chautemps]. For details of the controversy see: C. W. Newbury, 'The Formation of the Government General of French West Africa', *Journal of African History*, I (1960), 113–15.

[3] Minute on Grodet to M.C., 22 June 1894, MFOM Soudan V 3(a); minute on Grodet to M.C. 22 July 1894, MFOM Soudan I 6(b); Delcassé to Grodet, 12 Nov. 1894, MFOM Télégrammes Afrique, Soudan, 1894, Départ no. 73: 'Je vous renouvelle expression de ma confiance...'

that the Military's conduct often justified the harsh measures which were taken against them. Grodet could hardly be blamed for placing Lieutenant Mangin in thirty days' detention when this officer was found to have distributed slaves among his servants and interpreters.[1] The Military's deliberate refusal to co-operate with a civilian Governor was much more directly responsible for the Sudan's troubles. The *officiers soudanais* had enjoyed their independence for too long to surrender it lightly. They fought relentlessly to preserve their privileged position, and the whole edifice of civilian control eventually crumbled under their determined assaults. For Grodet was faced with an insuperable task. He stood alone and virtually unarmed against the concerted force of military insubordination. The Ministry's moral support and its approval for his disciplinary measures meant little when these measures had manifestly no deterrent value. Military power could only have been broken by a wholesale purge of the administration and the appointment of civilians to the key posts in the *cercles*. Yet, in the state of war for whose perpetuation the Military themselves were responsible, such a step was clearly impracticable. As long as the Military remained, the maintenance of security would continue to be a problem. It was a vicious circle from which neither Government nor Governor had any means of escape.

The consequences were predictable. Continued expeditions ruined any prospect of economic development. Hoping to encourage trade, Delcassé had opened the Railway to commercial use; but revenue from commercial charges did not average much more than 7,000 fr. a month during 1894.[2] Amid the devastation, only the slave trade seemed to flourish, and slaves were openly sold at all the French posts. At one point the Commandant of Beyla even included the proceeds of the sales in his monthly commercial returns.[3] The costs of military occupation continued to rise astronomically. The capture of Timbuktu completely wrecked the Sudan Budget. Troop reinforcements had to be sent and communications improved no matter what the cost, and Grodet was told to disregard financial considerations in the higher interests of

[1] See: Ebener, ordre no. 148, 16 Oct. 1894, Arch. Guerre, Soudan 4.
[2] Railway receipts, January–December 1894, MFOM Soudan XII 4(a).
[3] Grodet to Commandant, Bissandugu, 12 Sept. 1894, MFOM Soudan XIV 1(a); Grodet to M.C., 18 July 1894, *ibid*. The Governor did his best to suppress the trade but his injunctions could have little effect, for slaves formed an integral part of the Sudanese economic system under French rule just as they had before the conquest. See: Captain Maziller (Kayes), Rapport, 8 July 1894, Archives du Gouvernement-Général de l'A.O.F., Dakar, K 14. I am grateful for this reference to Dr C. W. Newbury.

security. As a result, he was forced to request additional credits totalling 5,700,000 fr. during the first ten months of his administration. By the end of 1894 Sudanese expenditure had reached the unprecedented level of 12,000,000 fr. a year.[1]

The Ministry's problems in Parliament increased proportionately. In June 1894 Delcassé assured the Budget Commission that his Ministry would in future be able to exercise effective control over costs through the civilian Governor.[2] But by then the Ministry's Estimates for 1895 had already been presented, and they totalled 9,400,000 fr. The occupation of Timbuktu, Delcassé explained, would itself cost more than a million a year, and the needs of military defence would make it impossible to cut back on garrison strengths.[3] Meanwhile, the immediate costs of the Timbuktu expedition also had to be met. In November 1894, four months after his confident declarations, Delcassé had to ask the Budget Commission for a supplementary credit of almost 4,000,000 fr. This time, the Commissioners were less obliging. Although they accepted the demand as indispensable, they approved it only because they recognised the fact that the Government had not been responsible for the expedition. At that, they reduced the credit by 100,000 fr. as a warning for the future.[4]

The difficulties of the civilian administration in the Sudan gave its militarist opponents in Paris new heart. Despite their temporary eclipse after the Bonnier massacre, Archinard and his supporters had not lost all their influence, and they certainly had no intention of giving up the fight. By the autumn of 1894 Grodet was again being regularly attacked in the militarist Press; *La Politique Coloniale* accused the Ministry of Marine of instigating this campaign against the principle of civilian control.[5] All the military party needed to topple the shaky structure of civilian rule was a major scandal, and Commandant Mon-

---

[1] Lebon to Grodet, 11 Feb. 1894, MFOM Télégrammes Afrique, Soudan, 1894, Départ no. 10; Grodet to *Colonies*, 6 Mar. 1894; same to same, 10 May 1894; same to same, 9 July 1894; same to same, 13 Sept. 1894, *ibid*. Arrivée nos. 21, 61, 78, 103.

[2] Procès-Verbaux de la Commission du Budget, séance du 18 juin 1894, AN C5547, p. 174. The declaration was made during the discussion of the supplementary credit of 2,289,800 fr. to cover the costs of the Macina campaign. See above: p. 215.

[3] Projet de Loi [Budget, 1895], 17 Mar. 1894, *J.O. Doc. Parl. Chambre*, no. 553, p. 472; Procès-Verbaux de la Commission du Budget, séance du 22 octobre 1894, AN C5447, pp. 416–17. The Minister admitted that the number of regular troops in the Sudan had more than doubled since 1891.

[4] Projet de Loi, 6 Nov. 1894, *J.O. Doc. Parl. Chambre*, no. 941, p. 1926; Cochery, Rapport, 13 Dec. 1894, *ibid*. no. 1071, pp. 2177–8.

[5] See: *Le Siècle*, 29 July 1894; *La Politique Coloniale*, 2 Aug., 11 Aug., 6 Oct. 1894, reporting the progress of the campaign.

teil's disastrous expedition against Samori gave them more than enough ammunition.

French relations with Samori during the early months of 1894 were confused. Bonnier's death and Richard's dismissal had cancelled out the Military's plans for a gigantic pincers movement and had allowed the *imam* to regain much of his strength. In January Captain Marchand, engaged in an exploration of the territories between the Ivory Coast and the Sudan, reported that Samori was preparing to attack Kong. At the same time, however, Governor Binger of the Ivory Coast declared categorically that 'Samori will never come to Kong either as a friend or as an enemy', and Paris was inclined to accept his assessment rather than Marchand's.[1] In March, moreover, Grodet announced that the *imam* seemed anxious to negotiate a new agreement with the French, and the Ministry cautiously allowed him to follow up the *démarche*.[2] But by August Marchand's continued reports about the threat to Kong were being taken much more seriously. Reversing his position, Binger now described an expedition against Samori as vital for the very survival of the Ivory Coast and urged the Government to act. Even Grodet admitted that the situation was critical.[3] Faced with the unanimous opinion of his local authorities, Delcassé decided to authorise a new campaign.

The Minister's most immediate problem was how to finance the operation, for he had recently been warned that no further credits were available for colonial expeditions.[4] By a happy coincidence, however, developments outside the Sudan provided the money just when it was needed. In May 1894, the publication of the Anglo-Congolese Agreement, an obvious attempt to bar French access to the Upper Nile, had incensed French public opinion, and in June the Chamber, spurred on by the *groupe colonial*, unanimously voted 1,800,000 fr. for 'the defence of French interests in Africa'. Although the credit was specifically

---

[1] Binger to Under-Secretary, 9 Jan. 1894 [Copy], AEMD Afrique 124; Under-Secretary to M.A.E., 24 Feb. 1894, MFOM Côte d'Ivoire IV 5 (b).

[2] Grodet to Lebon, 3 Mar. 1894, MFOM Télégrammes Afrique, Soudan, 1894, Arrivée no. 32; Lebon to Grodet, 6 Mar. 1894, *ibid.* Départ no. 20; Grodet to Delcassé, 2 June 1894; same to same, 27 July 1894, MFOM Soudan I 6 (b). Little progress was made because Samori refused to negotiate at a French fort or to accept a French Resident.

[3] Binger to Delcassé, 8 Aug. 1894, cited in: Rapport de la Commission d'Enquête, 14 Mar. 1896, MFOM Afrique III 21 (d); Grodet to Delcassé, 8 Aug. 1894, MFOM Soudan I 6 (b); same to same, 13 Aug. 1894, MFOM Télégrammes Afrique, Soudan, 1894, Arrivée no. 87.

[4] Dubard [*Inspecteur-Général, Contrôle*], Note, annexe 2 aux procès-verbaux de la Commission d'Enquête, séance du 24 février 1896, MFOM Afrique III 21 (c).

The Failure of the Civilian Experiment

intended for the Upper Ubangi, its general description enabled Delcassé to spend it on the Ivory Coast.[1] At the same time, an expedition under Commandant Monteil which was already on its way to the Congo provided the Minister with the necessary military force. Originally, Delcassé intended to have Monteil establish a French presence on the Upper Nile at Fashoda in the hope that Britain might thus be forced to begin negotiations on the evacuation of Egypt.[2] But Foreign Minister Hanotaux, determined to settle the Egyptian Question by diplomacy alone, overrode this bold plan, and in July 1894 Monteil was expressly forbidden to enter the Nile Valley. In August, when Hanotaux forced Leopold to repudiate what remained of the Anglo-Congolese Agreement,[3] the Monteil mission lost all its urgency; and on the 14th (the day the Franco-Congolese Agreement was signed) Delcassé obtained Cabinet approval for the diversion of the expedition to Grand Bassam.[4]

Monteil's new objective was to protect Kong and teach Samori the futility of continued resistance. The Commander, however, was ordered not to annihilate the *imam*'s forces. Indeed, if Samori agreed to recognise French suzerainty and accept a Resident, he could be allowed to carve out a new kingdom for himself on the borders of Sierra Leone and Liberia. Having restored military security, Monteil was to send political missions into the Niger Bend to link up with treaty-making expeditions moving north-west from Dahomey and so cut off the Gold Coast and German Togoland from the interior. As far as Delcassé was concerned, this was to be the Monteil expedition's most important task.[5]

Although the Minister had at first intended to bring the Sudanese columns into the operation, Grodet objected because Kong was too far

---

[1] In doing so, Delcassé had the backing of his Director of Defence; but his *bureau politique* considered the manœuvre irregular. See: J-L. Deloncle, Note, annexe 1 aux procès-verbaux de la Commission d'Enquête, séance du 4 février 1896, MFOM Afrique III 21 (c).

[2] The origins of the Fashoda expedition have been exhaustively studied. The fullest accounts are: J. Stengers, 'Aux origines de Fachoda: l'expédition Monteil', *Revue belge de philologie et d'histoire*, xxxvi (1958), 436–50; xxxviii (1960), 366–404, 1040–65; and G. N. Sanderson, *England, Europe and the Upper Nile* (Edinburgh, 1965), esp. pp. 114–90.

[3] German pressure had already brought about the effective abrogation of the clause leasing a corridor between Lake Tanganyika and Lake Albert to Britain.

[4] Delcassé to Monteil, 14 Aug. 1894, MFOM Afrique III 19(b); Deloncle, Note, annexe 1 aux procès-verbaux de la Commission d'Enquête, séance du 4 février 1896, MFOM Afrique III 21(c).

[5] Delcassé to Monteil, 14 Sept. 1894; same to same, 22 Sept. 1894; same to same, Instructions, 24 Sept. 1894, MFOM Afrique III 19(b). For the implications of Monteil's treaty making, see below: pp. 239–40.

away for the troops to campaign effectively, and Monteil was therefore warned not to expect any active assistance from the north.[1] Delcassé still hoped that the presence of French troops at Sikasso might at least block Samori's escape route in this direction; but Tiéba's successor, Ba Bemba, refused to accept a French garrison, and in November Grodet informed Paris that he could do no more than send him twenty rifles. When the Ministry made no comment, the Governor took no further action.[2] As always, he was much more preoccupied with the danger of military indiscipline. Anxious to prevent another Bossé, he ordered Commandant Dargelos at Bougouni to take no part whatsoever in the campaign, for he was convinced that the officers would deliberately provoke new hostilities in the hope of securing a *fait de guerre*.[3]

Meanwhile, the Monteil expedition was suffering the consequences of its hasty and inadequate preparation. Its sudden diversion to the Ivory Coast had disrupted its logistical services, and its supplies failed to arrive on time. When the column did set out, its advance sparked off a serious insurrection in the Baoulé valley. By January 1895 Monteil had still not made contact with Samori, and despite the insistence of the Ministry he had been unable to send out any diplomatic missions.[4] Worst of all, the expedition, irregularly financed to begin with, was much more expensive than anticipated. Both Bourdiaux (now Director of Defence at the Ministry of Colonies) and Governor Binger soon became disillusioned, and on the latter's advice Monteil was recalled in February.[5] By then, however, the expeditionary force had finally made contact with the *imam*, who proved to be just as formidable as ever. The French column was halted short of Kong, and in March it was obliged to retreat with heavy casualties. Monteil himself was severely wounded.[6]

[1] Delcassé to Grodet, 11 Sept. 1894, MFOM Télégrammes Afrique, Soudan, 1894, Départ no. 62; Grodet to Delcassé, 18 Sept. 1894, *ibid.* Arrivée no. 107; Delcassé to Monteil, Instructions, 24 Sept. 1894, MFOM Afrique III 19(b).

[2] Grodet to Delcassé, 10 Oct. 1894, MFOM Télégrammes Afrique, Soudan, 1894, Arrivée no. 116; Delcassé to Grodet, 24 Oct. 1894, *ibid.* Départ no. 71; Grodet to Delcassé, 3 Nov. 1894, same to same, 26 Nov. 1894, *ibid.* Arrivée nos. 128, 134.

[3] Grodet to Delcassé, 22 Dec. 1894; same to same, 16 Jan. 1895, MFOM Soudan I 7(a).

[4] Monteil to Delcassé, 4 Jan. 1895; same to same, 19 Jan. 1895, MFOM Afrique III 19(a). Monteil himself later ascribed his failure to the lack of sufficient planning and organisation. See: Monteil's testimony, annexes aux procès-verbaux de la Commission d'Enquête, séances du 1er février, 2 février 1896, MFOM Afrique III 19(a).

[5] Chautemps to Monteil, 18 Feb. 1895, MFOM Afrique III 19(b). See also: Rapport de la Commission d'Enquête, 14 Mar. 1896, MFOM Afrique III 21(d). Monteil himself blamed Binger for his recall. Monteil to Binger, 30 Mar. 1895 [Copy], AN 66 AP 10, Monteil Papers.

[6] Part of Monteil's report on the military operations of his column was later published as: P-L. Monteil, *Une page d'histoire militaire coloniale: La Colonne de Kong* (Paris, 1902).

The Failure of the Civilian Experiment

Grodet's rôle in the fiasco came under close scrutiny during the subsequent ministerial investigation. Because of Archinard's testimony, the Commission's report was less generous than it might have been. The Governor was criticised for his decision to halt the Richard expedition in January 1894, for his naïve faith in the sincerity of Samori's overtures, and for his general lack of interest in the Kong column. But the Commission did admit that he had kept the Ministry fully informed and had acted scrupulously according to his instructions; and it cleared him of any personal responsibility for Monteil's failure.[1] Unfortunately, its verdict came too late to save the Governor. In January 1895 the Dupuy Government had fallen once more, and Delcassé had been replaced as Minister of Colonies by Emile Chautemps. Although Chautemps had more than once declared his opposition to military expansion when *rapporteur* for the Colonial Budget, his first concern on coming to office was to dissociate himself from his predecessor's policies. Nor did he have Delcassé's resolution. The public outcry over his decision to recall Monteil more than satisfied his appetite for controversy over Sudanese affairs.[2] Grodet's less than heroic part in the Kong expedition greatly strengthened the militarists' hand, and when they mounted their final assault on the civilian administration of the Sudan, Chautemps avoided further complications by adopting a policy of pre-emptive surrender.

The debate on the Colonial Budget in March 1895 heralded Grodet's downfall. With the connivance of Archinard, the right-wing Deputy Le Hérissé launched a virulent personal attack on the unfortunate man, trotting out all the old charges against him. The Governor, he claimed, had been responsible for the Goundam massacre and had tried to hide the fact by truncating official despatches. His hostility and unwarranted harshness towards the Military were responsible for the deplorable state of Sudanese affairs; his inactivity had contributed to the failure of the Kong expedition. And when his administration of the Sudan was seen in the light of his earlier career—his scandalous Governorship of Martinique, his known association with the Panama swindlers, his inauspicious Governorship of Guiana—then his manifest unfitness for high office could no longer be questioned. After praising Chautemps, Le

---

[1] Archinard's testimony, annexe 3 aux procès-verbaux de la Commission d'Enquête, séance du 20 février 1896, MFOM Afrique III 21 (c); Rapport de la Commission d'Enquête, 14 Mar. 1896, MFOM Afrique III 21 (d).

[2] E.g. *Le Siècle*, 10 Feb. 1895; *La Politique Coloniale*, 26 Feb. 1895; *Le Temps*, 4 Mar. 1895; *Le Figaro*, 5 Mar. 1895.

Hérissé asked him to investigate these charges and proposed a nominal reduction of 1,000 fr. on the Sudan Budget to demonstrate the Chamber's desire for a reform in the colony's administration.[1] The Minister made no attempt to defend his subordinate. Just three days before, he had spent a most uncomfortable afternoon answering criticisms about Monteil's recall, and he had no wish to prolong the agony. He thanked Le Hérissé for his kind words, accepted the reduction of 1,000 fr. and promised that nothing would deter him from carrying out a full investigation. When the Budget Commission itself declared that a civilian administration could not function properly until peace had been established, Le Hérissé's battle was won, and his amendment was passed by acclamation.[2] Although Grodet's friends in the Senate did rally to his defence, Chautemps refused to discuss the matter any further.[3]

The Minister's performance rendered the Governor's position completely untenable; and when he requested sick-leave in April, he was promptly recalled. Parliament's determination to reduce costs and public disquiet about the state of civilian–military relations, Chautemps explained, made it imperative to introduce wide-ranging administrative reforms. Under the circumstances, no temporary replacement could be appointed while Grodet recuperated in France. This unfortunate but necessary change, he added rather hypocritically, in no way detracted from the Governor's valuable service in Africa.[4] But the Minister had clearly capitulated to militarist pressures, and as the fortunes of Grodet fell so those of Archinard began to rise. Within a week of the Budget Debate, Chautemps was consulting him about the proposed reorganisation of the Sudan. When news of Grodet's recall leaked out, the militarist Press jubilantly announced that Archinard would be sent to fill the vacancy. Although *La Politique Coloniale* at first refused to credit the rumour, it too soon admitted that the Colonel was going back to the Sudan.[5]

Yet all these predictions turned out to be inaccurate. On 16 June

---

[1] *J.O. Déb. Parl. Chambre*, séance du 4 mars 1895, pp. 693–9. Le Hérissé's charges were based on information contained in Archinard's confidential notes about the Timbuktu expedition.   [2] *Ibid.* pp. 699–702. See also: *ibid.* séance du 1er mars 1895, pp. 641–2.
[3] *J.O. Déb. Parl. Sénat*, séance du 5 avril 1895, pp. 376–7, 380–4.
[4] Grodet to Chautemps, 18 Apr. 1895, MFOM Télégrammes Afrique, Soudan, 1894, Arrivée no. 32; Chautemps to Grodet, 30 Apr. 1895, MFOM Dossier Administratif, Grodet.
[5] *La Politique Coloniale*, 16 Mar. 1895; Archinard to Chautemps, 18 Mar. 1895 [Copy], Archinard Papers; *L'Estafette*, 16 May 1895; *La Patrie*, 16 May 1895; *L'Autorité*, 31 May 1895; *La France Militaire*, 2/3 June 1895; *La Politique Coloniale*, 16 May, 21 May, 30 May, 1 June 1895.

The Failure of the Civilian Experiment

President Faure signed a Decree uniting Senegal, Guinea, the Sudan and the Ivory Coast into the federation of *Afrique Occidentale Française*, under the authority of a civilian Governor-General with direct control over Senegal and overall responsibility for civilian and military affairs. The western portions of the Sudan were detached to Senegal and the remainder placed under a civilian Lieutenant-Governor. Conflicts of authority between neighbouring Governors and the failure of the Kong expedition, during which 3,000 troops had stood idle in the Sudan, Chautemps explained, made it essential to impose unity of command over political and military affairs. Something had to be done about the anarchy into which the West African colonies, especially the Sudan, had slipped.[1] Despite the theoretical perpetuation of civilian rule, the reforms were a clear victory for the Military. Archinard was in fact offered the Lieutenant-Governorship of the Sudan, and even when he refused it no civilian was appointed.[2] Instead, the post was given provisionally to the *Commandant-Supérieur des Troupes du Soudan*, Colonel Trentinian, who was to hold it for the next four years.

The Minister's grandiose administrative system pleased nobody. The Budget Commission criticised him for not consulting Parliament about his reforms nor seeking the credits needed to pay for them.[3] The militarist Press condemned the maintenance of civilian control; *L'Autorité* denounced the appointment of a civilian Governor-General as 'a return to the vomit'. The colonialists were still more disenchanted. *Le Siècle* and *Le Temps* criticised the scheme as a costly, badly planned and impractical exercise in over-centralisation. *La Politique Coloniale* dismissed it as a last-minute fabrication whose only effect was to destroy the autonomy of the coastal colonies. The whole spectacle, it remarked ungraciously, was rather like that of a mouse trying to give birth to a mountain.[4]

Nor did the Minister's troubles end there. In March, the Senate Finance Commission had already reduced the Sudan Budget for 1895 to 9,000,000 fr., a cut of almost 400,000 fr.[5] In June, when Chautemps asked for a supplementary credit of 2,000,000 fr. to cover those costs of the Timbuktu campaign which were still outstanding, the Budget

---

[1] Chautemps, Rapport au Président de la République, and Presidential Decree, 16 June 1895, MFOM A.O.F. VII; *J.O. Déb. Parl. Sénat*, séance du 17 juin 1895, p. 627.

[2] *La Politique Coloniale*, 13 June 1895. The post was then supposed to have been offered to the Prefect of the Haute-Garonne, Laroche, who also refused it.

[3] Procès-Verbaux de la Commission du Budget, séance du 17 juin 1895, AN C5548, pp. 68–9.

[4] *L'Autorité*, 17 June 1895; *Le Siècle*, 20 June, 28 June 1895; *Le Temps*, 17 June 1895; *La Politique Coloniale*, 15 June, 20 June 1895.

[5] Morel, Rapport, 26 Mar. 1896, *J.O. Doc. Parl. Sénat*, no. 49, p. 152.

Commission, for the first time in fifteen years, rejected it outright. Six months before, the *rapporteur-général* pointed out, the Government had accepted a reduction of 100,000 fr. on a similar demand; now it maintained that its original estimates were inaccurate and could not even explain precisely where the discrepancy had occurred. At the same time, the Commission threw out the Minister's request for a credit of 380,000 fr. to cover the unforeseen costs of the Monteil expedition because the campaign had been launched without Parliamentary approval and financed with a credit voted specifically for the Congo. The fact that Delcassé had been responsible for the misappropriation did not make the Commissioners any more sparing in their criticism of his successor.[1] The unfortunate Chautemps was attacked on his Sudanese policy from every quarter. In the Senate he was formally questioned about the Military's alleged atrocities and about the wholesale distribution of women captives to the *tirailleurs*. He admitted the practice, insisting that it was entirely voluntary on the part of the 'épouses libres'; but his explanations were treated with the contempt they deserved.[2] In the Chamber Paul Vigné, a prominent critic of military abuses, repeated the charges and ridiculed the Minister's new Federation. During the debates about the Kong expedition, Delcassé accused him of personal responsibility for its failure. Even Le Hérissé, while approving the limited restoration of military influence, attacked him for not going nearly far enough. Despite Chautemps's desperate pleas, the Chamber adjourned both the Sudan and the Kong credits, a step which amounted to their rejection.[3]

But the Government's embarrassment did not disturb Archinard. After the arrival of Chautemps, he had regained much of his former influence over Sudanese affairs. Better still, the appointment of Jean-Louis Deloncle to the *Conseil d'Etat* in May removed his most dangerous enemy from the Ministry.[4] He could thus afford to turn down the offer of the Sudan. At the end of July 1895 he joined the Ministry of Colonies as Director of Defence in place of Bourdiaux. Within a year he was promoted to Brigadier, thus becoming one of the youngest Generals in the French Army.

[1] Procès-Verbaux de la Commission du Budget, séances du 17 juin, 18 juin 1895, AN C5548, pp. 67–9, 73–9; Cochery, Rapport, 18 June 1895, *J.O. Doc. Parl. Chambre* no. 1394, pp. 767 ff.
[2] *J.O. Déb. Parl. Sénat*, séance du 17 juin 1895, pp. 619–29.
[3] *J.O. Déb. Parl. Chambre*, séance du 26 juin 1895, pp. 1856–64; séance du 27 juin 1895, pp. 1878–1902. Supplementary credits on the Budget of 1894 had to be voted by 30 June 1895.   [4] *B.C.A.F.*, May 1895, p. 174.

9

The Last Years of Military Rule, 1895-9

With the incorporation of the Sudan into the West African Federation and the appointment of Archinard to the Directorate of Defence, the Military's victory seemed complete. Grodet's recall removed the greatest threat to their privileged position in the colony; the new Lieutenant-Governor, a military man, could be expected to treat them with more sympathy. Back in France, Archinard was becoming increasingly prominent in colonial circles. After 1895 he regularly attended the meetings of the *Comité de l'Afrique française*, and he even turned up at the annual banquets organised by his old enemies in the *Union coloniale*. As Director of Defence, he was again able to exert his influence over the formulation of Sudanese policy. 'Despite the Government-General...', *La Politique Coloniale* was to complain in 1896, 'Sudanese affairs are still being run from Paris by the military oligarchy which is daily taking over the Pavillon de Flore.'[1]

But not all the consequences of the civilian experiment could be undone. The Military's independence in the Sudan had traditionally rested upon its isolation. A measure of administrative integration through the Federation was the price they had to pay for their return to power. More seriously, the standstill imposed during Grodet's administration had not been universally applied; elsewhere in West Africa the pace of expansion continued to accelerate as the policy-makers sought to make the dream of a Chad empire come true. In the wake of the Congo explorers, Governor Brazza occupied the Sangha valley and Casimir Maistre established French influence in the region of the Mayo-Kebbi.[2] During his survey of the Say–Barruwa line, Monteil found that British influence over Sokoto was negligible, and on his return in 1893 he called for a modification of the line so as to give France Kuka and

[1] *B.C.A.F.*, June, July 1895, July 1897; *La Politique Coloniale*, 16 May 1896.
[2] See: M-A. Ménier, 'La marche au Tchad de 1887 à 1891', *Bulletin de l'Institut des Etudes Centrafricaines*, n.s. no. 5 (1953), pp. 5–18; M. Blanchard, 'Français et Anglais au Niger (1890–1898)', *Le Monde Français*, XII (1948), 409–23.

Katsina.[1] Although Mizon's expedition up the Benué in 1890 had not been successful, he was sent out once more in 1892 and managed to sign treaties of protectorate both with Muri and with the emir of Yola.[2] Mizon's unsavoury activities in Muri eventually forced Delcassé to recall him, but the Colonial Department still urged the Quai d'Orsay to ratify his treaties, provisionally at least, so that they could be used to extract further concessions from the English.[3] In reply to British protests about the explorer's alleged violation of the 1890 Agreement, the Quai d'Orsay flatly denied that the recognition of French influence north of the Say–Barruwa line in any way implied a reciprocal recognition of British influence south of it.[4] The French maintained their pressure throughout 1894. British attempts to block the southern routes to Chad by partitioning Bornu and Adamawa with Germany were quickly brushed aside. By the Franco-German Agreement of March 1894 France gained title to the southern shore of the lake, including both banks of the Chari, the territories of Baghirmi and Wadai, the major portion of the Sangha valley, and the town of Bifara on the Mayo-Kebbi, a navigable tributary of the Benué.[5] During abortive discussions with Britain later in the year, Foreign Minister Hanotaux, backed by the Colonial Ministry, refused to renounce French claims to Bornu and Adamawa and offered to recognise the bilateral character of the Say–Barruwa line only if it were redrawn so as to place northern Bornu, including Kuka, in the French sphere.[6]

[1] Monteil to Delcassé, 7 Apr. 1893 [Copy], AN 66 AP 9, Monteil Papers.

[2] As in 1890, Mizon posed as a strictly scientific and commercial explorer, but there can be no doubt about the political nature of his mission. E.g. Under-Secretary to M.A.E., 14 Dec. 1893 [drafted by J-L. Deloncle], MFOM Afrique VI 106(g): '...le côté politique de l'entreprise était pour ainsi dire laissé dans l'ombre.' For Mizon's activities along the Benué, see: Flint, *Sir George Goldie and the Making of Nigeria*, pp. 173-9.

[3] Delcassé to Mizon, 4 July 1893, MFOM Afrique III 16(a); Under-Secretary to M.A.E., 14 Dec. 1893 [drafted by J-L. Deloncle], MFOM Afrique VI 106(g).

[4] Dufferin to Develle, 30 Oct. 1893, *D.D.F.* x, no. 410; Projet de réponse, encl. in M.A.E. to Under-Secretary, 24 Jan. 1894; Under-Secretary to M.A.E., 2 Feb. 1894; Casimir-Perier to Dufferin, 9 Feb. 1894, encl. in M.A.E. to Under-Secretary, 19 Feb. 1894, MFOM Afrique VI 115(c). The Quai d'Orsay was at first prepared to accept the Say–Barruwa line as excluding French influence from Sokoto, but at the insistence of the Colonial Department it eventually denied that the line had any reciprocal character whatsoever.

[5] The texts of the Anglo-German Agreement of 15 November 1893 and the Franco-German Agreement of 15 March 1894 are printed in Hertslet, *op. cit.* III, 913-15; E. Rouard de Card, *Traités de délimitation concernant l'Afrique française* (Paris, 1910), pp. 8-11.

[6] Note du Ministre, 5 Sept. 1894, *D.D.F.* XI, no. 234; Phipps [British chargé] to Hanotaux, 17 Sept. 1894; Note [drafted by J-L. Deloncle], 29 Sept. 1894, AEMD Afrique 131; Note du Ministre, 29 Sept. 1894, *D.D.F.* XI, no. 237. The principal issue during the discussions was the future of the Upper Nile, and the talks collapsed when the two sides failed to reach agreement on it. This episode in Anglo-French diplomacy is described in:

French activity in the Niger Bend was similarly intensified. Before he left the Colonial Department, Etienne had already considered the possibility of turning French possessions on the Slave Coast into a base for expansion inland. After a new outbreak of fighting in the spring of 1892, Colonel Dodds was sent to break the power of Abomey, and plans were drafted for the extension of French influence as far north as Say. Once the conquest of Dahomey was complete, Delcassé ordered Governor Ballot to send treaty-making expeditions north-east into Borgu and north-west towards the Sudan and the Ivory Coast. By the spring of 1895, in an atmosphere of growing international tension, Captain Decœur had signed treaties with Nikki and Kiama, and Ballot had followed up to establish a chain of fortified posts throughout Borgu; a detachment from the Decœur expedition had occupied Say; and Captain Toutée had built Fort d'Arenberg on the Niger below Bussa. British protests against these incursions were summarily rejected. 'Nobody can contest the right of a European state to send missions into Africa, be they commercial, scientific or even political', Hanotaux maintained; any disputes which arose would have to be settled at the conference table.[1]

The advance from the coast had a special significance for the Military's position in the Sudan. Despite his aversion to the *officiers soudanais*, Delcassé did not hesitate to achieve his political objectives in the Niger Bend by military means. His expeditions were not the simple diplomatic missions which the Government had favoured in the past. The Monteil of the Kong column with 300 men under his command was a far cry from the explorer who had set out for Chad with a party of ten. Decœur was not another Binger; he had 150 *tirailleurs* with him when he moved into Borgu. But the Minister of Colonies was absolutely determined to prevent the creation of another Sudan in the south. He

Robinson and Gallagher, *Africa and the Victorians*, pp. 333–5; and A. J. P. Taylor, 'Prelude to Fashoda: The Question of the Upper Nile, 1894–5', *English Historical Review*, LXV (1950), 52–80.

[1] Dufferin to Dupuy, 1 Jan. 1895; Courcel to Hanotaux, 28 Mar. 1895; Hanotaux to Courcel, 29 Mar. 1895, *D.D.F.* XI, nos. 325, 412, 416. For French policy in the Niger Bend, see: C. W. Newbury, 'The Development of French Policy on the Lower and Upper Niger, 1880–98', *Journal of Modern History*, XXXI (1959), 25–6; M. Blanchard, 'Théophile Delcassé au Pavillon de Flore', *Le Monde Français*, XIII (1949), 3–34; G. Ganier, 'Les rivalités franco-anglaise et franco-allemande de 1894 à 1898', *Revue française d'histoire d'outre-mer*, XLIX (1962), pp. 181–261. For the British reaction, see: Flint, *op. cit.* pp. 216–32; M. Perham, *Lugard, the Years of Adventure* (London, 1956), pp. 473–557; F. D. Lugard, 'England and France on the Niger, the Race for Borgou', *Nineteenth Century*, May 1895, pp. 889–903.

realised the importance of maintaining strict control over his agents on the spot, and he was careful to choose either known opponents of the Sudanese *clique* like Monteil or personal favourites like Toutée.[1] The leaders of his expeditions all knew that their tasks were political rather than military, and they all operated in territories which were beyond the limits of Sudanese military influence. While Grodet held his head-strong officers in check, Delcassé turned Dahomey into the principal base for military expansion in West Africa, and here at least Chautemps followed the same policy. His instructions to Chaudié and Trentinian dealt almost exclusively with organisation and economic development; the continued extension of French influence was entrusted to Alby, Baud, Bretonnet, Decœur and Toutée, all of whom were based on Dahomey, which was not included in the new Federation.[2]

At the Directorate of Defence, Archinard grasped the significance of these changes and was not pleased by them. He saw that the days when the Military could fulfil their ambitions in the Sudan alone were past; henceforth the opportunities for real campaigning would lie in the east. If the Military were to benefit from them and at the same time regain their influence over the course of African expansion, they would have to bring the Sudan back into the mainstream of the Government's African policy. The Director of Defence acted accordingly.

THE SUDAN AND THE OCCUPATION OF THE NIGER BEND

Despite the growing importance of Dahomey, the Sudan was never completely excluded from the Government's expansionist policies. Even the Military's most violent critics admitted that the capture of Timbuktu would enable France to establish her sway over the northern regions of the Niger Bend. The Colonial Department ordered Grodet not to neglect 'the progressive extension of our sphere of influence', and the Governor himself called for a rapid if peaceful advance towards Say.[3] British activities on the northern frontiers of the Gold

---

[1] Blanchard, 'Théophile Delcassé au Pavillon de Flore', *loc. cit.* p. 18; Binger's testimony, annexe aux procès-verbaux de la Commission d'Enquête [Monteil expedition], séance du 8 février 1896, MFOM Afrique III 21 (c): 'Il [Delcassé] ne voulait pas prendre d'officier ayant servi au Soudan sous les ordres du Colonel Archinard.'

[2] Chautemps to Trentinian, Instructions, 6 July 1895, MFOM Soudan I 9(a); Chautemps to Chaudié, Instructions, 11 Oct. 1895, MFOM A.O.F. I 1.

[3] *La Politique Coloniale*, 29 May 1894 (quoting interviews with Vallon and François Deloncle); M.C. to Grodet, 21 Apr. 1894, MFOM Télégrammes Afrique, Soudan, 1894, Départ no. 29; Grodet to Delcassé, 22 July 1894, MFOM Soudan I 6(b).

Coast underlined the need for speed. The Native Agent Fergusson was already engaged in negotiating treaties with the chiefs of Mossi, Gurunsi and Dagomba, and in July 1894 Grodet transmitted alarming rumours about the arrival of a strong British expedition at Bobo-Diulasso.[1] At first, Delcassé hoped that Monteil might be able to forestall the threat; but when the Kong expedition proved unable to carry out its diplomatic tasks, Chautemps had to call on Grodet to establish the necessary protectorates over Yatenga, Lobi, Mossi and Gurunsi.[2] In February 1895 Grodet sent Commandant Destenave to secure the relevant treaties. But the ruler of Mossi, the *naba* of Wagadugu, refused to have any dealings with the French, and since Destenave had been forbidden to use force, he did not press the issue. By October the Ministry was forced to admit that its attempts to extend French influence by peaceful means had so far met with little success.[3]

Destenave's failure gave Archinard the chance to press for policies more congenial to his restive officers in the Sudan, and he immediately drew up plans for an expedition against Wagadugu. Both Chaudié and Roume, the head of the Ministry's administrative division, opposed the scheme on the grounds of cost and security; but Archinard continued to agitate for an invasion of Mossi, and his more belligerent views gained the support of the new Minister, Guieysse.[4] Accordingly, Captain Voulet was sent to Wahiguya, Mossi's second city, and in September 1896 he occupied Wagadugu as well. He then moved south to Sati, capital of Gurunsi, signed a treaty with its chief, and returned to Wagadugu. In February 1897 he left Wagadugu once more, made contact with a mission from Dahomey and helped it to establish French influence over Gurma.[5] Meanwhile, Destenave garrisoned Wagadugu, built a fort at Wahiguya, sent Lieutenant Chanoine to occupy Sati and

---

[1] Same to same, 30 July 1894, *ibid.*

[2] Monteil to M.C., 19 Jan. 1895, MFOM Afrique III 19(a); Chautemps to Grodet, 9 Feb. 1895, MFOM Télégrammes Afrique, Soudan, 1895, Départ no. 4.

[3] Grodet to Destenave, 20 Feb. 1895, cited in Grodet to Chautemps, 20 Feb. 1895, MFOM Soudan I 7(a); Destenave to Governor of the Sudan, 10 May 1895 [Copy], MFOM Soudan I 6(*bis*); same to same, 13 July 1895, MFOM Soudan III 3(c); Notes pour le Président de la République, 8 Oct. 1895, MFOM Sénégal I 96(*bis*).

[4] Archinard, Note pour la 1ère direction, 24 Oct. 1895; Roume, Note pour la direction de défense, 20 Nov. 1895; Archinard, Note pour la 1ère direction, 3 Dec. 1895, MFOM Soudan I 6(*bis*); Chaudié to M.C., 17 Jan. 1896, MFOM A.O.F. I 1; Archinard, Note pour la 1ère direction, 15 Feb. 1896, MFOM Soudan III 3(c); Guieysse to Chaudié, 26 Dec. 1895, MFOM A.O.F. I 5.

[5] Trentinian to Chaudié, 20 Feb. 1896; Chaudié to Trentinian, 22 Apr. 1896, encl. in Chaudié to M.C., 1 May 1896, MFOM Soudan I 9(b); Chaudié to M.C., 25 Nov. 1896;

then moved north with his main force into Dori and Yagha. In May a detachment from his column under Captain Betbeder reoccupied Say.[1]

Archinard's new policies of military expansion threw the Sudan back into the arena of international rivalry. For a time in 1895 it seemed that Anglo-French disputes might be settled in a spirit of mutual accord. Decœur's courteous dealings with the Royal Niger Company and Toutée's withdrawal from Fort d'Arenberg greatly eased the tension and cleared the way for negotiations. Ambassador Courcel had already suggested a resumption of talks on the Niger and on 'other petty questions' which remained in dispute, and after Toutée's withdrawal Salisbury agreed to reconvene the Anglo-French Boundary Commission. In January 1896 discussions were reopened.[2] But French hopes for an amicable settlement in no way lessened their determination to secure the widest possible extension of their projected West African empire. Although the Ministry of Colonies was now prepared to accept the bilateral nature of the Say–Barruwa line and to recognise the Anglo-German Agreement of November 1893, its price was the revision of the Lagos–Dahomey boundary so as to give France access to the Lower Niger, the revision of the Say–Barruwa line to give her Kuka, and the recognition of her influence over the eastern shore of Lake Chad as far as the Chari. In addition, Britain would have to pay compensation for the losses incurred by Mizon, guarantee freedom of navigation along the Niger more effectively than she had in the past and accept the union of Dahomey and the Ivory Coast. No meaningful negotiations were possible on these terms, but the French delegates refused to budge from them. Discussions quickly degenerated into acrimonious wrangling over the validity of each side's treaties in the Niger Bend, and when the French rejected the final British offer in April 1896, the talks were broken off.[3]

---

same to same, 9 Dec. 1896; same to same, 23 Mar. 1897, MFOM A.O.F. I 1; Voulet to Governor of Dahomey, 20 Feb. 1897, MFOM Soudan III 3 (c). For an account of Voulet's expedition, see: *B.C.A.F.*, August 1897, pp. 253–66.

[1] Scal to Chanoine, 4 Mar. 1897, MFOM Afrique III 37 (c); Trentinian to Chaudié, 16 May 1897; Chaudié to M.C., 18 May 1897, MFOM Soudan IV 5. Destenave's report was published in *B.C.A.F.*, *Renseignements Coloniaux*, December 1898, pp. 213–24.

[2] Courcel to Hanotaux, 10 Apr. 1895, *D.D.F.* XI, no. 443; same to same, 14 Aug. 1895; same to same, 29 Sept. 1895; same to same, 23 Oct. 1895; Salisbury to Courcel, 29 Nov. 1895; Courcel to Berthelot, 15 Jan. 1896, enclosing Joint Declaration, *D.D.F.* XII, nos. 128, 161, 181, 217, 274. See also: Flint, *op. cit.* pp. 229–30.

[3] M.C. to M.A.E., 7 Feb. 1896; same to same, 20 Feb. 1896, MFOM Afrique VI 133 (b). The minutes of the Commission are to be found in MFOM Afrique VI 134 (b). Any

The Sudan and the Occupation of the Niger Bend

The French advance on the ground now assumed formidable proportions. Troop movements from the Sudan into Mossi and Gurunsi were accompanied by a new series of expeditions from Dahomey, and in the spring of 1897 Commandant Bretonnet occupied Bussa.[1] At the same time, Guieysse's successor as Minister of Colonies, André Lebon, sent Captain Cazemajou on a provocative mission to strengthen French influence along the Say–Barruwa line. As far as possible, the explorer was to stay north of the line, but if necessary he could follow Monteil's itinerary and confirm the treaties which his predecessor had negotiated. Having reached Chad, he was to establish friendly relations with Kuka and sign a treaty of protectorate with the conqueror of Bornu, Rabih Zubair. He was then to proceed along the north-east shore of the lake until he met an expedition under Commandant Gentil which was moving north from the Congo. Following the spirit of his instructions, Cazemajou crossed the Niger south of Say, signed a treaty of protectorate with Argungu, and then announced his intention to visit Sokoto.[2]

As in the past, the impetus behind these energetic measures came from the Pavillon de Flore. Lebon was the one who ordered Captain Voulet to advance through Gurunsi and launched the Dahomey columns on their provocative drive towards the Lower Niger. In occupying Bussa, Bretonnet disobeyed his orders, but the Minister of Colonies refused to disavow the action and urged the Quai d'Orsay to postpone any talks on the dispute until all his expeditions had reached their objectives and so enabled the French to negotiate from strength.[3] The Cazemajou expedition was also his work. The Foreign Ministry had given its assent only on his specific assurance that the explorer would in no circumstances enter the territory of Sokoto, and it was understandably indignant about the apparently deliberate deception. But Lebon offered no apologies and made no excuses for the tone of his

---

prospect of an agreement was, of course, made much more unlikely still by the start of the British invasion of the Sudan in March 1896. For an account of the negotiations in their general diplomatic context, see: J. D. Hargreaves, '*Entente Manquée*: Anglo-French Relations, 1895–6', *Cambridge Historical Journal*, XI (1953), 65–92.

[1] Lebon to Hanotaux, 19 Jan. 1897, MFOM Afrique VI 142(a). See also: Flint, *op. cit.* pp. 241–2, 265–6.

[2] Lebon to Cazemajou, Instructions, 22 Feb. 1897, MFOM Afrique III 25; Cazemajou to Lebon, 1 Nov. 1897, MFOM Missions 11, Cazemajou; same to same, 28 Dec. 1897; same to same, 26 Jan. 1898, MFOM Afrique III 25.

[3] Lebon to Hanotaux, 4 Feb. 1897; same to same, 17 Mar. 1897; same to same, 22 Mar. 1897; same to same, 11 May 1897; same to same, 17 June 1897, MFOM Afrique VI 142(a).

16-2

instructions. Although he agreed that the Argungu treaty could not be ratified immediately, he refused to take disciplinary action against Cazemajou and left it up to the Quai d'Orsay to decide how far the explorer's diplomatic gains could be upheld.[1]

The obstinacy of the French Colonial Ministry, however, was more than matched by the new intransigence of its British counterpart. The arrival of Joseph Chamberlain at the Colonial Office in 1895 revolutionised British policy in West Africa. Like the policy-makers in Paris fifteen years before, the Colonial Secretary saw the West African interior as a vast undeveloped estate to be secured for Britain's future benefit through the direct action of the State. Under his administration, West Africa ceased to be a mere pawn in Britain's Egyptian strategy and became an intrinsically valuable territory whose possession was considered worth fighting for.[2] Determined to reverse 'the present policy of drift', Chamberlain took resolute steps to meet the dangers of French expansion. Discarding the traditional—and ineffectual—policy of diplomatic protest, he set out to beat the French at their own game: to answer each of their provocations in kind and to check all their advances with superior British force. In September 1895 he sent a military expedition against Ashanti, at least partly in order to keep the northern territories of the Gold Coast out of French hands. In June 1897, after the French had occupied part of Gurunsi, he authorised Governor Maxwell to negotiate with Samori, to reinforce his northern garrisons, and if necessary to occupy Bonduku in the French sphere.[3] On the Niger frontier, he pressured Goldie into an invasion of Nupe and Ilorin at the end of 1896; and after the French occupation of Bussa he sent his newly organised West African Frontier Force to camp on the French lines of communication. By now, Chamberlain seemed bent on precipitating a conflict. Although he warned Goldie in July 1897 that Britain would never actually fight for Bussa or Mossi, he told his Under-Secretary of State that the Niger and Gold Coast hinterlands had

[1] Hanotaux to Lebon, 21 Dec. 1896; Lebon to Hanotaux, 27 Jan. 1897; same to same, 5 Feb. 1897, MFOM Afrique III 25; same to same, 14 Mar. 1898, *D.D.F.* XIV, no. 84; Hanotaux to Lebon, 28 Mar. 1898; Lebon to Hanotaux, 1 Apr. 1898, MFOM Afrique VI 149(c); same to same, 18 Apr. 1898; Hanotaux to Lebon, 28 Apr. 1898; Lebon to Hanotaux, 9 May 1898, MFOM Afrique III 25. The Quai d'Orsay was so upset by the incident that Hanotaux's successor, Delcassé, refused to pay its share towards the cost of the mission. See: Delcassé to M.C., 5 Jan. 1899, MFOM Missions 11, Cazemajou.

[2] The best analysis of Chamberlain's policy towards West Africa is Robinson and Gallagher, *Africa and the Victorians*, pp. 395–402.

[3] Chamberlain to Maxwell, 22 Nov. 1895, cited *ibid.* p. 400; same to same, 26 June 1897, cited in Sanderson, *op. cit.* pp. 317–18.

to be protected 'even at the cost of war', and he seemed positively delighted by the prospect that some French provocation might give his troops the chance to retaliate.[1]

The equally uncompromising attitude of local French commanders almost made Chamberlain's wish come true. In Borgu, *tirailleurs* and Hausas were soon facing each other with fixed bayonets, and when the British planted the Union Jack outside Kiama, then occupied by the French, a major battle seemed only a stray rifle-shot away.[2] Further west, where Archinard had managed to push his *soudanais* to the fore, the two sides came even nearer to blows. In the wake of Voulet's advance, troops had been sent to occupy Buna and Wa on the northwest frontier of the Gold Coast. But the British did not recognise French claims to the towns, and in December 1897 Colonel Northcott ordered their garrisons to withdraw. When they refused, he bustled them out.[3] Smarting under this humiliation, the French commander, Commandant Caudrelier, immediately ordered the *tirailleurs* back and refused to evacuate his positions despite Northcott's increasingly violent threats. Both Lebon and Governor-General Chaudié approved Caudrelier's firm stand, and the latter gave him permission, once all attempts at conciliation had failed, to resist any new British aggression by force.[4] Not to be outdone, the British Government refused to accept responsibility for the consequences of French provocations, and for a time an armed clash seemed almost inevitable.[5]

In the end, however, the peace was kept, and the disputes in the Niger Bend were settled by negotiation. For the crisis was a very unreal one, provoked not by the importance of the issues involved but by the absurd military posturings of the Colonial Ministries and their local

[1] Chamberlain to Goldie, 1 July 1897, cited in Perham, *op. cit.* p. 633; Chamberlain to Selborne, 28 Sept. 1897, cited in J. L. Garvin, *The Life of Joseph Chamberlain* (London, 1934), III, 208; see also: Perham, *op. cit.* p. 639.

[2] *Ibid.* pp. 676–97.

[3] Chaudié to M.C., 12 Nov. 1897; same to same, 21 Nov. 1897, MFOM Télégrammes Afrique, Sénégal, 1897, Arrivée nos. 171, 176; Northcott to Boulard [Commander of the French garrison at Buna], 15 Dec. 1897; Northcott to Caudrelier, 26 Dec. 1897; Caudrelier to Northcott, 21 Dec. 1897; same to same, 7 Jan. 1898, MFOM Côte d'Ivoire IV 6(d); Chaudié to Lebon, 16 Jan. 1898, MFOM A.O.F. I 2.

[4] Chaudié to Lebon, 18 Jan. 1898, MFOM A.O.F. VI; same to same, 20 Jan. 1898, MFOM Télégrammes Bureau d'Afrique, 1898, Arrivée no. 3; Lebon to Chaudié, 21 Jan. 1898, *ibid.* Départ no. 6; Chaudié to Lebon, 24 Feb. 1898, MFOM Côte d'Ivoire IV 7(a).

[5] In April, Lieutenant Sigonney actually protested that his troops had been fired on by the British garrison at Sapeliga, but his report turned out to be inaccurate. Sigonney to Northcott, 9 Apr. 1898; same to same, 10 Apr. 1898; Northcott to Sigonney, 11 Apr. 1898; same to same, 21 Apr. 1898, encl. in Ballay to M.C., 11 July 1898, MFOM A.O.F. I 2.

agents. When the situation threatened to get completely out of hand, the more prudent counsels of the Foreign Ministries reasserted themselves. Although Salisbury had been forced to approve his Colonial Secretary's West African policies in order to keep the Liberal Unionists in the government, his own priorities remained firmly centred on Egypt and the Upper Nile. Once Kitchener had been launched upon the invasion of the Sudan and Marchand had set out for Fashoda, a much more serious African crisis was on the cards, and it was important to have petty squabbles on the Niger out of the way before it broke. Salisbury himself regretted the breakdown of the West African talks and tried hard to revive them. In October 1896 he hinted at the possibility that Dahomey could be given access to the Lower Niger; in January 1897 he declared himself ready to reconvene the Joint Commission; and when he visited Paris in March, he suggested that the two sides submit their differences to arbitration.[1]

The Quai d'Orsay was just as anxious for a reasonable arrangement. Ambassador Courcel had no doubts about the proper order of French priorities in Africa. Egypt was the key issue which divided Britain and France and the one which had to be settled to French satisfaction. The ridiculously exaggerated Niger question was merely an unnecessary complication. At the first sign of British moderation, therefore, the Ambassador urged the Foreign Ministry to resume negotiations and so 'remove this dead weight...on our general relations with England'.[2] Hanotaux was inclined to agree; as early as 1895 he too had dismissed the Niger question as 'useless'. After the departure of Marchand, he became just as anxious as Salisbury to clear the decks for the coming confrontation; only the obstinacy of the Pavillon de Flore prevented him from taking up the Prime Minister's offer in January 1897.[3] By the autumn, moreover, even Lebon had become sufficiently alarmed by the British military build-up in West Africa to urge a resumption of talks, and in October the Niger Commission was again called into session.[4] This time, French demands were much more modest. After some initial

[1] Courcel to Hanotaux, 3 Oct. 1896, *D.D.F.* xii, no. 468; Salisbury to Monson, 12 Jan. 1897, encl. in Hanotaux to Lebon, 21 Jan. 1897; Courcel to Hanotaux, 18 Mar. 1897, encl. in same to same, 21 Mar. 1897, MFOM Afrique VI 142(a); Note du Ministre, 26 Mar. 1897; Communication de M. le baron de Courcel, 26 Mar. 1897, *D.D.F.* xiii, nos. 166, 167.
[2] Courcel to Hanotaux, 29 Sept. 1895, *D.D.F.* xii, no. 161; same to same, 11 Dec. 1896, *D.D.F.* xiii, no. 40; same to same, 26 Jan. 1897 [Copy], MFOM Afrique VI 142(a).
[3] Hanotaux to Courcel, 27 Sept. 1895, *D.D.F.* xii, no. 157; Hanotaux to Lebon, 21 Jan. 1897; Lebon to Hanotaux, 4 Feb. 1897, MFOM Afrique VI 142(a).
[4] Lebon to Hanotaux, 6 Oct. 1897, *ibid.*

fencing, their delegates offered to give up French claims east of the Niger and recognise the Anglo-German Agreement of November 1893 in return for access to the Lower Niger, a reasonable settlement in the Niger Bend, and recognition of their claims to the eastern shore of Lake Chad. By January, they had abandoned their claims to Bussa and agreed to consider British proposals for the creation of a free-trade area to include the Ivory Coast and Dahomey.[1]

Much of this new moderation was due to the psychological effect of Chamberlain's aggressive policies. By January 1898 Ambassador Courcel was in a panic over rumours that some British politicians were seeking to provoke a major conflict in West Africa, and he warned Hanotaux in March that Salisbury was no longer in control of the wilder elements in his Cabinet.[2] Hanotaux too was convinced that the British were deliberately trying to provoke a rupture in Anglo-French relations, and he was not prepared to risk the consequences. Accordingly, when Salisbury protested against the activities of Cazemajou and threatened to eject the offending explorer from the British sphere by force, Hanotaux gave him the most abject assurances that France fully recognised British influence over Sokoto.[3] Lebon tried to put a somewhat braver face on the situation, but he too appreciated the danger of war and quickly sent more cautious orders to his West African commanders.[4]

There was more to the French retreat, however, than a simple loss of nerve. By 1898 the weakness of their military position in West Africa could no longer be ignored. In Dahomey, where their total force (including auxiliaries) numbered 2,000, they could feel relatively confident; but in Mossi and Gurunsi their strength was hopelessly overstretched. In December 1897 the Lieutenant-Governor of the Sudan reported that the troops available for military operations in the Volta region were at an absolute minimum; by February 1898 the need to send a relief column to Kong and an expedition against Sikasso had reduced their numbers still further.[5] Meanwhile, the British were steadily

[1] The proceedings of the Commission are to be found in MFOM Afrique VI 142(b).

[2] Courcel to Hanotaux, 28 Jan. 1898; same to same, 12 Mar. 1898, *D.D.F.* xiv, nos. 32, 80.

[3] Hanotaux to Courcel, 1 Feb. 1898; same to same, 21 Feb. 1898, *ibid.* nos. 35, 59. See also: Monson to Hanotaux, 21 Feb. 1898 [Copy], MFOM Afrique IV 38(c); same to same, 25 Feb. 1898, *D.D.F.* xiv, no. 61.

[4] Lebon to Hanotaux, 9 Apr. 1898, MFOM Afrique VI 149(c); Lebon to Chaudié, 26 Jan. 1898, MFOM Télégrammes Bureau d'Afrique, 1898, Départ no. 9.

[5] Lieutenant-Governor, Sudan, to Lebon, 3 Dec. 1897, MFOM Soudan I 9(c); Chaudié to Lebon, 16 Nov. 1897, MFOM Télégrammes Afrique, Sénégal, 1897, Arrivée no. 173; same to same, 24 Feb. 1898 on the occupation of Kong, MFOM Côte d'Ivoire IV 7(a). See below: pp. 252–3.

reinforcing their positions, and by November 1897 they were supposed to have a thousand men in the vicinity of Buna. In March 1898 the French military attaché in London informed Paris that 7,000 uniforms had been shipped to Lagos and that 2,000 Zulus would be brought up from Natal if necessary. The fact that the notorious Colonel Lugard had been appointed to command the West African Frontier Force did not reassure him. 'It seems more than likely', he warned, 'that the British are preparing to take vigorous action [in West Africa].'[1] It would have been unthinkable for the French to risk a military confrontation in these circumstances. As their *chargé* in London pointed out, 'no matter how fantastic some of the reports from West Africa might be, it is certain that British forces there...overwhelmingly outnumber ours.'[2]

The signature of the Anglo-French Agreement on 14 June 1898 settled the Niger disputes to the general satisfaction of both sides. British influence in 'Nigeria' was confirmed by the recognition of the Say–Barruwa line's bilateral character. The new Lagos–Dahomey frontier laid the bogey of a French political presence on the Lower Niger. With the creation of a free-trade area from the Ivory Coast to the Cameroons frontier, Britain secured what Salisbury had once described as the principal objective of his West African policy.[3] The French fared only marginally worse. They lost Ilo and Bussa and with them any hope of an independent outlet to the Lower Niger, but they were granted the lease to land for two trading posts on the river and one in the Delta. They lost Bornu; but adjustments to the Say–Burrawa line facilitated their access to Chad from the west, and recognition of their influence over the eastern shore of the lake confirmed the union between the Congo and the rest of their African empire. In the Niger Bend they lost parts of Borgu and Gurunsi but kept Nikki and Mossi. They too gained satisfaction on their most important objective: free passage between the Sudan, the Ivory Coast and Dahomey. Wa, for which the local commanders had once been ready to fight, was given to the British without any visible qualms; Buna was kept as a consolation prize.[4] Once Chamberlain had taken charge of British policy in West Africa, the French could not have secured a more favourable settle-

---

[1] Same to same, 16 Nov. 1897, MFOM Télégrammes Afrique, Sénégal, 1897, Arrivée no. 173; Dupontavice to Minister of War, 10 Mar. 1898 [Copy], MFOM Afrique VI 149(c).
[2] Geoffray to Hanotaux, 30 Apr. 1898, encl. in Hanotaux to Lebon, 6 May 1898, *ibid.*
[3] Hanotaux to Lebon [*sic*: Courcel], 8 Feb. 1898, enclosing telegram from Salisbury, 28 Jan. 1898, *D.D.F.* xiv, no. 45.
[4] The text of the Agreement is printed in Hertslet, *op. cit.* ii, 785–92.

ment without the risk of war, and nobody, not even the zealots of the Pavillon de Flore, considered an African empire worth such a price. In their determination to save face at all costs, the Military had for a moment brought France perilously close to the brink; but once the politicians realised the limitations on their African policy, the crisis quickly passed. The Agreement of 1898 effectively completed the diplomatic partition of West Africa. With it, the Military's last excursion into the uncongenial realm of international affairs also came to an end.

COMMERCE AND CONQUEST IN THE SUDAN

While the Military were satisfying their appetite for action beyond the Niger, the Sudan itself was moving slowly along the road to commercial development. In deciding to federate the West African colonies, Chautemps had hoped to establish a more rational basis for their economic exploitation. His instructions to Governor-General Chaudié emphasised the overriding importance of creating the most favourable conditions for the growth of trade. Success, Chaudié was warned, would henceforth be measured by 'the prosperity of the territories united under your authority'. The colonies had to be made to pay for themselves; all other considerations, humanitarian or otherwise, were secondary. The Governor-General was ordered to handle the question of slavery with extreme caution, especially in the Sudan where domestic slavery formed an integral part of the economic structure. He was to be equally circumspect in dealing with the slave trade; for the *dyulas* were the Sudan's only important com᠁ ᠁rcial middlemen, and the prosperity of the colony would continue to depend on their co-operation until a more efficient transportation network had been created. Traditional policies towards Islam were also reversed, and Chaudié was instructed to gain the friendship of the Muslims, who were undoubtedly the most enlightened, the most energetic and the economically most advanced element in the population.[1]

To the Government's immense satisfaction, its efforts finally began to bear fruit. Chaudié agreed wholeheartedly with the spirit of his instructions and made sure that his local authorities in the Sudan knew exactly what was expected of them.[2] More important, Trentinian proved to be the Ministry's most loyal and competent military collabo-

[1] Chautemps to Chaudié, Instructions, 11 Oct. 1895, MFOM A.O.F. I 1.
[2] Chaudié to Trentinian, Instructions, 16 Nov. 1895, MFOM Soudan I 9(b).

rator since Gallieni. Although the Lieutenant-Governor's record on the slave trade was not spotless, he accepted the Government's new Muslim policy and applied it energetically.[1] Under his administration peace was maintained, and the commercial position rapidly improved. The value of Sudanese exports, a mere 300,000 fr. in 1895, increased tenfold over the next three years. Local revenue, 1,300,000 fr. in 1893, totalled more than 3,000,000 fr. by 1898.[2] Revenue from railway charges showed a similarly encouraging rise, and by 1896 the Ministry felt confident enough to ask Parliament for permission to extend the line beyond Bafoulabé. Work proceeded well, and in 1897 plans were drafted for completing the line to the Niger by 1904 or 1906. To meet the increased cost, Parliament authorised a loan of 1,000,000 fr. a year from the *Caisse de la Dette* and raised it to 3,200,000 fr. in 1899.[3] Since 1895 work had also been in progress on a road from Konakry to the Upper Niger which was to facilitate commercial movement between the Sudan and Guinea.[4] By the turn of the century the Sudan was beginning to acquire the efficient communications system so essential for its economic development.

Much more significantly, the new administration managed to control the costs of Sudanese occupation. Although the 1895 Estimates, 9,000,000 fr., were again exceeded by 1,000,000 fr., the final expenditure was still some 2,000,000 fr. lower than the previous year's.[5] Encouraged by these figures, the Ministry cut its Estimates for 1896 by 100,000 fr. and accepted a further reduction of 450,000 fr. imposed by the Budget Commission.[6] Incredibly enough, the new credit proved more than sufficient. Profiting from the relatively calm state of his colony, Trentinian was able to realise substantial savings on the cost of trans-

---

[1] Trentinian to Commandant, Northern Region, 19 Dec. 1898; Trentinian to Commandant, Niger–Volta Region, 24 Dec. 1898, *ibid.*

[2] *B.C.A.F.*, April 1897, p. 126; Note, n.d., MFOM Soudan XIII 3; Annexe aux procès-verbaux de la Commission [on the reorganisation of the Sudan], séance du 12 septembre 1899, MFOM A.O.F. VII.

[3] Procès-Verbaux de la Commission du Budget, séances du 24 juillet 1896, 10 octobre 1896, AN C5553, pp. 689, 736; Siegfried, Rapport, 11 July 1896 [*sic*], *J.O. Doc. Parl. Chambre*, no. 2055, pp. 1235–6; Riotteau, Rapport, 20 July 1897 [*sic*], *ibid.* no. 2695/6, p. 1813; Le Hérissé, Rapport, 16 Jan. 1899, *ibid.* no. 619, p. 391. See also: Rougier, Rapport, 28 Jan. 1899, MFOM Soudan XII 8 (b).

[4] The construction was begun at the colony's expense, but after 1896 it was granted an annual subvention of 100,000 fr. This subsidy was withdrawn in 1899.

[5] Projet de Loi, 16 Jan. 1897, *J.O. Doc. Parl. Chambre*, no. 2195, p. 21.

[6] Procès-Verbaux de la Commission du Budget, séance du 8 octobre 1895, AN C5548, p. 331. Several members of the Commission were in favour of reducing the Estimates by 900,000 fr.

portation and supply and to produce a budgetary surplus for the first time in the Sudan's history.[1]

But the growth of international tension in the Niger Bend and the failure to break completely with the traditional patterns of military expansion soon nullified the effects of Trentinian's economies. Despite its emphasis on commercial development, the Government could not afford to neglect the serious problems of security created by the disastrous expedition to Kong. After Monteil's retreat, Samori's forces had occupied Bonduku and had threatened both Bobo-Diulasso and Sikasso. Archinard, now in charge of the Ministry's defence policies, prescribed the standard military remedies. Although he did not favour an immediate offensive, he rejected any thought of negotiation and called for a decisive campaign if ever the *imam* tried to return to the Sudan or to advance deeper into the Ivory Coast. Chautemps approved his Director's hard line and ordered Chaudié to keep two companies of *tirailleurs* ready for action should the need arise.[2]

For a time, it seemed that a conflict might be averted. Samori's attempts to carve out a new kingdom for himself in the hinterland of the Ivory Coast had provoked strong local resistance and made it essential for him to avoid additional difficulties with the Europeans. After his defeat of Monteil, therefore, he tried to establish friendly relations with the Gold Coast. When his overtures were rebuffed, he turned to the French, offering to lay down his arms and accept any territory which they were prepared to give him.[3] Both Chaudié and the new Minister of Colonies, Guieysse, were willing to respond, and in March 1896 a mission under Captain Braulot was sent with an offer to recognise Samori's authority over the provinces of Djimini and Diamanko in return for the payment of an indemnity and the acceptance of a French Resident with escort. Unwilling to allow a European military presence in his territories, Samori rejected the offer and refused to meet the treaty-makers; but he continued to assure the French of his peaceful

[1] Chaudié to M.C., 13 Apr. 1897, MFOM Télégrammes Afrique, Sénégal, 1897, Arrivée no. 56; Projet de Loi, 18 May 1897, *J.O. Doc. Parl. Chambre*, no. 2429, p. 1235. The surplus amounted to 730,000 fr.

[2] Archinard, Ligne de conduite à suivre à l'égard de Samory, 29 Aug. 1895, MFOM Côte d'Ivoire IV 4; Chautemps to Chaudié, Instructions, 11 Oct. 1895, MFOM A.O.F. I 1. For Samori's activities after the failure of the Kong expedition, see: Kouroubari, 'Histoire de l'imam Samori', *loc. cit.* pp. 564–5; H. Labouret, 'Les bandes des Samory', *Afrique Française, Renseignements Coloniaux* (1925), pp. 341–55.

[3] Howard [British *chargé* in Paris] to Hanotaux, 26 Sept. 1895, *D.D.F.* XII, no. 156; Chaudié to M.C., 7 Jan. 1896; same to same, 9 Mar. 1896, MFOM Télégrammes Afrique, Sénégal, 1896, Arrivée nos. 4, 27.

intentions.[1] Paris also remained anxious to avoid war. The Sudanese authorities were forbidden to garrison Bobo-Diulasso or Kong; bnt when the *imam* renewed his overtures, Braulot was sent out to occupy Buna.[2] When he reached the town, however, Braulot found it already occupied by one of Samori's lieutenants who refused him entry. He then retired towards Lokosso and met the *imam*'s son, Sarantyeni-mori, who offered to accompany him back and clear up the misunder-standing. On the way, the *sofas* suddenly turned on the party and massacred it.[3] A showdown was now inevitable. Although Lebon was still reluctant to force the issue, he recognised the need to avenge Braulot's murder and sent troop reinforcements to the South-East Region. At the end of October 1897 Commandant Caudrelier occupied Bobo-Diulasso, and in January 1898, at the height to the crisis over Buna and Wa, his troops engaged the *sofas* at Kong.[4]

In the midst of their conflict with Samori, the French had to send an expedition against Sikasso as well. Relations with the town had not been cordial ever since Tiéba's successor, Ba Bemba, had refused to accept a French garrison in 1894. The need to maintain a common front against Samori had prevented an open breach, and as late as June 1897 the Sudanese administration was still confident that Ba Bemba would provide reinforcements for a campaign against the *imam*.[5] But in February 1898 a French mission under Captain Morisson was igno-miniously run out of town. Chaudié immediately warned the Ministry that the maintenance of French prestige along the whole south-eastern front made it essential to avenge the insult, and Lebon reluctantly authorised a punitive campaign. In April Trentinian's temporary replacement, Lieutenant-Colonel Audéoud, set out with a strong column, and he took Sikasso by storm on 1 May. Both sides suffered

---

[1] Same to same, 11 Mar. 1896, MFOM Côte d'Ivoire IV 5(d); M.C. to Chaudié, 18 Mar. 1896, *ibid.*; same to same, 24 Apr. 1896, MFOM Côte d'Ivoire IV 4; Chaudié to M.C., 10 July 1896, MFOM Télégrammes Afrique, Sénégal, 1896, Arrivée no. 71; same to same, 25 Nov. 1896, MFOM A.O.F. I 1.

[2] Chaudié to M.C., 7 May 1897, MFOM Télégrammes Afrique, Sénégal, 1897, Arrivée no. 69; same to same, 14 May 1897, MFOM A.O.F. I 1; M.C. to Chaudié, 13 May 1897; same to same, 2 July 1897, MFOM Télégrammes Afrique, Sénégal, 1897, Départ nos. 54, 90. In sending Braulot to Buna, Lebon hoped to profit from Samori's recent defeat of a British column.

[3] Chaudié to M.C., 18 Aug. 1897; same to same, 19 Sept. 1897, *ibid.* Arrivée nos. 112, 122.

[4] M.C. to Chaudié, 20 Sept. 1897; same to same, 24 Sept. 1897, *ibid.* Départ nos. 104, 106; Chaudié to M.C., 26 Oct. 1897, *ibid.* Arrivée no. 157; same to same, 24 Feb. 1898, MFOM Côte d'Ivoire IV 7(a); same to same, 31 Mar. 1898, MFOM Soudan I 9(d).

[5] Trentinian, Rapport, 14 May 1897, MFOM Soudan I 9(c); Lamary to Chaudié, 28 June 1897, encl. in Chaudié to M.C., 1 July 1897, MFOM A.O.F. I 1.

heavy casualties; Ba Bemba committed suicide, and his capital was put to the sack.[1]

The capture of Sikasso and the signature of the Anglo-French Agreement left the French free to settle their accounts with Samori. The *imam*'s position was by now desperate. European pressure and local opposition had prevented him from consolidating his hold over his new empire; constant fighting had reduced his once powerful armies to small bands living precariously off the countryside. French successes at Kong and Sikasso persuaded him that further resistance was useless, and in August 1898 he made a final attempt to negotiate, offering to disband his followers and retire back to the Upper Niger. After some hesitation, however, the Ministry decided to hold out for his total submission. A few days later, a French column surprised him in his camp and took him prisoner, thus bringing the Military's longest and most difficult campaign to a successful conclusion.[2]

But the Military's victory was expensive. The resumption of large-scale operations after 1896 threw Sudanese finances into disarray once more. Encouraged by the results of Trentinian's prudent administration, the Ministry had made substantial reductions in its Estimates for 1897 and 1898;[3] but the consequences of continued expansion and Anglo-French tension soon made themselves felt. In March 1898 the Ministry had to ask for a supplementary credit of 485,000 fr. to pay for the reinforcement of the columns in the Niger Bend. In December it was forced to admit that the Anglo-French crisis, the capture of Sikasso and the final campaign against Samori had thrown out its calculations by more than 2,000,000 fr.[4] In 1899 the Estimates were exceeded by 4,380,000 fr., the worst figures since Timbuktu. Although the need to mobilise reserves during the Fashoda crisis accounted for a large part of the increase, the cost of occupying the territories captured during 1898 still made up almost half the total.[5] By October 1899 the

[1] Chaudié to M.C., 13 Feb. 1898; M.C. to Chaudié, 15 Feb. 1898, MFOM Soudan IV 6; same to same, 11 Mar. 1898, MFOM Télégrammes Bureau d'Afrique, 1898, Départ no. 30; Chaudié to M.C., 18 May 1898, MFOM A.O.F. I 2.

[2] Ballay to M.C., 31 Aug. 1893, MFOM Télégrammes Bureau d'Afrique, 1898, Arrivée no. 110; M.C. to Gov. Gen., 2 Sept. 1898; same to same, 26 Sept. 1898, *ibid.* Départ nos. 129, 142.

[3] The Estimates were cut to 6,212,000 fr. (excluding 768,000 fr. earmarked for railway-construction) for 1897, and 6,180,000 fr. for 1898.

[4] Projet de Loi, 21 Mar. 1898, *J.O. Doc. Parl. Chambre*, no. 3123, pp. 852–3; Projet de Loi, 20 Dec. 1898, *ibid.* no. 553, p. 556.

[5] The Estimates for 1899, after reductions imposed by the Budget Commission, totalled 6,165,000 fr. but expenditure rose to 10,545,000 fr. Of the increase, some 2,457,000 fr. was the result of troop mobilisations. See: Boudenoot, Rapport, 14 Feb. 1900, *J.O. Doc. Parl. Chambre*, no. 1422, pp. 526 ff.

Sudan's financial position was again causing the Ministry 'the most serious embarrassment'.[1]

The traditional problem of civilian–military relations also remained unsolved. Although the reorganisation of 1895 had greatly improved the Military's position in the Sudan, their subordination to a civilian Governor-General did little to ease the frictions which had so plagued the colony during Grodet's administration. Chaudié and Trentinian worked together remarkably well; but not even the enlightened Lieutenant-Governor could free himself completely from his professional background. On more than one occasion he had to be reminded of the Government's determination not to permit any unnecessary campaigning.[2] After Trentinian's resignation in April 1897, relations between the Military and the Governor-General rapidly deteriorated. Anxious to see the restoration of civilian rule in the Sudan, Chaudié opposed the appointment of Colonel Lamary as Trentinian's replacement and accepted him only when Trentinian himself agreed to resume his command after a period of convalescence in France.[3] The Governor-General's apprehensions proved well founded; Lamary waited less than three weeks before requesting permission to occupy Kong and Bobo-Diulasso. Chaudié vetoed the proposal, and Lamary reluctantly accepted the decision. But three months later he took the Ministry's demand for an investigation into the circumstances of the Braulot massacre as a personal insult and immediately resigned.[4]

Chaudié's dealings with Lamary's successor, Lieutenant-Colonel Audéoud, were even less friendly. The new Lieutenant-Governor had no intention of co-operating with his civilian superior and addressed his demands for troop reinforcements directly to the Ministry of Colonies. Chaudié's reprimand, delivered with the Minister's full approval, soured Audéoud's disposition still further, and when Paris rejected his observations on the excessive sick leave granted to civilian personnel, he too resigned. Only a reaffirmation of official confidence and his inscription on the *tableau d'avancement* persuaded him to change

[1] M.C. to Gov. Sen., 7 Oct. 1899, MFOM Télégrammes Afrique, Sénégal, 1899, Départ no. 206.

[2] M.C. to Chaudié, 30 Mar. 1896, MFOM Soudan I 9(b); Chaudié to M.C., 2 May 1896, MFOM A.O.F. I 1; M.C. to Chaudié, 3 May 1897, MFOM Télégrammes Afrique, Sénégal, 1897, Départ no. 50.

[3] Chaudié to M.C., 21 Apr. 1897, MFOM Soudan I 9(e); same to same, 18 May 1897, MFOM A.O.F. I 1.

[4] Lamary to Chaudié, 28 June 1897; Chaudié to Lamary, 30 June 1897; same to same, 1 July 1897, cited in Chaudié to M.C., 1 July 1897, MFOM A.O.F. I 1; same to same, 3 Oct. 1897, MFOM Télégrammes Afrique, Sénégal, 1897, Arrivée no. 131.

his mind.[1] The Lieutenant-Governor soon carried his insubordination to absurd lengths. He flatly refused to comply with an order to stop levying customs dues on goods entering the Sudan from the neighbouring colony of Guinea and wrote directly to Paris for a confirmation of its instructions. In October 1898 he again threatened to resign, this time over the appointment of a civilian to supervise the colony's finances. When the Ministry confirmed its orders about customs duties, Audéoud immediately left the Sudan, disregarding the Minister's threat to punish him if he abandoned his post.[2] Acting Governor-General Ballay, however, was glad to see the last of him. Audéoud, he complained, had systematically neglected to inform him of every major political and military development in his colony.[3]

THE END OF MILITARY RULE

By 1898 all hopes for an improvement in the Sudan's prospects had vanished as costly military campaigns and bitter administrative squabbles again became the dominant characteristics of the colony's affairs. It was now obvious that the federative system had failed to cope with the Sudan's chronic problems any more effectively than the earlier experiment with civilian rule. If the cost spiral were to be controlled and economic progress resumed, a new form of organisation would have to be adopted. Once more, the rôle of the Military was called into question, and this time the issue was not to be decided in their favour.

The Military's declining fortunes in the Sudan were accompanied by the gradual eclipse of their influence in Paris. Despite Archinard's appointment as Director of Defence, the military party was never able to regain all its former control over Sudanese policy. Its victory in 1895 had brought it no respite from the denunciations of its enemies, and the publication of a brochure by Lieutenant-Colonel Humbert accusing Desbordes and Archinard of cowardice, disloyalty and indiscipline soon brought a new intensity to the anti-militarist attack. In 1892,

[1] Audéoud to M.C., 3 Dec. 1897, MFOM Soudan I 9(c); Chaudié to M.C., 16 Dec. 1897, MFOM A.O.F. I 1; M.C. to Chaudié, 14 Jan. 1898, MFOM A.O.F. I 2; same to same, 28 Mar. 1898; Audéoud to Chaudié, 22 May 1898; M.C. to Ballay, 6 Aug. 1898, MFOM Dossier Administratif, Audéoud.
[2] Ballay to M.C., 7 Oct. 1898; same to same, 15 Oct. 1898; same to same, 21 Oct. 1898, MFOM Télégrammes Afrique, Sénégal, 1898, Arrivée nos. 137, 141, 145; M.C. to Ballay, 21 Oct. 1898; same to same, 26 Oct. 1898, *ibid*. Départ nos. 155, 160; Audéoud to Ballay, 26 Oct. 1898, encl. in Ballay to M.C., 31 Oct. 1898, MFOM A.O.F. I 2.
[3] Same to same, 31 Oct. 1898, *ibid*.

Humbert claimed, Desbordes had deliberately held back his promotion because he had obeyed the orders of the Under-Secretary, not those of his military superiors. At the same time Archinard, the man responsible for all the Sudan's troubles, had been promoted by virtue of *faits de guerre* no more brilliant than his own. And, when he had complained of this injustice to the Minister of Marine, Desbordes had him placed in sixty days' detention.[1] The habitual extravagance of Humbert's language made it easy for Desbordes to dismiss his charges as fantastic,[2] but the aggrieved Colonel refused to be put off. Throughout the following year, he levelled a constant stream of invective against his alleged persecutors. To help the campaign along, *La Politique Coloniale* regularly opened its columns to him, and the recently founded *Dépêche Coloniale* also lent its support.[3] In reply, Archinard made only one hesitant and ineffectual attempt at a rebuttal; thereafter he prudently kept silent.[4]

Surprisingly enough, Humbert's bizarre tactics succeeded. By 1897 Archinard's position at the Ministry of Colonies was becoming extremely precarious. In July, reports reached Paris of a serious military reverse at Rhergo, north of Timbuktu, where a troop of *spahis* had been massacred by Tuareg raiders from Hoggar. Humbert blamed Archinard for the disaster and called for the punishment of those responsible for the policy of military conquest; *La Politique Coloniale* supported the accusation, and Lebon himself was sufficiently alarmed to order a full investigation of the affair.[5] Two months later, news of the Braulot massacre added more fuel to the anti-militarist fire, and the Minister felt obliged to order another investigation.[6] The public controversy aroused by Humbert's campaign, the Rhergo massacre and the death of Braulot soon turned Archinard into a distinct political liability, and in October 1897 the Director of Defence was posted to Indochina as

---

[1] G. Humbert, *Le général Borgnis-Desbordes et le colonel Humbert de l'artillerie de marine* (Paris, 1896). See also: *La Politique Coloniale*, 16 May 1896, 23 June 1896, 17 Nov. 1896, for attacks on the *officiers soudanais*.

[2] Desbordes, interview with *Le Gaulois*, 17 Nov. 1896.

[3] *Le Soir*, 28 July, 30 July, 1 Aug., 16 Aug., 8 Sept., 3 Oct. 1897 [articles by Humbert]; *La Politique Coloniale*, 17 Nov., 21 Nov. 1896; 30 Aug., 3 Sept., 23 Sept., 29 Oct., 4 Nov., 18 Nov. 1897 [articles by Humbert]; *La Dépêche Coloniale*, 31 July, 7 Oct., 8 Oct. 1897.

[4] *Le Soir*, 29 July 1897 [article by Archinard].

[5] Chaudié to Lebon, 14 July 1897, MFOM Télégrammes Afrique, Sénégal, 1897, Arrivée no. 95; Lebon to Chaudié, 21 July 1897, *ibid*. Départ no. 75.

[6] Same to same, 24 Sept. 1897, *ibid*. Départ no. 106. Three days before, the anti-colonialist Deputy Paul Vigné had warned the Minister of his intention to interpellate the Government about recent disasters in the Sudan. Vigné to Lebon, 21 Sept. 1897, MFOM Soudan I 9(c).

Commander of the *Brigade de Cochinchine*. His departure exposed Desbordes to the full force of the anti-militarist offensive. In August 1898 Humbert published a second pamphlet repeating his charges and demanding the immediate convention of a formal court of honour to try the Inspector-General. Humbert's language was by now demented, but *La Politique Coloniale* took him seriously and predicted that his appeals for justice would not go unanswered.[1] It was not entirely mistaken. Less than a month later, Desbordes too was posted to Indochina as *Commandant-Supérieur des Troupes*.

The eclipse of the *clique Desbordes* drove another nail into the coffin of military rule. By 1898 the *officiers soudanais* were coming to the end of their usefulness. After the conclusion of the Anglo-French Agreement, the destruction of Sikasso and the capture of Samori, there could no longer be any excuse for maintaining 4,000 troops in the Sudan. Both Parliament and the Ministry could read the writing on the wall. In December the Minister of Colonies again assured the Chamber that 'the era of conquest is definitely closed', and to hold him to his promise the Budget Commission cut the 1899 Estimates by 40,000 fr. Now that Samori was no longer a danger, it claimed, troops could slowly be withdrawn from the Sudan and expenditure correspondingly reduced.[2] When Trentinian was sent back to repair the damage done during his absence, he was left in no doubt about the nature of his duties. The new Minister of Colonies, Guillain, warned him that the period of conquest and military expansion was over; in future, economic development was to be the rule. Because of the Fashoda crisis and the threat of war with England, the Sudan would for the moment remain in military hands; 'but this military occupation', Guillain added, 'cannot be prolonged indefinitely and must prepare the way for the eventual establishment of a really effective civilian administration'.[3]

Shortly thereafter, the political repercussions of the Voulet–Chanoine expedition dealt the Sudanese military empire its *coup de grâce*. Despite the strength of British reactions to the Cazemajou mission, the Ministry of Colonies had refused to abandon its attempt to extend French

---

[1] G. Humbert, *Plainte officielle contre le général Desbordes: Pour La Justice* (Paris, 1898); *La Politique Coloniale*, 1 Sept., 17 Sept. 1898.

[2] Projet de Loi, 20 Dec. 1898 [supplementary credits], *J.O. Doc. Parl. Chambre*, no. 553, p. 556; Procès-Verbaux de la Commission du Budget, séance du 1er décembre 1898 [1899 Budget], AN C5642, p. 147; Doumergue, Rapport, 16 Jan. 1899, *J.O. Doc. Parl. Chambre*, no. 609, p. 263.

[3] Guillain to Gov. Gen., Instructions pour Trentinian, 10 Nov. 1898, MFOM Soudan I 9(d).

influence along the Say–Barruwa line. By the summer of 1898 plans had been drafted for a new series of expeditions to Lake Chad. Gentil was again to move north from the Congo; Captain Lamy was to advance south-east across the Sahara from Algeria; Voulet and Chanoine, the conquerors of Mossi and Gurunsi, were to join them from the Sudan. The signature of the Anglo-French Agreement did not affect the plan, and in July 1898 Voulet was ordered to survey the new boundary, skirt the north-east shore of Chad, link up with the Algerian and Congolese columns, and help them to establish control over Kanem and Baghirmi.[1] The Government's West African experts were unanimously opposed to the expedition. Trentinian, then in Paris, objected to its size; a column of three hundred armed men, he complained, could hardly be described as a diplomatic mission. Ballay warned that the resources of the Sudan had been completely exhausted by the recent campaigns and that porters would be extremely difficult to find. Even the more adventurous Audéoud predicted rebellion and certain disaster if the expedition travelled overland.[2] But their warnings were disregarded.[3] The consequences were even more terrible than Audéoud had foreseen. By February 1899 French Residents in the eastern sectors of the Niger Bend were reporting that the expedition, in its desperate attempts to find porters, had adopted a policy of deliberate terrorism and had left a trail of carnage in its wake. Although these reports were not transmitted to Paris, the Ministry soon learned the news through unofficial channels.[4]

Guillain's first reaction was to throw a shroud of absolute secrecy

[1] M.C. to Voulet, Draft Instructions, 11 July 1898; M.A.E. to M.C., 13 July 1898; same to same, 25 July 1898; M.C. to Voulet, Instructions, 27 July 1898, MFOM Afrique III 37(b). The Ministry of Colonies had at first intended to send Voulet further east into Wadai, Darfur and ultimately to Fashoda; but this plan was cancelled at the insistence of the Quai d'Orsay.

[2] Trentinian, Note pour le 1er bureau, 17 Feb. 1898, MFOM Missions 49, Voulet–Chanoine; Ballay to M.C., 12 July 1898, MFOM Missions 11, Voulet–Chanoine; Audéoud to Ballay, n.d., encl. in Ballay to M.C., 13 July 1898, *ibid.*

[3] The expedition had an impressive collection of supporters. Both the Pavillon de Flore and the Quai d'Orsay were firmly committed to the realisation of the Chad Plan. The *Comité de l'Afrique française* promised its financial support, and even President Faure was said to have exerted his influence on Voulet's behalf. D'Arenberg to Gov. Gen., 23 June 1898, MFOM Missions 110, Voulet–Chanoine; *La Dépêche Coloniale*, 6 Sept., 5 Oct. 1899; *L'Estafette*, 7 Oct., 11 Oct. 1899.

[4] Crave, Rapport, 2 Feb. 1899; Grandeyre, Rapport, 15 Feb. 1899; *idem*, Rapport, 1 Mar. 1899; *idem*, Rapport, 1 Apr. 1899, MFOM Missions 110, Voulet–Chanoine; Note confidentielle, 30 June 1899, MFOM Afrique III 38 (a). News reached Paris through Lieutenant Peteau, a junior member of the expedition who had quarrelled with his superiors and had been sent back to Kayes. Peteau then sent his Deputy in France a full account of the atrocities, and the latter transmitted his report to the Ministry.

over the whole affair. When an investigation confirmed the extent of the atrocities, he sent Lieutenant-Colonel Klobb to relieve Voulet but ordered him to complete the mission; if necessary Klobb was to take the incriminated officers with him.[1] At the same time, Trentinian was privately warned to prevent the publication of any information whatsoever about the incidents.[2] But a scandal of such proportions could not be hidden indefinitely, and when Voulet murdered Klobb as the latter tried to relieve him of his command, further suppression of the news became impossible. By September, most of the relevant details had been made known.[3]

Predictably, *La Politique Coloniale* made good use of the scandal in its campaign against the *officiers soudanais*;[4] but the dimensions of the affair soon outgrew the simple issue of Sudanese military indiscipline. By an unfortunate coincidence, Voulet's accomplice was the son of General Chanoine, the Minister of War whose sudden and treacherous resignation in October 1898 had brought down the Brisson Ministry. In this indirect fashion, the question of the Military's future in the Sudan became enmeshed in the most violent phase of the Dreyfus affair. Not surprisingly, nationalists and militarists denounced the Voulet scandal as a *dreyfusard* invention, a nefarious plot to injure the former Minister of War by blackening the reputation of his son. The right-wing Press denied all the charges, tied itself in knots trying to prove that Voulet could not possibly have murdered Klobb, and accused 'a coterie of Anglophiles' of deliberately sabotaging the mission in order to discredit the Army.[5] Even the unfortunate Klobb was dragged into the controversy. François Coppée and Jules Lemaître, the intellectual lights of the *Ligue de la Patrie Française*, offered to pay for his memorial service, and his widow gladly accepted. Every effort was made to turn the occasion into a public demonstration of nationalist grief. The church was packed by

---

[1] Dubreuil, Rapport, 22 Apr. 1899; Salaman, Rapport, 8 May 1899, MFOM Missions 110, Voulet–Chanoine; M.C. to Gov. Gen., 16 May 1899, MFOM Télégrammes Afrique, Sénégal, 1899, Départ no. 107. Guillain later admitted that he had issued these instructions in the hope that the guilty parties might atone for their crimes by meeting a glorious death on some battlefield. *J.O. Déb. Parl. Chambre*, séance du 23 novembre 1900, p. 2272.

[2] Guillain to Trentinian, n.d., referred to in Trentinian to Vimard, 23 May 1899, cited in Vimard to Gov. Gen., 7 Oct. 1899, MFOM Afrique III 38(a); Undated Note, MFOM Missions 49, Voulet–Chanoine. Vimard was at the time acting Lieutenant-Governor while Trentinian was again away on sick leave.

[3] Articles about the murder of Klobb began to appear in the middle of August. Grandeyre's report on the assassination was published in *Le Figaro*, 2 Oct. 1899.

[4] *La Politique Coloniale*, 29 Aug., 5 Sept., 14 Sept., 16 Sept., 21 Sept. 1899.

[5] *La Patrie*, 26 Aug. 1899; *L'Estafette*, 24 Aug., 12 Sept., 17 Sept., 20 Sept., 23 Sept., 30 Sept., 3 Oct., 4 Oct., 11 Oct. 1899.

anti-dreyfusards; Monteil, the recent 'nationalist and anti-cosmopolitan' candidate for the Presidency, acted as master of ceremonies; the most prominent wreath on display bore only one name: Déroulède.[1]

The Military's involvement in this domestic crisis was to have fatal consequences. 1899 was a turbulent year in French politics. The emotions released by the Dreyfus affair and the confrontation at Fashoda were running high; the Republic itself seemed in danger of falling to a military *coup-d'état*. On 16 February President Faure had died in less than dignified circumstances, and at his funeral Déroulède had made another ludicrous attempt to march on the Elysée. To meet the threat from the Right, the Republicans closed ranks; and after the assault on President Loubet at Auteil, Dupuy stepped down for the last time in favour of Waldeck-Rousseau and his *gouvernment de la défense républicaine*. The Sudan was one of the first casualties of its counterattack. On 6 September the new Minister of Colonies, Albert Decrais, set up a Commission to study the administrative reorganisation of French West Africa. The Sudan's continued financial difficulties and the unfavourable publicity aroused by the Voulet scandal, he told the Commissioners, made it more essential than ever to bring 'the era of conquests and expeditions' to an end. The Commission was therefore to advise him on the policies most suited to the colony's 'pacification and economic development'.[2]

Of its members, only Trentinian retained his faith in the Sudan's economic viability and called for the maintenance of its autonomy. To save the colony, he drew up a scheme of preferential tariffs and troop reductions which he claimed would cut expenditure by 3,000,000 fr. a year without requiring any change in the administrative system. But even Trentinian accepted the need to reduce the Sudan's ridiculously overextended frontiers and agreed that certain regions could be placed under civilian control.[3] His colleagues were determined to go much further. Governor-General Chaudié would accept nothing less than complete reorganisation; both geographically and economically, he claimed, most of the Sudan formed part of the hinterland of the coastal

[1] *La Dépêche Coloniale*, 10 Oct., 19 Oct. 1899.
[2] Procès-Verbaux de la Commission..., séance du 8 septembre 1899, MFOM A.O.F. VII. The Commission was composed of Roume [*directeur des affaires d'Asie*], Binger [*directeur des affaires d'Afrique*], Guyho [*inspecteur des colonies*], Drouhez [*chef du bureau militaire du Ministre*], J. Decrais [*chef de cabinet du Ministre*], Chaudié, Ballay and Trentinian.
[3] Procès-Verbaux de la Commission, *ibid.* See also: Trentinian to M.C., 9 Jan. 1899, MFOM Soudan I 9(e).

colonies and should rationally be attached to them.[1] After consultation with Ballay and Binger (now head of the African Department), he presented an alternative proposal, based on a plan drafted by Commandant Destenave, for reducing the Sudan to two military districts and partitioning the remainder between the neighbouring colonies.[2] His views prevailed and were embodied in the Commission's final conclusions which he himself drafted.[3]

In his report, Chaudié paid the conventional tributes to the Military's achievements but stressed that their primary task of establishing unchallenged French supremacy had been successfully completed. To satisfy the need for economy, the interests of commercial development and the repeated demands of Parliament, the pacified territories now had to be brought under civilian control. Civilian Governors could deal far more effectively with economic problems than even the most conscientious military man. The dismantling of the Sudan's command structure and reductions in garrison strengths would realise a saving of more than 1,500,000 fr. without prejudice to Trentinian's proposed economies. Most important of all, the new organisation would confirm the authority of the Governor-General over the territories under his command, prevent further unauthorised military expeditions, and check the all too human desire of serving officers to distinguish themselves by 'ever glorious but sometimes useless feat[s] of arms'.[4]

On the whole, the Commission's recommendations were well received. The Military's opponents and the majority of the West African traders were of course delighted. Both *La Politique Coloniale* and *La Dépêche Coloniale* came out strongly in favour of the proposed changes; the Chambers of Commerce of Dakar, Saint-Louis and Rufisque all passed resolutions expressing their approval; and a host of commercial Houses, including the *Comptoir colonial français* and the influential *Compagnie française de l'Afrique occidentale*, assured the Minister of their full support.[5] Only the right-wing Press and those merchants who held the

---

[1] Such a scheme had long been favoured by the coastal trading interests. See: *La Politique Coloniale*, 10 May 1894; Le Cesne [Secretary, *Union coloniale*] to *La Politique Coloniale*, 26 Mar. 1895.

[2] Destenave, Projet d'organisation de la boucle du Niger, 15 Nov. 1898, MFOM A.O.F. VII; *idem*, Projet d'organisation politique, administrative et défensive de l'A.O.F., Arch. Guerre, E.M.A. 57.

[3] Procès-Verbaux de la Commission, séance du 12 septembre 1899; Chaudié, Rapport au Ministre des Colonies, 26 Sept. 1899, MFOM A.O.F. VII.

[4] *Ibid.*

[5] The relevant letters, resolutions and newspaper cuttings are to be found *ibid.*

contracts for supplying the Sudanese garrisons campaigned against any diminution of the Military's influence, and their views carried little weight at the Ministry.[1] The Commission's report was duly approved, and on 17 October 1899 the Decree reorganising French West Africa was signed. The Sudan was partitioned between Senegal, Guinea, the Ivory Coast and Dahomey, which was now included in the Federation. Two districts based on Timbuktu and Wagadugu remained in military hands, but these were placed under the political control of the Governor-General.[2] In future, military operations would be restricted to the remote regions of the far north-east; for all practical purposes the 'era of conquest' in the Western Sudan was over.

Officially, Decrais justified the reorganisation on strictly economic grounds, and his report to the President of the Republic contained all the stock phrases about the Military's brilliant accomplishments. But Binger gave a more accurate account of the factors behind the decision to dismember the Sudan. Its two main objectives, he claimed, were to strengthen the political powers of the Governor-General and to extend civilian control over territories previously under military rule. In practice, the Governor-General's authority over the Sudan had never been more than nominal; the colony's real master had been the Lieutenant-Governor. As the senior officer, he alone could command the obedience of the troops which were stationed there; but as a senior officer he could never free himself completely from certain military attitudes. This undesirable situation could not be corrected simply by appointing a civilian Governor; Grodet's administration had been proof enough of that. The only solution, Binger concluded, was 'to abolish the office of Lieutenant-Governor and with it the Sudan itself. There was no other way to suppress this West African State within the State.'[3]

---

[1] *La France Militaire*, 24 Aug., 14 Sept., 15 Sept. 1899; *La Patrie*, 11 Sept., 10 Oct., 13 Oct. 1899; *L'Eclair*, 14 Sept., 22 Sept., 12 Oct. 1899; *L'Echo de Paris*, 15 Sept. 1899; *Devès et Chaumet et al.* to M.C., 11 Sept. 1899, MFOM A.O.F. VII.

[2] Decree, 17 Oct. 1899, *ibid.*

[3] Decrais, Rapport au Président de la République, 17 Oct. 1899; Binger, Note pour le Ministre, n.d., *ibid.*

10

Conclusion: French African Policy and Military Imperialism

'We have behaved like madmen in Africa', lamented President Félix Faure after the humiliation of Fashoda, '[having been] led astray by irresponsible people called the colonialists.'[1] The judgement was harsh but not unfair. The African policies of the Third Republic were seldom the product of rational calculation; the attempt to force the British out of Egypt by raising the *tricolore* over an inaccessible sandbank on the Upper Nile was merely the most striking example of the illusory goals which her statesmen pursued.[2] Sudanese policy was based on equally unsound premises. For most of the nineteenth century, France mistakenly assumed that the legendary wealth of the West African interior would justify the extension of her influence and ultimately the establishment of her dominion over it. Dazzled by the vision of a Sudanese Eldorado, she set out to transform the interior into a magnificent new empire, and this remained her basic objective until she had extended her sway to Lake Chad. The Republic paid dearly for the luxury of her imperial ambitions in West Africa; in the two decades after 1879, Sudanese expansion cost her some 130,000,000 fr.[3] Yet she was never able to realise an adequate return on her investment. The very policies she adopted prevented her from securing the profits she so ardently desired. Military conquest did not lay the foundations for commercial development; indeed, by aggravating political instability and disrupting established patterns of trade, it positively hastened the Sudan's

[1] Félix Faure, Mémoires, November–December 1898, pp. 385–6, Faure Papers; also cited in [Félix Faure], 'Fachoda', *Revue d'histoire diplomatique*, LXIX (1955), 34.

[2] The folly of the Nile strategy had been recognised long before Marchand finally set out for Fashoda. E.g. Chautemps's statement to the Budget Commission, 18 June 1895, AN C5548: 'La prétention d'agir sur le Haut-Nil à l'aide des troupes est une idée folle, une chimère dangereuse pour le budget...Une action sérieuse sur le Haut-Nil est à écarter. Chaque tonne de marchandise coûte plusieurs milliers de francs pour arriver jusqu'au Nil. A quel chiffre limiter la dépense?'

[3] This estimate is based on the total credits voted specifically for the Sudan between 1879 and 1899.

economic decline after 1880.[1] Yet the Sudanese myth survived all the disappointments which the French suffered, and although their policies passed through many periods of hesitation and discouragement, the prospect of an African empire retained its grip upon their imagination. As late as 1904 Paul Leroy-Beaulieu was still describing the Chad Basin as 'one of the jewels of Africa'. . . a new Egypt, perhaps an even greater Egypt'.[2]

Colonialists must take much of the blame for creating the political climate in which the myths of Sudanese expansion could flourish. The visionaries of empire in the Geographical Societies, in the Press and in Parliament generated the enthusiasm which swept over the Trans-Sahara Railway project, and their agitation forced the Government to claim the Congo as another avenue into the interior. A decade later, their successors preached the same imperialist message through the *Comité de l'Afrique française*, formed specifically to work for 'the union around the shores of Lake Chad, of French possessions in the Sudan, in Algeria-Tunisia, and in the Congo'.[3] Throughout the period, the success of their propaganda revealed the extent of popular support for their objectives. Sudanese expansion did not arouse the same anti-colonialist passions as did the invasion of Tonkin or the occupation of Tunisia. Few doubted the potential importance of the Trans-Sahara Railway or criticised the decision to advance into the Western Sudan. Many later condemned the failures of railway-building and the scandalous administration of Sudanese finances, but virtually nobody questioned the Government's political objectives. Only in the 1890s did opposition to Sudanese policy reach significant proportions, and even then the most ferocious critics were often champions of a still more ambitious African empire. The conquest of the Western Sudan was not planned or carried out in an atmosphere of public indifference or hostility; French empire-building in West Africa, whatever its failings, was popular.[4]

But popularity was not its most significant characteristic. Public opinion did not make African policy, nor was imperialism the product of the popular imagination. The policy-makers were dreaming of an African empire long before the colonialists began their agitation. Their dreams shaped the course of Sudanese expansion for half a century

[1] See: Miège, *op. cit.* III, 375–459; C. W. Newbury, 'North African and Western Sudan Trade in the Nineteenth Century: A Re-evaluation', *Journal of African History*, VII (1966), 233–46.
[2] P. Leroy-Beaulieu, *Le Sahara, le Soudan, et les chemins de fer transsahariens* (Paris, 1904), p. 353.
[3] D'Arenberg, Circular Letter, 15 Jan. 1896, AN 81 AP 6 IV, Rambaud Papers.
[4] Cf. Hargreaves, *Prelude to the Partition*, pp. 198–200, 278–9.

before the 1860s. After 1879, through the efforts of Freycinet and Jauréguiberry, they did so again. Freycinet kept the vision alive during the difficult years of the mid-1880s. After 1887 Etienne gave it substance by transforming the vague schemes of his predecessors into a clear-cut policy. Delcassé and Lebon carried his Chad Plan through to its conclusion. The 'colonialists' who mattered in the political life of the Third Republic were the Ministers, the Under-Secretaries and their permanent officials. Together they comprised the 'official mind' of French imperialism. What their thinking on African questions reflected was the imperialism of the French official mind.

For the African policy of the Third Republic was nothing if not imperialist. It had its origins in the vague aspirations of an earlier age, but its essential features were peculiar to its own time. The policy-makers of the Restoration, the July Monarchy and the Second Empire were informal imperialists. They envisaged nothing more than a loose commercial empire in the Western Sudan. They hoped to bring the interior within the French orbit through the gradual and peaceful advance of trade, influence and civilisation. They wished to secure the benefits of its wealth without incurring the expense or the responsibility of its rule. They had no desire to adopt the costly methods of military conquest. The revolution in African policy after 1879 occurred with the change in official thinking on the crucial questions of cost and military effort. Freycinet and Jauréguiberry were the revolutionaries. Both men were firmly convinced of the intrinsic value of African territory and preoccupied with its future development. Both were obsessed with the dangers of European competition in a continent about to be partitioned and determined that France should seize her rightful share of the spoils. Both considered it the duty of the Government to stake the political claims which traders and investors could later exploit. Freycinet, the railway-builder, recognised the importance of bringing Europe's technological expertise to bear upon the development of Africa. Jauréguiberry, the military man, saw the imposition of political hegemony and military security as the necessary preconditions for economic development. Freycinet pledged the technical and financial resources of his Government; Jauréguiberry undertook to create the empire by military means. Theirs were the vital decisions. By accepting the financial and military burdens involved in empire-building on a grand scale, they inaugurated the era of French imperialism in West Africa.

The French were not the only ones to pursue imperialist policies in

West Africa. In the early nineteenth century British statesmen, scientists and explorers had entertained equally high hopes about the future prospects of the Sudanese interior. After 1895 Joseph Chamberlain was to make the development of a tropical African empire an equally important objective of his Government. Indeed, his 'doctrine of tropical African estates' was a mirror-image of the policies which Freycinet and Jauréguiberry had introduced fifteen years before.[1] But this difference in timing is crucial. European imperialism, it has been argued, was not a factor in the partition of West Africa. Policy-makers on both sides of the Channel were supposedly preoccupied with the traditional concerns of *haute politique*: the maintenance of the Mediterranean balance and the security of the routes to the East. Their West African policies are therefore explained in terms of their grand strategies in North Africa and particularly in Egypt; and imperialist manifestations in West Africa such as Chamberlain's doctrine or the Chad Plan are described as an attempt to pay for the administration of an existing empire or as a convenient rationalisation of advances already made.[2] Whatever the validity of this argument for the British experience in West Africa, it cannot explain the nature of French policy there. France had begun to build her West African empire long before the Suez crisis broke the liberal entente and gave a new intensity to old rivalries in Egypt and the Mediterranean. The imperial idea dominated French strategy in the West African interior and helped to fashion her policies along the West African coast throughout the late nineteenth century. Indeed, it could be argued that French imperialism, far from being a consequence of the Partition, was itself one of its principal causes.

But French imperialism was not the product of the official mind alone. Jauréguiberry's policies were neither new nor entirely his own. Faidherbe had drawn up the plans which he approved in 1879, and Brière was the one who persuaded him to approve them. Once the Minister had authorised a military advance, moreover, his military agents quickly seized the initiative. In the Western Sudan, the Military formulated their own policies and generated their own expansive force which often carried them far beyond the limits envisaged by their metropolitan employers. They perpetuated the 'era of military expansion' for a decade after Paris had first called for it to be closed. They conquered

---

[1] The best account of Chamberlain's doctrine is given in Robinson and Gallagher, *Africa and the Victorians*, pp. 395-402.

[2] Cf. *ibid.* pp. 408-9; *idem*, 'The Partition of Africa', *loc. cit.* pp. 611, 620-2.

vast territories at times when the emphasis in official policy was squarely on consolidation. They turned their colony into an exclusive military preserve, destroying the Government's most cherished hopes for commercial development and undermining all its efforts to control the cost of their activities. For twenty years they, not the Ministries, were the final arbiters of the Sudan's destiny. They determined the pace, the extent and the nature of the conquest. Paris had called on them to establish the military security it considered essential for the achievement of its economic objectives. It had never intended them to carve out a specifically military empire in the Western Sudan. Yet this was precisely what they did.

In part, the *officiers soudanais* owed their influence to the confused state of French military administration at the time. Until the creation of the Colonial Army in 1900, control over the *infanterie* and *artillerie de marine* remained dangerously split between various Government departments. The Inspectors–General remained the effective masters of the two corps, and after 1890 these were men with Sudanese experience. Brière, Desbordes and their associates were the real masters of the Sudan as well. Through a web of intimate personal relationships and through their powers over postings and promotions, they commanded the loyalty of their subordinates on the spot and wielded a *pouvoir occulte* which could at times completely overshadow the legitimate authority of the Government.

The confused state of French political life, particularly in the realm of civilian–military relations, also worked to their advantage. As long as French troops were actively engaged in military operations, they enjoyed considerable immunity from metropolitan attack. It was difficult for a politician to criticise a soldier who was defending French interests overseas without risking the accusation of cowardice or treachery. It was all the more difficult for a member of the Government to do so when the enemies of the Republic were all too anxious to denounce his criticisms as an attack upon the whole sacrosanct military structure. No Ministry felt secure enough lightly to provoke a major controversy over such a politically dangerous issue. Only when military indiscipline led to disaster did the *officiers soudanais* become the objects of general censure, and even then they retained the support of the militarists and of most politicians on the Right.

Ultimately, however, the Military found their greatest source of strength in the Government's own policies of expansion. By entrusting their execution to its military agents, Paris became the captive of its local commanders. Difficulties of communication made it impossible to issue detailed instructions or to deny them the right to interpret orders in the light of existing circumstances. As the conquest proceeded, they became the experts on whose advice the Government was forced to rely; they supplied the information on which its plans were based. When their tours of duty in the Sudan were over, they were often seconded to important advisory and executive positions within the policy-making structure itself. As the men on the spot and as key figures in the metropolitan bureaucracy, the *officiers soudanais* acted as a remarkably effective pressure group and exerted a direct influence on the formulation of policy. When local commanders failed to extort the Government's approval for their plans, they could always resort to the tactics of the *fait accompli*, knowing that their actions would not be disavowed. For everyone accepted the maintenance of military security as the over-riding priority. It was axiomatic that a retreat under any circumstances was unthinkable, because any sign of French weakness or lack of resolution could only encourage their enemies and so endanger the very existence of the colony. No matter how strenuously Governments objected to an unauthorised advance, they had to accept its consequences. Their only sanction was to dismiss the offending commander and face the political storm which was bound to follow. By the time Paris summoned up the necessary courage, the Military were too firmly entrenched for the mere appointment of a civilian Governor to breach the defences of their independence. The imposition of civilian authority at the top was of little consequence when military influence pervaded every branch and every level of the administration. To break the military stranglehold on Sudanese affairs, Paris finally had to break up the Sudan itself.

The nature of French policies also determined relations with the African states of the Sudanese interior. Those who dismiss the significance of imperialism for the partition of Africa also discount its relevance for the European occupation of the continent. France, they maintain, had no real desire for a West African empire; instead, she was driven to extend her political control partly by the independent activities of her military agents but mainly through a series of unplanned encounters with the reviving Islamic polities which confronted her. The local crisis is thus advanced as the dominant factor in the expansionist process, and the conquest is described as little more than a reluctant European response to the forces of uncompromising, religiously inspired African resistance.[1] But such an interpretation clearly exaggerates the significance of Muslim recalcitrance. At no time were the reactions of the Sudanese empires to European expansion determined primarily by their religious character; their military strength and internal cohesion were always the decisive factors. When the French advance first began in the late 1850s, the Tokolor *jihad* was reaching its height. Umar's obligations as a religious leader may have contributed to his declaration of war; but it was the military power at his command which enabled him to challenge his European adversaries for supremacy along the Senegal. When the challenge failed and he diverted his advance towards the Upper Niger, he did not hesitate to conclude a truce with them. By the 1880s when the Military embarked upon their conquests, Tokolor fortunes had been completely reversed. The religious enthusiasm of the original *jihad* had been lost; factional strife after the death of Umar had dissolved the cohesion of his empire; *talibé* desertions had sapped its strength, and Bambara rebellions were undermining its security. Its ruler was no longer a militant religious reformer but an essentially secular potentate struggling desperately to save the empire from total collapse. The declining importance of Ahmadu's religious position may have given him more scope for collaboration with the French; his political and military weakness gave him no other choice. Certainly, he appreciated the dangers of European expansion, and he waged a determined economic and diplomatic campaign in defence of his territorial integrity. But his opposition was never violent. Indeed, he looked on the French as potential allies against his rebellious subjects, and he gave them generous concessions in return for their spurious promises of military aid. As the rebellions grew fiercer and the Sultan's position more precarious, so his determination to avoid war increased. By 1887 he was ready to compromise what remained of his religious authority by accepting a French protectorate. The French moreover were fully aware of Ahmadu's impotence in the face of their expansionist designs. The Military never ceased to assure Paris of his inability to resist their advance, and they often based their policies on this assumption. French assessments of Tokolor weakness contributed much more to the conquest than did their fears of Tokolor strength.

In military terms, the Samorian empire presented by far the most

---

[1] This interpretation is advanced most forcefully in Robinson and Gallagher, 'The Partition of Africa', *loc. cit.* pp. 609, 619–20.

serious challenge to French ambitions in the Western Sudan, yet Samori's religion was not a crucial factor in his resistance. Although the *imam* was a devout Muslim, his power rested upon the strength of his armies rather than of his faith. The secular nature of his empire, a dynamic military state geared to territorial expansion and based economically upon the slave trade, gave him the incentive to oppose the French advance; the training and discipline of his *sofas*, not their religious fervour, gave him the capacity to do so. But not even Samori was uncompromising in his hostility. Having abandoned the struggle in the Senegal–Niger valley, he too accepted French protectorate in order to secure European support against his African enemies. He too preferred a negotiated settlement to a war *à outrance*. When all efforts to arrive at a peaceful solution failed and the French attacked, both he and Ahmadu resisted as best they could. But their resistance was a consequence of French aggression, not one of its causes.

The Military's independent initiatives undoubtedly provide a partial explanation for the conquest. The *officiers soudanais* had a definite professional interest in seeking action. They were drawn to the Sudan by the opportunities it afforded for *faits de guerre* and for the rapid promotions that went with them. Prospects of a brilliant career led them to accept the hardships of colonial life and gave them the incentive to perpetuate or if necessary to provoke conflict. To a degree, the conquest was simply the work of ambitious officers whose professional future depended upon the constant demonstration of their military ability. The context in which they operated intensified their aggressiveness. The Military in the Western Sudan were field-commanders in a theatre of war. The problem of military security was their dominant concern, and total military victory was their only solution to it. The doctrine of pre-emptive attack had obvious attractions for men who were hypersensitive to the potential danger of organised African opposition. The fact that the potential enemies were Muslims heightened their fears and strengthened their determination. For the Military's attitude to West African Islam was conditioned by the long history of Franco-Muslim conflict in Africa. The Algerian experience, transmitted through Faidherbe, coloured their thinking and made the actual disposition of a ruler like Ahmadu irrelevant to their calculations. To the Military, Ahmadu was the representative of a totally alien faith and culture with whom there could never be any compromise. The Sultan's weakness did not lessen their fears of an anti-European *jihad*. His efforts at conciliation could not shake their conviction that Muslims, because of their religion, were bound in the end to resist the advance of European civilisation and that France could never feel secure until the spectre of the *jihad* had been laid.

But the conquest of the Western Sudan was not simply the product of the Military's personal ambitions or their preoccupations with security. The logic of French African policy also permitted no other outcome. A genuine *rapprochement* with the African empires of the Sudanese interior was possible only as long as French ambitions were limited to the peaceful extension of influence and trade. Once dominion as well as trade became the goal, their eventual subjugation became inevitable. On this the policy-makers and the Military were agreed. Neither could envisage the Sudan as having more than one master, even if they differed on who the master was to be. Both considered the imposition of unchallenged European political control essential, whether for economic development or for military security. Before the 1890s, Paris was no less firmly committed to the overthrow of Ahmadu and Samori than its military agents; the principal disagreement between them was on the question of timing. Thereafter, the policy-makers grew more concerned to maintain the peace which they considered necessary for commercial development, but the maintenance of political supremacy remained their first priority. The Military, for whom dominion was less a prelude to development than an end in itself, were less hesitant still. In the final analysis, the motives for the conquest are to be found not in any combination of local crises but in the considerations which led the policy-makers and their agents to create a French empire in West Africa, in the imperialism of the official and military minds.

But local factors cannot be left out of the reckoning. Muslim rebellion in southern Algeria had helped to scuttle the Government's more grandiose schemes of African empire in the 1860s and did so again in the early 1880s. In the Western Sudan, the final confrontation with Islam was delayed for a decade after the conquest began, for not even the Military wanted a war until they were sure of winning it. Since the days of Faidherbe, official policy had been to advance gradually, if possible in co-operation with the Muslims, until the occupation of the Senegal–Niger valley and French control over the Niger left them incapable of effective resistance. By 1883 this objective had been achieved; but the French then found themselves too precariously established along their line of forts to contemplate a further military advance. Thereafter, the difficulties of transportation and supply resulting from the failure to build the railway, military complications with Samori, and the insurrection of Mahmadu Lamine gave the Tokolor empire a new lease on life. Only in 1888 was Gallieni able to complete the consolidation of the Sudan and thus set the stage for Archinard's conquests. Meanwhile, the realities of power in the Western Sudan forced the French to revise their assessments about their opponents. Even the Military came to see that Samori and his *sofas* were much more dangerous than Ahmadu's supposed fanaticism. They were not mistaken. When the overthrow of Ahmadu left them free to mount their final onslaught against the Samorian empire, the *imam*'s military skills and the success of his guerrilla tactics enabled him to maintain his independence until the end of the century.

Nor was the influence of the local factor entirely negative. France owed her own success in the Western Sudan to the use she made of African troops. The *tirailleurs*, accustomed to local conditions, able to withstand the effects of the climate, well armed, well trained, and stiffened by European cadres, were by far the most effective fighting force in the area. In relying on local manpower, however, the French were obliged to adopt local methods of warfare. Except for its veneer of European discipline, the whole military machine was modelled on African lines. Basically, there was little difference between a *sofa* and a *tirailleur*. The prospect of plunder was the principal reason why the latter served the French, and the regular distribution of captives was the most efficient way to secure his continued loyalty. That female prisoners were euphemistically called *épouses libres* did not make them any less a form of payment. When Grodet tried to stamp out the practice by punishing some of the officers responsible, the main concern of his military commanders was to prevent the news from reaching the *tirailleurs* lest they be encouraged to desert.[1] The immense problems of transportation created by the lack of an efficient communications system were met by enforced porterage. The dreary lines of chained bearers which accompanied the Voulet–Chanoine expedition were the same as those which followed the armies of Samori. The much vaunted *villages de liberté*, supposedly the Military's chief contribution to the fight against the slave trade, were little more than a means of alleviating the labour shortage along the supply lines. Freed slaves who were not sent to the villages where they could be used as porters were usually con-

[1] Ebener, Ordre no. 148, 16 Oct. 1894, Arch. Guerre, A.O.F. Soudan 4.

scripted into the *tirailleurs* just as prisoners had been drafted into the armies of Umar.[1]

Military rule was similarly African in character. The subject states, created as instruments of security and bases for continued expansion, were no more progressive in their internal organisation than the political systems which they replaced. The client chiefs, deriving their authority from the military might of their European masters and practically uncontrolled in the details of their government, enjoyed unfettered powers over their subjects, and they abused these powers as blatantly as they dared. Military administration did little to alter or improve the economic foundations of the Sudan. In lands devastated by half a century of war, the slave trade was the most lucrative branch of commerce, and the Military accepted it as such. Regular slave markets were held under the walls of the French forts long before the chaotic days of Grodet's governorship.[2] Archinard gave the traffic administrative recognition by levying the conventional *oussourou* or ten per cent duty on the slave caravans, and Trentinian resumed the practice after 1895.[3] In the end, military rule brought little benefit either to France or to the African. The real beneficiaries of the conquest were the conquerors themselves. They created an empire distinguished not so much by being French as by being military, and military along essentially African lines. They gave France title to territories more impressive for their size than for their wealth; they secured for themselves 'a *domaine réservé* where the officer was king, sultan and prophet, no more nor less than a Samori or a Rabih'.[4]

Yet the military empire of the Western Sudan contained the seeds of its own destruction. Its foundations rested upon the Military's ability to control the pace of French expansion and to maintain their exclusive mastery over the colony's affairs. They tried to do so by keeping the Sudan out of the mainstream of French African policy, but this was possible only as long as the Chad Plan remained a collection of pro-

---

[1] D. Bouche, 'Les villages de liberté en A.O.F.', part I, *Bulletin de l'I.F.A.N.*, série B, XI (1949), 526–40, esp. 529: 'Il est bien certain que le motif qui fit généraliser les villages de liberté c'est qu'ils étaient une excellente solution au problème des porteurs et de la main d'œuvre, bien supérieure, en tout cas, au système qui consistait à aller chercher les gens, les armes à la main, chaque fois qu'on en avait besoin, pour les voir fuir à la première inattention, système lent, compliqué et aléatoire.'

[2] Viard, Renseignements sur le Sénégal, 12 May 1887, AEMD Afrique 85. See also: Desbordes, Note, 10 Sept. 1886, MFOM Sénégal IV 87(d).

[3] Bouche, 'Les villages de liberté', part II, *loc. cit.* XII (1950), 142–5.

[4] *La Politique Coloniale*, 21 Sept. 1899.

jected lines on a map. Once steps were taken to fill in the blank spaces, the Sudan was bound to become part of a larger empire, and the Military's private domain was bound to be nationalised. As the Chad Plan came to dominate French strategy after 1890, the Sudan's isolation, and with it the Military's influence, was progressively eroded. By 1895 the *officiers soudanais* had even lost their position as the principal agents of military expansion. Ironically, the diversion of the military advance from the Sudan to Dahomey marked the beginning of their downfall.

The Military's single-minded pursuit of the conquest was to prove equally fatal to them. Driven on by their prejudices and ambitions, they subordinated all other considerations, commercial or humanitarian, to the establishment of their hegemony and turned the Sudan into an expensive, economically unproductive backwater. But as concentration on economic development began to produce more satisfactory results along the coast, the politicians grew less tolerant of the mounting costs and continued stagnation of the interior. As the Military's abuses became more widely known, their pretensions to act as a civilising force were destroyed, and the ranks of their enemies were swelled. By the end of the century the *officier soudanais* stood virtually alone, deprived of his influence in the Ministry, supported only by right-wing extremists and denounced by the very colonialists whose good-will he should have enjoyed. There was ironic justice in the fact that the Voulet–Chanoine expedition, undertaken against the advice of the Sudanese authorities and operating beyond their control, provoked the scandal which finally discredited them.

In the end, however, what sealed the Military's fate was the very success of their policies. They had always argued the case for conquest on the grounds of security. The need to crush all opposition, potential or real, was their basic justification for military domination. By 1899 they had achieved their goal, but in the process they had destroyed the only valid reason for their continued mastery. In a very real sense, when Samori fell, the Military fell with him. This was perhaps the greatest irony of all.

List of Sources

I. MINISTÈRE DE LA MARINE ET DES COLONIES

The Colonial Archives are now administratively part of the Archives Nationales (Section Outre-Mer); but they are still housed at the Ministère de la France d'Outre-Mer, Rue Oudinot.

A. *General Classification*

Correspondence relating to Africa is classified under a special system by geographical area and subject. Only the general classes consulted are listed here; specific references to individual dossiers are given in the footnotes.

Afrique: III (Explorations, Missions); IV (Pays étrangers); VI (Affaires diplomatiques); XII (Transport, Communications).

Sénégal: I (Correspondance générale); III (Explorations, Missions); IV (Expansion territoriale et politique indigène); VI (Affaires diplomatiques); XII (Transport, Communications); XVI (Troupes).

Soudan: I (Correspondance générale); II (Documents, Publications); III (Explorations, Missions); IV (Expansion territoriale et politique indigène); V (Affaires militaires); VI (Affaires diplomatiques); VII (Administration); IX (Budgets); XII (Transport, Communications); XIII (Commerce et industrie); XIX (Inspections).

Côte d'Ivoire: IV (Expansion territoriale et politique indigène).

A.O.F.: I (Correspondance générale); VI (Affaires diplomatiques); VII (Administration).

B. *Fonds Missions*

Missions:

2, Soleillet 1877–86
4, Monteil 1890–2
6, Mizon
9, Clozel 1893–6
10, Foureau 1896
    Chanoine 1897
11, Cazemajou
    Voulet 1897
    Voulet–Chanoine
12, Binger 1887–91
15, Soleillet 1876–9
    Gallieni 1879
    Mousnier 1879
    Carrey 1880
    Lenz 1880

16, Gallieni 1880
17, Abd-el-Kader
18, Gallieni 1886–7
20, Guillaumet 1894
    Baillaud
36, Hourst 1893
40, Archinard
49, Voulet–Chanoine
50, Borgnis-Desbordes 1881–2
    Borgnis-Desbordes 1882–3
109, Derrien 1880–1
    Monteil 1884–5
110, Voulet–Chanoine

List of Sources

c. *Registres de Télégrammes*: *Afrique*

Sénégal, 1889–99
Soudan, 1893–5
Bureau d'Afrique, 1898–9

D. *Dossiers Administratifs*

Archinard, Audéoud, Brière de l'Isle, Canard, Delanneau, Faidherbe, Gold-scheider, Haussmann, Servatius, Vallon.

2. MINISTÈRE DES AFFAIRES ÉTRANGÈRES, QUAI D'ORSAY

A. *Correspondance Politique*

Allemagne: 59–60, 97, 115–16
Angleterre: 850–2, 896–9, 905–21
Grande Bretagne: n.s. 11 (Relations avec la France), n.s. 29 (Empire Britannique)
Maroc: 50

B. *Correspondance Politique des Consuls*

Angleterre, Freetown: 53, 70–1, 74
           Manchester: 78–9

c. *Mémoires et Documents, Afrique*

Sénégal et Dépendances:

1852–5, Afrique 46	1883–4, Afrique 84
1856–67, Afrique 47	1885–7, Afrique 85
1868–75, Afrique 48	1886–9, Afrique 122
1876–8, Afrique 49	1890–1, Afrique 123
1879–82, Afrique 50	1892–4, Afrique 124

Possessions Anglaises de la Côte Occidentale:

1866–80, Afrique 56	1888–9, Afrique 128
1881–2, Afrique 57	1890–2, Afrique 129
1883–7, Afrique 86	1893–4, Afrique 131

Notes Générales: 1843–85, Afrique 74, 75
Conférence de Berlin: 1884–5, Afrique 109

3. MINISTÈRE DE LA GUERRE (ARCHIVES HISTORIQUES DE L'ARMÉE, SECTION OUTRE-MER), Vincennes

A.O.F. Soudan 1–2, 4
E.M.A. 57

4. MINISTÈRE DES TRAVAUX PUBLICS, ARCHIVES NATIONALES

F^{14} 12436–8 (Chemin de Fer Transsaharien)

List of Sources

II. PARLIAMENTARY ARCHIVES

1. COMMISSIONS PARLEMENTAIRES, CHAMBRE (SÉRIE C), ARCHIVES NATIONALES

A. *Commission du Budget*

C   2842, 2844–6, 2849–50, 3150, 3152, 3173, 3175–7, 3302, 3304–6, 3314, 3316, 5380–3, 5441, 5443, 5445, 5447, 5547–8, 5553, 5555, 5624, 5625

Documents adressés à la Commission du Budget

5380, 5442, 5462

B. *Commission de l'Armée*

C   2806, 5375, 5435, 5541–2, 5618

C. *Commission des Traités*

C   3393, 5515, 5673

D. *Commission Parlementaire d'Enquête* (1871)

C   2874

E. *Commission sur le recrutement de l'Armée* (1877)

C   3148

F. *Commission des Colonies* (1895)

C   5565

G. *Projets de Loi*

C   3171, 3181, 3221–2, 3300, 3303, 3311, 3321, 5390, 5436, 5440, 5442, 5446, 5463, 5543, 5546, 5550, 5556, 5567–8, 5621

2. BUDGET REPORTS

AD   XVIII^f 888, 892, 893, 900, 913, 916, 918, 922

III. PRIVATE PAPERS

Archinard Papers (in the possession of Madame Entremont-Archinard)
Etienne Papers (Bibliothèque Nationale, n.a.fr. 24327)
Faure Papers (in the possession of Monsieur François Berge)
Freycinet Papers (Ecole Polytechnique)
Mizon Papers (Bibliothèque Nationale, n.a.fr. 10726–7)
Monteil Papers (Archives Nationales, 66 AP)
Rambaud Papers (Archives Nationales, 81 AP)
Documents relatifs au Sultanat de Ségou (Bibliothèque Nationale, n.a.fr. 25070)

List of Sources

IV. OFFICIAL PUBLICATIONS

Journal Officiel de la République Française

Ministère des Affaires Etrangères, *Documents diplomatiques français*, Ière serie. 14 vols. Paris, 1929–54.

Ministère des Affaires Etrangères, *Documents diplomatiques: Affaires du Congo et de l'Afrique occidentale, 1884–5 [Livre Jaune].*

Ministère des Affaires Etrangères, *Commission Supérieure pour l'examen du projet de mer intérieure dans le sud de l'Algérie présenté par le commandant Roudaire.* Paris, 1882.

Ministère de la Guerre, Direction des Troupes Coloniales. *Les armées françaises d'outre-mer.* 21 vols. Paris, 1931. [The more important volumes in this series are listed under their individual authors in the Bibliography.]

Ministère de la Marine et des Colonies. *Recueil des Traités: Afrique* [formerly MFOM Afrique I].

Ministère de la Marine et des Colonies. *Bulletin Officiel de la Marine et des Colonies.*

Ministère de la Marine et des Colonies. *Sénégal et Niger, la France dans l'Afrique occidentale, 1879–83.* Paris, 1884.

Ministère des Travaux Publiques. *Documents relatifs à la mission dirigée au sud de l'Algérie par le lieutenant-colonel Flatters.* Paris, 1884.

Ministère des Travaux Publiques. *Documents relatifs à la mission dirigée au sud de l'Algérie par Monsieur A. Choisy.* Vol. I. Paris, 1895.

V. NEWSPAPERS AND PERIODICALS

The following list contains only those journals consulted systematically over a period of time. References to individual articles in other journals are given in the footnotes.

Bulletin du Comité de l'Afrique Française (1891–9)
L'Avenir de la Marine et des Colonies (1882–3)
L'Autorité (1893–5, 1899)
La Dépêche Coloniale (1897–9)
L'Eclair (1893–5, 1899)
Le Figaro (1893–5, 1899)
La France Militaire (1893–5, 1899)
Le Jour (1893–5, 1899)
Le Journal des Débats (1893–5, 1899)
La Libre Parole (1893–5, 1899)
Le Matin (1893–5)
La Patrie (1893–5, 1899)
La Politique Coloniale (1892–9)
Le Siècle (1889–95, 1899)
Le Temps (1893–5, 1899)

Bibliography

Abun-Nasr, J. M. *The Tijaniyya, a Sufi Order in the Modern World*. London, 1965.

Alis, H. [Henri-Hippolyte Percher]. *A la conquête du Tchad*. Paris, 1891.

Nos Africains. Paris, 1894.

Archinard, L. *Le Soudan français en 1888–1889*. Paris, 1890.

— *Le Soudan en 1893*. Le Havre, 1895.

le général Arlabosse. 'Une phase de la lutte contre Samory, 1890–1892.' *Revue d'histoire des colonies*, vol. xx. 1932.

Atger, P. *La France en Côte d'Ivoire de 1843 à 1893. Cinquante ans d'hésitations politiques et commerciales*. Dakar, 1962.

Azan, P. *Conquête et pacification de l'Algérie*. Les Armées Françaises d'Outre-Mer. Paris, 1931.

Ba, J. H. and Daget, J. *L'empire peul du Macina, 1818–1853*. Paris, 1962.

Bayol, J. 'La France au Fouta Djallon.' *Revue des Deux Mondes*, December, 1882.

Beaudza, L. *La formation de l'armée coloniale*. Paris, 1939.

Béchet, E. *Cinq ans de séjour au Soudan français*. Paris, 1889.

Benoit, C. *Histoire militaire de l'Afrique occidentale française*. Les Armées Françaises d'Outre-Mer. Paris, 1931.

Berge, F. *Le sous-secrétariat et les sous-secrétaires d'état aux colonies: Histoire de l'émancipation de l'administration coloniale*. Paris, 1962.

Bernard, A., and Lacroix, N. *La pénétration saharienne, 1830–1906*. Algiers, 1906.

Bernard, F. *Deux missions françaises chez les Touareg en 1880–1881*. Algiers, 1896.

Binger, L. G. *Du Niger au Golfe de Guinée*. 2 vols. Paris, 1892.

Blanc, E. 'Notes sur les Diawara.' *Bulletin du Comité des Etudes Historiques et Scientifiques de l'Afrique Occidentale Française*, vol. VII. 1924.

Blanchard, M. 'Français et Anglais au Niger (1890–1898).' *Le Monde Français*, vol. XII, 1948; vol. XIII, 1949.

— 'Théophile Delcassé au Pavillon de Flore, 1893–1894.' *Le Monde Français*, vol. XIII. 1949.

— 'Administrateurs d'Indochine.' *Revue d'histoire des colonies*, vol. XXXIX. 1952.

— 'Administrateurs d'Afrique noire.' *Revue d'histoire des colonies*, vol. XL. 1953.

— 'Correspondance de Félix Faure touchant les affaires coloniales, 1882–1898.' *Revue d'histoire des colonies*, vol. XLII. 1955.

Boahen, A. A. *Britain, the Sahara, and the Western Sudan, 1788–1861*. Oxford, 1964.

Bonnier, G. *L'occupation de Tombouctou*. Paris, 1926.

Bouche, D. 'Les villages de liberté en A.O.F.' *Bulletin de l'Institut Français d'Afrique Noire*, série B, vol. XI, 1949; vol. XII, 1950.

Bibliography

Bovill, E. W. *The Golden Trade of the Moors.* 2nd ed. London, 1963.
— (ed.). *Missions to the Niger.* Vol. I. Cambridge, 1964.
Boyer, G. *Un peuple de l'ouest soudanais, les Diawara.* Mémoires de l'Institut Français d'Afrique Noire, no. 29. Dakar, 1953.
Braibant, C. (ed.). *Félix Faure à l'Elysée.* Paris, 1963.
Braudel, F. *La Méditerranée et le monde méditerranéen à l'époque de Phillippe II.* Paris, 1949.
Broussais, E. *De Paris au Soudan, Marseille, Alger, Transsaharien.* Paris, 1891.
Bruguière, M. 'Le Chemin de Fer du Yunnan: Paul Doumer et la politique d'intervention française en Chine, 1889–1902.' Part I. *Revue d'histoire diplomatique,* vol. LXXVII. 1963.
Brunschwig, H. *Mythes et réalités de l'impérialisme colonial français, 1871–1914.* Paris, 1960.
— *L'avènement de l'Afrique noire.* Paris, 1963.
— 'Le parti colonial français.' *Revue française d'histoire d'outre-mer,* vol. XLVI. 1959.
— 'Les Origines du Partage de l'Afrique Occidentale.' *Journal of African History,* vol. V. 1964.
le maréchal Bugeaud. *De la colonisation en Algérie.* Paris, 1847.
Cady, J. F. *The Roots of French Imperialism in Eastern Asia.* Ithaca, 1954.
Caillié, R. *Travels through Central Africa to Timbuctoo.* 2 vols. London, 1830.
Capperon, L. 'Bouët-Willaumez en Afrique occidentale et au Gabon, 1836–1850.' *Revue maritime,* n.s. 89. 1953.
Carette, E., and Renou, E. *Recherches sur la géographie et le commerce de l'Algérie méridionale.* Exploration scientifique de l'Algérie, no. 2. Paris, 1844.
Caron, E. 'La Marine au Niger.' *Revue maritime et coloniale,* vol. XCIX. 1888.
Carrère, F. and Holle, P. *De la Sénégambie française.* Paris, 1855.
Carroll, E. M. *French Public Opinion and Foreign Affairs, 1870–1914.* New York, 1931.
Catala, R. 'La question de l'échange de la Gambie britannique contre les comptoirs français du Golfe de Guinée.' *Revue d'histoire des colonies,* vol. XXXV. 1948.
Cecil, Lady G. *Life of Robert, Marquis of Salisbury.* 4 vols. London, 1931–2.
le commandant Chailley. 'La mission du Haut-Soudan et la drame de Zinder.' *Bulletin de l'Institut Français d'Afrique Noire,* série B, vol. XVI, 1954; vol. XVII, 1955.
Chalmin, P. *L'officier français de 1815 à 1870.* Paris, 1957.
Charbonneau, J. *La jeunesse passionnée de Gallieni.* Vichy, 1952.
Chauveau, J. 'Mizon à Yola.' *Revue d'histoire des colonies,* vol. XLI. 1954.
Clemenceau, G., and Schirmer, H. (eds.). *Georges Périn, 1838–1903: Discours politiques et notes de voyages.* Paris, 1905.
Coquery-Vidrovitch, C. 'Les idées économiques de Brazza et les premières tentatives de compagnies de colonisation au Congo français, 1885–1898.' *Cahiers d'études africaines,* no. 17. 1965.
Crowe, S. E. *The Berlin West Africa Conference, 1884–1885.* London, 1942.
Cultru, P. *Histoire du Sénégal du XVe siècle à 1870.* Paris, 1910.

Bibliography

Curtin, P. D. *The Image of Africa: British Ideas and Action, 1780-1850*. Madison, 1964.

Darcy, J. *France et Angleterre, cent années de rivalité coloniale: l'Afrique*. Paris, 1904.

Delafosse, M. *Haut-Sénégal–Niger*. 3 vols. Paris, 1912.

— 'Traditions historiques et légendaires du Soudan occidental.' *Afrique Française, Renseignements Coloniaux*. 1913.

Delavignette, R. and Julien, C-A. *Les constructeurs de la France d'outre-mer*. Paris, 1946.

Delcourt, A. *La France et les établissements français au Sénégal entre 1713 et 1763*. Mémoires de l'Institut Français d'Afrique Noire, no. 17. Dakar, 1952.

Demaison, A. *Faidherbe*. Paris, 1932.

Depont, O. and Coppolani, X. *Les confréries religieuses musulmanes*. Algiers, 1897.

Descostes, F. *Au Soudan, 1890–1891*. Paris, 1893.

Duchêne, A. *La politique coloniale de la France*. Paris, 1928.

— *Un ministre trop oublié: Chasseloup-Laubat*. Paris, 1932.

Duponchel, A. *Le Chemin de Fer Trans-Saharien, jonction coloniale entre l'Algérie et le Soudan; études préliminaires du projet et rapport de mission*. Montpellier, 1878.

— *La colonisation africaine, état actuel de la question*. Paris, 1890.

Duveyrier, H. *Les Touareg du Nord*. Paris, 1864.

Emérit, M. *L'Algérie à l'époque d'Abd el-Kader*. Paris, 1951.

— 'La crise syrienne et l'expansion économique française en 1860.' *Revue historique*, vol. CCVII. 1952.

Emily, J. 'La fin d'Ahmadou Sheicou.' *Communications de l'Académie des Sciences Coloniales*, vol. VIII. 1926–7.

Esquer, G., and Boyer, P. 'Bugeaud en 1840.' *Revue africaine*, vol. CIV. 1960.

Eugène Etienne, son œuvre coloniale, algérienne et politique, 1881–1906. Ed. *La Dépêche Coloniale*. 2 vols. Paris, 1907.

Faidherbe, L. L. C. *L'avenir du Sahara et du Soudan*. Paris, 1863.

— *Le Soudan français—chemin de fer de Médine au Niger*. Lille, 1885.

— *Le Sénégal, la France dans l'Afrique occidentale*. Paris, 1889.

[Faidherbe, L. L. C.] *Annales sénégalaises de 1854 à 1885*. Paris, 1885.

Fage, J. D. 'Some Thoughts on State-Formation in the Western Sudan before the Seventeenth Century.' *Boston University Papers on African History*, vol. I. Boston, 1964.

Faure, C. 'Le premier séjour de Duranton au Sénégal, 1819–26.' *Revue de l'histoire des colonies françaises*, vol. IX. 1921.

[Faure, F.] 'Fachoda.' *Revue d'histoire diplomatique*, vol. LXIX. 1955.

Feis, H. *Europe, the World's Banker, 1870–1914*. New Haven, 1930.

Flint, J. E. *Sir George Goldie and the Making of Nigeria*. London, 1960.

Frey, H. *Campagne dans le Haut-Sénégal et le Haut-Niger, 1885–1886*. Paris, 1888.

de Freycinet, C. *Souvenirs*. 2 vols. 3rd ed. Paris, 1912–13.

Froelicher, J. *Trois colonisateurs: Bugeaud, Faidherbe, Gallieni*. Paris, n.d.

Bibliography

Fyfe, C. *A History of Sierra Leone*. Oxford, 1962.

Gallieni, J. S. *Voyage au Soudan français (Haut-Niger et pays de Ségou) 1879–1881*. Paris, 1885.

— *Deux campagnes au Soudan français, 1886–1888*. Paris, 1891.

Gallissot, R. 'La guerre d'Abd el-Kader ou la ruine de la nationalité algérienne (1839-1847).' *Hespéris-Tamuda*, vol. v. 1964.

— 'Abd el-Kader et la nationalité algérienne.' *Revue historique*, vol. CCXXXIII. 1965.

Ganiage, J. *Les origines du protectorat français en Tunisie (1861–1881)*. Paris, 1959.

Ganier, G. 'Les rivalités franco-anglaise et franco-allemande de 1894 à 1898.' *Revue française d'histoire d'outre-mer*, vol. XLIX. 1962.

— 'Lat Dyor et le chemin de fer de l'arachide, 1876–1886.' *Bulletin de l'Institut Français d'Afrique Noire*, série B, vol. XXVII. 1965.

Garvin, J. L. *The life of Joseph Chamberlain*. 3 vols. London, 1932–4.

Gautier, E. F. 'Documents d'archives soudanais concernant le général Gallieni.' *La Géographie*, vol. XLII. 1924.

Gazeau de Vautibault. *Le Transsaharien*. Paris, [1879].

Gille, G. 'Les capitaux français et l'expédition du Mexique.' *Revue d'histoire diplomatique*, vol. LXXIX. 1965.

Girardet, R. *La société militaire dans la France contemporaine, 1816–1939*. Paris, 1953.

Gooch, R. K. *The French Parliamentary Committee System*. New York, 1935.

Gouilly, A. *L'Islam dans l'Afrique occidentale française*. Paris, 1925.

Gros, J. *Paul Soleillet en Afrique*. Paris, [1888].

— (ed.). *Les voyages de Paul Soleillet dans le Sahara et dans le Soudan en vue d'un projet de chemin de fer transsaharien, racontés par lui-même*. Paris, 1881.

Guillaumet, E. *Le Soudan en 1894, la vérité sur Tombouctou*. 2nd ed. Paris, 1895.

Guiral, P. 'L'opinion marseillaise et les débuts de l'entreprise algérienne.' *Revue historique*, vol. CCXL. 1955.

Halévy, D., and Pillias, E. (eds.). *Lettres de Gambetta, 1868–1882*. Paris, 1938.

Hallett, R. (ed.). *Records of the African Association, 1788–1831*. London, 1964.

Hanotaux, G. *Histoire de la France contemporaine*. Vol. IV. Paris, 1908.

Hanotaux, G., and Martineau, A. (eds.). *Histoire des colonies françaises et de l'expansion de la France dans le monde*. Vol. IV. Paris, 1931.

Hardy, G. *La mise en valeur du Sénégal de 1817 à 1854*. Paris, 1921.

— *Faidherbe*. Paris, 1947.

Hargreaves, J. D. *Prelude to the Partition of West Africa*. London, 1963.

— '*Entente Manquée*: Anglo-French Relations, 1895–1896.' *Cambridge Historical Journal*, vol. XI. 1953.

— 'Towards a History of the Partition of Africa.' *Journal of African History*, vol. I. 1960.

— 'The Tokolor Empire of Ségou and its Relations with the French.' *Boston University Papers on African History*, vol. II. Boston, 1966.

Hertslet, E. *The Map of Africa by Treaty*. 3 vols. 3rd ed. London, 1909.

Bibliography

Hiskett, M. 'Material relating to the State of Learning among the Fulani before their Jihad.' *Bulletin of the School of Oriental and African Studies,* vol. XIX. 1957.

— 'An Islamic Tradition of Reform in the Western Sudan from the Sixteenth to the Eighteenth Century.' *Bulletin of the School of Oriental and African Studies,* vol. XXV. 1962.

Hogben, S. J., and Kirk-Greene, A. H. M. *The Emirates of Northern Nigeria, a Preliminary Survey of their Historical Traditions.* London, 1966.

Holas, B. 'Un document authentique sur Samory.' *Notes africaines,* no. 74. 1957.

le lieutenant de vaisseau Hourst. *La Mission Hourst.* Paris, 1898.

Humbert, G. *Le général Borgnis-Desbordes et le colonel Humbert de l'artillerie de marine.* Paris, 1896.

— *Plainte officielle contre le général Desbordes adressée au Ministre de la Marine: Pour la Justice.* Paris, 1898.

d'Ideville, H. *Le maréchal Bugeaud d'après sa correspondance intime.* 3 vols. Paris, 1882.

Joalland, P. *Le drame de Dankori.* Paris, 1930.

Johnston, H. A. S. *The Fulani Empire of Sokoto.* London, 1967.

Julien, C-A. *Histoire de l'Algérie contemporaine: La conquête et les débuts de la colonisation (1827–1871).* Paris, 1964.

— (ed.). *Les techniciens de la colonisation.* Paris, 1953.

de Kersaint-Gilly, F. 'Essai sur l'évolution de l'esclavage en A.O.F.' *Bulletin du Comité des Etudes Historiques et Scientifiques de l'Afrique Occidentale Française,* vol. VII. 1924.

Kouroubari, A. 'Histoire de l'imam Samori.' *Bulletin de l'Institut Français d'Afrique Noire,* série B, vol. XXI. 1959.

Labouret, H. *Monteil, explorateur et soldat.* Paris, 1957.

— 'Les bandes de Samory.' *Afrique Française, Renseignements Coloniaux.* 1925.

de Loppinot, A. 'Souvenirs d'Aguibou.' *Bulletin du Comité des Etudes Historiques et Scientifiques de l'Afrique Occidentale Française,* vol. II. 1919.

de La Roncière, C. *La découverte de l'Afrique au moyen âge.* Mémoires de la Société Royale de Géographie d'Egypte. 3 vols. Cairo, 1924–7.

Leaman, B. R. 'The Influence of Domestic Policy on Foreign Affairs in France, 1898–1905.' *Journal of Modern History,* vol. XIV. 1942.

Lebon, A. 'La boucle du Niger, 1896–1898.' *Revue des Deux Mondes,* September, 1900.

Lecerf, P. E. *Lettres du Soudan* [posthumous publication by his father]. Paris, 1895.

Le Chatelier, A. *L'Islam dans l'Afrique occidentale.* Paris, 1899.

Legassick, M. 'Firearms, Horses and Samorian Army Organization.' *Journal of African History,* vol. VII. 1966.

Leroy-Beaulieu, P. *De la colonisation chez les peuples modernes.* 3rd ed. Paris, 1885.

— *Le Sahara, le Soudan, et les chemins de fer transsahariens.* Paris, 1904.

Bibliography

Lokke, C. L. *France and the Colonial Question: A Study in Contemporary French Opinion, 1763–1801.* New York, 1932.

Lugard, F. D. 'England and France on the Niger, the Race for Borgou.' *Nineteenth Century,* vol. XXXVII. 1895.

McKay, D. V. 'Colonialism in the French Geographical Movement, 1871–1881.' *The Geographical Review,* vol. XXXIII. 1943.

Mademba, A. 'Au Sénégal et au Soudan français; le Fama Mademba.' *Bulletin du Comité des Etudes Historiques et Scientifiques de l'Afrique Occidentale Française,* vol. XIII. 1930.

Mage, E. *Voyage dans le Soudan occidental.* Paris, 1868.

Mangin, C. 'Lettres du Soudan.' *Revue des Deux Mondes,* May–June, 1930.

Mantran, R. 'Une relation inédite d'un voyage en Tunisie au milieu du 19ᵐᵉ siècle.' *Cahiers de Tunisie,* no. 11. 1955.

de la Martinière, H. M. P., and Lacroix, N. *Documents pour servir à l'étude du nord-ouest africain.* 4 vols. Lille, 1894–7.

Marty, P. *Etudes sur l'Islam et les tribus du Soudan.* Vols. II, IV. Paris, 1920.

— *Islam en Guinée, Fouta Djallon.* Paris, 1921.

— *Etudes sénégalaises (1785–1826).* Paris, n.d.

— 'Une tentative de pénétration pacifique dans le sud marocain en 1839.' *Revue de l'histoire des colonies françaises,* vol. IX. 1921.

Masson, A. 'L'opinion française et les problèmes coloniaux à la fin du Second Empire.' *Revue française d'histoire d'outre-mer,* vol. XLIX. 1962.

Masson, P. *Histoire des établissements et du commerce français dans l'Afrique barbaresque, 1560–1793.* Paris, 1903.

— *Marseille et la colonisation française.* Paris, 1912.

le commandant Mattei, *Bas-Niger, Bénoué, Dahomey.* Grenoble, 1890.

Maunoir, C. and Schirmer, H. (eds.). *Journal de route de Henri Duveyrier.* Paris, 1905.

Méniaud, J. *Les pionniers du Soudan, avant, avec et après Archinard, 1879–1894.* 2 vols. Paris, 1931.

Ménier, M-A. 'La marche au Tchad de 1887 à 1891.' *Bulletin de l'Institut des Etudes Centrafricaines,* n.s. 5. 1953.

Miège, J-L. *Le Maroc et l'Europe (1830–1894).* 4 vols. Paris, 1961–3.

le commandant Mircher. *Mission de Ghadamès: Rapports officiels et documents à l'appui.* Algiers, 1863.

Monteil, P-L. *De Saint-Louis à Tripoli par le Lac Tchad.* Paris, 1895.

— *Une page d'histoire militaire coloniale: La Colonne de Kong.* Paris, 1902.

— *Quelques feuillets de l'histoire coloniale.* Paris, 1924.

— 'Contribution d'un vétéran à l'histoire coloniale.' *Revue de Paris,* vol. XXX. 1930.

Monteil, V. *Les officiers.* Paris, 1958.

— *L'Islam noir.* Paris, 1964.

Monteilhet, J. *Les institutions militaires de la France, 1814–1932.* Paris, 1932.

Murphy, A. *The Ideology of French Imperialism.* Washington, 1948.

Newbury, C. W. *The Western Slave Coast and its Rulers.* Oxford, 1964.

Bibliography

Newbury, C. W. 'The Development of French Policy on the Lower and Upper Niger, 1880–1898.' *Journal of Modern History*, vol. XXXI. 1959.
— 'The Formation of the Government General of French West Africa.' *Journal of African History*, vol. I. 1960.
— 'Victorians, Republicans and the Partition of Africa.' *Journal of African History*, vol. III. 1962.
— 'North African and Western Sudan Trade in the Nineteenth Century: A Re-evaluation.' *Journal of African History*, vol. VII. 1966.
— 'The Protectionist Revival in French Colonial Trade: The Case of Senegal.' *Economic History Review*, 2nd series, vol. XXI. 1968.
Newland, C. H. 'The Sofa Invasion of Sierra Leone.' *Sierra Leone Studies*, vol. XIX. 1933.
Parsons, F. V. 'The North-West African Company and the British Government.' *Historical Journal*, vol. I. 1958.
Pasquier, R. 'Les débuts de la presse au Sénégal.' *Cahiers d'études africaines*, no. 7. 1962.
Perham, M. *Lugard*. 2 vols. London, 1956–60.
Péroz, E. *Au Soudan français, souvenirs de guerre et de mission*. 4th ed. Paris, 1891.
— *Au Niger, récits de campagne, 1891–1892*. Paris, 1894.
Person, Y. 'La jeunesse de Samory.' *Revue française d'histoire d'outre-mer*, vol. XLVIII. 1962.
— 'Les ancêtres de Samory.' *Cahiers d'études africaines*, no. 13. 1963.
— 'L'aventure de Porèkèrè et le drame de Waïma.' *Cahiers d'études africaines*, no. 18. 1965.
le général Philebert and Rolland, G. *La France dans l'Afrique et le Transsaharien*. Paris, 1890.
Pisani-Ferry, F. *Jules Ferry et le partage du monde*. Paris, 1962.
le capitaine de Polignac. *Résultats obtenus jusqu'à ce jour par les explorations entreprises sous les auspices du gouvernement de l'Algérie pour pénétrer dans le Soudan*. Algiers, 1862.
Porter, C. W. *The Career of Théophile Delcassé*. Philadelphia, 1936.
Power, T. F. *Jules Ferry and the Renaissance of French Imperialism*. New York, 1944.
Quinquaud, J. 'La pacification du Fouta Djallon.' *Revue d'histoire des colonies*, vol. XXVI. 1938.
Quiquandon, F. 'Dans la boucle du Niger (1890–1891).' *Bulletin de la Société de Géographie Commerciale de Bordeaux*, nos. 19, 20. 1891.
Raffenel, A. *Voyage dans l'Afrique occidentale*. Paris, 1846.
— *Nouveau voyage dans le pays des nègres*. 2 vols. Paris, 1856.
Rambaud, A. (ed.). *La France coloniale*. Paris, 1886.
— 'Les Français au Soudan d'après le colonel Gallieni.' *Revue politique et littéraire*, vol. XLVIII. 1891.
— 'Au Soudan.' *Revue politique et littéraire*, vol. XLVIII, 1891; vol. XLIX, 1892.
— 'Le Soudan français et le colonel Archinard.' *Revue politique et littéraire*, 4e série, vol. I. 1894.

Bibliography

Rambaud, A. 'Tombouctou et le Soudan français.' *Revue politique et littéraire*, 4ᵉ série, vol. I. 1894.

— 'Le commandant Lamy.' *Journal des Savants*, vol. I. 1903.

Reclus, M. *Jules Ferry, 1832–1893*. Paris, 1947.

Reinach, J. *Le ministère Gambetta, histoire et doctrine*. Paris, 1884.

Renouvin, P. 'Les origines de l'expédition de Fachoda.' *Revue historique*, vol. CC. 1948.

le général Requin. 'Un soldat et un apôtre: Archinard.' *Cahiers Charles de Foucauld*, no. 29. 1953.

Révillon, T. *Camille Pelletan*. Paris, 1930.

Rinn, L. *Nos frontières sahariennes*. Algiers, 1886.

Robert, A., Bourloton, E., and Cougny, G. (eds.). *Dictionnaire des parlementaires français*. 5 vols. Paris, 1889–91.

Roberts, S. H. *The History of French Colonial Policy, 1870–1925*. 2 vols. London, 1929.

Robinson, R. E. and Gallagher, J. *Africa and the Victorians: The Official Mind of Imperialism*. London, 1961.

— 'The Imperialism of Free Trade.' *Economic History Review*, 2nd series, vol. VI. 1953.

— 'The Partition of Africa.' *New Cambridge Modern History*, vol. XI. Cambridge, 1962.

Robiquet, P. *Discours et opinions de Jules Ferry*. 7 vols. Paris, 1893–8.

Rogers, L. 'Parliamentary Commissions in France.' *Political Science Quarterly*, vol. XXXVII. 1923.

Rolland, G. *Le Transsaharien, un an après*. Paris, 1891.

Rouard de Card, E. *Les traités de protectorat conclus par la France en Afrique, 1870–1895*. Paris, 1897.

— *Les territoires africaines et les conventions franco-anglaises*. Paris, 1901.

— *Traités de délimitation concernant l'Afrique française*. Paris, 1910.

al-hajj Saïd. *Tarikh Sokoto*. Tr. O. Houdas. Publication de l'Ecole des Langues Orientales Vivantes, 4ᵉ série, vol. XX. Paris, 1901.

Saint-Martin, Y. 'Les relations diplomatiques entre la France et l'empire toucouleur de 1860 à 1887.' *Bulletin de l'Institut Français d'Afrique Noire*, série B, vol. XXVII. 1965.

— 'L'artillerie d'El Hadj Omar et d'Ahmadou.' *Bulletin de l'Institut Français d'Afrique Noire*, série B, vol. XXVII. 1965.

— 'Une source de l'histoire coloniale du Sénégal: Les rapports de situation politique (1874–1891).' *Revue française d'histoire d'outre-mer*, vol. LII. 1965.

Salenc, J. (tr.). 'La vie d'El Hadj Omar.' *Bulletin du Comité des Etudes Historiques et Scientifiques de l'Afrique Occidentale Française*, vol. I. 1918.

Sanderson, G. N. *England, Europe and the Upper Nile, 1882–1899*. Edinburgh, 1965.

Saulnier, E. *La Compagnie du Galam au Sénégal*. Paris, 1921.

Schefer, C. (ed.). *Instructions générales données de 1763 à 1870 aux Gouverneurs et Ordonnateurs des établissements français en Afrique occidentale*. 2 vols. Paris, [1927].

Bibliography

Schefer, C. *La grande pensée de Napoléon III.* Paris, 1939.

— 'La "Conquête Totale" de l'Algérie, 1839–1843.' *Revue de l'histoire des colonies françaises,* vol. IV. 1916.

Schirmer, H. *Le Sahara.* Paris, 1893.

— 'Pourquoi Flatters et ses compagnons sont morts.' *Bulletin de la Société de Géographie de Lille,* vol. XIII. 1896.

Schnapper, B. *La politique et le commerce français dans le Golfe de Guinée de 1838 à 1871.* Paris, 1961.

Smith, H. F. C. 'A Neglected Theme of West African History: The Islamic Revolutions of the Nineteenth Century.' *Historians in Tropical Africa* (Proceedings of the Leverhulme Inter-Collegiate History Conference, September, 1960). Salisbury, 1962.

Smith, M. G. *Government in Zazzau.* London, 1960.

Soleillet, P. *Avenir de la France en Afrique.* Paris, 1876.

— *L'Afrique occidentale, Algérie, Mzab, Tildikelt.* Avignon, 1877.

— *Voyage à Ségou, 1878–1879.* Ed. G. Gravier. Paris, 1887.

Stengers, J. 'Aux origines de Fachoda, l'expédition Monteil.' *Revue belge de philologie et d'histoire,* vol. XXXVI, 1958; vol. XXXVIII, 1960.

— 'L'Impérialisme Colonial de la Fin du XIXᵉ Siècle: Mythe ou Réalité?' *Journal of African History,* vol. III. 1962.

Suret-Canale, J. *L'Afrique noire occidentale et centrale.* Paris, 1958.

— 'El Hadj Omar.' *Présence africaine,* 1958.

Taylor, A. J. P. 'Prelude to Fashoda: The Question of the Upper Nile, 1894–5.' *English Historical Review,* vol. LXV. 1950.

Terrier, A., and Mourey, C. *L'œuvre de la Troisième République en Afrique occidentale.* Paris, 1910.

Thiriet, E. *Au Soudan français: Souvenirs, 1892–1894.* Paris, 1932.

Thorson, W. B. 'Charles de Freycinet, French Empire-Builder.' *Research Studies of the State College of Washington,* vol. XII. 1945.

— 'Reappraisal of a Diplomatist.' *Historian,* 1945.

Titeux, E. *Saint-Cyr et l'école spéciale militaire en France.* Paris, 1898.

le commandant Toutée. *Dahomey, Niger, Touareg.* Paris, 1897.

Traoré, D. 'Les réclamations de Samory et de l'état de Kong.' *Notes africaines,* no. 47. 1950.

Trimingham, J. S. *Islam in West Africa.* Oxford, 1959.

— *A History of Islam in West Africa.* London, 1962.

Trumelet, C. *Histoire de l'insurrection dans le sud de la province d'Alger.* 2 vols. Algiers, 1879–84.

Tyam, M. A. *La vie d'el Hadj Omar.* Tr. H. Gaden. Mémoires de l'Institut d'Ethnologie, no. 21. Paris, 1935.

Vajda, G. 'Contribution à la connaissance de la littérature arabe en Afrique occidentale.' *Journal de la Société des Africanistes,* vol. XX. 1950.

Vignes, K. 'Etude sur la rivalité d'influence entre les puissances européennes en Afrique équatoriale et occidentale depuis l'Acte Générale de Berlin jusqu'au seuil du XXᵉ siècle.' *Revue française d'histoire d'outre-mer,* vol. XLVIII. 1962.

19-2

Bibliography

Vivarez, M. *Le Soudan algérien: Projet de voie ferrée trans-saharienne.* Paris, 1890.

Waldman, M. R. 'The Fulani *jihad*—a Reassessment.' *Journal of African History*, vol. VI. 1965.

Willis, J. R. '*Jihad fi sabil Allah*—its Doctrinal Basis in Islam and some Aspects of its Evolution in Nineteenth-Century West Africa.' *Journal of African History*, vol. VIII. 1967.

Zuccarelli, F. Le régime des engagés à temps au Sénégal, 1817–48.' *Cahiers d'études africaines*, no. 7. 1962.

Index

Index

Bambaras (*cont.*)
196, 197; rebel against French, 184, 198 n. 1, 201
Bambuk, 26, 56, 76, 144, 145
Bandiagara, 194, 197, 200, 225
Baoulé, river, 232
Bayol, Jean, 154, 155, 157
Bayol Treaty, 102, 153
Beledugu, 49, 75, 76, 80–2, 84, 86, 94, 120, 147–50, 180; *see also* Bambaras
Benty, 47
Benué, river, 102–4, 123, 169, 238
Berlet, A., 92
Berlin Conference (1884), 125, 127–8, 138
Betbeder, Captain, 242
Beyla, 225, 228
Bifara, 238
Binger, Louis-Gustave: expedition and treaties in Niger Bend, 154–5, 157; Governor of Ivory Coast, 230, 232; member of Commission on reorganisation of West Africa, 260 n. 2, 261, 262
Bismarck, Count Otto von, 125–7
Bissandugu, 158, 185
Bobo-Diulasso, 241, 251, 252
Bodian, 197, 198, 201
Boilève, Lieutenant-Colonel C. E., 115, 117
Boissy d'Anglas, F. A., 223
Boiteux, Lieutenant H. G. M., 217–18, 220
Boké, 47
Bondu, 26, 40, 59, 134, 144, 147, 190
Bonduku, 155, 244, 251
Bonnacorsi, Captain, 225
Bonnetain, Paul, 210
Bonnier, Lieutenant-Colonel Etienne: appointed *Commandant-Supérieur*, 216; and capture of Timbuktu, 217–21; death, 221
Bonny, 103–4, 122
Borgnis-Desbordes, General Gustave
career: appointed *Commandant-Supérieur*, 72, 87, military adviser to Colonial Department, 112, 117, 120–1, 140 n. 4, 143; Inspector-General, *artillerie de marine*, 186 n. 2, 189–90, 213; posted to Indochina, 257
military advance to the Niger, 84, 87–100, 108–12
and capture of Timbuktu, 218
attitude to Islam, 95–100, 118, 120
relations with: Archinard, 174, 178, 182, 186 n. 2, 210, 213; Bonnier, 216; Brière, 88, 143; Delcassé, 213; Gallieni, 80 n. 3, 95, 143; Humbert, 255–7
Borgu, 239, 245, 248
Bornu, 104, 160, 169, 170, 238, 243, 248

Bossé, 225
Bouët-Willaumez, Admiral L. E., 26
Bougouni, 216, 232
Bourdiaux, Colonel H.: head of Upper Senegal Bureau, 92; acting Governor of Senegal, 115; member of Sudan Commission (1889–90), 172; Director of Defence, 232; opposes British expansion, 123; supports military expansion, 115, 172; relations with Archinard, 174; relations with Desbordes, 92
Brass River, 122
Braulot, Captain, 251, 252, 254, 256
Brazza, Pierre Savorgnan de, 104, 237
Bretonnet, Commandant H. E., 240, 243
Brière de l'Isle, General Louis-Alexandre: early career, 56; Governor of Senegal, 55–60; recalled, 86; Inspector-General, *infanterie de marine*, 143, 189, 267; and Southern Rivers, 57; and Senegal–Niger Railway, 68–72; and Gallieni missions, 72–83, 95; and occupation of the Niger, 84–6, 87–8, 266; attitude to Islam, 57–8, 72–4
relations with: Archinard, 174, 178, 190; Delcassé, 213; Desbordes, 143; Gallieni, 143, 190
Briquelot, Commandant J. E., 191, 192, 198
Brisson, Henri, 70, 131, 164
Bubakar Saada, 40, 59, 134, 146
Bugeaud, General T-R., 8, 20–1
Buna, 245, 248, 252
Buré, 119, 133, 139, 147
Bureau du Haut-Fleuve, *see* Upper Senegal Bureau
Bussa, 243, 244, 247, 248

Calabar, 103–4
Canard, Governor of Senegal, 90–1, 109
Caron, Lieutenant J. E., 151, 219 n. 1
Casimir-Périer, Jean, 222
Cassagnac, Paul Granier de, 204, 212
Caudrelier, Commandant P-C., 245, 252
Cayor, 33, 34, 42, 45, 55, 136
Cazemajou, Captain G. M., 243–4, 247, 257
Chad, lake: expansion towards, 104–5, 169–70, 237–8, 242–3, 258, 263–5, 273–4
Chad Plan: and Anglo-French Agreement (1890), 159–62, 167–8, 238; and Franco-German Agreement (1894), 238; and Anglo-French Agreement (1898), 242, 247, 248; Archinard and, 198; Etienne and, 156–8, 157–9; Soleillet and, 105; public opinion and, 162–6, 264
Chamberlain, Joseph, 244, 246, 266

Index

Chanoine, Lieutenant C. P. J., 241, 257, 258-9, 274

Chari, river, 160, 238

Chasseloup-Laubat, J-N., marquis de, 32-3, 34, 44

Chaudié, Governor-General, French West Africa: instructions from Chautemps, 240, 251; and occupation of Buna and Wa, 245; and capture of Sikasso, 252; drafts report of Commission on re-organisation of West Africa, 260-1

Chautemps, Emile: attacks costs of military expansion, 204, 205; becomes Minister of Colonies, 233; capitulates to military pressure, 233-6; and creation of A.O.F. 235, 249; Niger Bend policy, 241

Civilian–military relations, 9, 51, 57, 216-18, 254-62, 267; see also Opposition to military

Clemenceau, Georges, 107

Clément-Thomas, Governor of Senegal, 153, 180-2

Cloué, Admiral G. C., 84-6, 95

Colonial Army, see Armée coloniale

Colonial Budgets, 3 n. 5; see also 'finances' under Senegal and Sudan

Colonial Department: organisation of, 6, 12, 103, 132, 189; relations with Foreign Ministry, 138-9, 168, 243; relations with Ministry of Marine, 213, 222; relations with military, 13, 208-9, 213-14, 222

Colonial policy in West Africa: influenced by groupe colonial, 206; influenced by public opinion, 63, 105; powers of Under-Secretary for Colonies over, 6-8; priorities of, 51-3, 100-6, 120-30; imperialist nature of, 65-6, 82-3, 106, 265-6

Combes, Colonel A. V. A.: campaigns against Samori, 118-20, 134, 136, 191-2

Comité de l'Afrique française, 166, 169, 206, 208, 211, 237, 264

Commandant-Supérieur du Haut-Fleuve: post created, 72; duties redefined, 190

Compagnie française de l'Afrique centrale, 169, 170

Compagnie française de l'Afrique équatoriale, 102, 123

Compagnie française de l'Afrique occidentale, 261

Compagnie du Sénégal, 102, 123

Congo, French: Brazza Treaty and, 104-5; access to Lake Chad from, 105, 160, 237, 264

Congrès colonial national, 163

Coronnat, General P. G. P., 222

Couchard, J. P. J., 222, 223

Courcel, baron A. de, 125-8, 242, 246, 247

Cousin, Paul, 208

Crampel, Paul, 169

Daba, 94

Dagana, 28

Dahomey: Etienne and consolidation of, 157, 239; base for expansion into the Niger Bend, 239, 240, 242, 246, 248, 274; West African free-trade area, 247, 248; becomes part of A.O.F., 262

Dargelos, Commandant V., 232

Decœur, Captain H. A., 239, 240, 242

Decrais, Albert, 2, 260, 262

De Lamothe, Governor of Senegal, 184-8, 190, 227

Delanneau, Commandant P. L., 121, 135

Delanneau, Governor of Senegal, 90, 110

Delcassé, Théophile: attacks Ribot's African policy, 165; Under-Secretary for Colonies, 193; Minister of Colonies, 227; member of groupe colonial de la Chambre, 206; member of Union coloniale, 209; and Timbuktu campaign, 218, 223; and Monteil expedition, 230-3, 236; Niger Bend policy, 239-40; Sudanese policy, 215; attitude to military, 203-4, 205, 213, 223, 239; relations with Archinard, 192, 193, 194, 209-14, 239; relations with Desbordes, 213

Deloncle, François: member of Sudan Commission (1889-90), 172; member of groupe colonial de la Chambre, 206; member of Union coloniale, 208; and British expansion, 163, 164; and Chad Plan, 162 n. 1, 163, 165; and military, 172, 204-8

Deloncle, Jean-Louis, 209, 214, 236

Departmental Commissions: West Africa (1850), 28; Vallon (1882), 110; re-organisation of Sudan (1889-90), 171-3; Monteil expedition (1896), 233; West Africa (1899), 260-1

La Dépêche Coloniale, 256, 261

Déroulède, Paul, 204, 260

Desbordes, see Borgnis-Desbordes

Destenave, Commandant G. M., 241, 261

Diafunu, 49

Diakha, 145

Diambouku, 49

Diana, 145

Diéna, 201

Dimar, 45

Dinguiray, 49, 152, 196, 199

Dio, 75, 84

Index

Dislère, Paul, 92, 213
Djimini, 155, 157, 251
Dodds, Colonel A. A., 239
Dreyfus Affair, 259–60
Drumont, Edouard, 213
Ducos, T. J. E., 28
Duponchel, Adolphe, 61, 63

Ebener, Lieutenant-Colonel, 226–7
Egypt: British policy towards, 244, 246; French policy towards, 126–7, 165, 231, 246, 263
Epouses libres, 236, 272
Erimakono, 191–3
Etienne, Eugène: president of *groupe colonial de la Chambre*, 206; Dahomey policy, 157, 164, 239; Futa Jallon and Southern Rivers policy, 152–3, 171, 199; Niger Bend policy, 155–8; and Hinterland theory, 158, 162; and Chad Plan, 164, 167, 169–70, 204, 265; and capture of Segu, 156, 168, 171, 180–2; and campaigns against Samori, 184–6, 188, 204; attitude to military expansion, 171, 180, 204, 206, 212; relations with Archinard, 179, 182, 185, 189; conflict with Foreign Ministry, 168
Faidherbe, General L. L. C.: early career, 28–9; influence of Algeria on, 29, 39; and the occupation of Senegal, 28–35; and Niger Plan, 35, 39–44, 53, 59, 104–5, 266; and expedition to Timbuktu (1884), 120; and Binger expedition, 154; attitude to Tokolor Empire, 37, 39–44
Falaba, 192
Falémé, river, 24, 59, 147
Farana, 191
Fashoda, 246, 253, 257, 263
Faure, Félix, 123–4, 129, 204, 263
Ferry, Jules, 4, 125–30, 138
Flatters, Colonel P. F. X., 66, 67, 102
Fort d'Arenberg, 239, 242
Franco-Congolese Agreement (1894), 231
Franco-German Agreement (1894), 238
Franco-Prussian War limits colonial expansion, 3, 45, 60
Frey, Lieutenant-Colonel H. N., 132–7, 139, 140, 141, 143, 147
Freycinet, Charles de: and African expansion, 64–6, 138, 265; and Trans-Sahara Railway, 63–7; and Upper Niger protectorate, 138–41, 142
Fuladugu, 75
Fulani Empire, 47, 66
Futa: hostility to French of, 34, 42, 45, 55,

109, 117, 120, 181, 195; Brière's campaign in, 57–8; source of reinforcements for Tokolors, 41, 49, 78, 175, 176
Futa Jallon: Anglo-French rivalry in, 151–3, 156; extension of French influence into, 102, 123, 152–3, 171, 172, 180; and Senegal–Sudan dispute, 227

Gabon, 44, 51
Galé, 133
Galiber, Admiral C. E., 131–2, 136, 137, 139
Gallieni, Lieutenant-Colonel Joseph Simon: *Commandant-Supérieur*, 141, 143; reappointment vetoed by Brière, 190; member of Sudan Commission (1889–90), 172; and Senegal-Niger Railway, 68; mission to Segu, 72–83, 95; and consolidation of Sudan, 144–50, 171, 272; and expansion into Futa Jallon and Southern Rivers, 151–3; attitude to Islam, 75, 80, 149, 175; attitude to trade, 144; relations with Archinard, 174–5, 199–200; relations with Colonial Department, 175
Gambia: French hope to obtain, 43, 44, 51–2, 101, 155; Gallieni stops Bambuk trade with, 145–6; relations with Tokolors, 77; Gouldsbury treaty with Futa Jallon, 102
Gasconi, A-S., 57, 61, 124 n. 2
Gentil, Commandant E., 243, 258
Geographical societies, 60–2, 264
Germany: Franco-German colonial cooperation, 125–7; French reaction to Anglo-German Agreement (1890), 159, 160, 168
Glele, 157
Goubanko, 84, 88, 97
Goundam massacre, 221–3, 226, 233
Grand Bassam, 51, 155, 231
Great Britain: West African policy of, 52, 77, 123–30, 138, 244, 266; Ferry avoids conflict with, 125–8; military build-up in West Africa, 246–8
Grodet, Albert: early career, 213, 215–16; appointed Governor of Sudan, 210, 211; recalled, 234; and capture of Timbuktu, 216–23; and Monteil expedition, 230–3; Niger Bend policy, 240–1; relations with military, 224–33
Groupe colonial de la Chambre, 166 n. 1, 206, 230
Guéliba, 191
Guidimaka, 97, 134–6, 141, 143
Guieysse, P., 241, 243, 251
Guillain, A., 257–9

Index

Index

Richard-Toll, 28
Rigault de Genouilly, Admiral, 51
Rio Nunez, 47, 51
Roads: Médine Bafoulabé, 68, 69; Konakry
–Upper Niger, 250
Rodier, Captain F. P., 137
Roume, Etienne, 241, 260 n. 2
Rousseau, Armand, 131, 132, 134, 138
Rouvier, Maurice, 62, 103, 105

Saboné, 180, 181
Sabouciré, 59, 76
Sadi-Carnot, F., 210
Saldé, 30
Salisbury, Robert, 3rd Marquess of, 159,
161, 164, 242, 246, 247, 248
Sambala, 40–1, 59
Samori: formation and organisation of
empire, 98–9; conflict with Sikasso, 119,
147, 150; relations with Ahmadu, 180,
181, 204; relations with British, 139,
150, 184, 186, 188, 191–2, 244
relations with French: Desbordes's campaigns against, 90, 94, 99–100, 111–12;
Combes's campaign against, 118–20;
Frey's campaign against, 132–3; Tour-
nier treaty with, 133, 139, 140, 141, 143,
147; Péroz treaty with, 147–8; renewed, 176, 177, 183; Archinard's campaigns against, 183–6, 191–3, 204, 208;
Humbert's campaign against, 186–9;
Bonnier's campaign against, 216–17,
224; Monteil expedition against, 230–3;
Braulot mission to, 251–2; captured,
253; nature of French policy towards,
150, 175–6, 269–70
Sangha, 237, 238
Saniokhor, 45
Sansanding (Upper Niger), 188, 193, 196,
197, 198, 201
Sarantyenimori, 252
Sati, 241
Say, 239, 240, 242
Say–Barruwa Line: and Anglo-French
Agreement (1890), 160; Delcassé's
views on, 165; Monteil survey, 170,
237–8; French demand revision, 242;
Cazemajou mission, 243, 247, 257–8;
and Anglo-French Agreement (1898),
248
Segu: Tokolor conquest of, 36; Bambara
rebellions in, 47, 135; French campaign against, 156, 168, 177–82; Diara
dynasty restored, 196; rebellions against
the French, 184, 188, 201, 205; base for
expansion, 197

Seignac, Governor of Senegal, 115, 119, 132,
137
Senegal: early colonisation of, 23–8; occupation of, 28–35; expansion under
Faidherbe, 39–44; autonomy of Sudan
from, 173, 190; dispute with Sudan,
227; becomes part of A.O.F., 235
finances, 30, 33, 45, 55, 57
trade, 27–8, 33, 45, 55
Senegal–Niger Railway: planned, 60–72, 74,
80, 81; given priority, 92, 113; subordinated to military needs, 106, 108,
136; slow progress of construction,
109–10, 115; work suspended, 116, 117;
recommenced, 142, 144; progress under
Gallieni, 145; Bafoulabé reached, 146,
177; Sudan Commission recommends
against extension, 172–3; opened to
commercial use, 228; extension to
Niger approved, 250; costs, 84–5, 91,
106, 109–11
Senegambian Triangle, 43, 44, 51–2, 101,
152, 155
Sénoudébou, 26, 28, 59, 144
Servatius, René, 93, 112
Le Siècle, 163, 207, 209, 222, 235
Sierra Leone: Boundary Agreement (1882),
103, 123–4; Boundary Agreement
(1891), 192; relations with Samori, 139,
184, 186, 188, 191–2, 244; relations
with Tokolors, 77
Siguiri, 113, 146, 150, 152, 172, 184, 185,
224
Siné, 31
Sikasso: war with Samori, 147, 150, 187–8,
251; French support for, 150, 183;
treaty with French, 150; refuses French
garrison, 232; French expedition
against, 247, 252–3; see also Ba Bemba,
Tiéba
Slave Coast, 157, 239
Slave trade, 200–1, 228, 249, 272–3
Sokoto, 66, 160, 237, 238 n. 4, 243, 247
Soleillet, Paul, 61, 63, 105
Southern Rivers: early protectorates, 47;
French control threatened by British,
55, 103, 123; outlet for Sudanese trade,
153, 171; see also Brière, Etienne,
Gallieni, Jauréguiberry
Spuller, J., 168
Sudan: early history, 15–20; Departmental
Commission (1889–90), 171–3; auto-
nomy, 173, 190, Archinard's admini-
strative policies in, 195–202; becomes
part of A.O.F., 235; reorganisation
and partition (1899), 260–2

295

Index